ENCYCLOPEDIA OF SPORTS

Volume - 1

SPORTS MANAGEMENT

ENCYCLOPEDIA OF SPORTS

Volume - 1

SPORTS MANAGEMENT

Edited By:
Y.K.REDDY
SURESH PADMANAVIA

SRISHTI BOOK DISTRIBUTORS
NEW DELHI (INDIA)

IBSN 978-81-89948-15-3 Vol-1
ISBN 978-81-89948-20-7 Set

Published by :
SRISHTI BOOK DISTRIBUTORS
4378/4-B-202, 2nd floor,
J.M.D. House, Ansari Road,
Daryaganj, New Delhi-110002
E-mail : srishtibookdistributors@yahoo.co.in
Ph. 011-23284904

***Edition* : 2009**

Rs.1000 (Each Volume)

Printed at
Suman Printers
Delhi-110093

Preface

Sports Management is a field of education and vocation concerning the business aspect of Sports. Some examples of Sports managers include the front office system in professional sports, college sports managers, recreational Sports managers, sports marketing, event management, facility management, sports economics, Sports finance, and sports information.

Sports Management is the study of planning, supervising and organizing various sporting activities like international and domestic tournaments for cricket, football, hockey, golf, and several other games. Sports Management Courses in India inculcates leadership qualities in an individual and helps him or her to coach, manage and train sportsmen coming from various fields of sporting activity.

As the Sports industry continues to grow and evolve at a dramatic rate, the goal of providing a comprehensive, current, concise introductory book on Sports Management becomes an enormous task. We have attempted to do just that, in providing our readers (students, professors, and practitioners alike) with this edition of *Sports/Management.*

This is a book intended for use in introductory Sports management courses. The focus of these courses, and this book, is to provide an overview of the Sports industry and cover basic fundamental knowledge and skill sets of the Sports manager, as well as providing information on Sports industry segments for potential job employment and career choices.

CONTENTS

CHAPTER 1

INTRODUCTION

The time has come for sports organizations to appoint experienced managers as full-time CEOs. Professional qualified managers bring administrative expertise, high networking and people-management skills that are essential for this role. Industry is replete with managers with a deep passion for sports who would surely be keen to meet this challenge.

Experienced CEO's would be able to direct the day-to-day functioning of the sports bodies efficiently and also leverage their connections to bring in industry sponsorships for players and events. They can tackle the high pressure competitive environment of sports and use their people management skills to improve the functioning of national teams. A critical and neglected aspect of growing the sports at the grassroots level will be addressed by a professional CEO. Hiring and creating a network of management professionals to manage the Sports at the regional level by creation of infrastructure will add to the growth of the Sports at the local level. Equally importantly this will create a "career ladder" for retired sportspersons and bring on-board management graduates who would like to make their profession in sports. Can we now hope for the era of the professional manager in Indian Sports scene? If sports is your passion, you do not necessarily have to keep it on the inside track. You get to stay in touch with the activities revolving around your favourite Sports and at the same time, use your brains to handle the managerial and administrative part of it. Sports has been a popular career in the West for sometime, but in India it has yet to come up in a big way. You can opt for being a professional player; a physical education instructor; a coach; an umpire or referee. You could even take up and practice sports medicine; or you could opt for sports journalism if you like to write. Or, better still take up a career that is a mix of sports and marketing or business. This is specialist area that is becoming increasingly popular today, it's the area of sports management and administration. Sports management combines work as an agent along with the business and marketing aspects of the Sports.

Work profile:

You can opt for being a professional player; a physical education instructor; a coach; an umpire or referee. You could even take up and practice sports medicine; or you could opt for sports journalism if you like to write. Or, better still take up a career that is a mix of sports and marketing or business. This is specialist area that is becoming increasingly popular today, it's the area of sports management and administration. Sports management combines work as an agent along with the business and marketing aspects of the Sports.

Sports agents and managers:

All successful and well-known players of Sports have their own personal managers or agents today. Even upcoming sports persons often employ managers to take care of their career growth. As a sports agent or manager, you will have to keep a track of your clients' schedules, look after activities such as their career progression, business promotion and even media and public relations. Administrative affairs such as budgeting, finance and other logistics have to be taken care of, often.

Sports administrators:

Many private and government-sponsored sports institutions employ qualified officials to manage their work at various levels. Most of these officials, particularly the senior ones, usually are sports teachers, coaches who have experience in managing sports activities. Therefore, as a sports administrator, your basic responsibility would be the planning and management of sports activities and events, from time to time.

Leisure and Sports-club management:

Today, all clubs, hotels and resorts boast of sports facilities and leisure centres. The work here would require you to handle administrative work, including that of managing accounts, planning, preparing schedules and timetables, and arranging for specialised coaches as per the requirement. There is an increasing demand for specialised sports centres which cater to a particular Sports. Such facilities often combine other leisure activities along with stay and catering facilities to ensure membership and usage. Golf clubs and resorts as well as adventure sports or other leisure activity centres require trained personel to manage and promote these sporting activities.

Training:

The academic programme leads to several objectives being fulfilled concurrently, wherein you have the opportunity to acquire business know-how in relation to Sports and leisure and improve your knowledge of economics at a high international level.

Eligibility:

You can take up any course of study at graduation level to be eligible for the sports management postgraduate diploma course. You could go in for a Bachelor's in Physical Education (BP Ed) or related course in the particular sports of your liking. The Sports Authority of India conducts courses in physical education that you can take up. Pursuing courses in business or administration will help too.

Institutions:

Post Graduate Diploma In Sports Management (PGDSM) is presently available at only two recognised universities in India:

Alagappa University, Karaikudi, Tamil Nadu offers a one-year PGDSM

Eligibility: Candidates who have passed BP Ed and NIS diploma exams. Application form and prospectus can be had from Director, Directorate of Distance Education, Alagappa University, Karaikudi-623003.

Indira Gandhi Institute of Physical Education and Sports Science, New Delhi offers a one-year PGDSM

Eligibility: 40 per cent marks in Bachelor's degree and sports achievements. Seats (50) Notification comes up in the month of June. The last date for application is in July.

Several private colleges and institutions are now introducing diploma courses in sports management. Several institutions abroad offer courses in sports management too, both at the undergraduate and postgraduate degree and diploma levels. You may even be eligible for a sports scholarship in the United States if you play at state or national level in any Sports. The UK, France and several other countries offer courses in sports management.

Personal attributes:

To be successful in this profession, you need to have: a liking for the Sports; commitment to the Sports and to the profession; energy and enthusiasm; patience; perseverance and sporting spirit. Most importantly, you must have good communication and business skills. It's particularly satisfying if you have an keen interest in sports, but are not able to make it to a competitive level. Even sports-persons who have given up active playing can utilise their experience and pursue a career in sports management.

All successful and well-known players of Sports have their own personal managers or agents today. Even upcoming sports persons often employ managers to take care of their career growth. As a sports agent or manager, you will have to keep a track of your clients' schedules, look after activities such as their career progression, business promotion and even media and public relations. Administrative affairs such as budgeting, finance and other logistics have to be taken care of, often. Many private and government-sponsored sports institutions employ qualified officials to manage their work at various levels. Most of these officials, particularly the senior ones, usually are sports teachers, coaches who have experience in managing sports activities. Therefore, as a sports administrator, your basic responsibility would be the planning and management of sports activities and events, from time to time. Today, all clubs, hotels and resorts boast of sports facilities and leisure centres. The work here would require you to handle administrative work, including that of managing accounts, planning, preparing schedules and timetables, and arranging for specialised coaches as per the requirement.

There is an increasing demand for specialised sports centres which cater to a particular Sports. Such facilities often combine other leisure activities along with stay and catering facilities to ensure membership and usage. Golf clubs and resorts as well as adventure sports or other leisure activity centres require trained personel to manage and promote these sporting activities. The academic programme leads to several objectives being fulfilled concurrently, wherein you have the opportunity to acquire business know-how in relation to Sports and leisure and improve your knowledge of economics at a high international level.

You can take up any course of study at graduation level to be eligible for the sports management postgraduate diploma course. You could go in for a Bachelor's in Physical Education (BP Ed) or related course in the particular sports of your liking. The Sports Authority of India conducts courses in physical education that you can take up. Pursuing courses in business or administration will help too. To be successful in this profession, you need to have: a liking for the Sports; commitment to the Sports and to the profession; energy and enthusiasm; patience; perseverance and sporting spirit. Most importantly, you must have good communication and business skills. It's particularly satisfying if you have an keen interest in sports, but are not able to make it to a competitive level. Even sports-persons who have given up active playing can utilise their experience and pursue a career in sports management.

Sports, like so many other areas of life and business, changes radically and very quickly in this modern age. The Sydney Olympics have had a major impact on the profile of Sports worldwide, and have left a massive 'feelgood' factor which has influenced governments worldwide. In the UK, the government has had much more impact on the delivery of Sports through various initiatives and guidance like how lottery and other funding should be focused and delivered. There is a massive new emphasis on Sports in schools, and the government has begun to see Sports as a tool in tackling social problems. These changes can often seem remote to people operating at local level, but in truth they have a major impact across all levels of sports delivery in the country. A change in focus for the lottery, for example, can mean that access to sports funding at a local level can change quite radically.

In India with the solitary gold in Beijing Olympics by Abhinav Bindra has opened up new hopes for the participants and the administrators. Sports management and administration is truly a growth business. Now is an exciting time to be involved in Sports and the future looks just as promising—if not more so.

Background

"Sports is the unalienable right of every person."

—European Sports Conference

Sports is the most precious commodity we can hand on to the next generation. *—Ron Pickering (1930-91), BBC commentator and sports coach*

The level of participation and degree of excellence attained within a given Sports is dependent, at least in part, on how that Sports is organized. Sports has traditionally been organized in an *ad hoc* way, relying on volunteers who are committed to their particular Sports. It is now clear that to encourage higher levels of participation and international excellence, new ideas about organizing need to be diffused to those involved in the management of Sports.

—*Newell and Swan (1995)*

It is to be emphasized in this introduction that this text is written from a practitioner's point of view. The contents are meant to be of assistance to the student and practitioner of the business of sports administration and management—it is to be hoped that all practitioners continue to be students of their business as well. While it could be seen as a movable feast, certain common requirements are likely to persist over the next decade or more as Sports undergoes major changes influenced by television, money and increasing professionalism, as well as the increasing pressure on volunteers in terms of time and our societal changes in terms of job roles and commitments.

Someone else coming from a specific interest area or from an academic viewpoint might well come up with quite different contents and emphasis in a book on the same subject, but this does not invalidate this text, which offers a personal preference and rank of importance of the subjects included. Sports has the power to change the world, the power to inspire, the power to unite people in a way that little else can. —

Nelson Mandela, in a speech at the Rugby World Cup, 1995

As stated, this book is written to be of practical help to practitioners working in the field of Sports and physical recreation, as well as of benefit to students of sports management and administration. It is intended to be an academic support, as well as a managers' handbook applied to the sports management and administration business. Very little has previously been written on the subject, and many people come to the work with little prior specific knowledge and little direct guidance—merely a great deal of the essential ingredients, enthusiasm and energy, or administrative experience gained elsewhere.

The consideration of the history and the social structural context of Sports is merely to give a background to the situation in which the sports manager or administrator works. As in any practical management situation, it is essential for the practitioner to be aware of his or her environment. A manager who ignores this environment and the specific setting is in danger of producing unrealistic practices unsuited to the situation in which they operate. This contextual understanding is vital but need not be a theoretical concept—rather, it entails a realistic analysis of the organizational and external environment, which guides good practice.

It is also to be hoped that a good manager will be able to apply the suggested practices, procedures and thinking to a variety of situations. For example, an identified weakness in the implementation of the Compulsory Competitive Tendering process within local authorities was that many operating direct services organizations saw their role as being solely to manage their facilities, while the client side was regarded as the agency which would develop Sports and consequently increase the usage and numbers using the facilities. This approach has proved to be flawed and it is clear that facility managers must allocate time to developing usage, and consequently the development of Sports, if they are to see a sustained increase in user figures. It is quite wrong for sports facility managers to concern themselves only with the present and solely with facility and procedural management, forgetting about the developmental role. They must think more broadly and take a longer term strategic view if substantial progress is to be achieved and sustained.

As we move forward, there is no doubt that the base of Sports is still very much in the hands of the volunteer. However, the situation must change if we are genuinely to treat our Sports more like a business—in a more professional and full-time manner. This surely is the only recipe for success. The administrators and managers of Sports must take it as seriously as the participants, have the same full-time commitment, and receive payment if they are to progress to the proper level of administrative support and managerial practice. A massive voluntary effort is put into Sports. Its importance should not be diminished; rather, it should be boosted by a growth in the numbers of full-time professional managers supporting the effort.

The past years have seen significant growth in the area of Sports Councils initiatives, as well as a rapid increase in the number of local authority development officers being appointed to promote and administer Sports. It is likely that the next 20 years will see a significant growth of professional sports administration, at a national and local level (this trend has already started), and that the training of these professionals, coupled (hopefully) with a constantly growing band of volunteers, will be crucial to improving the performance of our sports people throughout the world at all levels of competition. The development of vocational qualifications will mean that practitioners will be able to become qualified in sports administration as well as sports development, facility management and operations, and coaching. This will mean a considerable improvement in the potential for on-the-job training and assessment leading to a qualification. This initiative will help fuel the growth of a strong qualified profession of people employed in managing and administering Sports and recreation.

Sports administration will never be the highest paid occupation, and it will always require a tremendous amount of commitment and energy, but it can be very rewarding and will be done better by people given necessary training and support, as well as all the background knowledge that is available. In particular, management of the voluntary sector is an integral part of the target market, as well as the management of professionals working within their own operation or, as often happens, in close partnership with the voluntary sector. Indeed, the management of the relationship between the paid professional and the volunteer is referred to on many occasions. The dynamic of this relationship can be fundamentally improved if everyone involved takes a professional attitude (regardless of payment) and adheres to the principles.

Sports has been defined as the institutionalization of skill and prowess. Sports is also about personal development, team development, community and society development. In recent years the government has also become keen to use it as a tool for social change. Sports has further been defined (Coakley, 1994) as 'an institutionalized competition that involves vigorous physical exertion or the use of relatively complex physical skills by individuals whose participation is motivated by a combination of intrinsic and extrinsic factors'. Such definitions go to some lengths to distinguish Sports from recreation, play and spectacle. Certainly sports administrators and managers (aside from team managers) should not see their role and input as limited to 'competitive' Sports, at least in the narrow sense.

Sports and Politics

There have been many famous examples over the years of Sports being involved in politics, and of major international conflicts or controversies affecting Sports. For example, the Soviet invasion of Afghanistan in 1979 led to the boycott, by many countries, of the Olympic Games in Moscow in 1980. Further, and perhaps more famously, there has been the boycott of South Africa at national sporting level, even in traditional sports such as cricket and rugby, in order to influence its policy on apartheid. There can be little doubt that ultimately this, allied with sanctions, had a fundamental impact in changing South African policy. It is intriguing to venture that the white population of South Africa had such a desire for sports involvement that they would eventually cede the exclusive 'right' to govern their country in order to take part in Sports at the highest level.

It is also quite ironic that events such as South Africa winning the World Rugby Cup in 1995 have proved to be unifying factors in identifying the soul of the new South Africa. The appearance of Nelson Mandela in a Springbok jersey was, in itself, a remarkable statement about the change in political and social attitudes in South Africa. The recent Cricket World Cup controversy ('should England play in Zimbabwe or not?') is a further illustration of the strong link between politics and Sports. It seems ironic that the Prime Minister could appear on the same platform as Robert Mugabe at a conference, but the cricket team couldn't visit his country. In this case, is appeared that Sports was the only weapon being used.

Many more traditional sports thinkers and participants have felt that politics should not be involved in Sports because Sports is about some of the more idealistic aspirations of the human race, whereas the activities of politicians and politics are less than tasteful. However, since both affect humankind so fundamentally, it is difficult to separate them. This is proved true from Olympic to local level. The role of local authority politicians in the UK should not be underestimated in terms of the control they have over a significant spend in the support of Sports, in terms of facilities, staffing and performance. Local authority funding is crucial to Sports in the UK, and ultimately the decisions as to where this funding is allocated are made by local politicians for political reasons. It is naïve to believe that at a local level Sports is not tied up with politics.

Equally, there are some 'political issues' that need to be considered in terms of relationships with sponsors or other funding sources. For example, certain sponsors might not be happy to be associated with a Sports where drug-taking was thought to be prevalent, or where there was the potential for child abuse, or, indeed, in past days where some performers, e.g. the occasional rogue rugby player, would go and play in South Africa. There is also a significant debate in the UK about the relationships between sports and within sports themselves. This is certainly non-party-political, but there can be major clashes between lobbies or interest groups over how Sports as a whole, or particular sports, should be run. On a number of occasions such behaviour has been seen in paid and voluntary situations to the severe detriment of the particular Sports and its participants. Additionally, issues such as gender equality and racism are political issues in society as a whole and therefore become significant issues within Sports.

Funding from the National Lottery is now being used as another weapon to encourage clubs (especially the more traditional ones, such as bowling and golf clubs) to introduce an equal opportunities policy, and not to display traditional discriminatory positions, particularly against women. The issue of racism in Sports is perhaps most clearly seen on the football pitch and on the terracing, but is often used by groups with other interests as a vehicle to display their bigotry—shouting abuse at particular individuals or devising racist chants where they feel they are hidden by the mass of the crowd. Issues such as nationalism and patriotism can also be linked substantially to Sports, sometimes positively and sometimes negatively. There can be no more classic case of negative nationalism affecting Sports than the 1936 Olympics, which Hitler tried to make a vehicle for his Aryan superiority views. Equally, as mentioned earlier, South Africa's Rugby World Cup victory (and Scotland's Grand Slam title in 1990) had a unifying effect. The feelgood factor generated in Sunderland by the team's FA Cup win in 1973 was significant for the whole community at a time of economic recession.

The role of central government in Sports in the UK is principally concerned with providing the policy framework and establishing financial guidelines. It does not concern itself with direct service delivery, leaving that to the local authorities and sports bodies, with the sports councils setting the strategic direction. The UK is one of the few countries in Europe (and indeed beyond) that does not have the full post of Minister for Sports, although there is within the Department of Culture, Media and Sports (DCMS) a post for a junior minister with this title. Most other countries have this post clearly identified and given cabinet rank, perhaps linked with education, youth or culture. The devolved governments in Scotland, Wales and Northern Ireland also have a junior minister with Sports as part of their responsibility.

This leaves the DCMS junior minister effectively only responsible for Sports in England, and can cause some confusion in implementing policies across the UK where appropriate. It is interesting to note that after the arrival of John Major in Downing

Street, the policy involvement of the top rank of government, i.e. the Prime Minister, altered significantly. Through his personal interest in Sports he had some influence on the national curriculum in schools through the Department of Education and Employment, where he felt that team games were not sufficiently included—a belief he shared with the then Minister of Sports, Ian Sproat.

This led to several initiatives throughout the UK, such as the Youth Sports Trust, where significant government policy and resource direction were involved—although often no additional funding was granted, except through the National Lottery. The election of a Labour government in May 1997 brought about significant changes in sports policy. They have continued John Major's enthusiasm for Sports and, in the year 2000, increased the allocation of money into the revenue funding of the National Sports Councils in the UK—the first significant increase for many years. Allied to this funding increase, however, is an underlying change of policy emphasis—towards 'Sports for all' and participation, especially through schools.

Parameters and Definitions

Sports was born of a man's highest ideals and has been around for 33 centuries, which is longer than any other religion, culture or sub-culture; and must be defended and harnessed for its values.
Ron Pickering

The council of Europe's *European Sports* Charter, adopted in 1992, defines Sports as 'all forms of physical activity which, through casual or organized participation, aim at expressing or improving physical activity fitness and mental wellbeing, forming social relationships or obtaining results in competition at all levels' (Council of Europe, 1992). It is important to be clear about what is meant by the key terms used in this text. As with almost any word or concept, contrasting meanings and interpretations can be adopted by different individuals or groups on varying occasions. For the purposes of this text the following definitions and meanings will be adopted.

- Where the term recreation is used, it is understood that the recreation is of a physical nature.
- Recreation is seen as the physical (when related to Sports and usually the allied mental) re-creating (renewing) of the body and the person.
- Sports is seen as a physically active pastime participated in at a wide variety of levels, under agreed rules; not necessarily, but often, in a competitive setting; at the very least competing against oneself.
- Activity is the specific thing which is done to exert the energy—in this text its use will be a Sports of some sort.

According to Elvin (1993), Sports includes:

1. Elements of competition
2. Physical activity
3. Aspects of organization
4. The influence of outcome on quality of experience

He further differentiates between Sports and recreation by stating that in recreation:

1. The focus is on activity *per se*
2. Satisfactions is gained primarily from the quality of the experience.

Such a distinction as Elvin makes may be of some interest in certain areas of operation and perhaps should be recognized, but for managers and administrators the exact definitions are not crucial. It is, however, clearly important to recognize the level of commitment, 'seriousness' and performance at which people are involved in their Sports. Their demands may not be as high if they merely want to participate for the sake of participation and enjoyment as opposed to seeking some type of improvement in performance and some sort of specific outcome. It is vital that the level of provision that managers and administrators provide is the same in terms of standard and consideration for everyone concerned, regardless of level. But it is helpful to understand what the participants' perceptions and expectations are.

There may be some who think that a sports provider can lessen the quality of thought going into the process, or reduce the standard of provision, merely because it is concerned that the sports people are there to participate rather than perform to a high level. It is the job of a professional administrator to provide to the highest level at all times for all groups of customers, regardless of standard, ability or objectives. The European Sports for All Charter (Council of Europe, 1990) gives the following classification. A great range and variety of activities is covered by the term 'sport', which they subdivide into four broad categories.

1. Competitive games and sports which are characterized by the acceptance of rules and a response to an opposing challenge.
2. Outdoor pursuits in which participants seek to negotiate some particular terrain (signifying in this context an area of open country, forest, mountain, stretch of water or sky). The challenges derive from the manner of negotiation adopted and are modified by the particular terrain selected and the conditions of wind and weather prevailing.
3. Aesthetic movement which includes activity in the performance of which the individual is not so much looking beyond himself and responding to man-made or natural challenges, as looking inward and responding to the sensuous pleasure of patterned bodily movement, for example dance, figure skating, forms of rhythmic gymnastics and recreational swimming.
4. Conditioning activity, i.e. forms of exercise or movement undertaken less for any immediate sense of kinesthetic pleasure than for long-term effects that the exercise may have in improving or maintaining physical working capacity and rendering subsequently a feeling of general wellbeing.

Another example is given by Rodgers (1978): 'Ideally, all the four following elements are present in a Sports, and the first two are always present. Any Sports involves physical activity, it is practised for a recreational purpose, there is an element of competition and a framework of institutional organization.' It is generally difficult to categorize Sports and recreation (for the purposes of this book it is probably better to say physical recreation) definitively. To some extent, like beauty, Sports is in the eye of the beholder, and in addition some of the beliefs expressed and feelings held come from the perspective of the viewer.

In essence, the theoretical definition of Sports and physical recreation is not key to the administrator or manager; their concern is the support of the efficient involvement of others in their chosen activity. Some type of restrictive definition is not helpful and does not assist anyone. The aim of sports administration is to involve people efficiently, effectively and enjoyably, and to avoid excluding them through administrative bureaucracy, or indeed through any restrictive definition of the activity involved.

The History of Sports

This is not the appropriate place for an in-depth study of sports history, but history in every situation is very important in guiding present and future practice—setting it in a realistic context and perspective. This is as true of sports administration and management as it is of other areas of activity. A great deal is said about the history of Sports, but there has been limited study of the area, especially in the less well-known 'minority' sports. There is a great deal of conjecture and supposition over sports participation and development in some quarters, without a great deal of factual information to back this up. Sports officials are famous for sweeping statements.

It is interesting, for example, to note that the current much-debated commercialization of Sports first appeared a long time ago. The late Victorian era, for example, saw 70,000-80,000 people at a race meeting and a situation where top jockeys such as Fred Archer could earn the equivalent of over £1,000,000 in today's money during their career. During the period 1906-14 there were never fewer than 100,000 spectators at a Scotland versus England soccer match, so there was a demand and a commercial aspect to many sports, especially the major ones. There had been, in the earlier Victorian era, some significant changes in the format of some sports to bring them into line with the desires of the population and the challenges facing them. Horse races, for example, had been shortened to enhance interest and increase the number of races that could be staged on each race day. Rugby union and rugby league had split in conflict over the issue of payment, and professional Sports was beginning to develop. In 1890 the players of Glasgow Celtic went on strike for more money at a time when soccer was officially an amateur game.

While this professionalism brought about some pressures in Sports which led, for example, to saliva tests for drugs in 1910 and various other accompanying problems which continue to the present day, it would be wrong to suggest that there was a relaxed or happy state in such sports before they became professional. Before professionalism many sports were violent, disorganized and strongly sexist as well as unethical, with, for example, W.G. Grace—a supposed amateur—ending up as a millionaire. The real need for a study of sport's history is to challenge these myths and relate it more closely to the social and economic history of the country. Much more could be done to examine the economic effect of Sports and to look at the effects of Sports on society historically.

There are also some well-supported, if possibly flawed, arguments that, during the middle of the nineteenth century, Sports was used as an instrument of social control to indoctrinate and pacify the working classes. This argument has some inherent weaknesses, since in most situations the actual exchange and interaction between the upper and lower classes is limited. While there was a significant participation of a variety of classes in

Sports they tended to be in different sports and, even where they did play together, this was usually limited to the playing fields and did not extend to the clubhouse—in the case, for example, of golf and cricket.

Many working-class people did take part in Sports but these tended to be the more traditional sports such as quoiting, while the upper classes continued to have their own sports to participate in and dominate. If there was to be real social control then there would have had to be close contact and this, in large part, did not take place. Any real student of Sports should also be a student of sports history and be aware of the background of Sports in general and specific sports in particular. There is room for a great deal of further study in a wide variety of sporting texts. Such a study would be useful to improve the guidance of present and future practice in sports administration and management as in many other areas such as sports performance and coaching. It is genuinely beneficial for everyone involved in a specific Sports to have an awareness of its history and traditions, while never being a slave to either. Such knowledge allows even participants to put all their effort into perspective; to realize that others have done it before them and that there is a strong tradition of Sports behind them and supporting them. It is somewhat humbling and very useful in getting our present commitment into context to examine the past of any Sports and to understand that there is a background of participation, commitment and involvement that stretches back for many years—in some cases many hundreds of years.

Additionally, it helps modern-day participants and administrators put their performances in perspective when they realize that many achievements were made by their predecessors with much less suitable equipment and facilities. A historical understanding can also make many performers have more confidence in themselves when they realize that there has been a great deal of activity in their Sports before them and often there is a strong history of participation. For example, gymnastics and table tennis, which now may not seem major sports, have significant past participation levels and in some cases very successful histories.

For all the participants in a competition at the grass-roots level of Sports, it is inspiring to know they are joining a select band of performers who have performed successfully in a variety of arenas worldwide over many years. Such a context is meaningful for everyone involved in the Sports and helps encourage a commitment for the future. Far too often Sports is seen only in its modern setting and not for the considerable history it has given to the nation, the individual and many different communities. The setting of history can also help individuals in realizing their relative unimportance in any given sports setting, perhaps bringing in a little much-needed humility and supporting the belief that no individual or team can ever be bigger than the Sports itself—a key value which must underpin all successful and effective sporting participation and administration. To ignore history is stupid but to rely on it too much is dangerous—learn from it; don't live in it.

Trends in Sports Participation

Sports administrators must always be aware of trends in sports and the resulting effects on participation. Change can be rapid, e.g. the onset of many people retiring early; or predictable, e.g. the reduction in numbers of young people. In any such instance, sports management must react or, better still, anticipate. Published research by Gratton and Tice (1994) indicates that 'between 1977 and 1987 indoor Sports has shown the fastest rate of increase in participation, with 60 per cent more adults taking part in at least one indoor Sports compared to a 13 per cent increase in those taking part in at least one outdoor Sports. The average frequency of participation is also steadily increasing.' This published research also mentions that:

- The average age of participants increased across all activity groups
- The percentage of retired participants increased dramatically for virtually all activity groups
- The percentage of female participants increased in all activity groups except those taking part in only outdoor Sports.

Part of this information was produced through study of the General Household Survey and, although this takes only a sample of the population, it gives a general indication of trends that appear to be prevalent in Sports participation and the related habits of the population at that time.

Interestingly, the administrative base of organized Sports continues to be under national governing bodies, whereas the growth of participation centres on informal and casual sports. Activities and sports such as walking, swimming and golf have large participation levels outside any recognized organizational base. Even where there is a significant governing body in any Sports, e.g. athletics, there is only a minority of participants in formal membership of the governing body.

It is also interesting to note that while governing-body membership has remained static in recent years there continues to be a growing number of small clubs coming into existence. These clubs are still dependent on a large voluntary support basis but indicate a significant existence of sporting interest which is not allied to either local authorities or national governing bodies. This raises the issue of how such more formalized organizations relate to mass participation and involvement on the informal basis.

Another interesting trend has been the rise in overall participation by women, though just to state that would be simplistic, because, within this overall trend, there has been a continuing change towards female participation in keep fit and aerobics, which have seen a 33 per cent increase in a three-year period. Meanwhile there has been some decline in other, more traditional, outdoor activities, to the benefit of indoor sports where women appear to be participating in larger numbers. Women do seem still to be constrained by their lack of uncommitted time and money in comparison to men, and Sports still seems in many situations to be dominated by men and not yet seen as a significant part of women's role in our society.

Almost inevitably, with changing demographic trends, the fastest growing area of sports participation is that of middle-aged and older people. This ties in with the growth in activities such as walking, swimming, bowls and golf. People under 30 tend to participate in the more active and team sports where there are still some problems such as school/club gaps, leading perhaps to lower-than-desired levels of participation and poor standards in some sports. There is, however, a significant participation at an even younger age group—for example, under 16 in sports such as basketball and volleyball.

In terms of social class it would appear that there has been a narrowing of the gap between participation by unskilled manual workers and the professional group in recent years. There is still the issue that some lower social class groups remain relatively disadvantaged and have low participation rates, particularly women in the semi-skilled and unskilled groups. It is interesting to note that this variation is not true across sports as, for example, soccer reflects little difference while golf and squash do.

There also seems to be a small but noticeable difference in participation in the southern parts of Great Britain and particularly greater female participation in the most southerly parts of England—from the east Midlands down. The difference is not enormous but is noticeable, and perhaps is some reflection of the social class factors mentioned above, as well as perhaps reflecting the economic wellbeing of certain areas and the sports facilities provided. Research such as the General Household Survey means that administrators are now better able to identify participation trends in Sports in the UK, and it is important that they look at these trends on a regular basis.

Pricing of Sports Participation

Research by Coalter (1993) indicated that the cost of entrance into sports facilities is a relative, rather than an absolute, determinant in deciding participation. Relatively speaking, the costs of entrance to a range of common Sports-physical recreation facilities are low. This would seem to indicate that the high subsidy culture which exists in the UK is comparatively successful in supporting participation levels. Coalter concludes by saying: It is more useful to view the decision to participate not as a simple economic one, but as indicating an order of priorities, in which the major enabling facility and resource is not just money but time. Decisions to participate are taken within the context of the relationship between values, attitudes and lifestyle factors. It would seem that for most people the actual and perceived cost of sports participation is not simply money but time.

The Economic Impact of Sports

Clearly Sports rests on an economic foundation. Harry Edwards in Sociology of Sports Journal, 1973. The trend in spending indicated by the General Household Survey information suggests an increased participation in Sports and implies a significant impact of spending on Sports for the economy as a whole. Fashion can also have an effect; recently, for example, baseball hats have become trendy, and for many years sports trainers have been popular footwear for daily use. Other implications are raised, e.g. the ability of local authorities to maintain their contribution to Sports with the changes in their powers, the current reorganization and cutbacks in central government support for local government. The lottery, however, has seen a significant increase in spending throughout the country, particularly in the construction industry, architecture and various other project-related spin-offs to the funding raised through the lottery and spent through the Lottery Sports Fund:

The lottery trends are positive but there are threats to spending and it is interesting to set it in context. The economic impact, however, is certainly an argument in support of Sports and the growth it continues to foster for the economic health of the nation. The other key point is that such studies did not attempt to gauge or evaluate the benefits to the productivity of the nation as a whole, of a population made fitter by their participation in Sports; nor, indeed, do they tend to look at the contribution of Sports to the welfare of society. An investigation into both these items would be interesting and perhaps would provide another argument for central government to increase support of Sports.

Sports Clubs

Arguably the most crucial factor in the operation and survival of Sports i is the sports club. The nature of these clubs varies in different sports, geographical locations, facility bases and traditions, but typically they are localized, single-Sports clubs organized by volunteers and living almost hand to mouth from a limited contribution of members' subscriptions, local authority support and other income raised through the contacts or efforts of club members. Some clubs are quite affluent due to recreational play income and relatively high fees—such as golf clubs. Some survive quite healthily through income from bars or other social activities, e.g. bowling clubs or tennis clubs. One of the most difficult areas of Sports to fund is that of youth Sports, especially developing talent, due to the necessity to look to many members to provide the large part of the funds to support the development of future excellence in a few.

The club base is very often made up of a group of parents, friends or experienced performers who administer the club for the benefit of the participants, which they will probably be themselves. There may be support from the local authority, local sports council or other agency. There will be some requirement to affiliate to the local sports council, join the national body to participate fully in the widest range of sports opportunities, and while this may bring some benefits—technical advice, coaching support, competitive outlets—there will also be some cost implications.

The typical model for sports clubs in the UK has very much tended to be single Sports, while sports not necessarily independent (especially in facility use), e.g. many athletics clubs and swimming clubs, use a variety of facilities for their training. This model is not typical of much of western Europe, where community-based multi-sports clubs are much more common. Throughout Holland, Scandinavia, Spain, Germany and France, clubs such as hockey, football and rugby share changing and social facilities as well as playing fields, and there may also be allied indoor facilities for basketball, volleyball, handball, etc.

This type of multi-Sports club is rare in the UK and is much envied by a number of clubs who would see such an amalgamation as quite healthy. It should be noted that there have been some, mostly unsuccessful, attempts at amalgamation in the UK on a local basis, but it would appear that differing histories, social traditions and expectations have caused some practical problems in drawing clubs together effectively. This is a model, however, favoured by many and it is quite likely to be pursued in the future, especially as economic demands place additional difficulties on clubs. Current lottery funding arrangements tend to favour such logical facility developments, which are often beyond the means of one club on its own.

The multi-Sports club does appeal in the sense of combining all resources—not just physical or social, but also in terms of personnel and joint fundraising efforts, etc. The difficulties arise when any funds raised have to be disbursed and significant debate can take place as to how this should be done, pitting one Sports against another or one group against another. The voluntary nature of sports clubs in the UK has been their strength for many years but looking at the fast-changing sporting scene, both domestically and internationally, one has to debate whether the small club units functioning on a voluntary basis can continue to support the development of Sports at a time when individual performers can aspire to be paid tens of thousands of pounds for one appearance.

This dichotomy of individual wealth set against club (and indeed governing body) poverty seems to identify an issue which will cause significant problems for sports in the next ten years at least. The professionalization of athletics and rugby union among others will necessitate serious reconsideration of how such sports are administered at local and national level. The scale of the finance available will mean substantial changes in the operation of the volunteer as opposed to the paid administrator at all levels of Sports. Individuals or teams, paid thousands of pounds, even up to hundreds of thousands of pounds, will not easily coexist with spare-time volunteers in delivery terms. The response time required by paid top performers is short and rightly demands appropriate efficiency from the sport's administration.

This debate will evolve and develop but it seems likely to be performer-and finance-led rather than dictated by the Sports administrators or lower-level participants. For example, the greater funds available have already meant that individuals have been attracted to larger clubs through financial inducements and this trend will continue, further endangering the smaller clubs by removing the cream of the players and encouraging the player to look for (at the very least) substantial expenses packages. It will not seem much of a reward to hard-working volunteers in the local rugby club if everyone they encourage and develop through the early stages (in a voluntary capacity) departs as soon as they show any serious promise, to look for substantial sums of money in a more lucrative club setting. The movement towards buying success even at club level must be a major disincentive to volunteers in the other 'feeder' clubs.

Sports Clubs' Effectiveness

Some interesting lessons can be drawn from research by Koski (1995), who studied 835 Finnish sports clubs in an attempt to analyse their organizational openness and effectiveness. Koski examined five dimensions of effectiveness:

- Ability to obtain resources
- Internal atmosphere
- Efficiency of the throughput process
- Realization of aims
- General level of activity.

He felt that all dimensions except internal atmosphere were interrelated, and his findings indicated that many of the features of effectiveness were largely linked to the size of membership, ideological orientation and organizational environment. Perhaps more worryingly, he found that success orientation was incompatible with a relaxed atmosphere. Finnish sports clubs are similarly independent and voluntary organizations; they are not connected with the school system as happens, for example, in

North America. Koski examined a wide range of clubs—some having only ten members, others having more than 5,000. Some are based on social considerations and social interaction, while others are highly commercial organizations where the main concern is entertainment. Koski feels that sports clubs differ significantly from organizations such as firms or entrepreneurial organizations. He defines effectiveness in relation to the achievement of the functions of the sports club.

Many are moving towards a service of business organization from being based on a non-commercial purpose. Increasing commercialization and business planning are the key developments identified, while there must still be a commitment to the basic ethos of Sports and sports participation. While the dimensions discussed in relation to sports clubs were the ability to obtain resources, internal atmosphere, the efficiency of the throughput process and the realization of aims, these must be underpinned by a high level of general activity, and club operation should be about input in terms of participation as well as financial outcomes.

At the end of his research Koski found that the number of sports disciplines supported by the club was associated with the ability to obtain income and the number of participants. Specifically, clubs specializing in fewer disciplines were more effective than those catering for many disciplines—specialist clubs were able to generate more income. In addition, members of these specialized clubs were more active in their participation in club activities. This movement towards specialized clubs with fewer Sports disciplines is a recent one in Finland—70 per cent of the clubs founded in the 1980s specialized in only one Sports, whereas the comparative figure in the 1930s was only 30 per cent. Koski found that, in general, clubs with clear values underlining their activities were more effective, particularly in their ability to obtain resources and in displaying a high general level of activity. He also found that the size of the club in terms of the numbers of members had a considerable influence in almost every dimension of its effectiveness. The power of the voluntary organization rests on its members—the more members the club has, and the greater the support, the more potential for action the club will have. In large organizations official positions are more sought after, therefore more competent and motivated people are available.

Koski felt that the most important factor of his research as it related to the development of sports clubs was that they must have a broader definition of effectiveness. Other organizations may be satisfied with a narrow set of goals as the means to assess their effectiveness, but voluntary organizations need to broaden their definition of effectiveness and measure it accordingly. Such a broad definition may require further research to generate easily quantifiable indicators of performance, though these may be adapted from effectiveness measures used by others, such as those used by non-profit-making firms.

Issues Facing Sports

Elvin (1993) highlights a number of issues that the Central Council for Physical Recreation (CCPR) has previously identified as management-related concerns or challenges for Sports. These include:

- The sale and subsequent loss of school playing fields,
- The competitive tendering, contract management and the effect on public facilities,
- The national non-domestic rates,
- The taxation on national governing bodies of Sports,
- The development of a coherent role for sports sponsorship,
- The availability of central government funds and
- The structure of Sports

Although these issues were first highlighted ten years ago, most of them still seem live. Perhaps now the following issues could be added:

- The impact of the National Lottery.
- The potential of the Institute of Sports and the mechanisms for implementing this.

- The potential change in government policy from excellence to participation.
- The apparent lack of volunteers coming through to administer Sports.
- The continuing development of international sporting standards
- The level of underskilled staff administering Sports (and indeed coaching it)
- The continuing difficulties in delivering through the new Sports Councils' structures.
- The restriction of local government spending and its impact on Sports and recreation.

As you can see, this list is lengthy and could probably grow daily. There are many problems—actual, perceived and potential—facing Sports, but as ever if they are faced up to in an aggressive and active way then achievements will be made.

Trends Affecting Sports

Being involved in Sports creates attention and, while some in smaller sports may complain about the lack of publicity and image, there is a significant public interest in many things (sometimes unpredictable) that affect Sports. The most recent, perhaps, has been the phenomenal impact of sports clothing (from shoes to hats) on general fashion trends, and this has fed back into Sports, making goods such as training shoes extremely expensive. It has also brought international fame and fortune for major trading names such as Nike, adidas, LA Gear and Reebok, which have become the significant players in the sports game. The amount of money being made by these companies is mind-boggling, and the pressures they can impose are significant in terms of both the fashion market and the influence they can exert commercially in the sports world.

However, recent troubles with ITV Digital and NTL, the telecommuni-cations company, largely caused by over-investment in football, show that such investment is hazardous. Sport's popularity and personalities can be transitory and should be treated with some caution. Obviously, sports organizations should exploit this popularity while they are on the top, but be aware that it won't last forever. In the UK, a lot of sports provision has traditionally been leased in the public sector and a continual government drive to reduce public spending has curtailed the level of provision that many local authorities, in particular, have been able to make. The situation eased just a little as the new century dawned, but given the demands of health, education and social services on public spending, it seems unlikely that Sports will get a great deal more public finance in the foreseeable future.

CHAPTER 2

The Sporting Society

> I think we have undervalued Sports and the place of it in our national life… You watch the morale rise in any Sports when we get a good team. People like Sports and they enjoy it; it is part of our national psychology.
>
> —*John Major, BBC TV Interview, August 1993*

It can be argued that Sports has always preoccupied the mind of humans, perhaps inordinately given its importance. Going back to the ancient Greeks and Romans, physical prowess in relevant sporting fields was seen as important and a mark of someone's characteristics and worth. This perceived status has always put it in the public eye and made it subject to scrutiny, comment and criticism. Even in modern times, apart from the period of the two world wars, the role of Sports and its importance in our society has been a matter of debate in the media and in all forums of society. The social meeting places (including public houses) of our culture constantly reverberate to animated discussions on the sporting prowess and success, or lack of it, of our national team or local favourites. This prominence of Sports has caused its own special problems on many occasions, and has led some dictatorial political figures to exploit its importance in the public mind for their own devious ends.

The marrying of many issues has led to a confusion for sports administrators and participants and has often given added pressure to their involvement. This, for example, can be seen in the relationship between Sports and politics and the participation of women in Sports. The purpose of this chapter is not to come up with definitive answers to any of the issues raised, but merely to identify relevant issues, put some differing views and indicate the possible implications for administrators. These are not matters where definitive answers can be easily provided, nor should they be, but administrators who see their operation in Sports as an island, unaffected by other societal issues, are working in a false situation which will lead to ineffective action.

The range of issues to be considered includes the role of women in Sports, the role of volunteers in Sports (more of which later), professionalism versus amateurism, the use of drugs in Sports, political influence in Sports, and the role and importance of Sports in our society.

Sports Diversity

One of the most interesting things about Sports is its sheer diversity. While many bemoan, with some justification, the lack of a co-ordinated and common approach to Sports, both across sports and within different governing authorities, the width of provision is beneficial for participants and probably allows a wider net to be cast, leading to most people getting caught in it at some time. This causes sizeable problems in terms of the management and administration of Sports, since it is delivered in so many different contexts. The agencies managing and delivering Sports come primarily from three sectors—private, public and voluntary. There are, within each of these, enormous variations and each specific variation can lead to different provisions in a variety of situations.

Within the public sector—by far the largest provider—there are two main operators: national government and local government. The role of the national government is in setting a policy, determining thinking and implementation through the sports councils. There are other government agencies that have an impact on sports provision. A considerable amount of money is spent in pursuing Sports through these agencies and it is generally spent in encouraging others, laying down policy, and what one may call 'pump priming'.

While the home country sports councils claim to be executive bodies, in the sense that they have money to spend and the power to spend it, they are in fact enablers, empowerers and communicators. This must always be remembered by those involved, as it helps clarify lines of communication and action, and assists in reducing duplication or confusion on the part of the sports manager, or even the sports participants. The roles of the national educational agencies can be significant, and sometimes are a little confusing.

It is always worthwhile, however, for the sports manager and administrators to be quite clear as to what motivation government has in supporting Sports and what specific emphasis is currently being applied. In recent years the pendulum of Sports has regularly swung between participation and performance, although there is often a wider dynamic in the sense that politicians may espouse support for mass participation as the key purpose, while happily standing in a photograph with the current Olympic champion—perhaps to bask in the reflected glory and to give support to Sports, but obviously not at a participation level.

The political impact on Sports must not be underestimated, and the effects of decisions of politicians, even on the usual government cutbacks, can be quite significant in terms of sports participation. Equally, decisions can have a major positive impact: for example, the National Lottery is a substantial benefit to Sports and should see an enormous return in terms of personnel employed in the provision of Sports in the UK. It is all too easy, but very dangerous, to minimize the impact of national government and politicians on sporting activity.

Local politicians and local government can also have an enormous effect on sports provision and management. In practice, the money spent by local authorities in support of Sports at all levels far outweighs the money directly spent out of central government funds. There is a common belief among some national agencies and politicians that they are the key players, when in fact the local authorities are the key providers for most sports participants. Their role is crucial and should never be underestimated.

Everyone involved in Sports will have clear examples of positive, active authorities providing meaningful and sizeable opportunities for Sports at all levels within their community. Other authorities, which have not seen their role in sports provision as being quite as large, will create more negative experiences, indicating how the withdrawal or the lack of local initiative and support can be significantly damaging and lead to under-provision in Sports. Local authorities, through relevant departments, can provide personnel and facilities to a variety of standards and levels. A trend in recent years, largely due to compulsory competitive tendering, has been for the amalgamation of generic direct services departments so that Sports has often become part of an overall department along with environmental health and other such direct services. This is a further rationalization of the larger leisure departments formed around 1975 in the last reorganization of local government, but it is not necessarily helpful to take all specialist expertise out at middle management level. Obviously, the thinking is that economies of scale can be achieved. While this may seem beneficial to all concerned, there are possible disadvantages of a larger department, with a general manager, getting others to deliver the services.

One of the disadvantages is that Sports may be fighting for funding and influence within a very large overall department, where it may be seen as quite a low priority compared to emptying dustbins or providing parks and open spaces. Equally, given that some significant amounts of finance can be obtained out of the general pot, there can be significant benefits to a large department in that the practitioner on the shop floor is allowed, with relatively little interference, to achieve their targets and plans. They are actually allowed to do things and make decisions without any bureaucracy above them interfering with progress. There can often be a bureaucratic limitation of work achieved in some local authorities because accountability is felt to be more important than action.

With the advent of unitary local authorities, the link of Sports to education poses another possible threat to its status, but equally provides new opportunities that could see a wider range of activities made available on a more co-ordinated and widely organized community basis. In the local, as in the national situation, the role of the politician is considerable in deciding what funds will be available to what specific facility or activity, and a good deal of convincing will often have to be done to get politicians to spend sizeable monies on Sports, as opposed to related leisure items such as arts, parks and environmental projects.

Role and Importance of Sports in Our Society

One of the major difficulties facing sports administrators and participants is the apparent lack of importance given to sporting participation at most levels.

> Whoever said Sports had nothing to do with politics made a very great mistake. —*Juan Antonio Samaranch, Past President, International Olympic Committee*

Recently the government, and other political parties, have started to talk about how much money is going into Sports through the National Lottery. This discussion is welcome and may be praised, but it prompts the question: If Sports, facilities, excellence, development, and even a British Academy of Sports, are so important, why is such provision left to the whim of the lottery ticket purchaser? If politicians really value Sports, surely some genuine commitment from the public purse should be made. While Chancellor Gordon Brown has allowed some increased revenue funding to the Sports Council, it is still not a budget priority.

> There must also be some justification for supporting Sports on other grounds: economic impact, the health of the nation, international prestige, and the national 'feelgood' factor, to name but a few. The biggest problem today is that the Olympic Games have become so important that political people want to take control of them. Our only salvation is to keep free from politics.—*Avery Brundage in Sports Illustrated, 1964*

Certainly for many of those who reach Olympic-medal level, fame and fortune can follow—though this tends to apply only to sports such as swimming and athletics and not to sports such as fencing, or even perhaps judo. For most people participation in Sports is only for their own benefit in terms of health and enjoyment. Even the potential health links and benefits are often underplayed by the government and certain health agencies, and while this relationship is growing, a robust funding link has not been established. The importance of Sports and the need for funding of Sports are beginning to be recognized by national government, and many now realize that the facilities available do not compare well with other countries, especially those in continental Europe and North America. The funding of Sports has always been low when set against many other items of government expenditure. It has never enjoyed the widespread political support that the arts, for example, have had.

The high status and position given to sports participants and coaches in the USA for example, has never been reflected in our society, and this may be seen as a significant weakness when activities seek publicity and resources. It is a considerable disincentive to participate if your achievements are not widely recognized. A former colleague—a Commonwealth athletics champion—reported how her status changed completely when she went to study at a university in the USA. Her success was widely acclaimed in local and national media, and, wherever she went to compete in the very competitive varsity matches, she became a media personality much sought after for interviews. Many sports media people in her native country would have struggled to know what event she took part in and the level at which she competed, but university-level success brought her fame in the USA.

The issue of high regard applies equally to the coach. In the USA a major college or league coach will be much sought after and very well rewarded in terms of status, standard of life and salary; whereas in the UK, only a very few can command payment outside professional Sports, and generally the status is low, despite efforts by all the UK sports councils and Sports Coach UK to change thinking on this issue. It has long been assumed in the UK that only past performers could possibly be sports coaches with any expertise, and no amount of training could substitute for this personal experience and playing ability. The notion that this past player would automatically become a coach or team manager and would not require any further substantial training has proved spectacularly unsuccessful in some of the major games in the UK.

Coaching has never been seen as a profession that can be entered by serious professional people in order to improve the quality of Sports. It has been seen as one aspect of voluntary support for many sports, therefore requiring substantial training or resources. Fortunately, this situation is beginning to change slowly as governing bodies, at all levels, increase their understanding of the requirement for coach education, and the National Coaching Foundation increases its work in educating coaches with generic coaching theory.

This lack of esteem and importance given to participation and coaching has spread to the area of administration, where the vast majority of sports administration, promotion and development has been left to volunteers on the assumption that they can, in their spare time, fit in all the necessary work and do the job required. Even the training of volunteers has only relatively recently started to be seriously considered by the Sports Councils, and, while training of coaches may have been limited, the coaching of administrators (whether paid or voluntary) was effectively non-existent until the 1990s.

The future will almost certainly see a growth in this area—indeed, it is hoped that this book may help towards that—but realistically Sports can only progress if everyone involved in it has been trained and has sufficient funding and support from many sources, to service and support the performance on the pitch or the games-hall floor.

The Benefits of Sports

Chris Gratton and Peter Taylor, in particular, have written at length on the economic impact of Sports and recreation, and their work is well worth reading for anyone who is advocating a case for Sports (Gratton and Taylor, 2000). In addition, Sports can offer major psychological and physiological benefits through participation. There is some evidence to indicate that physical health and wellbeing can be improved through regular sports participation, although this participation does not need to be of a highly competitive, aggressive or 'sweaty' nature. A vigorous walk or a relaxed swim can benefit general health a great deal and the notion that only lung-bursting aerobics can produce the type of health benefits required is misguided.

People participate in Sports for a wide variety of reasons, and the choice is theirs. It may be for competition, it may be for relaxation, it may be for enjoyment, it may be to get away from everything else, it may be for social reasons—the list is almost endless. The key for the administrator is to be realistic about why participants appear and to cater for them accordingly. Certainly anyone involved in Sports should be given a significant understanding of the benefits available and what they need to do to advance them or promote them to non-participants. There is also a need for all administrators involved in Sports to work hard to promote the benefits and equally to be ready to counter any perceived disadvantages, many of which are quite mistaken. For example, it has become quite widely accepted that drug-taking is a major problem in British Sports. This is not the case, and the few instances where it has been noted have revolved around a very small number of sports. Despite a major testing programme, very few of those tested have been found to take any performance-enhancing substances. The problem we face in our society with social drugs is much, much greater than the minimal problem that Sports may have with drug-taking to enhance performance.

Equally, the anti-competition lobby should, perhaps, be opposed. There is a constant argument that competition is damaging and that Sports promotes unhealthy competition, when in fact there is a strong argument that Sports promotes the more positive aspects of competition rather than the potentially damaging ones which can appear in other aspects of our society. It is an important role for those involved in Sports to be quite clear about the benefits and strengths of Sports and to advocate the case for participation in it. Another societal advantage of sports involvement is that if people are actively participating in Sports, at least they are not doing anything anti-social, e.g. vandalism or other forms of crime. This may appear negative, but it is a valid argument with a factual base—participation in Sports, even highly competitive Sports, is better than anti-social behaviour.

It was implied above that the economic benefits are better left to experts such as Gratton and Taylor (2000) to expound and examine, but one major factor has been the advent of the National Lottery. While a great deal of criticism has been expressed over the size of individual prizes, and the desti-nation of certain funds (e.g. the Churchill Papers), or the perceived tendency to centralize funding in London, there is no doubt that the money being diverted into Sports through the lottery has had a major economic impact not only for Sports, but also for the construction and other industries. This will help with economic regeneration in a number of areas. It is somehow perceived that money from the lottery is taken from people's pockets and is then won by a few, who immediately save it. This is true of only a certain amount of the prize money; the rest partly goes to the Treasury but will also be a significant spend in Sports and other areas. This will have a significant economic impact.

Additionally, now that the government allows some specified development programmes to be supplemented by the lottery rather than capital projects and individual excellence, occupational opportunities and development schemes in Sports stand to benefit enormously. The impact this is having on employment in the sports area is considerable. The economic impact continues to increase, and will certainly soon be another potential study for Gratton and Taylor.

The Aims and Objectives of Sports

There have been prolonged discussions about the aims and objectives of Sports and its suitability to communities, especially in the educational setting. Many have felt that competition was damaging and should not be encouraged through Sports or any other educational activity. The relationship between education, Sports, health and fitness has also been examined at length. While it is unclear what society's general view is, some members of the educational establishment (certainly during the late 1960s, 1970s and early 1980s) felt that Sports, due to its competitive nature, was damaging and encouraged some of the worst aspects of human behaviour.

The evidence for this is patchy and many would argue that since much of our behaviour is developed before the age of seven, children, who do not have direct experience of competitive Sports before that age, cannot be strongly influenced by it. Certainly there is an increasing amount of 'bad sport' in the media and that may be a factor, but it is likely that much of the influence occurs throughout childhood. Some, indeed, would argue that basic competition between human beings is an inherited trait, dating back to the time when humans had to hunt for food and compete with fellow humans in order to survive.

This argument may be equally flawed, but certainly Sports by its very nature is competitive and therefore can produce the bad as well as the good elements of competition. If Sports, like the rest of life, is seen as an individual challenge where one constantly tries to improve one's own performance, even in the team situation, then no damage will be noted, but if it becomes a competition against colleagues, then it is likely that societal and personal damage may occur. In essence, it is important to be aware of the personal challenge of Sports rather than the challenge against other persons.

Sports has also suffered because of its poor image in relation to certain pursuits, through violent and deviant behaviour, as well as other issues such as gender inequality and a lack of recognition of different cultures and ethnic origins, as well as the issue of élitism. It is undoubtedly true that Sports carries a great deal of historical and cultural baggage and has a tendency to be massively dominated by white, largely upper-class, men. There have been noticeable exceptions to this, as football (especially in the professional ranks), rugby league and to some extent sports such as table tennis, gymnastics and swimming have developed through more working-class origins. None the less, many of what were seen as the major games and individual activities have been dominated by the higher echelons of society and indeed have been dragged round 'the Empire' (now the Commonwealth) by the Oxbridge 'mafia'.

The Commonwealth Games have until very recently been a haven for sports of a more traditional nature, largely in the Corinthian ethos—these were the sports taken round the world by the old colonial British. Lawn bowls, shooting, rowing, wrestling and weight-lifting, as well as athletics and swimming, have been the mainstay of this quite traditional event. It would appear now that this event is changing to reflect the sporting balance of the nations involved, and seeing the introduction of activities for teams and of a more modern nature for many of the participating Third-World countries.

The issue of female participation has also altered dramatically in relatively recent times. The last years saw the advent of new events such as the Women's Soccer World Cup and, most recently, the Women's Rugby Union World Cup, both of which no doubt, in time, will grow to be significant sporting events, as a number of other sports owned or now shared by women have become. The old idea of Sports only being played by 'butch' women on hockey fields is outdated and does not reflect modern societal practices or beliefs.

The issue of race is much less clear, and has taken some time to develop. Part of the traditional imbalance of poor black boxers from the ghettos of the USA and other such stereotypes has gradually disappeared as black sportsmen and women have taken over many internationally recognized events and made them their own regardless of their country of origin. People such as Linford Christie, Tiger Woods and Martin Offiah have begun to break down any traditional barriers between cultures or ethnic origins as far as participation and strength of performance are concerned. There are still, however, some big issues over the participation of Britain's Asian community in Sports, even in football at professional league level.

Current Issues

Women in Sports

The role of women in Sports, as in so many other societal situations, has been very mixed. There has been a marked increase in the number of participants in recent years, but the importance of the role of women as top-level coaches and administrators has not always effectively increased to the same degree. Much of sport's hierarchy is still a male domain. There has undoubtedly been an increase in the number of female sports development officers, for example, though few of them have operated at the highest level within the home country sports councils, or the local authorities, or other key agencies in the sports field. There have been some notable exceptions such as Sue Campbell in the National Coaching Foundation and Youth Sports Trust, and now the DCMS (Department of Culture, Media and Sports), Dr Anita White in the English Sports Council, Sue Burgess in the Welsh Sports Council and Pam Scott in the Scottish Sports Council, but the role of women (as in so many other work situations) has not been balanced in terms of sports administration positions, relative even to (sometimes low) participation levels.

There is no doubt that women have not been fully represented in Sports in a variety of ways—as participants, coaches or officials. Even in sports such as gymnastics, in which around 80 per cent of the participants are female, the top official positions have often been held by men. Women have often felt discriminated against within the sporting sphere, and embarked on a long campaign through the 1970s and 1980s to increase their numbers in terms of participation. This has been successful, and figures indicate that the trend is significantly upwards. This increase is important and will very likely continue, though there are some sceptics who feel that the increase is somewhat contrived and involves only a limited number of Sports and physical activity areas, such as aerobics. There has been, however, a definite increase in the number of women participating over the past 30 years, whatever the Sports or the motivation, but there is still a great deal to be done to see an equality of action in many sporting areas. There are several major sports where women are still treated very much as second-class citizens, and in some cases they are almost not recognized at all.

Sports such as bowls and golf often still treat women in a very offhand manner, reminiscent of the way they were treated in every sphere in Britain in the nineteenth century. Women are not allowed to become full members of certain sports clubs, not allowed to play on certain days, not allowed to use certain facilities, etc. These situations are being fought against (in many cases by local authorities and sports councils in grant allocations) in order to ensure equality of treatment, but many are historically based and will only change in the face of continuing strong resistance.

Professionalism and Commitment

> The only true amateurs in Sports these days are those who are no good at it.
>
> —*Christopher Brasher, past athlete and director of the London Marathon*

The issue of professionalism has caused, and for many sports is continuing to cause, significant embarrassment and heart-searching. The debate over whether performers, coaches or even administrators should be paid is ongoing. Many sports, such as athletics, have decided to go open and make all performers eligible for some form of payment (whether into a trust fund or whatever). Others, such as rugby, are still engaged in heated debate as to the activities which may be paid for. Many who, until recently, fundamentally rejected the concept of being paid for playing the game, increasingly accepted that financial rewards are acceptable for many other aspects related to success on the playing field.

This debate also split the two hemispheres, with the south very much favouring open payment for participants. Now professionalism is here for players, and its effects have been dramatic. The long-term effects are not yet fully evident, but, as some had anticipated, the input of professional players appears to have made the rich stronger and the poor struggle. In Wales, the failure to face the 'who pays for this?' question has caused deep splits in the game's administration, while for Bristol in the English top league it has almost brought bankruptcy.

The more that the historian looks for the halcyon days of 'pure' amateurism, the more they recede from view. Tom McNab, sports historian, author and consultant—Scottish Athletics Conference, September 1997. Increasingly, commercial pressures in many sports are such that money is a, if not the, major consideration, and it seems inevitable that performers will demand their share of this money increasingly as time goes on. The necessity to obtain sponsorship and commercial support to secure the very existence of sports events and organizations means that Sports cannot continue to ignore the implications of that input. Some type of return and guarantee will be required by and from the performer, in terms of public appearances and marketing as well as good performances on the pitch or court; it means that he who pays the piper will be able to call the tune, and that the control of Sports will move from the participants to the financer.

Another major consideration in professionalism is whether the coaches and administrators should be paid and professional. Many would argue that the age of successful Sports based purely on voluntarism has passed. If the performers are to be highly paid, then surely all the people who support and enable their participation should be paid also?

Information Technology

The advent of information technology and related technological advances will have a significant impact on Sports, though perhaps not as much as it has in other forms of human operation such as the workplace and the home. There have already been many changes, resulting in the ability to collate membership information on databases, to video and play back performances and to fax and email information around the world. Such developments for all concerned are rapid and are multiplying each year.

These changes will have a major impact on Sports and in all its aspects throughout the world. Technological developments, and the global thinking accompanying them, will continue and will, in essence, benefit Sports and sporting links within and between nations. The ease of talking to someone on the other side of the world, and making arrangements, can only make the sports administrator's life easier and the management of Sports is potentially enhanced in the same way as other business areas. There are additional implications in terms of the personnel involved and the skills they require to face up to the world we live in today. Rapid advances also place additional stresses on those of the older generation, to ensure that they keep up or catch up, at least to some degree.

The benefits of the technology are potentially enormous, but so too are the implications in terms of confidentiality of information, recording of facts, record-keeping, direct mailing and many other aspects of sports administration. The arrival of the Internet and its ability to promote even easier worldwide communication has vast sporting potential. It could bring greater rewards for sports personnel with more international exposure, as well as easing the way for individuals world-wide to link together. Many individuals/stars now have their own website to publicize themselves and encourage their fanbase.

The potential for training individuals in sports administration and management over such an international computer network is significant and soon this aspect of training will match other initiatives in terms of creating training links and opportunities at home and abroad. In essence, information technology and all technological advances should be grasped with both hands by Sports for the benefits they could bring to the whole area, as they do to the rest of our society. If correctly handled and used to achieve agreed targets, these developments are hugely beneficial to Sports and its administration.

The Ethics of Sports

A great deal is made by many different agencies, coming from different viewpoints, of the ethics of Sports and the way in which it is abused by many people for a variety of reasons. Often the perceived negative aspects of Sports are emphasized, and good and correct behaviour (which often appears in the practical situation) is forgotten. As Sports England (1996) states, 'Sports is governed by a set of rules and, often unwritten, principles of behaviour which usually come under the banner of fair play. Sadly, it is often these principles which are not strictly adhered to in a range of sports.' The Council of Europe has produced a code of Sports ethics that covers a wide range of topics, defining fair play, suggesting who is responsible, suggesting what the governments can do to encourage it as well as, ultimately, the individuals involved in terms of personal behaviour and what to do when working with young people.

Key to the consideration of this text for the administration of Sports are the duties identified for sports and Sports-related organizations. These organizations are stated to have the following responsibilities.

- To establish a proper context for fair play.
- To publish clear guidelines on what is to be considered ethical or unethical behaviour and ensure that, at all levels of participation and involvement, consistent and appropriate incentives and/or sanction are applied.
- To ensure that all decisions are made in accordance with a code of ethics for the Sports which reflects the European code.
- To raise awareness of fair play within their sphere of influence through use of campaigns, awards, education material and training opportunities. They must also monitor and evaluate the impact of such initiatives.
- To establish systems which reward fair play and personal levels of achievement in addition to competitive success.
- To provide help and support to the media to promote good behaviour.

A number of special additional points are identified relating to young people, and all of these can be found in the *Code* of Sports Ethics published by the Council of Europe (1992b).

Competition

There is also the issue, highlighted by Elvin (1993) and others, of competition. As we have seen, this is often used to criticize Sports, and it is suggested that somehow competition is created by Sports rather than created by the human race and is therefore an integral part of Sports. While the very worst aspects of competition can be displayed through misplaced motives in sports participation, coaching and officiating, so, more often, can the very best qualities be demonstrated by competition in Sports. Sports can bring out controlled competitive human displays of a quality seldom seen in other aspects of human existence. The genuine camaraderie witnessed even after the most intense rugby confrontation, or the shared joy over a team-mate's outstanding athletics triumph, are examples of the many situations where Sports can control and build relationships, even from its base of competition.

Sports England (1999) suggests that Sports can make a contribution to 'the new policy agenda' by:

- Contributing to the reduction in youth crime
- Improving health and fitness
- Reducing truancy
- Making a positive contribution to young people's attitude to learning
- Assisting in community regeneration (especially by acting as a catalyst in multi-agency co-operation)
- Improving the environment
- Providing opportunities for 'active citizenship' via opportunities for volunteering.

Sports and Society

Aggression v. Team Spirit

There have been prolonged debates, moralistic and practical, about the benefits of Sports in modern society. Two diametrically opposed views exist—one is that Sports can encourage competitive and aggressive behaviour in the individual and therefore should be discouraged; the second is that the social mixing and teamwork encouraged in Sports are beneficial to the individual for their whole life—not just on the sports field.

Football hooliganism is probably one of the main manifestations of violence popularly associated with Sports, though clearly this is not associated with participants but rather spectators. Sports such as rugby also allegedly encourage violent behaviour and discourage people from participating through violent conduct that, to some, seems to be acceptable even within the broad laws of the game. The rugby unions would argue that this is not the case and that their game is strictly governed and in fact encourages fair play, obedience to the referee and controlled physical contact.

A number of other sports rely on a degree of self-confidence and physical presence but avoid any aggression, at least within the rules, and the officials are charged to keep aggression to a minimum. Aggression on the soccer pitch has become a major issue since the police and local authorities began to take an interest, even on occasion prosecuting individuals for assault and other such misdemeanours even though they occurred in a football context. Such behaviour, it is argued, is illegal and unacceptable regardless of the fact it happens under the guise of Sports.

While some would argue that the soccer authorities have been lukewarm about the action taken, this is not the case in most governing bodies, which have been quite strict about adhering to disciplinary standards and support their officials in doing so. Most sporting bodies give total support to officials and ban or suspend competitors who act in an aggressive or violent manner. Even boxing, an overtly violent Sports, has very strict rules about behaviour which are rigorously enforced by the referees and overseen by the medical profession. Indeed, one of the strong arguments in favour of boxing is that the physical discipline in terms of training and the control of aggression—the rules that it brings—actually benefit the participants rather than supporting or encouraging illegal aggression. The martial arts are increasingly popular with a range of ages. The argument for martial arts is that the primary aims are:

- To foster physical fitness and bodily control,
- To encourage self-discipline and an ability to defend oneself, without showing aggression or leading aggression but only responding to it.

A strong argument for Sports is that aggression can be controlled and beneficially handled in a way that is of long-term good for society rather than just an ego. Some psychologists argue that many people take part in Sports to allow their aggression to be taken out, for example, on a squash court or the rugby field rather than in any antisocial or illegal way. Such an outlet for controlled aggression benefits society in preventing potentially major conflicts between individuals as well as encouraging a level of fitness and health which is obviously beneficial to them. It is argued that these benefits to society far outweigh any possible problems caused through aggression brought about through Sports. The issue of Sports and its consequences for society with regard to violence is a sizeable one. Despite recent deaths in the boxing ring, shows of violence on the rugby field and civil prosecutions on the football field, the trend is still to believe that participation is a deterrent to violence rather than an encouragement of it.

Political Context

One of the outstanding features of Sports is that it has been an issue which is not highly politicized. It has never really become a political football, either at local or national level, and while politicians have clung to any success at the top level to claim some personal return in terms of publicity and image, it has never been given the same significance as it has in a number of other countries throughout the world. Nevertheless, the recent Cricket World Cup and England's refusal to play in Zimbabwe caused concern with politicians in the UK who didn't want them to go, and those in Africa who didn't want them to play. Sports is so important as media draw that it must have some political importance, since politicians want media coverage for their stance on sporting issues.

The commercial impact of Sports in the USA is substantial It is highly desirable for politicians to be seen to be supporting Sports, e.g. to give the opening signal to the Super Bowl or to be a close supporter of the Chicago Bulls. This political public credibility through being attached to Sports does not appear in the same way in the UK. John Major's interest in and, close link with, cricket did not necessarily make him a more popular leader or have a great effect on his rather grey image. No political party has ever claimed any significantly different attitude towards Sports as a key issue in its manifesto when looking for public support at elections. This is not something that appears to be highly rated by politicians or, they believe, the voting public. It is equally true to say that Sports has not been used in the UK at the other end of the political spectrum. At no time has any government—left-wing or otherwise—tried to use Sports to ameliorate the population or force them to consider Sports as a major instrument of governmental manipulation.

This is the type of system which did exist in the Soviet Union and in large parts of Eastern Europe for many years after the Second World War. Sports was seen as a means of keeping the population happy; keeping them fit so that they could be prepared to fight in the army as required; and to glorify the state through the success of particular sports performers. These highly structured Sports systems were an integral part of the state's operation and were very heavily funded and encouraged by the government. The position in the UK is quite different. Governments may make comments to indicate their joy about individual sporting successes and espouse support for Sports and the benefits it can bring. However, they will not produce significant sums of money to back up their claimed support and, in real terms, the money given to Sports is small.

The Labour Party has always said that it would give more money to Sports than the Conservatives. Given the opportunity to prove this, it has, but only to a limited extent. All politicians make some positive noises, but in real terms they have made little significant improvement in the funding of Sports in the UK. The advent of the lottery has brought massive injections of money into sports facilities and talented athletes, although the overall percentage and the actual amount going to Sports dropped significantly from 1999/2000 onwards. This is direct additional funding from individuals, not additional government funding support; indeed, the government grasps 12 per cent of all sales.

Sports and Health

Gratton and Tice (1989) came to the conclusion that 'the evidence seems consistent—Sports participants seem to be healthier. Labour will implement a national strategy for Sports dedicated to providing excellence at all levels. This will increase sporting opportunities and improve national sporting performances. We will tackle the decline in school Sports by ending the sale of playing fields and improving PE training for teachers.

- We will develop sporting opportunities for young people to help them foster a sense of their value to society and to help tackle the problems of youth crime. To achieve this we will set up a dedicated Youth Sports Unit within the Department.
- We will provide a more strategic approach to sports funding through existing government grants, the lottery and local authority services. By reducing bureaucracy and increasing effectiveness of delivery mechanisms more resources can be freed for Sports.
- We will focus on play opportunities for children by setting up a new National Lottery good cause for children and children's play.
- We will set up a Taskforce for Football to tackle the problems of the game.
- We will make the Football Trust a recipient of lottery money so that it may continue its essential work for football at all levels.
- We will appoint an advisory body to oversee the listed sporting events on television.

Its remit will be to ensure that top sporting events remain as accessible as possible for viewers across Britain.

- We will implement legislation to make the non-prescribed use of steroids in Sports as well as the supply of steroids illegal.
- We will legislate against ticket touting.
- We will use all the power of government to help bring major international events such as the World Cup and the Olympic Games
- Local authorities will be encouraged to develop and publish a leisure and sports strategy.
- Sports will continue to be a permanent good cause for the purpose of lottery funding.

The general conclusion of Gratton and Tice's study was that 'participation in Sports not only makes the participant healthier, but also provides an enriched quality of life by stimulating participation in a whole range of non-Sports leisure activities'. They felt that for government and other agencies the policy implication of this research was clear— 'greater emphasis should be placed on encouragement to take part in exercise as an important component of preventative healthcare'. This research was based on a number of pieces of leisure research and data, in particular the General Household Survey. It indicates quite strongly that participation in Sports, while not guaranteeing health in itself, can be a significant impetus to health or at least preventive healthcare. It would appear that there is a real need to increase our sports participation, if only because it will improve our health. One would hope that one day politicians will match the two, and realize that one way to save money on the health service is to spend money on Sports.

The importance of people just taking part in Sports for enjoyment, fitness and health should not be underestimated. Their motivation will often be as strong as those with a desperate desire to win. While most people look for some sort of challenge in Sports and/or satisfaction through a quality performance, at their own standard, it should be remembered that everybody is in there to be what might be more widely perceived as 'a winner'. The definition of winning is often a personal rather than a public perception—the feeling one gets if one has achieved the level of one's own best performance is often much more important and satisfying than any concern over beating others. Feelings of improved health and activity can also be a major incentive for Sports.

Where We Practise Our Sports

One of the most challenging and interesting aspects of sports management and administration is the vast range of situations in which this takes place. As mentioned above, it is important to note that we have a situation of sports management and organization within the private, public and voluntary sectors. Each of these has its own special problems and constraints from an ethical, as well as organizational operation point of view. There is an added dimension to much of Sports due to the facility base, and the possible constraints placed upon organizers by the sports facilities available for the participant. Many of the implications of management and administration are similar regardless of the facility, but equally a sizeable number of procedures and other factors will alter depending on the exact nature of the facility provision, and the demands that this puts on the skills of managers and other staff, as well as budgets.

Sports Facilities

The enormous range of sports facilities makes them almost too many to mention—Sports of some nature can take place in almost any indoor or outdoor facility. Many sports demand highly sophisticated facilities but others can take place, especially at the participation level, in the most rudimentary area with nothing but the bare essential equipment, or even adapted or invented equipment which approximates to the ideal. Football, for example, can be played in the Olympic Stadium in Munich or in the back garden—it can be played by one person with one improvised ball of paper or by 22 highly paid professionals using a top-quality ball. Both of these situations are Sports, and while one of them may require very little management and the other a great deal, there are levels between these, many of which require significant managerial, organizational and administrative input. The implications of the facilities must be recognized, however, and the desire of many sports people is to produce more sophisticated facilities.

They hope for a level of participation and performance which will improve given suitable facilities. This is why so many sports groups are spending much of their time and resources in seeking lottery funding and other possible support, in order to try to take their sport's facilities to an appropriate level to enhance numbers and excellence. Complex sports facilities can be very expensive in terms of capital construction costs, and often in terms of running costs as well. This causes problems for the organizations or agencies responsible for funding during the design and build stage, and on through to the service provision stage, on an ongoing basis. The range of facilities includes the following:

- *Playing Fields*—covering outdoor areas where Sports and activity take place, such as school playing fields, private club playing fields and public playing areas.
- *Recreation Areas*—these cover areas such as National Parks, outdoor education facilities, country parks, waterways and lakelands used by many different groups for a variety of activities, from hill walking to canoeing, from rock climbing to orienteering and sailing.
- *Artificial Surfaces*—this growing area includes surfaces provided for activities such as tennis, hockey and football on artificial turf. This facility is now used for an increasing number of sports, for example cricket. Considering British weather, it is likely that such use will continue to grow.
- *Athletics Tracks*—these are nowadays largely of a rubberized surface—running on an ash or grass track is no longer acceptable for anything beyond the most basic athletics.
- *Golf Courses*—there has been a substantial growth over the past 20 years in the number of golf courses provided. This continues, perhaps most noticeably in the past few years in terms of the private sector looking to capitalize on the popularity of this Sports, and farmers trying to maximize land use and profit. However, as for many sports, we are not willing to pay a high price and have a traditional view that golf is a game for everyone, played at a reasonable price, especially on local community courses. The number of people able to pay the high prices demanded by some of the exclusive clubs and the new private developments is limited, and this has led to a number of proposals for high-cost memberships and various shareholding schemes being unsuccessful.

- ***Stadia***—in this area there is a significant range of provision by private, public and voluntary sectors, particularly for soccer and rugby, but there are a number for athletics and some other less well known sports, such as shinty in the north of Scotland or hockey at one or two specialist facilities. There can be little doubt that we have been very poorly provided for in terms of big sports stadia and still has nothing which would match the large range provided in a number of countries in Europe or further afield.
- ***Specialist Facilities***—a growing trend in a wide variety of sports is to require specialist facilities for top-level competition or training. For example, cyclists must have a velodrome, and such a requirement pushed the government into providing appropriate facilities for Manchester to back up its Olympic bid. To reach world-class level, gymnastics needs a high level of facility provision (pitted landing areas) for training. Tennis, as a Sports, will only be successful if it has a continued significant growth in the number of indoor courts available.
- ***Multi-purpose Sports Halls***—a vast range of these halls exists, but investigations by the Sports Council have shown that we are still significantly short of such facilities. Also, because of their multi-purpose use they tend to be dominated by mass participation sports such as indoor football or badminton. Again, the specialist requirements for sports such as basketball and volleyball need to be recognized in the construction and management of such facilities.
- ***Swimming Pools***—swimming is undoubtedly the most popular specialist Sports, and there is a wide community provision of pools. They tend to be leisure pools or too small for high-level events. Swimming is far and away the UK's most popular (active) recreational 'sport' and obviously, with our inclement temperatures, it must be

done indoors. The growth of swimming pools in recent years has tended away from the traditional rectangular pools which cater for competitive or fitness swimming, towards the leisure pool with flumes and water slides and chutes to attract all the family. It is increasingly recognized at this time that provision of both types of facilities will interest a wider range of the population, keep an active customer base longer and provide better for the health and fitness of the community. Now many leisure pool constructions attempt to include a 25-metre learning or fitness pool alongside, or even integrated into, the overall design.

- ***Footpaths***—walking has many participants, but most do it more for exercise and fresh air than any specialist form of sports participation.
- ***Ice Rinks***—these facilities are very popular with a variety of client groups, being used by three main groups: curlers, ice skaters and ice hockey players. Programming can be difficult, as each of these groups feels that it is short of time or put off from certain times at the facility to allow for others. This natural dynamic causes significant problems on what is limited available, desirable ice time.

While the weather can be somewhat inclement, it seldom prevents participation in one Sports or another. We also have a significant outdoor resource in the form of our extensive coastline and vast areas of grassland and hillside, which can be walked and enjoyed by the whole population. This is a major benefit which we must protect for many reasons, including the health, fitness and sports participation of the community. This variety means that the sports manager has a responsibility for a very wide physical area in many situations.

CHAPTER 3

Role of the Voluntary Sector

Despite the problems with the voluntary sector in respect of development potential and its patchy response to external initiatives, it is too big to ignore. In particular,a research discloses a total adult sports volunteer force of 5.8 million people. The key characteristics of these volunteers in relation to the development of sports participation are their enthusiasm and social motivations. Harnessing these qualities in attracting new members/ participants is the challenge for Sports. Any initiative to engineer growth in participation in the voluntary sector, however, will involve a considerable degree of inefficiency because of the problems in the sector. Nevertheless, the voluntary sector should be treated seriously as an agent for driving up participation. To this end, Sports should actively seek resources to extend and improve VIP; create smart solutions to promoting activity development in voluntary sports organisations without increasing workloads; and expand sports development services in local authorities, particularly to stimulate school-club links.

Thus far the implications are rather bleak. Faced with a conspiracy of problems caused by societal changes and national institutions' requirements, voluntary sports organisations are hard pressed to deliver their core activities, and many are doing so with diminishing and increasingly hard-pressed volunteer resources. The scope for such organisations taking a lead role in developing participation in Sports seems as remote as hoping for significant extra funds for local authority sports development from the Exchequer. However, the picture is not all black and to give up on voluntary organisations as agents for the development of sports participation on the grounds above would be premature. Voluntary sports organisations which are of the contemporary/ formal type have the managerial skills and techniques to promote development and respond to external initiatives. In addition the research indicates:

- Whilst 40% of voluntary sports organisations have falling volunteer numbers, another 40% have increasing volunteer numbers.
- The majority of voluntary sports organisations contacted did not report volunteer recruitment difficulties.
- The most frequently identified reason for the increasing workloads in voluntary sports organisations contacted was not greater bureaucracy and persistent volunteer shortages, but rather increased activity, such as expansion of membership numbers, new junior sections, new female teams/competition, new veterans' teams/competition, and new events.

Therefore, expansion of participation is occurring in parts of the voluntary sports sector, because of increasing demand, combined with the capacity and willingness of voluntary sports organisations to accommodate expansion. To what extent such growth is at least in part facilitated with external assistance, rather than purely organic growth, is not known. Nevertheless, there are sufficient positives in the participation development potential of some voluntary sports organisations.

External Assistance for Voluntary Sports Organisations

The extent to which voluntary sports organisations show awareness and have made use of external assistance is one test of the possible extent of contemporary/formal organisations. This is particularly the case when one of the defining differences in such organisations is their attitude to external assistance. Many of the problems and constraints facing voluntary sports organisations cannot be solved from inside Sports – they are caused ultimately by societal changes and/or pressures from central government. Stimulating much of the voluntary sports sector to undertake new developments to help drive up sports participation will be very difficult against the backcloth of societal changes, institutional pressures, volunteer shortages, increasing volunteer workloads and volunteer recruitment difficulties.

Nevertheless, the voluntary sector is too big to ignore. According to the Sports England research there are well over 8 million members of voluntary sports clubs affiliated to NGBs, which is a substantial participation base. Even small rates of growth in this sector will represent significant increases in sports participation. More importantly, the research discloses a total adult sports volunteer force of 5.8 million people. These include volunteers contributing in unaffiliated sports organisations and those contributing informally for family and friends rather than within organisations. The key characteristics of these volunteers in relation to development of sports participation are their enthusiasm and social motivations. Harnessing these qualities in attracting new members/participants is the challenge for Sports. Any initiative to engineer growth in participation in the voluntary sector, however, will involve a lot of waste in the sense of inefficiency. This is because not all the sector is amenable to external policies and incentives – in fact probably a minority of sports organisations are likely to respond positively.

The inefficiency of policy delivery through the voluntary sector is exacerbated by the difficulty of identifying the appropriate targets - the contemporary/formal organisations which are receptive to development incentives. Thus some of the resources to stimulate participation development will 'fall on stony ground'. But this is not a new situation – many economic development initiatives suffer failures which at least partially offset the successes; many people trained in specific skills move to other vocations; some lottery projects fail; etc., etc. Nevertheless, an inefficiently stimulated voluntary sports sector may offer as good or better prospects for participation growth than a heavily constrained public sports provision sector, or a commercial sector with relatively narrow sporting interests. To this end, Sports should actively seek resources to achieve the following:

- Extension and improvement of VIP
- Smart solutions to promoting activity development without increasing workloads
- Expansion of sports development services in local authorities, particularly to stimulate school-club

Voluntary Organizations

The nature of Sports is that it operates on the basis of voluntarism. This reliance on volunteers probably has many weaknesses, but it certainly has many strengths. The professionalization of sports administration and governing body and club organization in Sports remains limited, despite their growth over recent years, and while some would argue that there is an ever-growing need to move towards a more professional attitude, most realize that it would be impossible to find the funds to pay the large number of people who work in sports administration in Britain. A massive voluntary workforce drives Sports forward in the UK, and it is important that everyone operating in the field, in a paid or unpaid capacity, understands the nature of voluntary organizations and the limitations which can be put on certain spheres of operation. For example, it is extremely difficult to be strictly businesslike and curtail individuals' right to speak at meetings if they are, at the same time, giving up a great deal of their own time to support the operation of Sports.

Such a sympathetic argument, however, is not a basis for supporting bad practice or for allowing people to talk forever on the same subject, going nowhere and benefiting no one. Individual volunteer officials can be seen as stakeholders in the business—the sports organization—through the input that they make, so they deserve to be heard and should always be considered. This never justifies not being businesslike about the manner in which organizations operate, but it does argue strongly against being ruthless in the operation of these principles—this may be justifiable (debatable!) in business situations, but it can never be seen as justifiable in the voluntary scene. While the principles in theory are the same, their implementation in practice should be softer.

The absolutely vital necessity for anyone working in a sports organization or a sports setting is to have a fundamental interest (not necessarily a technical knowledge, but an interest in the Sports) and an empathy with all the other people involved. It is not necessary to be a fanatic, and sometimes it is a distinct disadvantage because fanatics can become blinkered to new ideas and different ways of doing things. It is, however, quite important that people understand the fanaticism and the love that people have for a Sports so that they can relate to them on a meaningful level. There are many examples of people trying to come into the leisure scene, including Sports, and telling others how to operate, while clearly not understanding where the sports volunteer organization or agency is coming from in terms of interest and commitment. This is a recipe for disaster, and has proved extremely unsuccessful in a number of situations and caused a good deal of antagonism and upset within organizations.

A classic example of this is for an organization to appoint an administrator who has no understanding of the Sports. This can be fine, as long as they develop an interest and an empathy for the Sports and the people involved, and they come to understand the old concept that the participant is king. What simply does not work is the situation where the administrator believes that the filing system is the most important issue, and where efficient administration does not recognize the unique situation of Sports, as well as the quite remarkable commitment and interest of all the people involved in the body—paid or unpaid. There are many examples of this not working, and staff lasting only for a short period.

It also must be recognized that there are significant differences between sports organizations and other voluntary organizations—indeed, there can be noticeable differences between one sports body and another. It is always an error to assume that they are all the same and that they all have the same problems. This is simply not true. Many of the issues are shared, but they are never exactly the same and an open approach must always be taken—any attempt to approach such bodies with preconceived notions will be unsuccessful. There is no doubt that, as in many other situations, sports bodies and other voluntary bodies can learn from each other in many areas, but they should not automatically be regarded as the same.

The need for officials to understand the functioning of voluntary organizations generally, and sports organizations in particular, is vital, but it must be set in the context that each particular governing body and/or its situation is unique. Charles Handy (1988), in one of his many excellent books, Understanding Voluntary Organizations, examines voluntary organizations generally and looks at the people involved in the organization and how they should be organized. This and other such texts are well worth reading because they show other examples which illuminate the sports situation. They should not be taken as the definitive type of text on sports organizations—probably such a text has not yet been written—but there is always much to learn from such general management books and, in particular, one which relates to voluntary organizations, which share many problems whether they come from Sports, the arts, community care or charity situations. An individual studying voluntary organizations needs to look at the organization, its culture, the people involved and its internal and external relationships, as well as learning from other bodies with similar characteristics.

Sports is a Voluntary Concept

It is estimated that in the UK between one in two and one in five of the population are volunteers on a regular basis—that is, they make a weekly voluntary contribution to some organization, individual or group. This volunteering capacity is increasing rather than declining. This growth is in response to increasing personal involvement in community life, and the potential such involvement gives for personal development. The growth in voluntarism or the interest in volunteering reflects the change in our society in a number of ways:

- The removal of government or local authority intervention in a number of areas.
- The reduction of funding available for certain activities.
- The proliferation of new activities.
- The changing policies of government, e.g. community care, lottery funding.
- The increased number of retired (especially early retired) people.
- The growing desire to be of service to the community outside the workplace.
- The need to feel personal worth.
- The desire to benefit others.

All these factors have caused a significant rise in the commitment of volunteers, but their role is always threatened as pressures build on them, and initiatives to support them are always required. As mentioned elsewhere in the text, it is essential that volunteer support and training are given to maintain enthusiasm and interest where it exists or engender it anew in people who have not previously been involved in volunteering.

The voluntary ethic, although it is often decried, is important and will continue to be so for Sports and other areas of our society in the foreseeable future. It should not be underestimated or in any way demeaned. Any effort in this text, or elsewhere, should be to streamline it, improve it and focus it, but never to discourage it because it has such a lot to offer and is irreplaceable. Sports in the UK is said to have over 1.5 million volunteers involved, who give an average of 2.5 hours per week to their chosen activity.

National Governing Body Recruitment: A national governing body of Sports employs an administrator, and is having difficulty in retaining him/her. It has taken different approaches in making appointments:

- Recruiting someone from a Sports background with relatively little administrative skill or background experience.
- Selecting an administrator with sports background, but an extensive administrative CV.
- Choosing someone, previously a volunteer, who now wanted to move into 'running the sport' on a full-time paid basis.

All had their own problems, not identified during interview and selection or addressed in inducting the person into the post. The problems exist in a number of areas, which often include:

- Paid v. voluntary
- Little technical knowledge v. lots of technical knowledge
- Sports knowledge v. administrative knowledge
- Fact v. perception
- Commitment to Sports v. commitment to job
- Management v. leadership
- Short-term knowledge v. years of experience in the Sports.

Voluntary Ethos

Voluntary organizations by their nature tend to be very jealous of their *raison d'être* and guard their voluntary role and their independence very closely. They tend to believe that they are involved as volunteers to further the voluntary cause almost as much as they are there as sports administrators to further the sporting cause. There tends to be a belief that organization, administration and management should be in the hands of the volunteer and should not require the same level of competence and organization as business situations. A sort of 'slapdash' amateur attitude is felt to be acceptable because there is no compulsion or salary attached. This ethos of the administrative support service being self-justifying or acceptable for its own sake is the traditional feeling in many sporting organizations. Such a belief is incorrect and unjustifiable because it does not produce quality support or delivery for the performer and the organization.

The voluntary commitment shown is enormous, and should be matched by a serious, professional attitude being adopted by such people to a level that does not embarrass or cause the performers any difficulties, and will deliver their requirements on a quality and consistent basis. Proper management and administrative practices are vital to effective sports performance on the field of play, as are quality coaching and talented committed athletes. Ignoring the benefits of good business management may bring about a number of significant potential dangers to any sporting organization.

In particular, there will be an almost inevitable lack of strategic direction or vision in the organization. This in turn will lead to poor direction which follows from indifferent or non-existent planning and goal-setting. Individuals will often see themselves as slaves to the organization and to the cause, giving their time to perform basic short-term tasks without any view to the future, when they may no longer be involved, or without any vision concerned with what the organization could achieve for its participants in the future. Service for service's sake and short-term performer excellence are sometimes seen as more important than real long-term achievement, or building lasting foundations.

For the future this complacent belief can lead to inadequate co-ordination and administrative activity, and means that the organization will not function as effectively as it could. It could imply a lack of leadership and everyone will tend to push their own point of view and stick to it doggedly, because they have a major role in the organization and a background of service, rather than speaking with a view to achievement.

A key factor in much of this lack of management and planning is often a lack of understanding by many of the participants at all levels of sporting organization as to what exactly the organization exists to do and what each individual's role within that organization is—whether as an administrator, coach, player, manager, official or member of the medical staff, each individual should have a clear idea of what they are there to do within the overall organizational structure. Both individual and organizational goals should be quite clear and explicitly stated for all to be aware of and understand.

Voluntary Sports Organizations

Amis et al. (1995) studied a number of sports organizations in the USA and Canada with a view to examining the role of and relationship between staff and committees, and the internal relationships in the organization and their function. A few notable conclusions were reached, the first being that 'analysis of the data does nothing to disprove the contention that conflict is endemic in VSOs'. It was also felt that 'the organization's design must be thought of as a major contributing factor to conflict in VSOs'. The many pressures facing such organizations were identified and it was suggested that they were causing stress and conflict within the organization. The various sub-groups and subcommittees working within the organization almost inevitably conflicted with each other. The authors suggested that this 'increased susceptibility to conflict must be addressed if the organization is to function productively'.

In addition, the findings indicated that the voluntary nature of these organizations adds considerably to the potential for conflict. While the combination of voluntary leadership and professional expertise is an appealing notion, it is also highly problematic. The differing values and expectations of each group...make the voluntary, professional relationship inherently conflictual.

The findings of the study were that this conflict degenerates into major issues. The very structure and informality of such organizations, especially as they face financial and other resource restrictions, exacerbates existing problems. This study provides some very clear evidence that there are significant and difficult dynamics and conflict within voluntary organizations, but is unable to offer significant solutions because 'until the causes of conflict are understood the process of conflict management will remain unviable'. It does shed some light on the nature and scale of the conflict, but notes that further detailed research must be done to gain a deeper understanding of why such conflict exists and how it is caused. Such a study would substantially assist in identifying causes of, and hopefully in turn solutions to, the problems facing such organizations not just in North America, where this study took place, but in other areas such as the UK.

One final quotation from Amis et al. (1995) is very relevant for sports managers and administrators: 'it is worth reiterating that although the conflict may become manifest as a dispute between individuals, it is as a result of their membership in conflicting sub-units. The conflict remains, therefore, structural, not interpersonal.' This statement has major implications for sports managers in that they should perhaps be considering organizational structure and team operation more than personal or interpersonal skills. When considering the problems facing such voluntary sports organizations it is all too easy to rush off and blame various individual personalities, and strengths and weaknesses, without examining the structure of the organization and its inherent conflict creating mechanisms.

Management of Voluntary Organizations

Thibault *et al.* (1994) drew on various research sources to establish that, in essence, there had been very little research into voluntary sports organizations and their use of strategic planning had been very limited. The study set out to look at this lack of evidence of strategic planning and tended in its conclusions to support the notion of contingency, i.e., that there should be a good fit between the environment and the strategy undertaken—that the strategy should match the specific situation and need, because there is 'no universal set of strategic choices optimal for all businesses'.

The conclusion of Thibault *et al.* was in fact that people will have 'a better opportunity to successfully implement a strategy when it is congruent with the environment'. This clearly implies that every voluntary sports organization must consider its own situation before developing a strategy and should not necessarily follow the strategy or direction of another.

Thibault *et al.*'s research is very interesting. It follows and strengthens the belief that each situation or voluntary organization in Sports is different and should be assessed as such, and that the 'broad-brush approach' to sports organizations and any problems thrown up for administrators and managers is not appropriate. This finding matches the belief that voluntary bodies in Sports—clubs, governing bodies or other associations—have the right to go their own way and make their own policy, regardless of what others may wish them to do. The relationship with others in both the public and private sectors can be complex and often difficult for all partners to understand, but for volunteers autonomy is paramount.

Very often, the local authority or national sports council will wish the voluntary body to go in one direction—in line with a national or local 'political' policy—but that may not be what is perceived as being in the best interest by the volunteer. Ultimately, since much of Sports operates in a voluntary sphere, the volunteers' decision is the vital one. Sometimes the autonomy of voluntary organizations can be seen as a threat to politically motivated authorities or those with other perceptions as to the needs of the local community, who are, in short, coming at the provision of Sports from quite a different angle to that of a self-motivated, sports-specific voluntary organization.

As far as the private sector is concerned, their relationship with voluntary organizations can be mutually beneficial in terms of generating business for them, through sponsorship and other such commercial relationships. They may be involved in a partnership which can lead them to supplying goods or services at a cost to the voluntary organization and its members. This is often a more clear-cut relationship than that which involves policy—there is an identifiable bottom line.

The scope, sphere of operation and diversity of the voluntary sector are almost inestimable. There are thousands of voluntary groups working in a variety of sectors in the UK, and in Sports their numbers are enormous. It is very hard to estimate the number, but it is believed that around 10 per cent of the population give service to voluntary organizations and, in Birmingham alone, there are over 8,000 voluntary groups, of which three-quarters are concerned with Sports, cultural or social welfare activities (Badmin, 1992, 1993).

Research by Sports England (1996) suggested that over 1.5 million people are involved in providing sports opportunities, for themselves and others, in the UK. The areas of interest covered by Sports organizations include activities as diverse as wheelchair basketball, national dance, baton twirling, ice hockey and aerobics. Such organizations may have very different technical demands and requirements but, in essence, they have the same management requirements. Most draw on limited resources and finances, and they all put demands on a limited number of potential volunteers to keep them functioning. This commitment of individuals within the organization, which is remarked upon several times in this text, must be understood by people dealing with voluntary organizations in the sporting sector. The motivations and motives of volunteers and voluntary organizations are perhaps the key issues that need to be clearly understood by all who have anything to do with them.

Sports organizations may also have some unique characteristics that separate them from other voluntary sector organizations in terms of their very clearly determined role, the disciplinary control over participants and officials, and their need to link and liaise with other organizations such as district leagues, national bodies or even international bodies. Such differences mean that it is often difficult for any sports voluntary group to remain totally autonomous and independent except for solely recreational organizations. As soon as a higher level of competition or performance is involved, the body must become very complex.

Another key area of knowledge for a sports organization is to recognize where volunteers come from. They will often come from past performers or the parents of current performers, while it is rare, if welcome, that someone enters as a willing volunteer just because of some desire to promote the good of others, or some innate interest in a particular sporting activity. One could argue that the scarcity of volunteers in the latter group has been a weakness: that there tend to be too many individual vested interests, and people only last in sports administration for 50 years because nobody else will do the job. This view is perhaps a little negative when there are so many good people doing a high-quality job in a vast array of sports organizations, many of which have lasted for 100 years or more, totally dependent on quality voluntary effort. The pressure on the organizations and the volunteers themselves appears to be growing significantly, and is perhaps best explained as follows.

1. The diminishing availability of finance from local authority, government or commercial support, set against the constant driving up of the cost of participation in Sports, makes it more difficult for volunteers to have even their expenses met by the sporting organization. This creates costs for such voluntary administrators which many cannot bear for long.
2. The pressure in the workplace on many individuals has meant that they have very little spare time, and must consider using it in a paid way to help meet the growing cost of living.

In short, the lack of individual finance, the cost of Sports and the cost of living are all threatening the commitment, interest and availability of volunteers in a variety of areas. A growing number of people are asking why, if their time is to be used in support of others, it should be at considerable additional cost to themselves, at a time when they could perhaps be earning money instead of paying out money for no return (apart from their own enjoyment).

The role of the voluntary sector, and its relationship with the public sector at national and local level, is another 'life-threatening' or, at least, enthusiasm-diminishing aspect of work in sports voluntary organizations. There tends to be a view among the volunteers that the paid officials and organizations should be doing more for them and their sporting organization, through grant aid or substantial administrative support. At the same time there is often an unreal expectation from paid full-time officials as to what volunteers can achieve in the limited time they have available to commit to their organization. This divergence of positions and expectations can lead to strained relationships between organizations and individuals, in addition to the differences that the public and voluntary sector organizations may have, as outlined above.

The Nature of Voluntary Organizations

Voluntary organizations can often be self-perpetuating, especially if they are not focused. They should be open organizations that seek out change and look for new members at all levels, all the time—people with potential to help the organization function should be actively targeted and brought on board at every possible stage. There is a very common complaint of cliques and small introverted groups holding power within many sports organizations, and this can be off-putting for individuals that we should be looking to attract. It is in the nature of human beings that we do tend to socialize with people we know and are somewhat resistant to new people and their new ideas—we may feel threatened and often react in a negative fashion when someone tries to join in.

Again, it is crucial that the members of the organization know what the goals, individual and organizational, are and that everyone, new and old, is driving in the same direction. They must understand and allow for human quirks and differences, while not allowing these personal characteristics to destroy active achievement. If the goal is always to seek organizational improvement, then good people will always seek the support and involvement of others to get the task achieved. The role of team-building is vital and all the participants in sports administration need to be team workers so that they can pull together towards common aims, and involve all other willing volunteers.

Appreciation of group dynamics, as well as individual personalities, will help sports administrators recognize that each group needs different personalities to play different roles both formally and informally, and while they have their individual roles they also help the group function together—helping push forward a decision or showing the leadership what is required to achieve progress. It is always best that people are sympathetic and understanding to such processes and roles, especially informal ones, rather than resistant to them. An understanding that people have their views, desires and targets, individually as well as within the group, and that they have a role to play in the cohesion of the group, will help everybody work together for the benefit of the organization.

Organizational Structures and Personalities

Within the sports world there are a variety of structures—both formal and informal—and there can be conflict between them and the official structures or the structure recognized by outside agencies. Many informal structures are stronger, and in some ways more important, than the formal structure. Often one individual can dominate the sports setting: where this person is the club coach or the national governing body president, they can be the dominant figure leading the organization forward or holding it back. This strong individual can be a major benefit to an organization where he or she is working for its betterment, but there is a danger of some type of personality cult forming and one individual becoming too dominant. A good co-operative leader is extremely valuable, but an authoritarian or dictatorial individual could cause major problems for the organization, internally and externally.

Inevitably an organization will be associated with the personalities in it and, while they can be a major strength, no one personality should dominate or exclude all others. Regardless of their abilities, such domination will be limiting in some way and will detrimentally affect the organization's reputation. Sports, by its very nature, is personality-dominated and strength of character is one of the qualities it produces in people. Inevitably sports management and administration will be no different from performance on the squash court or hockey field in this respect. Equally, to continue the on-field analogy, individuals need to be part of a team to be most effective, regardless of their talents and abilities, because the sum achievement of many will always outweigh the efforts of one.

As mentioned, the key concept for all individuals involved in the organization, at whatever level, is for them to understand what tasks have to be performed for the most effective operation of the agency to the benefit of the Sports and those involved in it. In essence, it is always much better for any organization to be focused on the tasks to be performed and to take account of personalities and feelings than to be focused only on personalities themselves. It is important that individuals and structures are aimed towards achievement of the task in the most efficient and effective way.

To adopt a task-focused approach will be most effective, as long as such an approach allows individuals to show their true talents and allows others to realize their individual aims within the organizational structure. If we focus on the task then solving problems and making decisions becomes a great deal easier, and can, usually beneficially, be de-personalized. Many sports organizations have what might be referred to as the club—often social club—ethos. This is where a small group dominates the operation and involves others only when it sees fit. It could be seen as a series of concentric circles with fairly strict boundaries between them which are difficult to penetrate. There is often a real difficulty for individual members in penetrating the inner sanctum and having real effect on the operation of the organization.

While a central, small, active management group may be effective in getting things done, it always needs to be aware of what is happening around it and should be keen to draw other individuals into the organization and its activities, rather than fight hard, as many social groups do, to exclude others and their expertise. By keeping to a small clique you will inevitably restrict the activity of the organization to the aims of a few, which will be to its major detriment in the short or long term.

Such a clique can often build up round the club coach, manager or similar type of person, with a strong personality, views and commitment. Such people have a capacity to destroy rather than create small interest groups. It is essential for a sports organization to have a clearly identified structure—probably hierarchical, where each individual has a clearly identified role to play in achieving progress for the organization. This type of structure is perhaps a little dated because it relies on clearly defined levels of management, but it gets things done and means that people are quite clear as to what they are in the organization to do. It can be especially useful in 'spare-time amateur' organizations. In essence a highly structured organization can be quite helpful in that it helps clarify and delineate individual roles, and allows people to achieve their tasks within the clear structure.

It is vitally important that sports organizations have an open approach to involving everyone who has something to offer to the Sports and its participants. An attitude which excludes individuals is most inefficient, ineffective, divisive and damaging, and can create strife within the organization. The ethos of any sports organization is key in the sense that the morals, attitudes and standards it portrays will be carried right into the games hall or sports field, through its organizational structures. There is a moral side to sports administration and this must be understood and appreciated by all those involved, so that it can underpin everything that is undertaken. A dated 'public school' type of organizational belief and behaviour may be quite inappropriate to sports organizations in the twenty-first century, but still the principles of morality and fairness they brought to administrative and management roles as well as performance are essential to retain the very nature of Sports.

Governing Bodies

In terms of Sports in the UK undoubtedly one of the most significant influences is that of the national governing bodies. These organizations represent the clubs, districts and interested individuals who constitute sports participants at different levels in the UK—in other words, the very sizeable voluntary sector. These governing bodies can range in size from only a few people, in cases such as a minor martial art or hang gliding, up to thousands of members with a substantial professional organizational base in sports such as association football and rugby union. There can be many problems with the operation of these organizations since, as they act as the representative voice of a specific Sports at all levels, the demands on the organization are substantial. Responses to initiatives and developments such as coach education, government policy and sports council initiatives are many and varied and impose strains on often low-key, small-scale operations, largely made up of volunteers who sometimes are expected by larger professional organizations, such as the sports council, to respond very quickly.

This situation, where the organization is operating on a largely voluntary basis but is constantly dealing with many professional organizations, causes problems. Demands for immediate response can be damaging to function and operation as well as personal relationships. Many frustrations are created for paid staff involved in Sports or local authority personnel, private sector or national agencies because they cannot get a prompt answer from the national governing body, owing to the need to wait until the next committee cycle decides on governing body policy on any specific issue.

By definition the voluntary sector must be voluntary and largely depends on people giving up their spare time, but it must aim to take a professional attitude and, wherever possible, appoint professional people to implement the policies of the organization, as laid down by the volunteers involved. The more professionalized the organization, the more likely it is to be really effective and have the ear of the major players of the sports council (who have an enormous influence on the resources available to governing bodies and the sports they represent). There must always be a link between effectiveness and efficiency in terms of the costs imposed on the Sports by any type of central administration, but in essence professionalism is the aim and is largely beneficial, provided it is done in an efficient, cost-effective manner.

Another issue for governing bodies to consider is the relative age of the committee personnel and the participants. It appears inappropriate, as happens in so many places, for young performers to be 'governed' by much older people; performers at the age of ten may not benefit greatly from chief officials who are 50 or 60 years older than them—it can be very difficult for people to relate to performers where there is such a significant age gap, and indeed it is difficult for the performers to relate to them. Certainly mechanisms for participant input to administrative systems need to be devised.

There have been instances in the past where there has been a total lack of communication, and indeed understanding, between the individual participants and the sports organization. In some cases this is aggravated by an age gap and by a gap in time between the governing body personnel's actual participation in the Sports and their attaining some official post. Very often comments such as 'things were not like this when I was performing' will be made—a statement which displays astonishing naïvety and ignorance. It implies that sports participation remains the same despite the fact that everything round it is changing with time. Society in general moves on; so too must the requirements and provision for participation in Sports.

For example, to compare the commitment required from a rugby player to play first division or premiership rugby to that required to play in the top flight of rugby some 20 years ago is impossible. There are light years of difference in terms of the fitness levels and commitment required today, and with the professional game the gap is growing.

This tendency for ageing officials to try to relive their youth through others, or advise players how to cope with modern pressures which they themselves never faced, can cause rifts within sports organizations. Sensible sports administrators realize that they exist to support and help the performer but should not be reliving past performances or applying dated criteria as to how performers should behave in the modern era. Administrators should try to be sympathetic to the enormous pressures facing modern-day sports performers—it is difficult for an ageing amateur player to realize the major challenges faced by a young, highly paid professional, who is subject to enormous media and commercial demands. Administrators should try to have a feeling of sympathy, or empathy, for the performer facing such pressures, and try to keep up to speed with sporting developments in the fast-changing modern world.

Volunteerism and Change

It has been often and wisely stated that the only thing that is constant is change. This statement needs to be reiterated all the time to allow people to understand that the status quo is not an option, that things do not stand still, time passes, hair grows, human beings age and society changes.

Sports has to face up to almost constant change in our early twenty-first-century society—among the many factors that affect Sports dramatically are political changes, the ageing of our population, the advent of the National Lottery, the changing business climate, technological advances, creeping professionalism, international competition, the funding of Sports, sponsorship implications, media changes and pressures. With all these quite radical alterations surrounding us, Sports cannot stand still. Certainly there is a desire to keep some of the more potentially damaging changes from affecting Sports, e.g. the extraordinarily high commercial pressures and the fast-developing production of drugs. But the change must be faced up to and coped with in a positive way by sports organizations as for any other individual and organization in our society. There is no point in burying one's head in the sand and believing that things will not or cannot change.

Change is constant but we must try to anticipate and lead it, not just follow it. Structures should be put in place to allow change to be acted on promptly, and indeed anticipated wherever possible. A good example of this is the sports governing bodies that were ready to be first in line with lottery bids. Even before the legislation was through Parliament, some groups had already detailed the outline of their bid. Consequently they were successful and now have the concrete benefits drawn from their anticipation of a major initiative and how they could react to it, and exploit it to the benefit of their Sports. This is perhaps the key to change—to be positive and take any changes which will inevitably happen and turn them to your favour. Every threat can become an opportunity. To do this you require structures which are responsive to change and individuals who will see a clear way ahead, reacting positively as required and leading forward into the future, looking for change and its positive effects rather than fearing it.

Voluntary Commitment-paid Staff Dynamic

It is by no means essential to have been an excellent performer to be an excellent administrator; sometimes, in fact, it can be a disadvantage because such a view of Sports may be limited. It is vitally important to understand what Sports is all about, why people get involved, and why they get so keen and fanatical about it. For many people involved, Sports is the major consideration of their life outside work, and sometimes even ranks as a higher priority than their work. It is extremely important to them, and it is essential that administrators understand such a viewpoint and have an empathy for the commitment and interest that everyone involved in the activity shows.

Sometimes 'lack of commitment' or perceived 'lack of understanding' of full-time paid staff can cause a major clash with voluntary officials who feel that the whole of their life and interest is committed to this activity, and cannot understand when a paid official wants to leave a meeting before 11 o'clock at night, or not give the '110 per cent' commitment that they sense they themselves give to their Sports. They often forget that they probably do not give that same '110 per cent' commitment to their work or their full-time paid employment, but they expect it of their employee, just because they happen to be involved in Sports. More than once such a paradox has caused significant problems in sports organizations due to the lack of understanding of respective viewpoints, roles and commitments.

Sports is demanding and demands enormous commitment from all those involved in it—failure to understand the commitment and interest shown by the volunteer on the part of the paid worker will cause difficulties for all concerned. Equally respect for paid staff must be shown by volunteers, by understanding that their love (Sports) can be 'only a job'. Sports and sports interest is almost unique in terms of the passion it can engender and the all-consuming commitment it can produce, hence the legendary tale of the 'golf widow' where golf is put above all else. It is important to understand that the 4th XV rugby players are just as committed to their Sports and interested in it and will go to almost the same trouble as the top-level performer who may be playing in the modern day for hundreds of thousands of pounds—even millions in some sports. Commitment and interest in Sports cannot be measured in purely financial terms.

The nature of Sports is such that it engenders enormous passions and enthusiasms, and it is constantly helpful for individuals to empathize with such emotions because they have a major impact on management practices and procedures. The passion and commitment must be present within managers and administrators as well as within participants at all levels.

The commitment of sports performers to take part in Sports at all levels, through the coldest or the hottest of weather and at extreme personal inconvenience and expense, has to be matched by the understanding of the organizers—paid or voluntary. Perhaps this requirement for an understanding of the enormous commitment of the participants is the most important point in the whole of this book. If such an understanding, empathy and shared interest does not exist then the whole relationship between the performers and the administration will be based on misapprehension, confusion and misunderstanding.

Many people in sports administration have shared the commitment of the participants and given their life, just as enthusiastically, to the organization and support of Sports, in much the same way as participants give it to the playing on the field. Commitment is not the only thing required; it must be marked by professionalism and professional attitudes. However, the sheer joy of participation must be understood and beneficially experienced.

In a wider field of operation, the author has been involved in passing on management and operational advice to people in the Sports and leisure field, and has thrived on the basis of understanding the whole business and field of operation. Frequently business has been obtained because other management trainers and consultants do not have the specialist background, but more particularly, the understanding of the ethos, atmosphere and commitment of Sports and leisure. Staff, paid and voluntary, enjoy the company of others who share that enormous capacity for work and commitment to customer enjoyment.

After all, if you are going to be involved in an event or promotion, perhaps into the early hours of the morning, several days a week, or even over a period of weeks, then it is absolutely vital that the necessary understanding and commitment are there to drive you forward to produce the best quality of organization. As in any organization, the mission statement, aims and objectives must be clearly understood by everyone concerned, so that everyone is pulling in the same direction and knows where they are going and why they are there. Only in such a situation can you achieve and maintain the necessary levels of motivation to ensure successful professional operation by everyone involved.

How to Retain Volunteers

When asked to identify what they wanted from their involvement in Sports, a small group of voluntary sports officials suggested the following:

- Reward
- Involvement
- Encouragement
- Empowerment
- Value
- Information
- Training
- Interest
- Clear and agreed objectives
- Praise
- Debriefing
- Appropriate post
- Responsibility
- Acknowledgement
- Progress
- Feedback
- Opportunity to socialize.

CHAPTER 4

People Participation and Sports Development

Sports Development is an important emerging field of academic study with a distinctive contribution to make to wider social, cultural, economic and educational policies and practices. It is a process whereby effective opportunities, process, systems and structures are set up to enable and encourage people in all or particular groups and areas to take part in Sports and recreation or to improve their performance to whatever level they desire.

To define sports development is inevitably difficult, and it means different things to different people. Basically, sports development is about providing and improving opportunities for people to participate in Sports at whatever level to the best of their ability and in fulfillment of their interest. The basic principle is that sports development should give opportunities for people to participate in Sports as well as supporting the development of new facilities and activity sessions. The sports development process requires some underpinning values. These have been agreed by the Institute of Leisure and Amenity Management (ILAM) Specialist Panel to include, for example, the following.

- Achiever
- Administrator
- Adviser
- Communicator
- Contractor
- Coordinator
- Customer
- Deliverer
- Diplomat
- Educator
- Emissary
- Employee adviser
- Employer
- Evaluator
- Implementer
- Influencer
- Innovator
- Leader
- Liaison officer
- Manager
- Marketer
- Mediator
- Mentor
- Monitor
- Motivator
- Negotiator
- Organizer
- Partner
- Pawn
- Persuader
- Planner
- Provider
- Representative

- Researcher
- Strategist
- Student
- Subordinate
- Supervisor.

Even this list probably does not cover all the specific roles that the sports development officer can be called upon to perform in some radically different situations, varying according to venue, age group, economic, Sports and social settings, among others. This wide range of roles is one of the main motivators towards reducing the generalist role of the sports development officer—no one human being can be all of these at any one time or will have strengths in all of these areas. By limiting the requirements on technical knowledge to one specific Sports, and indeed to the politics of one particular Sports, the chances of success in delivery are probably greatly improved.

In order to perform these many roles, sports development officers will require a wide range of professional skills. They need to be competent in:

- Organizing
- Leading
- Communicating
- Evaluating
- Politicing
- Being patient
- Persevering
- Thinking
- Planning
- Researching
- Sourcing
- Selling
- Understanding
- Dealing with people.

Again a sizeable list, but arguably not yet comprehensive—there still appear to be gaps. Like any list of skills, all that the active, ambitious and driven sports development officer can do is try to match up as much as possible, and work to enhance and develop their skills at every opportunity. The sports development officer, with all these roles to fulfil and these skills to demonstrate, will get involved in the 'sports development process'. This is fundamentally about providing sporting opportunities for people of all ages, sizes, sexes, colours and creeds in a proactive way. It is about seizing the initiative and looking for opportunities to make the appropriate provision.

Sports development is certainly about facing up to change and getting voluntary groups to react positively to it and seize opportunities that arise. It is about being very focused and targeted on each specific project, whether or not the overall plan is specific-Sports or target-group focused. It involves working with partners and the (almost hackneyed) concept of partnership. To be effective, sports development officers must cultivate the skills to work with other people and be realistic in what they can provide. There needs to a dynamic, innovative approach to provision to influence and interest the experienced, almost embittered, sports participants and administrators. The job of enthusing them comes by providing genuine new ideas and approaches to which they can see some benefits.

Certainly, the concept of being able to use governing body or other organizational support to promote and publicize the activities of Sports is openly seen as beneficial, even by the older 'blazer brigade' because they are always keen to see their Sports getting the limelight (even if it is only so they can have some reflected glory themselves). They do see that everybody should be aware of and interested in their Sports and, in the vast majority of cases, they warmly welcome significant amounts of publicity. The ability of sports development officers to build local, regional and national networks of contacts and support for Sports is enormously important, and is one of the key strengths of what is still a relatively small profession. Sports development officers should also lead the way in creating opportunities for all levels and abilities in Sports—they must take the wider view and be interested in everyone, while some specific sporting bodies tend to be very much focused on élite performance and excellence groups.

The ability to be adaptable and flexible in approach to people and to projects is fundamental to sports development. Rigidity and pre-set notions of how everything must be done will be almost as damaging as the dreadful negativity which may come to some sports development officers as they face frustrations from their employers or their customers. This negativity and pessimism can totally overwhelm their work and influence their customers to the point of inactivity or indeed damage of existing activities.

It should always be recognized that sports development has a number of special problems and difficulties which make it a challenging profession and an area in which it is sometimes not easy to see achievement on some occasions. It must always be undertaken, though, in a proactive, positive manner. Basically, sports development is still a new concept to many people involved in Sports. The traditionalists have tended to see Sports as just existing rather than needing to be promoted, developed and enhanced in any active way, but today this is necessary and this is a difficult concept for some to grasp. People's experience of Sports is limited, and any desire to expand and bring innovation can sometimes be resisted.

Individuals working in sports development can really struggle if they do not receive support and direction from their superiors or their organization, as well as some sort of strategic planning support, leadership to keep them focused and time actually to achieve what is to be done. Sports development cannot be an overnight panacea; to be effective it will take time. There is little doubt that in the whole area of sports development there is a dramatic shortage of knowledge for the practitioner, politician and senior official. There is a need for this issue to be addressed by all the UK sports councils, and indeed by the educational institutions, which should be looking to provide more courses, up to and even beyond degree level, to support this developing area of activity in the UK (and indeed other areas of the world).

To be effective as a sports development officer, individuals have to be self-motivated and controlled; they need to be able to keep focus on a direction; work with enormous commitment; relate well to all different types of people; and, while opposing it, know how to deal with bureaucracy to get things done. In essence it would be wrong to discriminate strictly or to differentiate too heavily between sports development and sports management and administration, because sound administration and management are vital to effective sports development.

The Quality of Leadership in Sports

Some commentators link leadership closely with the idea of management. Some regard the two as synonymous, and others consider management a subset of leadership. If one accepts this premise, one can view leadership as:

- Centralized or decentralized
- Broad or focused
- Decision-oriented or morale-centred
- Intrinsic or derived from some authority

Any of the bipolar labels traditionally ascribed to management style could also apply to leadership style. Hersey and Blanchard use this approach: they claim that management merely consists of leadership applied to business situations; or in other words: management forms a sub-set of the broader process of leadership. They put it this way: "Leadership occurs any time one attempts to influence the behavior of an individual or group, regardless of the reason.Management is a kind of leadership in which the achievement of organizational goals is paramount."

However, a clear distinction between management and leadership may nevertheless prove useful. This would allow for a reciprocal relationship between leadership and management, implying that an effective manager should possess leadership skills, and an effective leader should demonstrate management skills. One clear distinction could provide the following definition:

- Management involves power by position.
- Leadership involves power by influence.

Abraham Zaleznik (1977),for example, delineated differences between leadership and management. He saw leaders as inspiring visionaries, concerned about substance; while managers he views as planners who have concerns with process.Warren Bennis (1989) further explicated a dichotomy between managers and leaders. He drew twelve distinctions between the two groups:

- Managers administer, leaders innovate
- Managers ask how and when, leaders ask what and why
- Managers focus on systems, leaders focus on people
- Managers do things right, leaders do the right things
- Managers maintain, leaders develop
- Managers rely on control, leaders inspire trust
- Managers have a short-term perspective, leaders have a longer-term perspective
- Managers accept the status-quo, leaders challenge the status-quo
- Managers have an eye on the bottom line, leaders have an eye on the horizon
- Managers imitate, leaders originate
- Managers emulate the classic good soldier, leaders are their own person
- Managers copy, leaders show originality

Paul Birch (1999) also sees a distinction between leadership and management. He observed that, as a broad generalization, managers concerned themselves with tasks while leaders concerned themselves with people. Birch does not suggest that leaders do not focus on "the task." Indeed, the things that characterise a great leader include the fact that they achieve. Effective leaders create and sustain competitive advantage through the attainment of cost leadership, revenue leadership, time leadership, and market value leadership. Managers typically follow and realize a leader's vision. The difference lies in the leader realising that the achievement of the task comes about through the goodwill and support of others (influence), while the manager may not.

This goodwill and support originates in the leader seeing people as people, not as another resource for deployment in support of "the task". The manager often has the role of organizing resources to get something done. People form one of these resources, and many of the worst managers treat people as just another interchangeable item. A leader has the role of causing others to follow a path he/she has laid out or a vision he/she has articulated in order to achieve a task. Often, people see the task as subordinate to the vision. For instance, an organization might have the overall task of generating profit, but a good leader may see profit as a by-product that flows from whatever aspect of their vision differentiates their company from the competition.

Leadership does not only manifest itself as purely a business phenomenon. Many people can think of an inspiring leader they have encountered who has nothing whatever to do with business: a politician, an officer in the armed forces, a Scout or Guide leader, a teacher, etc. Similarly, management does not occur only as a purely business phenomenon. Again, we can think of examples of people that we have met who fill the management niche in non-business organisations. Non-business organizations should find it easier to articulate a non-money-driven inspiring vision that will support true leadership. However, often this does not occur.

Differences in the mix of leadership and management can define various management styles. Some management styles tend to de-emphasize leadership. Included in this group one could include participatory management, democratic management, and collaborative management styles. Other management styles, such as authoritarian management, micro-management, and top-down management, depend more on a leader to provide direction. Note, however, that just because an organisation has no single leader giving it direction, does not mean it necessarily has weak leadership. In many cases group leadership (multiple leaders) can prove effective. Having a single leader (as in dictatorship) allows for quick and decisive decision-making when needed as well as when not needed. Group decision-making sometimes earns the derisive label "committee-itis" because of the longer times required to make decisions, but group leadership can bring more expertise, experience, and perspectives through a democratic process.

Patricia Pitcher (1994) has challenged the bifurcation into leaders and managers. She used a factor analysis (in marketing)factor analysis technique on data collected over 8 years, and concluded that three types of leaders exist, each with very different psychological profiles:'Artists' imaginative, inspiring, visionary, entrepreneurial, intuitive, daring, and emotional Craftsmen: well-balanced, steady, reasonable, sensible, predictable, and trustworthy Technocrats: cerebral, detail-oriented, fastidious, uncompromising, and hard-headed She speculates that no one profile offers a preferred leadership style. She claims that if we want to build, we should find an "artist leader" if we want to solidify our position, we should find a "craftsman leader" and if we have an ugly job that needs to get done like downsizing.we should find a "technocratic leader".Pitcher also observed that a balanced leader exhibiting all three sets of traits occurs extremely rarely: she found none in her study.

Bruce Lynn postulates a differentiation between 'Leadership' and 'Management' based on perspectives to risk. Specifically,"A Leader optimises upside opportunity; a Manager minimises downside risk." He argues that successful executives need to apply both disciplines in a balance appropriate to the enterprise and its context. Leadership without Management yields steps forward, but as many if not more steps backwards. Management without Leadership avoids any step backwards, but doesn't move forward.

One of the key features of sports operations on the field of play, and also the key to successful management of sports practice off the field, is leadership. Leadership must be provided in any industry to give direction and pull everyone together towards a common goal. If planning is to be effective, someone has to take everyone along with them towards the agreed target. Someone has to do the pulling together and forward, as well as the motivation of others to keep them going towards the same goal.

This is not the place to get into a long debate over the theories of leadership. In practical management terms it is academic whether managers are born, are made or just appear as the need arises. The key point for the organization is that leadership is shown and that it is encouraged rather than squashed at any point. Again, training will be key to produce a quality of leadership and to draw it out at all the points of the organization. It is important that leadership is encouraged and is trained, where it already exists, to be better. The style of leadership can vary from laid-back to authoritarian, depending on the organization and the situation. However, is an overly dictatorial presence is usually inappropriate in the voluntary situation, where we are trying to build a team. The leadership style has to match the requirement of any particular organizational situation, and the best approach is the one appropriate at that point in time.

One of the difficulties with many sports industry situations, especially that of the voluntary sector, is that there is a need for democratic operation, and democracy does not always produce clear policy or unity of purpose, or even the best situation for leadership potential to be demonstrated. Sports bodies must work hard to allow true leaders to come through despite any traditions or overarching democratic desires. Heading up any organization in the twenty-first century involves leadership skill. It is quite different from the traditional style of leadership as understood in the past. Today's leaders are required to focus and inspire a leaner, more demanding workforce. The structure of organizations has become flatter and most leaders' span of control has greatly increased. Leaders have to develop followers, increase their motivation, and activate and promote positive changes in both individuals and organizations. This can be particularly difficult in any sports situation, where many of the leaders are part-time, voluntary people. The dynamics of leadership are still very important and, while Sports itself can be a great producer of leadership and leadership skills in individuals, this should not be taken for granted. Like any other skill required in the sports management and administration area, it should be trained. A good deal of the leadership that can be achieved, and exploited, in a sports situation is down to personality and charisma. Many people involved in Sports are well endowed with appropriate personality traits and are well used to getting people to follow a leader. The ability to support, cajole, motivate and inspire people is part of this process, but this inborn characteristic is crucially important where change and vision are required.

Charisma, like beauty, has been said to be in the eye of the beholder, rather than something that can be worked on. It is, to some extent, the traditional 'charmer' linked to the almost manipulative individual who can 'convince' people that the chosen direction is the right one and make them follow this charismatic lead. In the area of sports management and administration, a great deal of effort is required to lead what is often a committed and determined band of people towards a common identifiable goal. The whole concept of leadership has been investigated by many intellectuals and put into action by many practitioners over a long period of time. The military influence in leadership is noted and scholars in the UK, such as Adair (1988), have elucidated militaristic applications of sound practice derived from theories of human behaviour.

Transactional or Transformational?

One American guru of leadership has identified what he calls transactional and transformational leadership (Bass, 1990). He sees transactional leadership as based merely on 'managing the status quo—the situation as it exists and competently organizing round about that'. He has suggested in various books that it is necessary for a good leader to go beyond the basic transactional level and move to transform individuals and organizations by carrying them beyond basic performance levels. Very few situations today remain static—certainly not sports organization—so it would seem that the transformational approach is the way to approach sports administration and management. Bass (1990) has identified four 'i's for such transformational leadership:

- Intellectual stimulation
- Individual consideration
- Inspirational leadership
- Idealized influence.

He identifies each of these as being vitally important, and it is suggested that Sports and recreation managers will benefit by putting such beliefs into practice, and that this will help them carry out their role in what is a very challenging atmosphere. Sports involves enthusiastic, dynamic people who need to have some significant inspirational leadership to get the best out of them, and this is best for the organization as well. Sports, like other businesses, requires improved leadership so that innovation can be heightened, change managed and entrepreneurship increased to make sporting organizations more effective. As with leaders in any situation, training and personal development are required to ensure that individuals can lead their organizations with creativity and into risk-taking situations, which is necessary in order to see progress achieved in the future. The sports fraternity sometimes believes that it has 'instant' leaders, and that they will come to the top naturally and make all the right decisions and take the right initiatives because of their sports participation.

This is obviously not always accurate, and support must be given to potential leaders to produce quality in the organization's operation. The training of individuals from a sports background must be linked to sound theory and knowledge if the organization is to progress in a time of change. The UK at the start of the twenty-first century is a place full of change and uncertainty, and many organizations face this situation with some trepidation. To go forward they need leaders who must be highly educated, trained and developed individuals—in sports organizations as elsewhere. The changes faced will not suddenly become easier but look likely to be set in a more confused cultural and global context calling for more innovative, creative and entrepreneurial leadership applications.

It is important that leadership, rather than supervision or control, is seen as the job of the manager. He or she should try to lead the staff forward, encouraging all team members to get involved and to get to a point where they are clear about the objectives of the organization. To use an old maxim: 'tell me and I may remember, show me and I may see, involve me and I will understand'. This type of approach is certainly the most effective leadership approach for Sports, as for so many other situations. Staff, particularly volunteers, cannot just be ordered about and must be involved in the decision-making and in agreeing a course of action.

Leadership Qualities in the Sports

There is a great deal of debate among both practising executives and academics as to what exactly constitutes good leadership. There is, however, some agreement that some technical expertise or ability in the area in which leadership is being practised will help gain respect and get people to follow the example given. This does not mean that they need to know it all, but they must show some understanding of the work that has to be undertaken and some knowledge of what is required to work in Sports. If, after all, the leader knew everything then perhaps he or she would do everything themselves. Certainly the importance of recognizing and empathizing with the commitment required for effective operation in sports administration is a crucial leadership skill. In addition, many different qualities are sought in a leader by different people.

There is, however, some agreement that good leaders tend to be extrovert, enthusiastic and have an 'attractive' personality and character which is appealing to others. In sports management and administration, the leadership qualities required are a bit like beauty—in the eye of the beholder. But here is a list of some of the qualities the author considers important:

- Technical knowledge (or at least credibility)
- Integrity
- Honesty
- Inspiration
- Commitment
- Enthusiasm
- Thick skin
- Willingness to work hard
- Love of Sports
- Administrative ability
- People skills
- Sense of humour.

A leader in any situation must be aware of individual needs, task needs and group-maintenance needs if the dynamics of the individuals and groups are going to be combined successfully to get the necessary tasks completed. This is a step beyond the basic concept of the hierarchy of individual needs espoused by Maslow (1954), which included:

- Physiological—the need to eat, drink and rest
- Safety—to be safe from danger and feel secure
- Social—have a feeling of ease with other people in friendship and belonging
- Esteem—self-respect and recognition by others
- Self-actualization—a feeling of achievement and personal development.

These are all valid, but need to be set in the group and task setting to see real achievement. Leadership must not be seen as dictatorship; it is a necessity to draw everyone together to get them pulling in the same direction rather than having them working in a disjointed way or towards the wrong objective. The leader's job is to bring cohesion and involve everyone from the beginning in the big decisions to be made. To be leader does not mean making all the decisions—group decision-making is preferable and promotes group responsibility and involvement. There may be some occasions when the leader has to take the final decision or make a decision on their own, but, particularly in the sporting sphere, the involvement of others will be vital to gain their support—as it is most likely that strong personalities will be involved. It is vital to remember that while leaders are often thought to have some innate qualities, they will also need to develop and add to these qualities. Adair (1988) has identified a number of skills which are relevant to the sports situation:

- Defining the task
- Having the ability to identify exactly what is required to be done
- *Planning*—making the necessary plans for the task to be carried out
- *Briefing*—telling everyone what their involvement is (in a shared discussion)
- *Controlling*—monitoring through the work to ensure that everything is proceeding according to plan
- *Evaluating*—having a realistic assessment of what is happening in the process and how close the successful completion of the task is
- *Motivating*—keeping everyone involved, enthusiastic and committed to fulfilling the task
- *Organizing*—ensuring that everyone is working in a planned co-ordinated way towards the end goal
- *Setting an example*—showing a commitment and enthusiasm which will encourage others to follow and so ease the functioning of the operation towards the end goal.

One area where Sports is often sadly lacking is that of establishing a training programme for its managers and administrators. It has tended to expect a high level of commitment and innate ability coming off the sports field into the organization, and so has tended to believe that Sports has people with the natural leadership ability and does not need to train or support them in any significant way.

This may be a major error, since the skills required for leading a team on the park are not necessarily the same, and most certainly not all the same, as those needed to head up a governing body or to be a manager of a sports organization. It is important that all sports bodies seek to develop leaders and encourage personal and professional development for those individuals, whether they are involved in a voluntary or paid capacity. The growth of the Running Sports programme by the sports councils for volunteers, and vocational qualifications implementation in sports administration for paid personnel, will both have a significant impact on the development of administrators and managers in the area of sports administration.

The importance of such initiatives cannot be overemphasized, as Sports must not expect people automatically to possess leadership skills; they have to be nurtured and supported. Following from this training and effective leadership development, it is hoped that everybody involved in the organization will work better as a team and work towards the common objective. This will benefit everyone involved in terms of personal satisfaction and will also produce the results the organization is looking for. Good leadership is the key to developing good teams, but the existence of a good leader does not automatically mean that the team will be effective. Other issues have to be considered and developed to produce a good effective team operation.

CHAPTER 6

Administrative and Controlling Agencies

MINISTRY OF YOUTH AFFAIRS AND SPORTS

The Ministry of Youth Affairs & Sports was initially set up as the Department of Sports in 1982 at the time of organisation of the IX Asian Games in New Delhi. Its name was changed to the Department of Youth Affairs & Sports during celebration of the International Youth Year, 1985. It became a Ministry on the 27th May, 2000. The specific subjects being dealt with by the Ministry are contained in the Order of the Government of India(Allocation of Business) Rules, 1961. The youth, i.e. those falling within the age group of 15-35 years constitutes nearly 40% of the total population of India. This group which is the most vibrant and dynamic segment of the country's population constitutes potentially its most valuable human resource. To optimally tap their constructive and creative energies, the Ministry pursues the twin objectives of personality building and nation building, i.e. developing the personality of youth and involving them in various nation-building activities. As most of the issues concerning young people are the functions of other Ministries / Departments, like Education, Employment & Training, Health and Family Welfare, etc., the role of the Ministry of Youth Affairs & Sports is to act as a facilitator and catalytic agent. Sports promotion is primarily the responsibility of the various National Sports Federations, which are autonomous. The role of the Government is to create the infrastructure and promote capacity building for broad–basing sports as well as for achieving excellence in various competitive events at the national and international levels. The Ministry's schemes are geared towards achieving these objectives.

Secretariat

The Ministry has a total sanctioned strength of 192. It consists of 16 Group 'A' Officers i.e. 1. Secretary, 2. Joint Secretaries, 3. Directors and 4. Deputy Secretaries, 1 Programme Adviser, 4 Under Secretaries (3 Under Secretaries have been promoted as Deputy Secretaries on in-situ basis) and 1 Principal Private Secretary. There are 72 Group 'B' posts (20 Gazetted and 52 Non-Gazetted), 75 Group 'C' posts and 29 Group 'D' posts. At present, 3 Section Officers are working as Under Secretaries on in-situ basis. Besides this, there are posts in the Personal Staff of Minister / Minister of State for Youth Affairs and Sports. There are 33 employees belonging to Scheduled Castes – 2 in Group 'A', 5 in Group 'B'(Gazetted), 6 in Group 'B' (non-Gazetted), 11 in Group 'C' and 9 in Group 'D'. Besides this, there are 9 employees belonging to Schedule Tribes working at present in this Ministry i.e. 1 in Group 'B' (Gazetted), 3 in Group 'B'(Non-Gazetted), 3 in Group 'C' and 2 in Group 'D'.

Subordinate Offices

National Service Scheme Organisation (NSSO) is the only Subordinate Office of the Ministry.

Use of Official Language (Hindi)

The Ministry has sufficient staff for implementation of the Official Language Policy and the Official Language Act, 1963. An

Official Language implementation Committee has been set up under the chairmanship of Joint Secretary to monitor the implementation of Official Language Act in the Ministry of Youth Affairs and Sports. To promote the use of Hindi in Official Work, all notifications, resolutions, general orders, circulars, memorandum etc. are issued bilingually. All name plates, notice boards, rubber stamps, seals, letter heads etc. are prepared both in Hindi & English. Letters received in Hindi are invariably replied to in Hindi.

The Ministry has been notified by the Department of Official Language, under Rule 10(4) for the maximum use of Hindi. A number of Sections of the Ministry have been specified under Rule 8(4) for the use of Hindi. Out of five Subordinate/ Autonomous offices under the purview of the Ministry four offices have been notified under Rule 10(4). The employees in the Ministry who do not possess working knowledge of Hindi are nominated for training. Similarly the clerks and stenographers who do not know Hindi typing & stenography are also nominated for Hindi typing and Hindi stenography training.

On the pattern of previous years, the Hindi Fortnight was celebrated during the current year in the month of September, in which a large number of officers/employees participated in the different competitions. In order to promote the maximum use of Hindi in the Ministry, appeal was issued at the level of Minister for Youth Affairs & Sports. Similarly the Hindi Fortnight was also celebrated in the Subordinate offices under the Ministry. On the occasion of the different Sports awards viz. Rajiv Gandhi Khel Ratna Award, Dronacharya Award, Arjuna Awards, Dhyanchand Award, Maulana Abul Kalam Azad Trophy etc were given by the Hon'ble President of India and like every year a book was also issued bilingually in both Hindi and English during this year (2001-2002). A Hindi Salahakar Samiti (Hindi Advisory Committee) under the chairmanship of the Union Minister of Youth Affairs & Sports for reviews progress in the use of Hindi.

Vigilance and Public Grievances

Vigilance and Public Grievance Cell in the Ministry of Youth Affairs & Sports works under the overall supervision of the Secretary, Youth Affairs & Sports. There is a Chief Vigilance Officer and a Director to assist the Chief Vigilance Officer in his day-to-day functioning. Each autonomous organisation and subordinate offices of the Ministry have their independent Chief Vigilance Officers to deal with vigilance and public grievances. During the year under consideration the Ministry has taken keen interest to redress the public grievances and taken quick steps to dispose off the pending vigilance matters. A vigilance awareness week was celebrated in the Ministry as well as in all the field organizations of the Ministry. During this week, various activities like debates, essay competitions, display of banners and films on the menaces of the corruption in the society, were undertaken. The Ministry has also prepared its citizen charter.

Library

The Ministry has a small departmental Library where publications of interest on subjects like sports and games, yoga, physical education, youth programmes, literature, law, rules, etc. are preserved for reference. At present, the library has 2703 publications including a good number of Hindi books. There are also a large number of other publications of importance, like sports and youth magazines, Annual and other Reports of various Ministries / Departments, audio and video-cassettes and thousands of photographs, etc.

NATIONAL YOUTH POLICY 1988

Introduction

1. Youth, in all ages, has been in the vanguard of progress and social change. Thirst for freedom, impatience for quicker pace of progress and a passion for innovation, coupled with idealism and creative fervour, saw the youth in the forefront of the freedom struggle in our own land.

If our youth was inspired by the call of the Father of the Nation in the first half of this century, the youth of today face the challenge of economic development and technological progress with social justice.

2. The youth of India, representing a third of our population, constitute a vital and vibrant human resource. They have a right, as well as an obligation, to participate actively in national development and in shaping the Destiny of the nation which is, in point of fact, their own destiny. Their problems are many and varied and their aspirations naturally high, in a country with a great past and greater promise for the future. The need, therefore, is to create increasing opportunities for them to develop their personality and their functional capability and thus make them economically productive and socially useful.
3. Such opportunities have to be created on a large scale, to cover a wide spectrum of areas of human endeavour; and they have to be made available to youth of all strata of society, particularly the disadvantaged. All national programmes should be directed to enable the youth to become a productive, self-confident and committed force for national development. These programmes must create adequate facilities for the all round development of youth and assist in their striving for excellence in all fields.
4. This calls for an integral and their-disciplinary approach, involving both government departments and organisations and sectors outside the Government such as the family, educators, leaders, voluntary agencies and youth organisations. The Central and State Governments have to provide adequate mechanisms supportive of this process.
5. It behaves the Nation, therefore, to assist youth in getting their due share in the country's life and progress, while equipping them to meet their obligations adequately. It is not an easy task, but it is a necessary task, in which not only the Government but the whole nation, including

individuals, institutions and organisations, have to be brought together in a spirit of creative enterprise, as envisaged in this National Youth Policy.

Objectives

6. The policy shall be directed towards the achievements of the following objectives:
   - To instill in the youth a deep awareness of and respect for the principles and values enshrined in our Constitution and a willingness to further the rule of law, with an abiding commitment to national integration, non-violence, secularism and socialism;
   - To promote among the youth the awareness of our historical and cultural heritage and imbue them with a sense of pride and national identify, together with a deep commitment towards their preservation, as well as the enrichment of the environment and ecology;
   - To help develop in the youth qualities of discipline, self-reliance, justice and fair-play, a burning concern for public weal, sporting spirit and above all, a scientific temper in their modes of thinking and action which, inter alia, will enable them to combat superstition, osbcurantism and the numerous social ills that beset the Nation;
   - To provide the youth with maximum access to education which, in addition to developing their alround personality imparts appropriate professional and vocational training with a view to enabling them to avail of employment and self-employment opportunities towards the aim of Bekari Hatao; and
   - To make the youth aware of international issues and involve them in promoting world peace, understanding and a just international economic order.

Plan of Action

7. The following shall represent the plan of action for the implementation of the National Youth Policy.

- Programmes aimed at inculcating knowledge of and respect for the Constitution of India, together with a sense of national integrity, cultural unity, democratic values and faith in socialism and secularism will form the care of all youth activities.
- Programmes seeking to create a thorough awareness of our history, freedom struggle, national development, achievements of modern science and technology and their applicability in overcoming socio-economic constraints and achieving faster progress, without losing our cultural identify and spiritual strength, will be implemented.
- Special efforts will be made to faster and develop contracts between youth from different parts of the country, with a view to inspire them to combat regionalism, communalism, linguistic chauvinism and other divisive and fissiparous tendencies, through participation in the programme of Antar Bharti.
- Meaningful programmes of mass education, formal and non-formal, will be undertaken, so that the benefits of education reach all young men and women, including non-student rural youth, with particular emphasis on the dis-advantaged sections of our society.
- Training programmes will be organised, aimed at imparting requisite skill to youth for self-employment, improving their employability and enhancing their productivity, while making them appreciate the dignity of labour.
- Programmes will be undertaken to offer opportunities to the youth for leadership training through personality development and character building, and for motivating them to voluntary social and community service.
- Promotion of physical fitness through mass participation in yoga, indigenous games and modern sports

will be made an integral part of all youth programmes, together with adventure activities calculated to develop the spirit of risk taking, team work and endurance.

- Youth parents will be particularly sensitized to their responsibilities and their own role as catelysts of social change, by being involved in movements against various social ills, harmful practices and superstitions, and by adopting the small family norm and appropriate family welfare measures.
- True to our great tradition of viewing the world as one family, programmes, enabling contacts and close links between the youth of India and their counterparts all over the world, will be expanded, to promote international understanding and strengthen world peace.

Outstanding work done by young persons and voluntary agencies in various fields will be recognised and rewarded through a system of awards, scholarships and the like.

Implementation

8. The Ministry of Human Resource Development (now Ministry of Youth Affairs and Sports), Government of India will be the Nodal Agency in the Government of India for the implementation of the National Youth Policy and providing such guidance and assistance as may be required.
9. Systematic and scientific monitoring and evaluation of the implementation of the Policy will be done, to provide insights into the needs, and aspirations of the youth of different levels and to assess the impact of the programmes and the expenditure thereon in relation to stated objectives. Monitoring and evaluation would be built into the system on an on-going basis and necessary mid-term corrections applied.
10. Maximum participation by non-governmental Institutions, public and private, will be encouraged, and in fact sought, in the mobilisation of youth in specific areas of

national development. Programmes of youth organsiations will be encouraged through financial and organisational support.

Co-ordination

11. The most important component of the youth programme will be the removal of the unemployment, both rural and urban, educated and non-educated. This shall inform all programmes for youth undertaken by all departments of Government, Central and State, as well as non-Governmental Agencies . This will be ensured by all these Agencies, working in unison and in mutual consultation and coordination. The Ministry of Human Resource Development (now Ministry of Youth Affairs and Sports), Government of India, will make all efforts to serve as a clearing house of data, information and ideas germane to process of coordination, while keeping infact the independent operational aspects of each of the Agencies.
12. The Central Government, State Governments and Voluntary Agencies will work in close coordination in the implementation of the National Youth Policy. Detailed exercised at the local level will be initiated in order to being about maximum utilisation of the State and Central facilities and to avoid duplication in all the spheres of activity that the Policy contemplates, and to evolve effective, responsive and responsible mechanisms for these purposes.
13. A Committee for National Youth Programmes (CONYP) will be set up, bringing together representatives of of the concerned Ministries, Departments and National Youth Organsiations, to advise the Department (Ministry) of Youth Affair and Sports in discharging its duties in the effective implementation of the National Youth Policy.

Conclusion

14. It is significant that the National Youth Policy is being launched in the year of the birth centenary of Pt. Jawaharlal Nehru. In the implementation of the policy,

the national and the Government will be guided and inspired by the philosophy and vision of Pt. Nehru, who was not only the rallying point of youth during the struggle for independence but also the man who become a symbol of resurgent youth in Independent India. With his world view of history and his modern, scientific temper working in unison with the traditions and heritage of this great country, Pt. Nehru was a great humanist who strove for the ideas of socialism, secularism and democracy. These cardinal principles and ideas enshrined in the Constitution to India will inform all programmes of action for implementation of this Policy, enabling the youth of India to march forward, with confidence in themselves and faith in the future, basing their convictions on our ancient heritage but utilising their skills, knowledge, energies and idealism to harness the fruits of science and appropriate technology in building a new and vibrant India.

NATIONAL YOUTH POLICY 2003

Preamble

1. The National Youth Policy, 2003 reiterates the commitment of the entire nation to the composite and all-round development of the young sons and daughters of India and seeks to establish an All-India perspective to fulfill their legitimate aspirations so that they are all strong of heart and strong of body and mind in successfully accomplishing the challenging tasks of national reconstruction and social changes that lie ahead.
2. The earlier National Youth Policy was formulated in 1988. The socio-economic conditions in the country have since undergone a significant change and have been shaped by wide-ranging technological advancement. The National Youth Policy - 2003 is designed to galvanize the youth to rise up to the new challenges, keeping in view

the global scenario, and aims at motivating them to be active and committed participants in the exciting task of National Development.

3. The Policy is based on recognition of the contribution that the youth can, and should, make to the growth and well-being of the community and endeavours to ensure effective co-ordination between the policies, programmes and delivery systems of the various Ministries, Departments and other Agencies. The thrust of the Policy centres around "Youth Empowerment" in different spheres of national life.
4. For India to occupy her rightful place in the Comity of Nations and to meaningfully discharge the manifold obligations thereto, it would be imperative to ensure the effective pursuit of youth development programmes which promote personality development and Qualities of Citizenship and enhance commitment to Community Service, Social Justice, Self-reliance, National Integration and Humanism, an inclusive view of the entire universe as enshrined in our ancient scriptures. The Policy, therefore, recognizes these inter-related values and principles as its basic premise.

Rationale

1. Since our national progress depends, crucially, on the ways and means through which the youth are encouraged and nurtured as a positive force for national progress and are enabled to contribute to socio-economic development, it is essential for an appropriate policy framework to be in place to harness the energies of the youth in this task.
2. Recognizing, further, that youth development is a multi-faceted concept, it is equally necessary that all the relevant agencies, including the Ministries and Departments of the Central and State Governments, and local self Government bodies and Panchayati Raj institutions devise their plans and programmes bearing these aspects and

features in mind. The Policy will facilitate a multi-dimensional and integrated approach in this behalf, with the State Agencies striving to accelerate the formulation and implementation of programmes.

3. An important indicator of the success of such programmes being the stake of the beneficiaries in the results of the same, this Policy also stresses that the youth of the country should enjoy greater participation in the processes of decision-making and execution at local and higher levels. Such participation would be facilitated by identifiable structures, transparent procedures and wider representation of the youth in appropriate bodies, with the emphasis being more on working with the youth than for the youth.

The Definition of Youth

1. This Policy will cover all the youth in the country in the age group of 13 to 35 years. It is acknowledged that since all the persons within this age group are unlikely to be one homogenous group, but rather a conglomeration of sub-groups with differing social roles and requirements, the age group may, therefore, be divided into two broad sub-groups viz. 13-19 years and 20-35 years. The youth belonging to the age group 13-19, which is a major part of the adolescent age group, will be regarded as a separate constituency.
2. The number of youth in the age group of 13-35 years, as per the 1991 Census, was estimated at about 34 crores, and about 38 crores in 1997, which is anticipated to increase to about 51 crores by the year 2016. The percentage of youth in the total population, which, according to the 1996 Census projections, is estimated to be about 37% in 1997, is also likely to increase to about 40% by the year 2016. The availability of a human resource of such magnitude for achieving socio-economic change and technological excellence needs commensurate

infrastructure and suitable priorities to maximize its contribution to National Development.

Objectives Of The National Youth Policy

The objectives of the National Youth Policy are:

- To instil in the youth, at large, an abiding awareness of, and adherence to, the secular principles and values enshrined in the Constitution of India, with unswerving commitment to Patriotism, National Security, National Integration, Non-violence and Social Justice;
- To develop Qualities of Citizenship and dedication to Community Service amongst all sections of the youth;
- To promote awareness, amongst the youth, in the fields of Indian history and heritage, arts and culture;
- To provide the youth with proper educational and training opportunities and to facilitate access to information in respect of employment opportunities and to other services, including entrepreneurial guidance and financial credit;
- To facilitate access, for all sections of the youth, to health information and services and to promote a social environment which strongly inhibits the use of drugs and other forms of substance abuse, wards off disease (like HIV/AIDS), ensures measures for de-addiction and mainstreaming of the affected persons and enhances the availability of sports and recreational facilities as constructive outlets for the abundant energy of the youth;
- To sustain and reinforce the spirit of volunteerism amongst the youth in order to build up individual character and generate a sense of commitment to the goals of developmental programmes;
- To create an international perspective in the youth and to involve them in promoting peace and understanding and the establishment of a just global economic order;
- To develop youth leadership in various socio-economic and cultural spheres and to encourage the involvement

of Non-Governmental Organizations, Co-operatives and Non-formal groups of young people; and

- To promote a major participatory role for the youth in the protection and preservation of nature, including natural resources, to channelise their abundant energies in community service so as to improve the environment and foster a scientific, inquisitive reasoning and rational attitude in the younger generation and to encourage the youth to undertake such travel excursions as would better acquaint them with cultural harmony, amidst diversity, in India, and overseas.

Thrust Areas of the Policy

1. *Youth Empowerment:* The Policy recognizes that in order for the youth to effectively participate in decision making processes, it is essential that they are better equipped with requisite knowledge, skills and capabilities.Towards this end, the Policy envisions the following:

Attainment of higher educational levels and expertise by the youth, in line with their abilities and aptitudes, and access to employment opportunities accordingly;

Adequate nutrition for the full development of physical and mental potential and the creation of an environment which promotes good health, and ensures protection from disease and unwholesome habits;

Development of youth leadership and its involvement in programmes and activities pertaining to National Development;

Equality of opportunity and respect for Human and Fundamental Rights without distinction of race, caste, creed, sex, language, religion or geographic location and access to facilities relating to Sports, Cultural, Recreational and Adventure activities.

2. *Gender Justice:* The Policy recognizes the prevailing gender bias to be the main factor responsible for the poor status of health and economic well-being of women in our society and that any discrimination on grounds of

sex violates the basic rights of the individual concerned and it, therefore, stands for the elimination of gender discrimination in every sphere. The Policy enunciates that:

(a) Every girl child and young woman will have access to education and would also be a primary target of efforts to spread literacy.

(b) Women will have access to adequate health services (including reproductive health programmes) and will have full say in defining the size of the family.

(c) Domestic violence will be viewed not only as violation of women's freedom but also as that of human rights.

(d) All necessary steps should be taken for women's access to decision-making process, to professional positions and to productive resources and economic opportunities.

(e) Young men, particularly the male adolescents shall be properly oriented, through education and counseling to respect the status and rights of women.

3. The Policy further enunciates that

(a) Action would be pursued to eliminate all forms of discrimination in respect of the girl child, negative cultural attitudes and practices against women, discrimination against women in education, skill development and training, and the socio-economic exploitation of women, particularly young women;

(b) Concerted efforts will be made to promote a family value system that nurtures a closer bond between men and women, and ensures equality, mutual respect and sharing of responsibility between the sexes.

4. ***Inter-Sectoral Approach:*** The Policy recognizes that an inter-sectoral approach is a pre-requisite for dealing with youth-related issues. It, therefore, advocates the establishment of a coordinating mechanism among the various Central Government Ministries and Departments and between the Central and State Governments, and the

community based organisations and youth bodies for facilitating convergence in youth related schemes, developing integrated policy initiatives for youth programmes and for reviewing on-going activities / schemes to fill in gaps and remove unnecessary duplication and overlap.

5. ***Information & Research Network:*** Youth development efforts in India have been hampered by lack of adequate information and research base. The Policy, therefore, suggests the establishment of a well organized Information & Research Network in regard to various areas of concern to the youth to facilitate the formulation of focused youth development schemes and programmes. The Rajiv Gandhi National Institute of Youth Development (RGNIYD) will serve as the apex Information and Research Centre on youth development issues. The National Youth Centre and the State Youth Centres will also serve as store houses of information for the youth. At the micro level, the Youth Development Centres under the NYKs will be equipped to serve as information centres for the local youth.
6. ***Privileges of Youth:*** The Policy acknowledges that the youth of the country should be assured of the following:
   - Appropriate education and training which enables them to render themselves socially useful and economically productive;
   - Gainful employment and adequate opportunities for personal development and advancement for those not currently in employment;
   - Requisite shelter and a clean environment, as also basic health services of quality;
   - Social defence and protection from all manner of exploitation;
   - Suitable participation in decision-making bodies which are concerned with issues relating to the youth and with socio-economic and cultural matters;

- Sufficient allocation of public funds for youth development;
- Access to Sports, Physical Education, Adventure and Recreational opportunities.

7. ***Responsibilities of Youth:*** The Policy exhorts the youth to fulfill their responsibilities, as are enumerated below:
    1. To contribute to sectoral, family and self development and to promote social and inter-generation understanding and gender equality;
    2. To extend respect to teachers and elders, parents and the family, in consonance with our cultural norms and traditions;
    3. To uphold the unity and integrity of the Nation, maintain peace and harmony, observe Fundamental Duties and respect the Fundamental Rights and Freedoms guaranteed under the Constitution to all sections of the people;
    4. To respect others' faiths and beliefs in the religious, cultural and social spheres and to different schools of thought and to neither exploit nor be instrumental in the exploitation of fellow citizens and other persons, especially women;
    5. To promote appropriate standards of ethical conduct in individual and social life, to maintain honesty and integrity of character and be committed to fight against all forms of corruption, social evils and practices.
    6. To preserve and protect the Environment; and
    7. To commit themselves to create a discrimination and exploitation free environment and to devote their time and energy in nation building activities.
8. ***Key Sectors of Youth Concern:*** The Policy recognizes the following areas as key sectors of concern for the youth:
    1. Education;
    2. Training and Employment;
    3. Health and Family welfare;

4. Preservation of Environment, Ecology and Wild life;
5. Recreation and Sports;
6. Arts and Culture;
7. Science and Technology; and
8. Civics and good Citizenship.

8. Education

1. The Policy acknowledges that the objective of providing appropriate education, which enables the youth to develop into good citizens of the country, should also suitably influence relevant actions of the Government and public behaviour.
2. It is recognized that the need of the educational system to instill, in the youth, an abiding sense of patriotism and in values oriented towards the unity and integrity of the country, equally calls for the elimination of violence in all forms, adherence to good moral and ethical values and respect and reverence for India's composite culture and national heritage.
3. This Policy emphasizes that the learning process should minimise the stress and strain, which the system may exert on students, especially in the early years. The thrust of the educational system, particularly in the early years, ought to be on learning, rather than on merely qualifying in examinations and memory-based tests. The Policy lays emphasis on outdoor learning as an integral part of the educational process and on Physical Education, Sports, Games and Adventure activities.
4. Academic institutions should be equipped with adequate sports and recreational facilities.
5. Education, above the secondary level, should have a high degree of vocationalisation so as to enable the youth to acquire such requisite skills as would augment avenues of employment for them; technical institutions need to be strengthened and their number increased keeping an eye on our country's emergence as a major force in information technology.

6. There needs to be greater uniformity in the educational system and standards in various parts of the country.
7. Closer links should be developed between the educational system and prospective employers, on an institutional basis and career counselling should be a part of the educational system, from the secondary level onwards. Programmes need to be undertaken for proper dissemination of information, amongst young men and women, in respect of career options.
8. Programmes should be undertaken to upgrade the existing skills of young artisans of traditional handicrafts and other products and for those who may wish to take up the same as a vocation. Education system should also have a rural orientation to address the varied needs of agriculture, agro – processing and other areas of rural economy.
9. Educational curriculum in schools should include information on health issues, including reproductive health, HIV-AIDS and also on population issues.
10. Youth clubs and Mahila Mandals should be encouraged to involve their members in programmes like "Sarva Shiksha Abhiyan" and Total Literacy Campaign for universalisation of primary education, and spread of literacy and to organize activities to promote book reading habits among the youth.

9. Training and employment

1. This Policy recognizes that the question of employment is, at present, of very serious concern for the Indian youth and that several social issues arise out of widespread unemployment and under-employment of the youth.
2. This Policy further acknowledges that the incidence of unemployment is more pronounced in the rural areas and in urban slums and calls for appropriate strategies and commensurate efforts to deal with it.

3. The current trends suggest that the growth rate of the labour force has been higher than the growth rate of population and that the growth rate of employment has not been in proportion to GDP growth.
4. The critical issues in this area include a mis-match between skills-requirement and employment opportunities, low technology levels, low wages and low productivity, occupational shifts in employment, under-employment owing to seasonal factors, excess labour supply in relation to demand, migration of the labour force from the rural to urban areas and limited participation of women in the work force, especially in the organized sector.
5. The incidence of unemployment has been accentuated by advances in technology and communications, to tackle which, opportunities for self-employment need to be created. Schemes to provide "seed money" to assist viable enterprises initiated by the youth need to be drawn up. A network of youth skill training centres would need to be established to build up the capacities of the young people for income generation activities.
6. Adequate funding for both pre-job and on-the-job training for youth by government as well as other stake holders should be ensured. For proper vocational guidance and career counselling, schools and colleges should pay adequate attention to this aspect as part of their co-curricular activities.
7. Government, in conjunction with youth organisations, will develop training programmes for young people in the rural areas, based on their needs. Special schemes would also be developed for young women, youth with disabilities and for young people returning from the urban to the rural areas, alongside flexibility in training systems and collaboration between training institutions and potential employers.

8. Co-operative schemes involving Self Help Groups of young people in the production and marketing of goods and services would be encouraged and strengthened, with government support. Banks and Co-operatives would be advised to make identifiable allocations of soft credit to young people and their Self Help Groups and micro-credit adopted as a strategy to enable young women and men, in the rural areas, to undertake fruitful economic ventures.
9. A Data Bank will be created to keep abreast of the employment opportunities being generated, as also the availability of young people, with the requisite skills, for the same;
10. Health
    1. The policy recognises that a holistic approach towards health, mental, physical and spiritual, needs to be adopted after careful assessment of the health needs of the youth.
    2. As per the youth population projections (based on the 1991 Census), about 21.4% of the total population in 1996 was estimated to be in the age group of 10-19 years; of these, about 78.4% lived in the rural and the remaining (21.6%) in the urban areas. The mean age of marriage in the rural areas was 21.56 years for males and 16.67 years for females. In the urban areas, the mean age for marriage was 24.32 years for males and 19.92 years for females. In other words, most women in India are married during the age of adolescence.
    3. The areas of focus of this Policy, in so far as health of the youth is concerned, are:
        - General Health;
        - Mental Health;
        - Spiritual Health;
        - AIDS, Sexually Transmitted Diseases, Substance Abuse; and
        - Population Education.

General Health

4. *Nutrition:* The policy recognises an urgent need for greater concentration on nutritional studies on the youth – particularly the young women and the adolescents and advocates all measures to lessen the differences between their daily average intake of energy and proteins and the recommended daily intake allowances (RDA). The Policy particularly emphasises on reduction of this gap, which is wider among the children of growing age as per Indian National Nutritional Profile, 1998.
5. The growth rate standard of Indian adolescents, measured in terms of Body Mass Index (BMI) viz. ratio between weight and height, is lower in India than in most of the industrialised nations. Iron deficiency and anemia are common, especially in girls. The growth-related requirements of adolescents often continue beyond the teenage years and overlap with the nutritional needs of early pregnancy, which has an impact on the health of new-born children, in addition to the mothers. Discriminatory practices in respect of girls also lead to lack of adequate nutritional intake, which results in malnutrition, anaemia and other micro-nutrient deficiencies in young girls which are more noticeable in the rural areas. These concerns need to be effectively tackled through appropriate measures, including awareness-generation programmes.
6. The Policy lays emphasis on the importance of hygiene and sanitation in promoting a healthy society. All efforts should be made to inculcate in the youth a sense of hygiene and sanitation right from early education. The youth on their part should be encouraged to organise mass awareness campaigns in their neighbourhood to promote better hygiene and sanitation. Their services should also be utilised in creating better sanitation facilities for the community, both in rural areas and urban slums.

7. Health education and health consciousness: This Policy strongly recommends introduction of health education in the curricula of regular / formal education in higher classes of schools and colleges, in non-formal education centres and in every other organised interaction with the youth. The policy advocates that every youth of India should clearly understand the what, why and how of good health within his or her socio – economic parameters. A policy of minimum physical exercise for all should be propagated.

(b) Mental Health

8. Lack of proper education often leads to mental depression. In an environment that is becoming complex and competitive by the day, the chances of young minds being afflicted with depression are ever rising. This is particularly so, among adolescents who are showing higher incidence of suicidal traits than even before. Against this background, this Policy advocates a system of education which teaches the youth to fight back rather than give in. It also recommends establishment of state–sponsored and free counseling services for the youth, particularly the adolescents.

9. Adolescence is a period of change and, consequently, one of stress, characterized by uncertainties in regard to identity and position in the peer group, in society at large and in the context of one's own responsibilities as an adult. The compulsions of parental approval often encounter the emerging aspirations of independence. Adolescents exhibit mood-swings and might even indulge in self-destructive activities, such as use of alcohol, drugs and violence; they need, therefore, to be treated with openness, understanding and sympathy and offered creative channels to harness their energies. This would necessitate training and capacity building of all professional groups including NGOs working with the youth belonging to this age group.

(c) Spiritual Health

10. Health of the mind should be coupled with the health of the spirit. Towards this, yoga and meditation should be propagated widely among the youth. Yoga, in particular, should be taught in the schools.

(d) HIV/AIDS, Sexually Transmitted Diseases and Substance Abuse

11. The Policy recognizes that the percentage of young people falling prey to substance abuse, STDs and HIV / AIDS being relatively higher, these issues need be tackled as, primarily, confronting the younger generation, particularly the adolescents who are most affected. Being highly impressionable, and, therefore, prone to high risk behaviour, they require proper education and awareness about reproductive health issues, including safe sexual behaviour. The Policy, therefore, advocates a two-pronged approach of education and awareness for prevention and proper treatment and counselling for cure and rehabilitation. It further enjoins that information in respect of the reproductive health system should form part of the educational curriculum. The Policy also stresses the need for establishment of adolescent clinics in large hospitals and similar projects in rural areas to address the health needs of the young adults.

(e) Population Education

12. The Policy recognises that a growing population is a serious national problem that has negated many of our achievements in the field of development. The youth have an important role to play in this sphere and can create greater awareness in this regard through community programmes.

13. Responsible sexual behaviour can be promoted through education in family-life issues and control of population. Pregnancy and childbirth, in the adolescent period, particularly for young women below 17 years of age who are living in unhealthy conditions and without adequate access to health services, has been a serious bio-medical

hazard.The adolescent age-group has to be sensitised in regard to the correct age for marriage and for the first pregnancy, sufficient spacing between births and limiting the size of the family. It is conceded that in spite of several initiatives taken by the Government, the social climate enjoins the young couple to produce their first child soon after marriage. This scenario is unlikely to change in the near or medium term. Entering into matrimony at the right age assumes critical importance in this context, apart from its healthy impact in checking the high rate of population growth.It is equally imperative that young adults be sensitised to their role and responsibilities as responsible parents. Ante-natal, natal and post-natal services of quality are also necessary for young women.

14. The following strategies should be adopted to provide better health services to the youth :
    1. Government, in co-operation with the Youth Organisations and NGOs, would promote the establishment of Youth Health Associations, at the grass-root level, to ensure proper sanitation, health and hygiene and would, in cooperation with Youth Organisations, develop Family Welfare Services for young people and provide counselling services;
    2. Programmes would be instituted, with the support of Youth Organisations and NGOs, to sensitise medical and para-medic students on the issues of health and hygiene and also in the IEC component of various disease control programmes; and
    3. Young people will be recognised as "Health Promoters".
15. The youth will also be involved in a structured manner in the following health-related activities:
    1. Construction of lavatories, water points, dispensaries and wells; cleaning of public places and related environment protection activities; community surveys and research on health-related matters;

2. Safe blood donation, nutrition and food production projects;
3. Information, education and prevention campaigns in respect of health concerns, such as malaria, malnutrition, STD (including HIV / AIDS), teenage pregnancy and abuse of alcohol and other harmful substances;
4. "Peer Education" will be an important element in promoting health services.

16. This Policy urges upon universal accessibility of an acceptable, affordable and quality health care service to the youth throughout the length and breadth of this country to be made available in close proximity to their places of residence. The youth should have this accessibility for themselves as well as for other vulnerable age groups whom they could help out.

1. The Policy recognises that children and young people are particularly vulnerable to the ill effects of environmental degradation. Unplanned industrialisation, which leads to pollution and to degradation of rivers, forests and land, adversely affects the young who have a vital stake in a healthy environment.
2. Considering the importance of community involvement in preservation of the environment, the Policy exhorts young people to play an increasingly significant role in mobilising the public, at large, in this national endeavour. The Policy also advocates motivating the youth to develop respect for Nature and to lead lifestyle which are less resource consumptive and more source conservationist.
3. The Policy recognises that women are seriously affected by environmental degradation resulting, inter-alia, in lack of potable water and scarcity of fuel wood.The migration of men to cities to seek employment often isolates the womenfolk who are left to fend for themselves.

4. Having regard to the above, the Policy highlights the following lines of concrete action:
   - Greater emphasis should be placed on environmental education in school curricula and training programmes should be arranged to inform teachers on environmental issues so as to enable them to instruct the youth suitably. Environmental education should also be a part of the outdoor learning process;
   - The participation of Youth Organisations in gathering environmental data and in understanding environmental issues would be encouraged as a means of improving their knowledge of immediate surroundings and accentuating personal concern towards proper environmental management;
   - Motivating the youth to establish nature and adventure clubs in villages and towns with a view to creating mass awareness towards protection of the country's biodiversity, and to work with local bodies and NGOs in planning and management of our forests, rural water bodies, common land and natural resources through active local participation.
   - Vocational training, in recycling of materials and managing waste materials, would be promoted so as to ensure that more young people may find a local source of livelihood and, at the same time, arrest degradation of the environment; and
   - Youth Organisations, at the grass root level, would be assisted in provision of training in agro-forestry, agriculture and traditional agricultural practices.
   - Promotion of both traditional and alternative technologies for water conservation and water harvesting through Youth organisations.

Sports and Recreation

1. Having recognised that the overall objective of the Policy is the all-round development of personality of the youth and noting that Sports, Physical Education, Adventure, Recreation and related activities might often be overlooked, this Policy strongly supports these activities as important areas of human resource development. No system of education could be considered successful, unless it addresses the urges and aspirations of the youth to be creative and appreciative of the manifold facets of nature and of social life.
2. The Policy, accordingly, enunciates that:
   - Sports and games be promoted as a mass movement by making it a way of life;
   - Sports, Games and Physical Education including Yoga, should be compulsory in all Educational Institutions;
   - Every educational institution should have adequate facilities for recreation, adventure and sports activities, including playgrounds;
   - Provision be made for common play grounds in the master plans of all civic and municipal areas;
   - At least one-fifth of the time spent by a student in an educational institution should be earmarked for outdoor activities;
   - Geographically disadvantaged areas would be extended additional support for the promotion of Sports and Games;
   - Rural, traditional and indigenous sports would be accorded special attention and it would be the responsibility of the Panchayat Institutions with the help of local youth organisations to develop and maintain infrastructure for this purpose. The involvement of organised youth bodies such as youth clubs under the NYKS, the volunteers of the NSS and the Scouts & Guides in the creation and maintenance

of sports infrastructure will go a long way in reducing the high cost of such infrastructure;

- A National Youth Festival will be held each year, starting at the Block level and culminating at the National Level;
- Youth Hostels would be constructed in as many places of historical and cultural interest as possible, to promote youth tourism;
- Youth Organizations devoted to such activities will be encouraged; and
- Adventure activities among the youth be promoted to inculcate qualities of leadership, resilience, courage, discipline and love for nature and the environment.

Arts and Culture

1. Activities connected with Arts and Culture provide recreation to individuals, sharpen their sensitivities and afford a vehicle to inculcate desirable ideals and values. The Policy recognizes the importance of Arts and Culture in a holistic approach to youth development and that Young People need to be sensitised to the great heritage of our country and provided with opportunities to understand and follow pluralistic forms of culture.
2. This Policy, therefore, enunciates the following:
   - The youth should be better enabled to imbibe the rich traditions and culture of India and sensitised to the need to preserve and enrich this extraordinary heritage. This will be sought to be achieved inter-alia through----
     - — inclusion of learning and appreciation of the country's rich heritage in art, architecture, music and dance etc. in the educational curricula at the school level;
     - — encouraging and facilitating through financial assistance in association with concerned State Govt./PRIs etc., visits to ancient monuments/

heritage sites during which attempt would be made to impress upon the young people the need for preservation of our ancient heritage by involving them in voluntary work for cleaning up the sites and surroundings and educating and motivating the local youth to protect such monuments against vandalism etc. The Ministry of Railways and State STUs will be persuded to offer concessional fares for such organised educational trips and for organising special services to such places, particularly during holidays;

— Encouraging and facilitating the visits of well known artists to educational institutions to impart lessons in appreciation through demonstrations/ workshops/performances;

— Encouraging and facilitating in association with State Govts./PRIs/NGOs attendance of young persons at performances by well known artistes in their respective areas.

4. A National Youth Centre would be established to provide young people with a common platform where they can express their opinions and views on various issues concerning them. Such a Youth Centre will also provide them with ample scope to give exposure to their creative genius and abilities in the fields of various cultural expressions like fine arts, music, theatre, film etc. State Youth Centres would be established, on similar lines, in the various States.

Science and Technology

1. As the adaptation of scientific and technological principles and developments, to maximise the use of local resources, are central to empowerment in the quality of life, the Policy recognises the importance of emerging, modern technologies, particularly in the field of infor-mation technology and electronic media, in enabling the youth to perform and achieve in all sectors of their interest.

2. The Policy also recognises that young scientists and technologists should be extended adequate facilities for research and that the contribution of the private sector in this field should be encouraged.
3. The National Youth Policy, therefore, provides for:
   - Review of policies in respect of the School Curriculum and the non-formal education sector so that Science may be popularised amongst all sections of the youth;
   - Support to providing exposure to the youth to the scientific temper and way of life;
   - Development of mechanisms within the system to identify and train gifted youth, as early as possible, in the fields of science and technology;
   - The best and the most positive use of information and communications technology, as well as all forms of media, including the electronic media, for youth development as well as for promoting and protecting the richness of our culture;
   - Promoting a multi-sectoral approach involving, inter-alia, the private sector and NGOs, to orient the youth towards scientific and technological studies and research;
   - Ensuring co-ordination between the various Government Ministries/Departments and Scientific Organisations/Institutions dealing with youth development programmes;
   - Upgrading science curricula in institutions of learning to inculcate the scientific approach amongst all sections of the younger generation;
   - Linking the projects of the young scientists to the problems of the people and ensuring better interaction between labs and the industry;
   - Documentation of the large repository of physical and knowledge based resources within the country to prevent their piracy by vested interests.

Civics and Citizenship

1. Human behaviour is significantly shaped by norms and values, which are a basis for attitudinal growth. The dominant features in the Indian Society, which impinge on the cultural and other values of young people, include areas such as family life, education, work and occupational activities, gender, class and ethnic relations, religion, mass communication, artistic and creative expression, sports, recreation, politics and the economic environment.
2. Anti-social behaviour is a manifestation of the absence of well-accepted values, attitudes and norms in the individual and in society which can reflect itself in crime, violent action, breakdown of parental authority in family life, corruption in public life, obscenity in the media, indiscipline in schools and in sporting activities and low productivity at the workplace.
3. The Policy, therefore, envisages the following strategies:
   - Embodying instruction in the values like respect for teachers and parents, adolescent and the aged besides religious tolerance, and compassion towards the poor and the needy. The concept of family as the basic and most important asset of Indian Society will be strengthened.
   - To motivate the youth to resist fragmentation of society on the basis of caste, religion, language and ethnicity and for promotion of democratic values enshrined in our constitution.
   - To mobilise the youth to create local pressure groups within the community to fight corruption at all levels and to ensure that the benefits of development reach those for whom they are intended and are not siphoned of by middlemen and the powerful.
   - Laying emphasis on the economic and social security of the youth belonging to underprivileged sections of our society and those who are mentally and physically challenged.

9. *Priority Target Groups:* This Policy will accord priority to the following groups of young people:
   1. Rural and Tribal Youth;
   2. Out-of-school Youth;
   3. Adolescents particularly female adolescents;
   4. Youth with disabilities;
   5. Youth under specially difficult circumstances like victims of trafficking; orphans and street children.

Broadbasing of Sports

Considering the key role of sports in national life and for inculcating national pride in the younger generation, the objective of broad basing, that is, universalisation or mass participation in Sports assumes special significance. It is imperative to ensure that the educational institutions, Schools and Colleges in both rural and urban areas; the Panchayati Raj Institutions, Local Bodies, the government machinery, the Sports Associations and Industrial Undertakings, as also the various Youth and Sports Clubs, including those of the Nehru Yuva Kendra Sangathan (NYKS) throughout the country are, and remain, fully associated with this Programme. Efforts will be made to promote and encourage women's participation in sports. The Union and State Governments, as well as the Sports Federations/Associations will endeavour to promote a "club culture" for the speedier development of Sports in the country.

In the National Sports Policy, 2001, high priority will be accorded to the development of Sports in the rural areas to harness the available talent and potential. In this context, the Village Panchayats/Gaon Sabhas as well as rural Youth and Sports clubs will be mobilized to facilitate development of the requisite infrastructure and for the identification of talent through an appropriate competition structure in the rural areas as also in the disadvantaged and remote parts of the country which appear to merit special consideration under various schemes including for the North East. Efforts will also be made for tapping such potential as swimming in coastal areas and Archery in tribal areas.

The available talent will be nourished and actively supported. Geographically disadvantaged Regions will be extended additional support for the promotion of Sports. There has been a strong tradition of Indigenous and traditional games in practically all parts of the country through ages. Indigenous games will be promoted through schemes related to rural sports.

Integration with Education

The integration of Sports and Physical Education with the Educational Curriculum, making it a compulsory subject of learning up to the Secondary School level and incorporating the same in the evaluation system of the student, will be actively pursued. A National Fitness Programme would be introduced in all Schools in the country, steps initiated to augment the availability of infrastructure, including play fields/ sports equipment and action taken to provide Physical Education Teachers in educational institutions through, inter-alia, the training of selected teachers in these disciplines. Specialized Sports Schools may also be set up. An appropriate Inter-school and Inter- College/University competition structure would be introduced at the National, State and District levels.

Infrastructure Development

The availability of adequate sports facilities throughout the country is basic to the development and broad-basing of Sports. In addition to the Union and State Governments, the sustained involvement of other agencies, including the Panchayati Raj Institutions, Local Bodies, Educational Institutions, Sports Federations/Associations. Clubs and Industrial Undertakings will be enlisted in the creation, utilization and proper maintenance of the Sports infrastructure. While existing play fields and stadia, both in rural and urban areas, will be maintained for sports purposes, the introduction of suitable legislation may be considered for providing open areas to promote sports activities. Steps would be taken to evolve low cost functional and environment-friendly designs in this regard, so that maximum benefits could be derived through relatively low levels of investment. Efforts will also be made to optimally utilize the available infrastructure and manpower and Special Coaching Cams organised, during the vacations, to provide intensive training to talented sports persons, even as they pursue their academic work.

Excellence in Sports

The Union Government would focus attention on achieving Excellence in Sports at the National and International levels. Various sports disciplines will be prioritized on the basis of proven potential, popularity and international performance. Particular emphasis will be placed on the development of such priority disciplines and the prioritization reviewed, from time to time. The IOA and the State Governments would also accord higher priority to such disciplines. In planning the development of various disciplines, the genetic and geographical variations within the country would be taken into account so that in areas of potential, in particular disciplines, timely steps may be taken to harness the existing and emerging talent. Centers of excellence will be set up to identify and train outstanding sportspersons including sports academies where young and talented sports persons will be groomed to achieve higher levels of performance in the international sports arena.

National Sports Federations (NSFS)

It is recognized that the management and development of Sports are the function of the Indian Olympic Association and the National Sports Federations, which are Autonomous Bodies and who, in turn, have affiliated State level and District level Associations. The Government and other concerned agencies and the Federations/Associations have, therefore, to work together harmoniously and in a coordinated manner to fulfil the objectives of the National Sports Policy, 2001. At the same time, the Indian Olympic Association and the various Sports Federations/ Associations will need to demonstrate orientation towards the achievement of results and ensure tangible progress in the field of Sports, keeping which in view, model bye-laws/organizational structures may be formulated for the NSFs, in consultation with them, and with due regard to the Olympic Charter, so as to make the functioning of the Federations/Association transparent, professional and accountable.

Acknowledging the importance of National Championships for developing competitive spirit and for talent-scouting, it would be incumbent on the Federations/Associations to hold Annual Championships in various disciplines in all categories, viz, Seniors, Juniors and Sub-Juniors (for both Men & Women) at the District, State and National levels. Each National Federation would draw up the Annual National Calendar of these events sufficiently in advance, every year, which would be compiled and published by the IOA. Greater emphasis will be placed on promoting the development of Sports amongst the juniors and sub-juniors and the more talented amongst them identified for Special Training and Support.

Effective participation in International Events, especially the Olympics, Asian and Commonwealth Games, is a matter of National Prestige. Participation in these Events has, so far, largely been restricted to those disciplines in which creditable performance is anticipated. The contingents to represent the country in such events need be chosen in due time, in the light of performance and promise, in National Championships and elsewhere. Long Term Development Plans (LTDPs) will be prepared for each Sports discipline, incorporating details of standard of performance, targeted levels of performance, participation in competitions at national and international levels, sports exchanges, scientific support and the holding of international competitions in the country. The implementation of the LTDPs will be reviewed periodically and the same would be continued, as a Rolling Plan year after year. The release of Government assistance would be considered on the basis of performance relating to the LTDP in question.

Scientific Back-up to Sports Persons

The significance of scientific-back up to Sports stands well established. Accordingly, action will be initiated to strengthen this area, in accordance with international standards. Experts would be associated with each Sports Discipline or Groups of Sports Disciplines, on a continuing basis, to provide the requisite support in terms of nutrition, psychology, medicine, pharmacology, physiology, bio-mechanics and anthrapometry as well as other branches of Sports Sciences. Suitable mechanisms would be introduced to achieve co-ordination between the laboratory and the field, that is, between the Coaches and the Sports Scientists, and particular care taken to ensure nutritional support to talented sports persons and to sustain their mental health and competitive spirit.

Appropriate research and development measures will also be initiated for the promotion of sports and to impart special skills to promising sports persons so that they are enabled to give of their best in international and other prestigious competitions. The SAI and other public and private organisations will be involved in such research and development programmes. The SAI and the NSFs would take coordinated steps towards the modernisation of the infrastructure required for the training of sports persons and to provide them with scientific support for achieving Excellence in Sports.

Sprots Equipment

Suitable measures will be initiated to ensure access to sports equipment of high quality. While the approach to import of equipment would, no doubt, bear the long term interests of the indigenous sports goods manufacturers in mind, the import of raw materials as well as finished sports goods of international quality should be permissible under Open General License. Similarly, Sports Federations/Associations and other recognized Organization involved in Sports Promotion, as also eminent Sports persons, may be extended exemption of customs Duty. The matter relating to exemption from sales Tax for Sports Goods and of free movement of raw materials and finished sports goods in the country would be pursued with the State Governments.

Training and Development of Coaches, Sports Scientists Judges, Referees and Umpires

The Policy recognizes that the standards of coaching and scientific back up in the country and those pertaining to umpires, judges and referees needs to be upgraded. Concerted steps will be taken to train Coaches, Sports Scientists, Judges, Referees and Umpires, in line with international standards. In addition to developing such expertise on an institutional basis, within the country, the deputation of promising persons to Training Courses, Conferences. Seminars, workshops and Tournaments abroad, so that they remain abreast of relevant developments in their fields, will be encouraged. Coaches would receive rigorous training for up-gradation of skills and may also be deputed overseas for the purpose.

Incentives to Sports Persons

Incentives provide recognition and financial security to distinguished sports persons, during and after their sporting careers, and also motivate the youth in the serious pursuit of sports activities. Adequate assistance will be extended for Insurance Cover and Medical Treatment in the event of such eventuality/requirement. Job reservation for sportspersons as per the prescribed categories will continue. Social Recognition, the Conferment of Awards and Honours at the National, State, and District levels, incentives in the form of Cash Awards and Avenues of Employment will be important elements of the National Sports Policy, 2001. Alongside sports persons, suitable incentives will be provided to Coaches, Judges and Referees for developing skills and enriching their experience.

Sports and Tourism

The Policy recognizes the inter-dependence and inter-relationship between the Sports and Tourism sectors, the integrated development of which is capable of generating very substantial revenues and ensuring a high volume of tourist traffic from within the country and from overseas, while simultaneously promoting a sports & fitness culture in the country. Adventure Sports, in particular, have great potential for the promotion of tourism. Towards this end, the concerned Ministries/Departments of the Union and State Governments, that is those handling Sports, Tourism and related subjects, will strive to draw up joint/unified Plans and Proposals for various parts of the country, with due reference to the possibilities in the North Eastern Region, and to execute these programmes in a systematic and coordinated manner.

Resource Mobilization for Sports

Insufficiency of financial resources has been a major constraint in promoting sports in India. While the Union and State Governments, would need to arrange higher budgetary provisions, special efforts are equally called for to mobilize corporate funds for the development of Sports in the country. Accordingly, corporate Houses would be approached and encouraged to adopt and support particular disciplines (as well as sports persons) in the longer term; for this purpose. Tripartite Agreements between the Government and the concerned Sports Federations and the Corporate Houses may be entered into for different Sports Disciplines. In the context of the Policy of Economic Liberalization, the Private/Corporate sectors would be more closely involved with the promotion of Sports, in general, and to build and maintain Sports infrastructure, in particular, with requisite emphasis on the latest technologies. A suitable package of incentives may also be evolved for this purpose. Eminent sports persons of established merit will be encouraged to set up and manage Sports Academies.

It may be recalled that a National Sports Development Fund has been created with initial contribution of the Union Government. All contributions (from within and outside the country) to this Fund have been extended 100% exemption from Income Tax. The mobilization of resources for the Fund will be strenuously pursued and the feasibility of exempting the incomes of Sports Federations and Sports persons (from sources other than employers) from payment of Income Tax explored. The revenues generated by the sale of Broadcasting Television Rights of Sports Events will be shared between the concerned Sports Federation/ Association and the Broadcasting/Telecasting agency, public or private, on mutually agreed terms, through appropriate revenue sharing arrangements.

Mass Media

The role of Mass Media is central to the popularization of Sports amongst the people at large. The Electronic Media, including the National Broadcasters, the Private Channels and the Print Media would be suitable mobilized for strengthening a Sports Culture in the country.

Globalisation

As a resurgent India confidently enters the New Millenium, Sports (and related activities) will be increasingly utilized as a medium for promoting cooperation and friendship in the Region, as also globally. Sports Exchange Programmes will be pursued with all friendly Nations, with emphasis, on the one hand on Advance Training for Sports persons and Coaches, Scientific Support, the latest Research Aids and Development of Infrastructure, and earning laurels for the country, in Sports and Games, on the other. The National Sports Policy, 2001 would be reviewed, periodically, in order, inter-alia, to incorporate changes/ modifications which may be necessitated by technological and other advancements in the field of Sports.

Partnerships and Liaisons

The private sector provides a significant range of opportunities, and since the advent of compulsory competitive tendering (CCT) and Best Value the relationship between the private sector and the local authority sector has become blurred in many situations. Much private sector provision is very limited and very specialized, focusing on activities that are specifically mass participation or have the potential to make significant returns. Examples of sports traditionally based in the private sector or which have developed under its auspices are snooker, professional football, rugby league, aerobics and fitness training. This list is not exclusive and is constantly growing as the commercial return for previously smaller sports increases, due to the potential for further publicity and television coverage caused by the vast growth in the media coverage—especially satellite and cable television.

The key issue about sports provision is not who provides it, but the increasing necessity for liaison between all parties due to the limited resources available, or, in the case of the private sector, the need to target customers and focus on efficient practice. There is a great deal of talk at present of networking partnership and liaison mechanisms—all of these are vitally important to successful projects run by any aspect of the industry. There needs to be a clear demarcation within these partnerships of who is doing what for whom, and what costs, in terms of time and finance, are attached to each partner in such an arrangement. Glib talk of networks and partnerships is all very well, but there need to be clear guidelines and specific means of operating within any such partnerships and networks if they are to be effective. Some of the guiding principles required to make partnerships work are:

- Clear project objectives
- Shared desire and commitment to achieve these objectives
- Honesty and trust
- Clearly allocated work roles
- Strong interpersonal relationships
- Dedicated hard work and effort.

The future of Sports is founded in partnerships between various agencies within and across industry sectors. It is beneficial to voluntary clubs to link into possible public sector (e.g. health authority) or private sector (e.g. bingo club) initiatives in order to benefit their sporting activities. As funding becomes more difficult and yet more and more essential for successful Sports at all levels, partnerships will become more and more crucial, and every opportunity to establish them must be pursued. Potentially there can be partners in many initiatives from unlikely sources, and viewing Sports in its widest community-benefit sense can often assist. The more traditional view of Sports as an élite performance activity is limiting and inappropriate. The implied public health benefits of Sports will suit certain people, including the media, local health boards and the social services. They would be much more interested in becoming involved and forming a partnership than they would where success for one or two individuals was the aim. The agencies that might want to become involved include:

- Enterprise companies/councils
- Tourist boards
- Private companies
- Health boards
- Local authorities
- Voluntary clubs
- National governing bodies
- Educational institutes.

Partnerships can bring together different organizations with their own aims to achieve agreed common goals. Through partnership everyone involved can be a winner. Increasingly networks—previously colloquially known as the jungle telegraph—have a role to play in sports administration. Primarily these are just about keeping in touch and learning from others active in the field of sports administration and management. This can be informal—through a telephone conversation or a chance meeting—or promoted formally at conferences or training seminars. Often these are encouraged or established by a national or regional sports council.

National Governing Bodies

Perhaps the key organizations involved in the provision of Sports are the national governing bodies (NGBs). These are the autonomous gathering together of the various sports clubs, individuals and organizations in specific sports. They represent the sports people with an interest in a particular Sports and are the main agency that represents the views of those sports participants. Governing bodies vary widely in nature and enormously in size, from small ones such as lacrosse or fencing to huge ones such as swimming, gymnastics or football.

Ultimately, regardless of all other agencies, these NGBs as amalgama-tions of sports participants are the key agencies in the co-ordination and provision of Sports. They do not always possess large amounts of money and may sometimes be lacking in direction, but they are the voice of each particular Sports. As such, they are consulted by other relevant partners such as the Foundation of Sports and the Arts, the various sports councils and local authorities.

Their role is enormously important—indeed it can be argued that without such an association representing the interests of any particular Sports, the future existence of that Sports may be jeopardized. This can be supported from the point of view of the body's role in the determination of rules and disciplinary procedures, or the interpretation of international rulings, or the co-ordination of international activities. In essence NGBs are made up of the individual participants (at whatever level of activity), officials and administrators, most of whom will also have a role in a local club or association, sometimes in a district or regional association as well as the national body. The officials of governing bodies are almost always voluntary and are under tremendous pressure, with work coming from a wide variety of sources, while being subject to the pressures of any democratic organization which has political (with a small 'p') moves and issues to resolve on an ongoing basis.

Most governing bodies of any size will also have a number of paid staff—including administrators, chief executives and clerical staff, as well as technical staff, national coaches and development officers. Only the latter staff will necessarily have deep technical knowledge about the performance and the rules and regulations of the Sports. For the former, it is more important that they have the ability to organize on a businesslike and professional basis. National governing bodies of Sports may be seen as autonomous gatherings of sports clubs and/or associations or individuals joining together to promote and represent a particular Sports. While these bodies vary significantly, e.g. from a large wealthy organization such as the Football Association to a relatively small and resource-short organization such as the Lacrosse Association, a number of distinct similarities and characteristics can be identified.

They are grant-aided— at least most receive money through the relevant sports council to support their activities. Only the larger, more affluent ones, e.g football and rugby union, do not receive a substantial portion of their running costs. They are autonomous— ultimately they are self-controlling and, while the sports council may fund them, and others may have views on what they should do, ultimately they decide internally for themselves.

They are voluntary— most governing bodies of Sports run largely on the basis of voluntary support in terms of staffing and assisting with organizational duties at events and promotions or even on a routine basis. A number now have significant numbers of staff on a paid full-time basis, but even they rely significantly on voluntary help from officials and administrators.

Pressure Group/lobby: One key role for any governing body is to operate as the public voice, speaking for that Sports and requesting, from all appropriate sources, support for and interest in that Sports and its participants.

Financed by Members: While support will be drawn from a wide variety of areas and commercial activities may be sizeable, the vast majority of governing bodies rely substantially on member contributions to ensure they have money available in order to function in their various roles.

***Amateur** (amateur in this sense means unpaid and spare-time—it should not be construed as 'amateurish'!):* Most governing bodies rely on committees, structures and functions undertaken by people in their spare time away from their normal form of employment. While, as mentioned above, many have employees, most are heavily dependent on this spare-time commitment.

Strong Public Sector Links: At both local and national level governing bodies of Sports rely substantially on their links with public sector bodies such as their local and national sports councils, and on sports development officers and others from these organizations to assist with projects and events.

Club Members: Most governing bodies have individual membership but many, in addition, have club members, and some even have regional or district associations in membership. The club structure is a key part of most governing bodies.

Individual Members: Ultimately many of the payments and much of the activity in support come from the individual members of governing bodies, whether through clubs, regional associations, or just by direct individual membership. The support of a mass of these members will be necessary for any successful governing body project.

Sports Council Links: Whatever the location of the national governing body, it will have to link with the Sports Council or one of the home countries' sports councils. This relationship is vital in terms of governing bodies relating the patterns of national development laid down by government through the sports councils and then working with sports council officials and programmes to achieve the aims of any such initiatives.

Democratic: In most cases governing bodies are truly democratic in allowing one member one vote on major constitutional issues, and ultimately in sanctioning development planning or direction changes. However, it is all too common for governing bodies to be dominated by limited 'cliques' which represent the views of only a small number of people. This may be because such a small group is influential, because they do all the work, or because there is apathy on the part of others. The principle of democracy certainly normally pertains and facing the annual general meeting is often the biggest problem of such dominant small groups.

Committees— Like many voluntary organizations, governing bodies tend to be dominated by committees and committee structures. This is often a very slow and inefficient way of making decisions, but allows for the democratic process to be implemented. The types of roles or duties that a governing body may undertake include:

- Administration of the Sports
- Marketing award schemes
- Staffing
- Servicing committees
- Producing publications
- Various membership services
- Producing teaching aids
- Organizing a coach education scheme
- Developing new initiatives
- Providing publicity
- Representation at national and local level
- International representation
- Providing a drug-control programme
- Event organization and management
- Providing and educating officials
- Framing, altering and applying the rules of the Sports
- Administering disciplinary procedures
- Organizing national squads or teams.

Increasingly, as society and Sports change, national governing bodies of Sports have a wide range of new challenges and future duties. These include:

- The preparing, delivering and monitoring of a corporate strategy
- Attracting more people into the Sports, in the face of growing competition from home-based leisure activities and even other sports

- Developing more effective partnership networks
- Improving media relationships and the image of the Sports
- Sourcing and servicing sponsorship arrangements and other commercial partnerships on an ongoing basis
- Enhancing self-reliance, particularly through training of administrators, officials and coaches
- Pressurizing policy-makers to support Sports in general as well as a particular Sports.

Whatever the future brings, it seems likely that the role of the governing bodies of Sports will continue to grow, and if they are proactive and organized then they will flourish. The future is a land of opportunities, and for those organizations properly prepared to meet them some progress and benefit will accrue. Certainly sporting bodies at all levels will have to get their form of planning right—they will have to be professional about their strategic planning to meet the challenges of tomorrow. Reviewing existing processes, focusing on direction and deciding on the methods of achievement are key issues for any governing body. Such a plan can vary in its requirements, but for most governing bodies it will probably involve the following steps to a greater or lesser degree.

1. A current situation audit assessing the present situation for the organization and the items which directly affect it—what is happening within and outside the governing body itself which impacts on its current and future operation. Such issues as the number of members, facilities available, government policies, national sports council policies, available finance, technological development, internal and external demands and needs will need to be considered.
2. Devising a corporate strategy—arising from an accurate professional assessment of the current situation, steps forward can be identified by bodies to see where they move to in the future. Key to this will be the identification of a mission statement—an overall reason for existing now and in the future.

Following on from this mission, a number of specific objectives can be identified—they will need to be:

- Specific
- Measurable
- Agreed
- Realistic
- Timed.

They will be structural or individual in nature. Arising out of these objectives a number of specific targets will need to be identified along with who is going to achieve them, how and when. The list of considerations for governing bodies will be long, but will include:

- Finance
- Target groups
- Marketing
- Coach education
- Government policy
- Staffing
- Sponsorship
- Event organization
- Media liaison
- External relations
- Competition
- Facilities
- Local authority relationships
- National sports council relationships
- Sports competition programme
- Society and demographic changes
- The role of volunteers and professionals
- Performance indicators
- Interim review stages.

These are just some of the topics that will be vital to producing a corporate plan which is useful and appropriate. As ever, Sports should study the procedures developed in other industries and where appropriate apply them to the sports business—even if it is largely voluntary.

Central Council of Physical Recreation (CCPR)

The CCPR is an independent voluntary body made up of around 240 governing bodies of Sports and other representatives in the area of physical recreation. It aims to represent these governing bodies in a variety of forums and support their work. A key role is representing their views to the sports councils and other public bodies in the field. It is widely regarded in government circles as a strong, independent voice for Sports and is consulted by government and others, including the media, when seeking a view of the voluntary sector. Additionally, the services offered by the CCPR, which include annual conferences, sports sponsorship advice and community sports leader award provision, are valued by a number of governing bodies and other agencies involved in the field of Sports and recreation.

There is, however, some doubt as to how representative the CCPR is. Certainly in Scotland, for example, it is not considered the representative organization for governing bodies in Sports—that place north of the border is taken by the Scottish Sports Association, which provides, on a smaller scale, similar services to the CCPR and speaks as the voice of Scottish Sports on behalf of the governing bodies.

Professional Bodies

There are a number of professional bodies involved in Sports in the UK, as well as a number which represent specific interest groups.

The British Institute of Sports Coaches

This institute (formerly the National Association of Sports Coaches) is a body set up to represent coaches. It has very close links with Spors Coach UK.

Institute of Leisure and Amenity Management (ILAM)

The Institute was formed in 1983 as a result of an amalgamation between various bodies operating in the Sports, leisure and recreation fields. Its membership is over 7,000 and is drawn from all aspects of the leisure field. While ILAM represents the wider view of the leisure profession, the sports influence within it is considerable. There is an active sports service, in addition to a panel which looks at contracting issues across the wide field of leisure, including Sports provision.

In essence ILAM's purpose is to represent and support the leisure professional in all aspects and to provide a lobbying voice for the needs of the profession and the whole sphere of leisure, including Sports. The Institute also has a role in identifying educational and training needs and providing appropriate qualifications and courses to answer these specific requirements. In addition, the Institute offers advice on careers and leisure policy locally and nationally, while working in partnership with a wide variety of other agencies to ensure that the Sports and leisure profession is recognized and listened to. Organizations such as the CCPR and the Sports Council wishing to ascertain the views of the profession will contact ILAM and also, where appropriate, the ISRM.

The work and strength of ILAM has grown significantly over recent years as the profession has increased in size. The role of Sports and sports development within the leisure profession has also grown, and it seems likely that this trend will continue with the presence of the National Lottery, the continuation (if on a smaller scale) of the Foundation for Sports and the Arts, and rather grudging and slow governmental recognition of the importance of Sports. All of these developments mean there will be a continued place for and growth in terms of the leisure and sports professional working through organizations such as ILAM.

The Institute of Sports and Recreation Management (ISRM)

Formerly known as the Institute of Baths and Recreation Management, the name was changed in 1993 in order to recognize the overall role this organization has in Sports and recreation, not just in swimming pool management. The focus is still very much on the technical issues and mechanical level course provision, but the ISRM's influence grows even though it tends to operate more at the operational than the managerial level—more with supervisors than directors of leisure. This pattern was historical—it arose from the older style of technical knowledge ('pool plant') bath managers who are now being overtaken by more managerial and less technical operators, as swimming pools become more sophisticated.

British Institute of Sports Administration (BISA)

BISA was formed in December 1993 in succession to the British Association of National Sports Administrators (BANSA), which was founded in 1977 by full-time administrators in national governing bodies of Sports. They saw the need to set up an organization to enable them to meet regularly, exchange information and expertise, and generate a corporate viewpoint on behalf of professional sports administrators. The formation of an institute has widened the objectives and membership to encompass the needs and wants of both professional and honourary sports administrators from the full range of backgrounds and organizations, including national governing bodies, national and regional sports organizations, and sports clubs and associations.

BISA has established itself as a responsible body which recognizes that sports administration is a very specialized and demanding profession. By organizing conferences, seminars and in-service training, BISA assists sports administrators to attain the very high standards required for British Sports to flourish at all levels. BISA gives sports administrators a chance to share solutions to common problems and to use their combined experience for the overall benefit of British Sports. Although other forums exist which give opportunities for sports administrators to meet, these invariably involve the administrators attending as representatives of their governing body or sporting organization.

Only through BISA do these administrators get the opportunity to attend in their own right, to represent themselves, and gain from each other the skills that are of particular relevance to their work.

Membership of BISA is open to all administrators of Sports and recreation, and currently includes people working for a wide variety of sporting organizations. BISA members include senior professional officers of national governing bodies, senior honorary administrators of national sports organizations, and members of staff of national, regional and local sports organizations and clubs. BISA has adopted a higher profile recently, so as to play a leading role on behalf of sports administrators at all levels. It is expanding its services in a number of essential areas of work, and intends to:

- Seek to increase its membership.
- Continue to play a full part in the development and promotion of the Running Sports training programme for all professional and voluntary sports administrators, at both national and local level, so as to improve the overall quality of sports administration.
- Continue to organize in-service training workshops for professional and leading voluntary sports administrators and provide the specialist high-level training part of the Running Sports programme for senior sports administrators.
- Continue to provide a forum for discussion of matters of mutual interest to sports administrators, including an annual conference focusing on matters of national significance in the field of sports administration.
- Perform the role of a professional institute and represent the views and needs of sports administrators on appropriate bodies, including the SPRITO National Council and Education and Training Committee.
- Provide an advisory service for sports administrators (professional and voluntary) on matters of personal

interest and concern, including personal employment issues.

- Promote the category of associate membership for voluntary sports administrators working at regional and local level.
- Consider operating as an assessment centre of S/NVQs in sports administration.
- Continue to draw on the knowledge, experience and expertise of the membership to benefit British Sports at all levels.
- Provide information to members regarding employment possibilities in sports administration.
- Seek recognition by appropriate bodies as the consultative body to represent the interests of sports administrators.
- Improve the status and recognition of the profession of sports administration by awarding honorary fellowships and granting fellowships and memberships on application, based on the known and proven knowledge and experience of candidates and by providing the quality control and regulation of standards for these awards.
- Establish courses leading to academic qualifications in sports administration, in co-operation with suitable educational institutions.

The National Association of Sports Development (NASD)

Formed only in 1998, this organization has begun to grow in importance due to its very specific nature and its direct communication channel to government. It has formed a strategic partnership with ISRM to try to service its members. It has, for many years (even before being formalized), held a two-day conference in Nottingham each year.

CHAPTER 7

Important Issues of People Management

A typical top-level sportsperson is young, physically gifted and extremely committed to both their own results and the success of their team. They will often share identical objectives with their team mates and be focused on a specific goal, whether this is an individual match or a longer-term competition. Their progress is highly visible, and both the individual and the team usually receive immediate feedback on their performance–even if, for some, this might be at the hands of the tabloid press. For the coach or manager, there are daily opportunities to discuss performance and explore actions to improve it. Also, the motivational strategies implemented by coaches read like a formula for how to find oneself in front of an industrial tribunal. If you're looking for a micro-managing bully, you could do a lot worse than start with many successful sports coaches.

By comparison, the leader of a senior business team is faced with a very different set of challenges. These may lie in the divergent personal perspectives and goals of their team members, most of whom will be older than the typical elite sportsperson. Succeeding in business also requires highly developed analytical skills and the ability to cope with many ambiguous, unpredictable tasks simultaneously.

In Sports, the parameters are fewer and more predictable. Although, just as in business, sports teams can employ better skilled team members, they can't suddenly decide to double the number of players on the field in a way your business competitor could suddenly decide to spend its entire annual advertising and promotions budget in one month.

Even defining winning and losing is more complex in business – is it about net profit, net margin, market share, return on capital employed, share price or shareholder added value? There may be value in using sports coaches or outdoor activities for motivational purposes. But for the serious business of securing long-term performance improvement from a senior team, training should be focused on three core issues: alignment of commercial goals and priorities and developing understanding of these within teams; clarity of team purpose and necessary procedures; and addressing team dynamics – although only if they're interfering with the agreement or achievement of business priorities.

As mentioned earlier, change and challenge face everyone employed or occupied in the sports industry, in whatever sector. In facing change the personnel and their response to challenge will be the key factor. The Audit Commission (1988) has stated that: 'the single most powerful reason why some organizations are consistently more successful than others is that their employees are better trained and more highly motivated than those of their competitors. They must feel that their contribution is valued by the organization in which they work.'

Performance Appraisal

Effective managers within any situation, especially one in which a tremendous commitment is required, should spend considerable time on developing their staff, recognizing their needs (both personal and in terms of job skill requirements), and do everything possible to support and train them to improve performance. The process of review in itself will lead to increased performance and, in turn, can improve staff morale. Through such appreciation, staff will feel that they are being taken seriously and that people are endeavouring to assess their training needs.

The attempt to produce motivated and trained staff implies that a number of steps are taken by managers at senior level and implemented at a lower level, by middle management and supervisory staff. A performance review system can be seen as threatening, but rather should be seen as supportive—the aim is to examine an individual's progress in a particular post, assessing achievements or failures, strengths or weaknesses. It is not a job-threatening but rather a job-strengthening intent. This performance review can take place in many situations and in a variety of ways, but, whatever the mechanism, it should be carried out by the direct line manager. Both should be clear of the details of the process and what it is aiming to achieve. Staff appraisal would certainly be a part of any performance review system.

It would include a review of the individual's past performance in the post, over a pre-set period (e.g. a year, six months, or three months), and would judge performance against previously identified objectives that both staff and employer would hope to have achieved within the post. Such a direct appraisal system is often wrongly seen as a potentially threatening or disciplinary situation, possibly even a conflict situation. This incorrect impression often grows because neither the person appraising nor the appraisee is trained or briefed as to how to handle the situation and what to expect. Staff appraisal sessions should:

1. Be set in the context of the aims of the organization overall,
2. Be limited to the specific job role and feelings of both parties,
3. Be undertaken by people who clearly understand the purpose of the appraisal sessions,

4. Emphasize the positive rather than the negative and look to the future rather than the past,
5. Identify achievement of past objectives and set future ones for a specific person in the post,
6. Be a two-way process so that there is some feedback from the person being appraised to their immediate line manager,
7. Leave both parties feeling they are part of a team operation and working towards the same ends,
8. Result in a confidential written record of the meeting, agreed by both parties, which should be retained by both as well as kept on file for future reference.

The appraisal system is intended to lead to more positive performance and beneficial team moulding. Any attempt by either party to focus on confrontation should be resisted, and the positive possibilities must be emphasized.

People Management

In the Sports setting the coach or team captain must be able to manage people if effective results are to be achieved. This is equally true of the manager or administrator within the sports industry. To achieve improved human performance it is necessary to create, initiate, maintain or coach individual and/or group motivation. The 'desire to perform', either as an individual or as a group, is key to performance. Managers must know where all the employees, workers, volunteers are coming from, and they must know where they are all meant to be going. They must recognize individual and team goals and help everyone to play their part in them. Individual goals may not always be exactly in tune with the organization, and that is another task managers must undertake—to try to get them both to head in the same direction.

The original thinker on motivation was Abraham Maslow. In the late 1930s he identified the levels of need. This is the classic structure of Maslow's hierarchy of needs: human wants must be recognized at all these levels and individuals' desires must be realized (Maslow, 1954). Not everyone will get to self-actualization, but it is something that many strive for, especially in the field of management and, indeed, that of sports performance. There are many other theories of motivation; for example:

- McClelland (1985) who talks about achievement, affiliation and power
- Herzberg *et al.* (1993) talk of maintenance factors and motivational factors, their thinking being that people must be maintained in a relatively cosy environment in terms of safety, security and status, while they would be developed through achievement, recognition and advancement.

Such theories are merely a context into which to set identification of what individuals are striving for. If this can be achieved, then more effective organization will be produced. Managers must understand that individuals look for fair treatment and equal opportunities to advance; they must recognize that money is not necessarily a key motivator. It may be an incentive, but is not the crucial motivation that many people are driven by—self-esteem and recognition are as important as finance. It is important to recognize that individuals working in various sectors of the industry may be motivated in different ways; for example, the motivation of someone working in public sports provision may be different from someone working in a governing body or in a private snooker club.

What Makes a Manager?

A group of staff working in the Sports and leisure business were asked what they identify as important for their manager. The results are interesting, and produce a worthwhile checklist for managers to gauge themselves against. A random list of items identified by staff as what they would want to see in their manager includes a range of skills and personal qualities such as:

- Being organized
- Always getting results
- Patient
- Approachable
- Decisive
- Interested
- Enthusiastic
- Assertive
- Communicative
- Listens and acts
- Firm but fair
- Punctual
- Confident
- Good motivator.

While this list is not, and probably could never be, comprehensive in all Sports situations, it is a useful checklist and managers should consider whether they are able to match up to what staff are looking for. Characteristics that staff would not like to see in their manager included:

- Selfcentred
- Moody
- Gossiping
- Dictatorial
- Intimidating
- Not understanding
- Looks down on people
- Poor attention to detail
- Lack of feedback
- Shy and nervous
- Fixed views
- Fails to value staff

This is another interesting list for managers to try to make a honest assessment of themselves against. These lists are just indicative, but might well be something that managers would consider in a quiet moment—how do they really measure up to what practising staff identify as the positive and negative aspects of their job performance?

Staff Appraisal

Part of any good staff management and development programme is an individualized appraisal system, either with the line manager or 360° (with subordinates, colleagues and superiors). There should be an opportunity for staff reviews and appraisals on a regular basis through direct contact of each staff member—whether voluntary or paid—with their relevant superiors to review their input into the organization and its functioning. The review is a two-way process where staff are encouraged to comment on the functioning of the organization and even their immediate superior's performance, as well as reviewing their own personal performance within the organization.

Such an individualized appraisal process should be seen as supportive and beneficial, not threatening. If properly undertaken it should see people building on strengths and moving forward into the future, not being threatened over poor performance—such situations, should they arise, need to be dealt with through disciplinary procedures and should not be the basis for a staff appraisal interview. If properly handled, staff appraisal will produce staff who are clear about their duty and the perceived perception of their performance and are well motivated to undertake their role because they feel their opinion is valued. If it is handled badly it can have the opposite effect, which can be detrimental to an organization. It is vital that all staff who undertake appraisal interviews should be trained in how to approach the whole issue in a positive manner.

It is equally important that all staff understand that appraisal is a positive approach, and that this message is loudly and clearly communicated to everyone involved. There is also an issue of organizational appraisal—a measure of the effectiveness of the organization overall, as well as specific projects, but this is a distinctly different issue from that of individualized appraisal, which can also be used to form the basis of an individualized training needs analysis and progressive personal development.

Staff Motivation

People in Sports are very highly motivated—from performer through to the Chairman of the British Olympic Association. People are motivated by many different factors to take part in sports administration, and these can include status, recognition, personal achievement, personal interest and even, to a very limited extent, financial gain. It is possible, however, as in many other work situations, to demotivate people and not be aware that we are doing so. Certainly it is important to ensure that some careful guidelines are followed in order to keep people involved and interested so that they are not lost to Sports, particularly scarce volunteer staff. People are much more likely to remain involved if they have:

- A clear sense of the purpose of the organization
- A clear sense of their role in the body
- The ability to manage their own input
- A set of predetermined guidelines
- A degree of authority, power and responsibility
- The opportunity to be challenged and to measure themselves against high standards.

It is important that the organization shows that it favours shared responsibility and co-operative working, ensuring that the power is jointly held so that everyone feels involved in achieving success for the organization. This is established through getting everybody working as a team member and co-ordinating the efforts of all and focusing them on established and agreed objectives. In terms of personal skills, any leader who is making any effort to motivate people must be careful to:

- Be an active listener
- Thank and compliment
- Provide rewards where possible
- Look for positive achievement

It is important to take account of what people say and give thoughtful, considered answers rather than rash, rushed responses which can be demotivating. It is equally important to be aware of what individuals want in return for their input and to give them enough responsibility and authority to make the post challenging and interesting, with a feeling that they are doing a worthwhile job. It is now realized that in order to obtain better performance, workers need to be motivated by more than fear or economic reward. The concern for quality consciousness, together with a greater market orientation, may be seen as the dominant concern for the private sector management in Britain since the 1980s. But the problem of motivation and commitment which it addresses is not new. It has been clearly identified that people will be happier in their work, and their commitment and effort will be increased, if they:

- Obtain a sense of achievement from what they are doing
- Have some responsibility for what they are doing
- Are recognized for their efforts and abilities
- Have a feeling of personal and career development
- Face some type of challenge
- Perceive their work as interesting or worthwhile.

Equally, people can be put off their job role and find work frustrating, less enjoyable and their motivation diminished due to factors such as:

- Overly bureaucratic structure
- Difficult superiors
- Poor physical surroundings
- Low wages and salaries
- Uncooperative colleagues
- Perceived incompetence of superiors and/or colleagues
- Their views not being listened to
- Lack of direction
- Dictatorial management
- Lack of involvement in the decision-making process
- Not knowing what the organization's aims are

- Being excluded by personal cliques
- Being overwhelmed by work
- Not being respected as part of the business.

An important issue in considering management and motivation of sports organizations is the degree to which voluntarism plays a part, and volunteers' ability as individuals to express their own views and play their own part. They are not compelled to do anything, even within the management structure, but do it on a voluntary basis and have the ultimate control over whether they contribute. This is a key aspect of the voluntary participation of individuals and groups in sports administration. It is a significant difference between Sports and business organizations and must always be recognized. It is not necessarily a weakness, and tends to lead to high degrees of motivation of the individual within a sporting structure—there is no control or compulsion, but there is enthusiasm.

For the sports person the desire to excel—to achieve their personal best and attain the highest standards of performance—is what drives them forward. This aim for achievement and personal and societal recognition is no bad thing: as an example, it can be copied by a quality administrator in the sports field, driving with the same ambition to be the best they can be in their role of supporting this dedicated sports person. They do not have to be high-level sports people themselves, but their motivation should be to be the best administrator they can.

It is very beneficial for the administrator constantly to remember where they are coming from and what they are there to do—to provide sporting opportunity so that everyone who wishes to can perform to the best of their abilities. This common bond of purpose, motivation and standards with the performers and all the participants is the ideal partnership all round. For the sports performer it is quite likely that their Sports will be the number-one thing in their life, and for many administrators it is the same. This is perhaps why people who go into sports administration for the payment, rather than the environment, often flounder: because their commitment falls short of that of the performer. It is fairly obvious that the more committed athletes are the more successful; this is generally the case for the sports organizer as well.

Delegation

Delegation is often done badly or not at all, because human beings have a tendency to believe that they can do things better themselves and it is simpler to do them that way rather than involve other people. This really is short-term thinking, and although in the short term things may be done better, eventually the system will break down. This is a recipe not for success but for frustration, both personal and organizational.

Delegating tasks means that the individuals who are receiving the tasks to perform require specific training. There will initially be a need for additional planning to ensure that there is a report-back system as well as clear parameters as to what has to be delegated. In the first instance delegation will take longer and tasks must be monitored on a regular basis, but in the longer term delegation will enormously aid organizational efficiency. Basically, delegation requires a clear statement of what has been delegated and why, and how the supervisory or report-back relationship will continue.

It is also important to make more time available for key personnel by allowing others to take on tasks. This will help the others' personal development and sense of achievement: given some sort of responsibility, most people are much more highly motivated. Particularly in the voluntary sports situation, if you can get 1 per cent out of 100 people it is going to create a great deal more than trying to get 100% out of one person. Delegation encourages people to feel responsible and be part of the organization or team, and will enhance their job satisfaction and enthusiasm for the tasks they are required to perform. Sports has a strong history of enthusiasm, commitment and dedication, but this commitment can only be effective if a strong organizational structure is established and tasks are performed at the appropriate level. Teamwork will be important, but this is often a clear and happy relationship for sports people. The clear identification of working roles, tasks and structures to be used helps achieve effective and efficient organization. Governing bodies of Sports can lose effectiveness through unclear or dated organizational structures and poor delegation—an old belief 'that everything is done better by myself'.

Delegation, if it fails, very often does so because the delegator does not have faith in the individual they are giving the work to and gives them the wrong tasks for the wrong reasons. It is important to delegate tasks for the right reasons and to the right person. It must be clear that they have the right skills (or at least are going to be trained in the right skills) and are given the necessary knowledge and confidence to undertake the tasks set. A lack of clarity, direction and leadership leads to poor organization and in turn a lack of effective and efficient operation. If any of these problems are apparent then the Sports and its participants will be damaged. As in any other business, good planning and thought combined with appropriate monitoring and leadership will ensure maximum achievement.

Communication

Communication may be defined as 'The giving, receiving or exchanging of information so that the material communicated is clearly understood by everyone concerned'. As far as organizations and managers are concerned, communication must be clear, frequent and involve everyone necessary. If the organization is to function smoothly then there must be clear lines of communication, in various forms, and everyone must know what these lines of communication are. Today we have the most advanced communications technology ever seen, and this brings about possibilities and potential benefits to many situations, not least the management of Sports in all its forms. The massive growth of electronic communications, including the electronic mail system, fax machines, mobile phones and computer communication, still must be set alongside the traditional (and essential) verbal and non-verbal communication which takes place between human beings for progress to be achieved harmoniously. In addition, in a sporting situation where we are trying to get in touch with our clients and potential customers, written and visual communication can be important. If communication is to be effective then it must be:

- Clear
- Concise
- Courteous
- Correct
- Complete
- Correctly directed.

Any blockage in the lines of communication will cause unnecessary delays in getting things achieved and will significantly damage customer relations, which for everyone involved must be the number-one priority. It should be emphasized that within many sports management and administration settings communication may be quite a complex process; it will not go solely from A to B, but may go from A to B to C, directly back to A and shoot off to D, at something of a tangent. This is caused by the informal 'jungle telegraph' which exists in so many places within Sports. Many people know others well because of the variety of contexts, different subject meetings, playing abilities, past contacts and informal networks, all of which are major factors in the industry. Communication can be vertical, horizontal, diagonal or, as mentioned above, it might be quite complex—almost like a spider's web or jigsaw network. In many cases this can be a benefit as long as managers are aware of the potential problems and/or benefits that exist in such an informal system and which, at times, may seem to work behind their back.

Getting the Right People

In sports administration, as in all other aspects of industry, it is important to get the right people in the right post. All too often in the past in voluntary sports organizations, for example, the treasurer has been an automatic appointment because they have been a local accountant or the secretary has been the least unwilling of the assembled AGM members, and the committee has been elected by those who were too slow to take their hands down from a previous vote. This sort of *ad hoc* appointment needs to be discouraged if progress is to be made in the planning and development of Sports at club, local and national level.

The future must lie in recruiting, through appropriate processes, the best people available for such posts, then training, appraising and supporting them through the process—as would be the approach in any other dynamic, progressive work situation. Adopting such an approach means that a job remit needs to be drawn up for every post, which should be drafted into an advertisement which is then placed in appropriate outlets ranging from the club noticeboard to the national association mailing or even the press. Only by doing this will it be possible to attract and select appropriate people to apply for the vacant post.

There will need to be application forms, CVs, references, interviews and all the other procedures normal in industry if this process is to be followed through. It is unrealistic to believe that every single step will be adhered to every time, but certainly in the case of national governing bodies and large sporting bodies such procedures should be adopted as opposed to *ad hoc* elections at poorly attended, geographically remote annual general meetings. Poor methodology militates in favour of domination of Sports by small groups, often out of touch with mainstream progressive developments, or people not always motivated by the best interests of the Sports. While this rigid 'quasi-industrial' regime may seem a little harsh, it has to be used for real progress.

The more positive side of posts should also be advertised, e.g. high-ranking national governing body officials may benefit from several international trips and the possibility of being selected for management posts at major international games such as the Olympics, as well as being listened to by government ministers, sports councils, etc. For any post there are some positive opportunities—these should be stressed so that it is not always the least unwilling who are attracted, because everything is painted black. Sports administration, like all other sports links or involvement, can offer some very enjoyable and positive times. The emphasis must always be on the positive to help attract the best people, because many quality people are available. Performance appraisal and support once the post has been filled are essential, mechanisms should be set in place to support and encourage staff (whether voluntary or paid), and management lines of communication should be clear.

The establishment of an appraisal system which allows people to have their progress in the post assessed and commented on is essential and allows them to make comments on the organizational setting where a paid official is often employed and managed by spare-time volunteers. This appraisal system in normal industrial situations may be on a monthly or six-monthly basis, but in a sports situation it is desirable that it happens at least monthly so that individuals are not left to feel isolated or under pressure.

The purpose of appraisal is to improve job performance and look at individuals' potential, based on objective standards or targets previously set. It is important that both the person being appraised and the appraiser are prepared for the session, preferably with a written and previously circulated agenda. Any criticism should be analytical, not personal and be aimed at supporting, helping and improving individual (and organizational) performance.

Work appraisals should be measured against a detailed plan previously agreed between the two parties and should match performance against previously set objectives. The issue of salary should not be negotiated during appraisal sessions, nor should they be set up as potentially threatening for either party. The aim is to see the individual and the organization develop harmoniously because the development of both will be beneficial to both. An appraisal system should not be seen as separate from ongoing day-to-day support for employees, since that too is essential to ensure that both develop well. Such systems are vitally important in Sports, where gossip and allegations can become the basis for widespread misperceptions.

There is a massive informal network in Sports and it must not be allowed to pressurize individuals or the organization excessively or unfairly. Only by adopting appropriate, businesslike mechanisms will such gossip be squashed. All appointment mechanisms and staffing procedures should be open and fair (in line with equal opportunities) and be widely recognized as appropriate for the organization.

Team Building

> It is very helpful for leaders (and indeed all members of a working team) to understand how groups and individuals function, and to beware the group dynamics within any group and their organization. This does not need to be a theoretical understanding but rather an awareness of how other people and groups function, when people are brought together. Every individual on the team is focused on the objective, which involves co-operating with others while carrying out your own particular set of duties.
>
> —*Hammer (1997)*

It is important that groups have a common goal and can see how they all, as a group and as individuals, are working towards this end. There can be a conflict in Sports of individual and group interests and understanding, as well as a lack of understanding of the concepts of interdependence and group consciousness—everybody must be working towards the same goals, in the same way, if team spirit is to be obtained consistently. Individuals need to see their role within the group but also to have a leader to involve them in the group and towards the fulfilment of the group objectives. The role of leadership is the key in achieving a successful creative group. One member of the group will have to show considerable leadership skills to put together a group of sports-minded people—often strong-willed and self-opinionated people—to achieve a set of agreed objectives to the benefit of the Sports involved. It is beneficial to give some consideration to concepts such as group creativeness, team development, structure and organization if there is to be any growth in the development of the group towards its common purpose.

Individual members must be aware of their roles, functions and responsibilities, and these must be clearly defined and written down to avoid any confusion. Individuals must see their role clearly themselves, with their own personal duties as well as their duties to help make the group function and achieve the task. It is also very important that the group, and the leader, recognize the abilities and the potential as well as the natural personalities of the individuals involved.

An awareness of how groups operate will be of benefit in the sports situation, especially because much of the administrative action is taken by groups and teams. Group practice in terms of how it normally operates and sets its programme, how it decides to go forward and how individuals use the strength of the group and recognize achievements and performance within it, is very important and should not be underestimated.

The ways that individuals within a group respond to authority and inter-relate are very important. In order to get group cohesion and everyone working together it is important to consider how individuals react within groups and see their respective roles. Sporting bodies are often made up of committees and subcommittees and therefore an understanding of group processes is very important for efficient functioning of the organization overall. The action of smaller groups and possible conflict, between individuals or even between sub-groups, are factors that must be considered.

There are a host of important matters to consider when looking at group processes, but cohesiveness, individual perceptions, conformity, competition, co-ordination, atmosphere, and structure are among the key issues to be aware of. Perhaps the most crucial overarching concept in terms of group processes and even team building is that of communication.The necessity of letting everyone find their role, being aware of others and ensuring that everyone knows quite clearly what is going on in the whole group is vitally important. Communication, in all its forms, is the key issue and a great deal of attention should be paid to getting the form of communication right, as this will ease many of the problems that can exist in group, and indeed organizational, functioning. This is even more true in the context of a voluntary body, where communication can be complex since individuals see each other spasmodically, as opposed to a normal work situation where they may meet on a more regular basis.

The other problem with groups is people—the human being is a complex animal and in its own way very difficult to legislate for. It reacts and functions in a complex manner and can cause many problems for itself and others. If we can promote strong interpersonal relationships and encourage skills in dealing with others then there is little doubt that we will be better able to withstand organizational problems that may arise, and difficult people who may cause problems. The balance between people is the key to getting things right—if individuals can co-operate then they will have a more effective organization.

It cannot, however, be expected that individuals will automatically come together easily, because often there is a conflict between people and groups or sub-groups. The pulling of such people and groups closer together and the removing of cohesion difficulties is a crucial role for the competent leader and can bring major benefits. In addition, increasing the skills of individuals will help them greatly in ensuring that they can contribute to group and organizational success by being able to relate well to others with high-level interpersonal skills in areas such as communication, listening and motivation.

It is vital to make this effort to build teams rather than just assume they exist, to give people the skills which they can use to work together and to work at group process and cohesion in order to get this co-operative effort. The key issue in building any team is to get a unity of purpose where there is a total commitment by all concerned to achieve the task or organizational efficiency. Any lack of understanding about objectives or lack of clarity about the aims of the organization will cause problems for the organization. Pulling towards a common aim helps with team building, as long as it is an agreed aim, and everyone is quite clear what it is.

Managers and administrators are trying to produce quality organization and administration for the performer in Sports. The cohesion of the group can add significantly to this common aim and development can be aided because we all have the same goals at heart. Within Sports there is likely to be a common objective and desire—whether it be for a specific rugby club to be successful or for more people to take part in lacrosse, it is likely that a number of people gathered together in a committee or subcommittee will share that purpose. This is most helpful in getting some cohesion into our operation and getting a unified drive towards achieving the set target. We have already considered exactly what the leader has to do to achieve this, and their role is crucial in getting things going for all concerned.

They must lead the way and concentrate group thinking on building a successful team, but they cannot be expected to achieve everything on their own. Good leadership will be beneficial not just for the leaders themselves but for everyone involved, and will help to achieve the objectives. In terms of getting the team correct, the selection of team members is a crucial step. There have been suggestions that selection in a democratic process such as an annual general meeting does not necessarily lead to the correct people being chosen. This, however, is the traditional method for most sports bodies, especially those of a large membership, and the consequences can sometimes be that people who are 'willing rather than able' are chosen. This can mean that they may not necessarily work together, although in some voluntary situations individuals are chosen (or unofficially pre-selected) by the existing committee because they can see that it may be possible to work with them. In a commercial situation selection would normally be very much on the basis of how individuals would fit into the team, and if it is perceived that they would not be helpful in achieving a task then they will not be selected, through interview or other processes. Selecting team members may seem an easy task but, depending on the situation, a great number of skills may be required for the team member; there will be a necessity for some type of technical knowledge and other attributes which will be beneficial to the Sports and its performers.

Unquestionably, the key considerations for any selection should be the ability of individuals to work as team members, and their personal attributes and skills which will help build a team towards the successful accomplishment of the task in hand. It is vital that the team is able to react well to problems or crises, and handle them—it should be able to identify what is wrong and do something concrete about it fast. In addition, it will be necessary to maintain the team morale once it is established and keep everyone focused on the end purpose, working at maintaining standards through supporting each other in a variety of situations that the group faces.

The continual definition or re-evaluation of roles within teams will also be beneficial to successful functioning and will cause individuals to be happier about their duties and responsibilities. If they have a clearly defined role, individuals will feel happier and more secure. This role may change from time to time in response to what the group actually needs or all the performers need. It is very important that the roles should not be static, but rather be seen as an ongoing requirement, with the possibility of changing or fine tuning as required to help the team achieve the identified tasks. Remember, teamwork is about:

- Motivation
- Achievement
- Confidence
- Challenge
- Goals
- Trust
- Openness
- Relationships
- Effectiveness.

Team Development

Six stages of team development have been identified (Chaudhry-Lawton *et al.*, 1993):

- Getting together
- Getting on
- Getting going
- Getting things done
- Getting stuck
- Getting out.

These points are all fairly self-explanatory, but we must be continually looking to develop our team strength and have everyone working together and understanding this process. Everything may not go easily immediately, but everyone working together must go through necessary processes to get things achieved. Research has indicated that team members have identified a sizeable list of ideas and comments as to why the teams they were in worked. These include:

- 'we got on well together—and socialize together'
- 'the leader was very clear about what he wanted, but was never bossy'
- 'loyalty'
- 'clear about what I had to do'
- 'it was enjoyable'
- 'I felt I counted and was valued'
- 'I knew what was going on'
- 'it was something we wanted to do'.

Chaudhry-Lawton *et al.* (1993) have taken such points and divided them into four main thrusts—clarity, commitment, communication and celebration.

Clarity: In terms of clarity, sports organizations are often found lacking, but if we analyse successful operations then we will always see complete clarity of organizational and individual aims.

Commitment: In terms of commitment, Sports is very fortunate and probably second to none, since few on-field participants or behind-the-scenes administrators lack commitment and most have notable determination to achieve.

Communication: This is an area in which there can be significant problems, especially within voluntary organizations, but even in full-time staff relationships. Because of the nature of Sports many of the people involved will be heading off in different directions on a regular basis, so getting the message through to individuals and various organizational committees and structures can be very difficult. This is a major problem for sports organizations and methods must be constantly examined to see if practices can be improved and updated to ensure that as much information as possible is passed on to all team members to ensure their clarity of objectives and understanding of current issues and tasks.

Celebration: Celebration, or one could say recognition and reward, is often ignored for people operating behind the scenes in Sports. Recent years have seen enormous changes for the on-field performers; the rewards now can be enormous and set individuals up for life totally due to their physical abilities. For workers in Sports behind the scenes the opposite is true—very often they have to put their own personal effort, commitment and time in for no reward whatsoever; indeed, it may cost them money. This makes it more difficult to enthuse such people and guarantee their commitment. Every effort must be made in an organization to recognize the supreme efforts of the volunteers and to give them whatever little rewards may be available in terms of merit awards, service to Sports awards, international trips, etc. Looking at team development in this way will assist in efficient management practice supporting participants in an effective drive towards success.

PERSONNEL MANAGEMENT

The management, training and development of personnel is the key quality of the sports industry and perhaps what marks it out from many others. All aspects of human resource development should be applied in the sports business as they are in others in terms of training people to bring out the best in them and to understand procedures and practices. In addition, all processes of personnel management in terms of consideration for staff, legal obligations to staff, health and safety, and employment regulations must always be adhered to and clearly understood. It is essential to ensure a happy staff in order to make it an effective staff.

The key difference in terms of personnel in the sports industry as opposed to others is commitment. The commitment will be driven by a host of agencies and will come from a variety of sources, but it will exist to a level not seen in the vast majority of other work situations (although it is also seen in some other employees who work for relatively small financial remuneration, sometimes not in great conditions, merely because of their considerable love of the activity). This commitment has a number of real benefits, but equally has a number of difficulties and dangers. Extreme commitment should be built on, while its tendency towards fanaticism or blinkered thinking should be discouraged as much as possible. Staff training will help here, as will appraisal and counselling. The management of people is basically what sports management and administration is all about. The human factor is a common thread to all aspects and situations—it is the essential ingredient to quality provision and operation.

In every situation the manager, or leader, will need to recognize the role of the people in the organization and encourage and support their positive input at all times. Concepts such as customer care come from quality staff operation at the delivery level every bit as much as, if not more than, they come from the thinking and action of the person at the top of the organization. The quality manager will recognize the role of individuals and groups of staff within any organization and will capitalize on their abilities, working with them to try to improve the provision given to all client groups. The manager in the human resource dimension will have many roles to fill, including those of:

- Leader
- Motivator

- Disciplinarian
- Role model
- Team builder
- Trainer
- Organizer.

Each of these roles has its own implications and means that managers must be multi-skilled and need to be trained, supported and encouraged by their superiors (even if these are a committee) if they are to perform their personnel functions well. Admiral Nelson is often quoted as saying: 'a happy ship is an efficient ship and an efficient ship is a happy one'. This is particularly appropriate in the sports industry, which is a service-based community provider that survives on delivery experiences in the physical activity arena for people. It relies on interpersonal relationships, personal commitment, enjoyment and participation. If the sports organization facility is not organized on the basis of Sports for participation and the enthusiasm of staff to provide for this, then it will fall short of the target for quality provision. The involvement of everyone in a co-ordinated dynamic effort to cater for customers is what the provision is all about, whether it be for a governing body or for a local sports centre.

The role of any individual charged with personnel support and development is to work with people to produce what the customer actually wants, while paying attention to the demands of staff in terms of motivation and satisfaction within their job. Often in the sports situation the demands of the customer can be extreme through their commitment to the Sports, and this can put unrealistic pressures on staff to respond seven days a week, 24 hours a day, because there will always be people wanting to take part in Sports at any time of the day and they will to some extent expect staff, especially paid ones, to be present at that time. A good manager will recognize the conflicting demands of the voluntary participant and the paid staff, or even the committed volunteer, who will sometimes want to turn off from the Sports and just go home—a view not often understood by the fanatical participant.

Such a relationship can lead to extreme stress on individuals, whether voluntary or paid, and be a disincentive to increasing their commitment and performance. The answer is to follow proper personnel procedures in all instances and ensure that from recruitment onwards appropriate 'industrial' procedures are followed. In particular in terms of staff, it is essential that an appraisal system is maintained so that there is an ongoing two-way review of job performance—this can often be useful in the voluntary sector. In order to retain staff we have to look at all the ways they are treated by all the agencies with whom they have contact, and what sort of reward and remuneration package they are given in return for the inevitable hassle they will face.

Well-thought-through personnel policies are essential for any sports organization as they are for any other successful business; they are perhaps just a bit more necessary because of the inevitable dynamic of conflict that can exist between customer and staff (voluntary or paid). A strong policy in this area will pay dividends in terms of the returns obtained from staff performance as well as staff retention.

CHAPTER 8

Strategic Management of the Organization

THE ROLE OF THE SPORTS MANAGER

The sports manager's role can vary enormously depending upon the setting, but the specific task of the manager will be to take general management functions and perform them in a sports setting. All management functions can apply in different situations at different times—the really skilful manager will know when each applies and will use that process appropriately. It is essential for sports managers to realize that they are managing in a sports situation, and that they should be applying the correct business principles and practices as appropriate and relevant to that situation, as colleagues will be doing in other industrial situations. There has been some delay in service industries generally in recognizing that they have to apply management principles, as do product-based industries. There has been a further gap in Sports realizing that it is actually a service industry, but now it is hoped these thought processes and then good practices will begin to be applied.

Skills of a Sports Manager

Sports managers will require a background knowledge in the process of management, but they will more particularly require a knowledge of Sports and the people involved in it. To be genuinely effective they will have to a have a feeling for the business of Sports, as well as management skills. In essence, sports management is all about managing:

- The workplace
- The people
- Day-to-day operations
- The facility
- The activity
- The development process
- Partnership working.

Sports management may be seen as a limited or short-term career for most professionals. While realistic careers and salaries are few and far between in the UK at present, in North America it is quite possible to see sports management as a significant career. If, as in other areas, this American pattern is followed in the UK then there is no doubt that sports management will become a genuine career opportunity in the UK very soon. Indeed, some would argue that this trend has already started.

General Management Approaches

It has been recognized in a number of settings that there are five general approaches to management.

1. The classical approach deals with the content, suggesting that there is core knowledge that each manager should possess. This includes the functions of planning, organizing and controlling.
2. The behavioural approach considers the role of the individual within the management process and identifies that each individual has needs, wants and desires. It considers that individuals are different and need to be appropriately treated.

3. Management science sets out to use mathematical approaches in management to get better efficiency; it relates to operational problems and methods of solving these.
4. The systems approach is based on designing a precise system of management made up of a variety of parts which must be brought together to function as a whole to meet the organization's objectives.
5. The contingency approach works on the assumption that there is no single best way to manage. The manager must be able to manage in different situations and recognize that organizations can vary in the best way.

There are always a variety of theories and ideas when managing in any given situation, and they should be applied at the appropriate time and in the appropriate manner.

QUALITY MANAGEMENT

Total Quality Management is a concept originating in Japan which has been extensively used by businesses throughout the Western world, particularly the USA and the UK. It is designed to produce increased performance through more efficient operation. There have been many definitions of the concept. In 1989 the British Quality Association stated that, Total Quality Management (TQM) is a corporate business management philosophy which recognizes customer needs and business goals as inseparable. It is applicable within industry and commerce. This generalist definition will suffice for purposes of Sports, management and administration, and allow a degree of interpretation by individuals in their own specific setting.

The concept of Total Quality Management has been enshrined in the management standards BS5750, ISO9000 and ISO9001. Many companies have striven to achieve these standards in a wide variety of industrial situations, and the general consensus has been that those who have made the effort to go through this process have found it to be worthwhile whether or not a certificate was achieved at the end.

In essence, the search for certification focuses the mind on company operational practices, and this in itself is beneficial. Quality management systems, however, should always be focused on the customer and the key issue is the satisfaction of customer needs in an efficient and consistently effective manner. In the search for quality management the manager should be looking for excellence in planning, control and implementation, focused on delivering at the end of the process what the customer wants.

To ensure quality planning a number of steps can be outlined:

- Determining who the customers are in general and specific terms
- Determining the needs of each sub-group of customers, in general and very specific terms
- Developing services and schemes which meet the identified needs
- Developing efficient processes to deliver these services on an ongoing and consistent basis
- Ensuring that all provision is delivered in an attractive and community-relevant way
- Ensuring that all relevant practicalities, such as health and safety, and other organizational policies are adhered to throughout the process.

Beyond the planning it is essential to carry such quality intent into high-quality delivery of service. This is fundamentally about taking the aims set down during quality planning to a set of specific measurable objectives and carrying this right through into practice. Operational procedures must always be set against these aims and objectives, and constantly monitored to judge their effectiveness and efficiency. A good manager will identify weaknesses quickly and take action to ensure immediate improvement in the service being delivered. Several times in this text, the issue of competition has been considered and it has been pointed out that it is a growing challenge to sports managers and administrators in a variety of situations. If any sports manager is to remain competitive then they must look to delivering the services required by properly identified customers in a quality manner. Quality, like beauty, is in the eye of the beholder, and only by monitoring the progress in terms of returns (both cash and attendance), as well as financial efficiency and sporting success (in terms of participation or excellence) of the organization, will the manager be able to see if true quality is being delivered.

Successful organizations can only achieve quality programmes and consistently improve on them if there is careful attention to detail and planning, and practice. This must involve all the staff, and particularly middle management, targeting certain areas of action for quick results and having an effective communication system throughout the organization to ensure that everybody is involved in the process. Sports organizations are often accused of having poor internal communication, and in an audit for quality achievement it will be identified that poor communication makes the achievement of policy absolutely impossible. For many, introducing appropriate internal and external communication is the first step on the ladder to achieving quality operation.

Organizations, in Sports as elsewhere, accepting Total Quality Management have as an important ingredient to their proper operation the identification of a number of key issues in this procedure:

- The establishment of clear aims and objectives
- Involvement and agreement of all the relevant people with these aims and objectives to ensure unity of organizational purpose
- Clearly established policies and, indeed, charters for customers and staff
- Identification of critical points in the achievement of successful oper-ations—both general and specific
- Aiming to become an organization which in its very culture believes in quality
- Clear identification of the supremacy of clients or customers in the drive for quality

- Clear identification of the role of individual members of staff or specific groups within the quality process.

The overall aims of installing quality management systems or practices are:

- An increase in customer satisfaction
- A reduction in costs
- An increase in market presence
- A reduction in accidents and staff absence
- Increased efficiency, productivity and profit
- Improved service delivery at all levels of the organization
- Increased participation and/or success at all levels
- Long-term stability and successful operation of the sporting organization.

In practical implementation terms the formation of a quality circle—internal or external—can be extremely useful in aiding the implementation of quality management systems. Such circles are made up of key staff within an organization or series of organizations who are working towards the implementation of quality procedures. Such groups give a real focus to the work to be undertaken and become a forum for ideas from inside and outside the organization to aid the process.

The key function such groups can fulfil is staff involvement, because without all of the individuals within the organization being involved, true quality will never be achieved. It must be felt to be a staff (paid or voluntary) initiative and potential benefit. Without a real commitment on the part of all the staff and a unity of purpose in the organization towards achieving quality, the whole venture is doomed to failure. For the sports organization, facility or service, the key is to devise a working action plan towards achieving the desired quality policy processes and practices. The desire to pass on the commitment of sports involvement and participation is not hard to find in such staff, but the realization that a lot of hard work and action are required makes this goal harder to achieve. Sports participants and sports staff like to see action rather than talk, and a working action plan can produce this.

This action plan should be enacted by all the staff and implemented on a controlled and ongoing basis with constant monitoring as appropriate. As mentioned above, a sound communication system in individual and organizational terms will be necessary to inform everyone what is going on at present, what is going to happen and what the results of all their efforts are. This process should be characterized by seven 'p's:

- Positive commitment
- Planning
- Participation
- Process control
- Problem identification
- Problem elimination
- Performance.

If these 'p's are put into practice, you will have a practical working performance quality management system which will be beneficial to customers, to staff and to the whole sports organization. Everybody will feel happier, more content and better pleased with their efforts and their treatment. Total Quality Management will be achieved with the managers, then all of the staff can give a total positive commitment, do the planning, operate the process, and be open to change and amendment throughout. Of necessity, this process can involve a lot of paperwork and logging of procedures that have to be followed and may be seen as a little tedious, but if everyone is clear as to what the end is, then they will become sufficiently committed to attend to the details required. This exercise can sometimes be slow and a little painful, but it will ultimately produce a result for everyone and will be of benefit to the organization or facility.

Fundamentally, it is essential, especially in the lower-key voluntary organization, that the concept of Total Quality Management be examined and some time spent examining potential benefits. The process can be time-consuming, but in practice efficient processes will be extremely helpful to the organization and its customers. Most of those who have been involved in the past have found it very demanding but in the end a useful tool for efficient organization and function. This will be as true in sports organizations as it is in many other industries. The exercise of examining management procedures and practices in itself is very worthwhile—self-examination is always useful and should be a constant process in any case. The examination of working procedures and practices should also be an ongoing process, not just a periodic review. The key aim is to ensure consistent and constant good management practice which must be the target for sports administrators and managers as it is for key staff in other organizations.

Providing quality in leisure services is about meeting customer needs, putting the customer first and delivering the service the customer wants. The exceeding of customer expectations is true quality customer service. The Sports Council (1984) considered four key areas of customer orientation:

- Finding out what the customer wants through effective communication
- Quality standards—specifying exactly what the customer might expect
- Quality of staffing systems—well trained and motivated staff providing a service through a good management system
- Quality process service provided through clear procedures clearly understood by all concerned.

This specifies very clear and simple models for those working in the field of Sports and recreation, and again emphasizes the importance of putting the customer first, clear communication between customers and staff, and clear procedures enabling quality processes to be carried out. In the field of quality there is much talk of customer charters (following on the Government's Citizen's Charter), but there are dangers that these can be seen as 'in vogue' at present and token gestures not really put into beneficial practice. It is essential that steps taken should be towards quality customer service, not merely a gesture in that direction. Quality management has a number of fundamental principles.

- There needs to a clear definition of quality agreed and understood by everyone in the organization.
- There needs to be a clear organizational structure which allows for the management and delivery of quality standards.
- The aim of quality organization and management is to remove all errors from the organization's performance.
- There needs to be some measurement of quality, including the comparative cost of not producing quality.
- There needs to be a total understanding that the concept is ultimately about competitive edge and quality delivery to customers.
- Managers must understand that significant staff training and involvement will be essential to ensure that there is effective understanding and delivery of quality principles and systems.

Additionally, quality has to do with a lot of principles and issues for everyone involved in the organization, and it requires individual and organizational commitment to ensure that the customer ultimately benefits. It is wrong to believe that quality can only come through the stamp of quality such as ISO9000 or following an Investors in People programme—these are structured methods but the certification or the public recognition should be secondary to the need for the organization to run effectively for the benefit of its customers. How this is actually achieved is a matter for everyone involved to have a view on and hopefully ultimately agree. In Sports and recreation, for example, a number of organizations have chosen to follow rigorously the vocational occupational standards route (collecting further employee vocational qualifications on the way) as a way to ensure that everything done by the individuals and the organization is done on a basis of competence in the workplace—this system, if totally understood and enjoying staff commitment, is another way to ensure quality for customers. Whatever the implementation method for producing quality, a number of significant items have to be considered. Some of the following concepts will have to be addressed before the programme is implemented or becomes effective:

- Commitment
- Cost-effectiveness
- Systems and structures
- Training
- Objective setting
- Performance indicators
- Overseeing
- Groups
- Quality circles
- Error elimination
- Recording mechanisms
- External advice.

Quality systems are sometimes perceived as being only about statistics, performance indicators and measurement mechanisms. This is very wrong, because while these measures are important, Sports and recreation is a people business about experiences, and sometimes a quality experience is required as much as an appropriate performance indicator. In essence, however, quality in many sports situations can be measured through the return of participants or other customer groups—a lack of quality in a Sports and recreation situation will certainly see the customers voting with their feet and not returning.

Sports and leisure facilities rely a great deal on return business, and steps must be taken to ensure that quality is always provided for customers so that they will return. Customers must be left in no doubt what is available to them, what is provided for them and who can help them through any participation programme they wish. Information will be a key aspect to quality in the Sports and recreation field, staff should be well informed, and customer care must be a key part of the business.

To know whether it is effective, any sports organization must have some type of performance indicators, as must individual administrators within the business. This does not mean setting unrealistic or overly demanding targets which simply cannot be reached or which are set by external agencies that lack specific knowledge. Nevertheless, if efficiency and effectiveness are to be fully emphasized and put into operation genuinely, then some type of quality check will be required. Quality should always be seen as something which pervades the whole organization and relates to everything involved in it—not only systems and procedures but also staff training and effective resourcing. The cost of quality should be seen as a positive rather than a negative influence, in that not having quality operation is going to cost more than adhering to quality, despite the fact that it takes time to establish the appropriate systems and organizational ethos in the early days.

Ultimately, everyone involved, no matter their place in the organization, must have the customer in focus and see that their role of satisfying customer needs, wants and desires in an efficient and effective manner is going to be crucial to delivering quality. Whether a member of staff is answering the telephone or putting across some complex customer information system, it doesn't really matter; the principle is the same—quality of effort and delivery will be vital to success.

It is somewhat ironic that Sports, which in many cases is measured by figures and times (statistics), is not always managed in the same way. Perhaps more measurable sets of targets in term of administration, as well as performance on the track or playing field, would assist in producing improved administration and management. Sports administrators should use the many statistics they assemble on a regular basis to help give some indications of performance. It is common for statistics on membership, participation levels, new members, international performance records, championship records, etc. to be recorded in Sports, and they can be the basis of some form of measurement of organizational achievement in administrative as well as technical terms. This would mean that performance indicators as judges of quality would not form an onerous task but would in fact be part of standard operational practice.

Other issues such as staff training or staff performance appraisal are worthwhile in themselves and should be implemented by an efficient modern organization for effective and efficient operation; they will improve the quality of the organization's functioning. It is crucial that staff appraisal, training and evaluation should be ongoing and not occasional or spasmodic. A fundamental principle of quality management is that there is consistency to the practice and it is not limited by time or commitment. Other initiatives, such as Investors in People (an initiative by the Department of Education and Employment), stress the input of personnel to quality organization and make great play of the motivation and training of staff to get them to achieve business goals. Adopting such a system can also be the impetus (or part of it) towards quality.

Practical Quality Considerations

Based on a now superseded standard, BS5750, some of the issues in practical terms that a sports manager/administrator would have to consider in order to go down the traditional quality management route and develop quality standards to the point of certification would be:

- The scope and field of application
- Quality system requirements
- Management responsibilities
- Quality systems
- Contract review
- Document control
- Purchasing
- Purchaser supplied product
- Product identification and traceability
- Process control
- Inspecting and testing
- Inspection, measuring and test equipment

- Inspection, test and status
- Control of non-conforming product
- Corrective action
- Handling, storage, packaging and delivery
- Quality records
- Internal quality audits
- Training
- Statistical techniques.

All of these may not seem appropriate initially, but when it is considered that the words may change slightly and the focus may move to services rather than products in the traditional sense, one begins to get the feel of the items to be covered in a formalized quality appraisal against national standards. The system might not always be appropriate, even in its new and revised editions, but the benefits of considering the headings are sizeable and can be translated well into the sports organization operation.

Strategic Management

Even the best plan degenerates into work. —*Anon*

In any sporting situation, public, private or voluntary, there is a need to establish a strategy for ongoing management and future development of the organization and the individuals within it. Sadly, the lack of strategic direction is often the downfall of the organization and, while mission statements and visions may be seen as fancy management jargon, they are beneficial to the function of a successful organization. If we do not know where we are going, how are we going to get there, and how will we know if we have got there? This is essential in facing up to change, which seems constant in the sporting situation. It is also essential if good customer service is going to be achieved, income targets met and facilities or services provided in an efficient and effective manner.

The strategy process any strategy development will look at:

- Establishing clear organizational aims and objectives
- Developing policies and communicating these to relevant parties

- Preparing appropriate documentation
- Establishing a system for a regular review of implementation of these plans.

Establishing a strategy should be a shared undertaking by all the staff members, voluntary or paid, and should be used as a tool to improve teamwork towards these jointly agreed objectives—ideally all employees should be involved in developing these objectives. A strategy which is not based on shared ownership involving all the participants will be much less effective—the imposition of such a strategy is certainly not the best way for successful organizational operation.

While there is a need for an overall plan, focusing on strategy and policy development, planning should be a concept which is taken into the practical situation and not just perceived as a theory. One of these applications is that of business planning, in particular preparing a business plan for relevant new initiatives, facility development, seeking finance or diversifying into new areas of operation.The key areas of any business plan are the aims and objectives, the methodology of achievement and the obtaining of resources, and the overall time-scale for the project. It is essential that sports managers, as with other industrial sectors, take business planning seriously for new initiatives and do not embark on new projects or schemes without having clear business plans laid out which can later be used as a measure of success or failure, as well as an ongoing performance guide and check.

A key issue in relation to business planning is to be sure that finance can be found to make the proposition viable, whether this is from income, sponsorship or local authority subsidy. Any business plan should bring forward detailed evidence that monies can be found in the short, medium and long terms to make the project viable and worthwhile from the commercial point of view—everyone can have great ideas, but only the proper planning will put them into practice effectively. If, when considering a business plan, things don't come together then in essence we should look for a new and different project. To quote from the Sports Council (1995-5): 'the development of a business plan is an invaluable discipline for managers and once developed and agreed, it becomes the implementation framework for the development operation of the project'. Such sound professional thinking should underpin all other operations within the Sports and recreation field. Only by such good practice will progress be made and easily monitored and measured.

Strategic Planning

The Sports Council (1994-5) goes on to say that a Sports and recreation strategy enables a local authority to:

- Ask itself some fundamental questions, i.e. undertake a service review
- Identify future needs and demands
- Assess performance.

In addition, the development Sports and recreation strategy will:

- Enable authorities to review policies and redefine them as necessary
- Modify and set clear objectives
- Identify distinct roles for each area of the service
- Form the basis of the facility management specification
- Indicate how provision in the authority can be integrated and co-ordinated
- Identify who can best provide the different aspects of the service—voluntary, private or public sector
- Give authorities regular appraisals and updates on current Sports and recreation provision
- Provide local authorities with a clear rational strategy for provision of a recreation service to the community (Sports Council 1994-5).

Sports development will be an integral part of this strategy but it will follow rather than lead. Strategic planning, facility planning and departmental organization will be key factors in ensuring that this Sports and recreation strategy can be implemented and if practical this will enable effective sports development as well as improved facility management. Strategic planning can be a difficult exercise for any organization, especially when it faces somewhat unpredictable change from external factors, as well as internal personalities and, in sporting situations, concepts such as volunteerism. This has a major effect on the planning process and implementation of operational business plans.

It is interesting to note that Peter Woods (of Direct Line Insurance fame) does not have a long-term business plan, but rather a rolling business plan which is reviewed annually and altered in light of changes and developments arising from the past twelve months and the likely future over the next twelve months—the longest term that he believes is likely to be predictable. His feeling is that a 'set in tablets of stone' business plan for three or five years, which does not respond to changes during that period, and is not reviewed annually, is more of a millstone than an effective business tool for a dynamic organization.

Mission Statements

Organizations benefit from having a mission statement which is clear and distinguishes their operation from others in the sector. The statement should change periodically to reflect change in the organization and the society in which it operates. A great deal of cynicism exists about business statements, but this should not be taken too seriously since in essence it is a good idea for everyone to know what the organization as a whole is up to. The mission statement for any organization can be set at a variety of levels and in fact it is very often better for the shopfloor worker to produce it than the managing director. It is certainly essential that the staff agree and understand it and that everyone pull towards this vision.

Depending on exactly what sector of the sports business you are operating in, the mission statement may well vary considerably, e.g. is your motivation for public service, private profit or voluntary satisfaction? A possible mission statement could be to:

- 'Establish hockey as the number-one family team game in Scotland'
- 'Provide sporting entertainment for potential business clients at a realistic price'
- 'Encourage the involvement of parents in supporting their young person's sport'.

Every organization needs to know what, in overall general terms, it is trying to do, and a mission is designed to specify this quite clearly so that everyone knows it and agrees it.

Organization

Organization is about establishing and maintaining practices and processes to maximize the performance of your sporting body by clearly identifying what each person within it has to do and ensuring that there is joint working—effective teamwork—as well as clearly defined roles within the prescribed structure. An appropriate organizational style will help clarify responsibilities and ensure clear lines of communication between individuals and sections within that organization. Such organization, in sports situations as with a number of other bodies, needs to be spelt out with power and authority within structures being definitively specified. The recognition of the potential need for change should exist in any vibrant organization, and this change should be pursued at any point where the structure is felt to be inappropriate, or where internal and external relationships are not clear.

Fundamentally, good organizational structure is about a clear chain of command and identification of specific responsibilities—such structures make organizations very much more effective than agencies in which everybody wanders about wondering what exactly their specific roles and tasks are. Clarity of roles and responsibilities makes it easier to delegate specific tasks. This should be done along with the delegation of the relevant power, authority and finance to allow the tasks to be undertaken in an appropriate manner—as we have seen, delegation is arguably the most important role of any good manager. This does not mean that the manager delegating tasks does not hold the ultimate responsibility; it means, rather, that the superior can spend time on work which may be even more vital to the organization. No effective top-level manager will be involved in dealing with trivia, or indeed any item which other members of staff have the time and ability (present or potential) to deal with.

Business Planning for Sports Bodies

Business planning is essential for sports bodies, as for any other organization wishing to achieve progress. The process involves examining, clarifying and documenting the current and future operation of the sports body. It doesn't need to be a lengthy or complex exercise—its extent depends on the size and nature of the organization. The process will need to be co-ordinated by an individual or small groups; through this they must consult widely before finalizing any report to ensure that it is truly reflective of the association's view. The compilers will need to drive it forward very hard to avoid any unnecessary delays.

Measuring Performance

Regardless of the type of operation that we are running, or the nature of the structures we have put in place to achieve our objectives, it is going to be important to measure how much we actually achieve. 'Performance indicators' is a term which has fallen into disrepute and causes some immediate antagonism because of a historical perspective related to the compulsion involved in competitive tendering in the sports business for local authorities. The principle, however, of having some clear indication of achievement and measures against which this achievement can be gauged is very sensible—it is certainly essential for an effective business, and it really is the measure of the efficiency of the business.

The problem with performance indicators is who dictates them and what is their nature. If sports administrators decide on and select their own performance indicators, then that seems to be quite acceptable and they can set them down realistically for six-month, twelve-month, 18-month or 36-month periods, or whatever seems appropriate, and they can judge performance against a set of clearly established guidelines.

The first measure of success is always against the objectives of the specific organization or project, bearing in mind that they will have had SMART (specific, measurable, agreed, realistic and timed) objectives set against them. Each of the quantities set down in the objectives will be measurable, e.g. an increase in membership of the organization by 10 per cent. Going beyond this it can be more difficult to measure achievement, but it is none the less important and failure to do so will certainly have an adverse effect on the performance of the administrator and staff involved.

It is always important to remember the principle that no measurement equals no management. Or, expressed another way: if you can't measure it, don't do it. While such statements may be extreme, they are accurate and reflect the need for competent managers and administrators to measure their individual and organizational performance. Quality, for example, can be measured through questionnaires on both efficiency and service quality—testing the economic use of resources and whether it is consistent provision in line with customer expectations.

The Complexity of Sports Management

The settings for sports management and administration are many and varied. They occur across a variety of sectors of the industry and are sometimes enacted in the most unlikely situations. In the private sector there is a vast range of areas where Sports and recreation are managed, e.g. health clubs, tourism attractions, corporate fitness situations, professional sports, as well as the related sporting goods manufacturing situations, the sports marketing and PR sectors, sports event management and sports management agencies.

The public sector has many of its own settings at local authority and national level. These range from local sports councils to major international sports complexes and can include dual-use school facilities and local village halls. The voluntary sector is enormous throughout the UK (1.5 million people in 1996) and its settings range from national and international governing bodies right down to local sports councils and clubs, in some cases very small clubs. The management role in the voluntary sector is often of the organization, but these organizations can sometimes run their own facilities on a small, or even fairly large, scale.

The range of facilities, which cuts across all the sectors, is enormous—they range from motor-car racing facilities to horse-racing tracks, from athletics tracks to swimming pools, from mountain faces to indoor climbing walls, from village greens to Lords, from croquet lawns to golf courses; the list is endless. In every setting, from international sporting arena to village bowling green, these facilities require a degree of expertise to be run efficiently and effectively. The functioning of all of them will benefit from a professional attitude to their management, even if the person doing the management is not a paid professional.

Planning

Any good manager in any situation will have to plan—Sports is no exception. There is a need to prepare for the future and to make the organization as efficient and conflict-free as possible. Good planning will effectively achieve both these aims and prepare the organization for change—a state which almost constantly faces everyone involved in Sports. Planning is the aspect of managing which establishes aims, targets, goals and objectives, and identifies the methods by which these targets can be achieved. Plans should be detailed and comprehensive, but should always be responsive and designed in adapted stages to cover both short-term and long-term operation. Planning should be based on detailed research and be specific and realistic to the organization being managed. While it is very easy to have business plans and to set the latest generic business standards, one of the key aspects of sports management is to remember that Sports, while it should be organized in a professional and businesslike manner, has this extra quality and element of commitment, desire, enjoyment and voluntary input which can never totally relate to purely business operation.

Objectives

In order to plan properly and to manage at various stages, a set of clear organizational objectives is vital, and a set of smaller objectives (or targets) for each individual and sub-group involved would be helpful to organizational process. Wherever objectives are used they need to be SMART: specific, measurable, agreed, realistic and timed. A number of other terms could be applied to objectives in a sports management situation, such as understood, clear, simple, financially accurate, manageable and unambiguous; all of them must be set into an achievement timetable identifying critical points along the way.

Time spent on devising these objectives and careful planning related to them is time well spent; it is time which will be repaid later because it will help eliminate wasteful and misdirected effort. Good planning in a sports situation should produce a strategic plan for the overall organization, as well as specific plans for any separate parts of the organization, and the necessary administrative procedures should be clearly laid down for the achievement of previously set, and agreed, objectives.

Control

Any effective organization must have controls of some sort which will ensure that what is desired is what is delivered. The structures must be in place to ensure that the objectives are achievable, and the mechanisms in place to ensure that achievement can be undertaken, but there will have to be a degree of monitoring and control to ensure on an ongoing basis that implementation is going as planned. Control may be looked upon in three aspects: recent past performance, current performance, and feedback from previous experience. Controlled techniques can help monitor capital, resource, personnel selection, procedures and practices as well as the budgeting process. For some organizations employee selection could be seen as the most important primary control technique. Care taken in designing accurate job descriptions and using appropriate advertising outlets, as well as efficient and effective interview techniques, will help put the right people in the right posts—a vital control step for any organization driving for efficiency and effectiveness.

Additionally, reporting systems for staff involved through incident reports and other routine procedures can help monitor employees on a daily basis, and again such practical control techniques are part of any sound agency operation. Obviously, the checking of financial data and its careful analysis, coupled with any other information returns, will help in controlling the organization's operation. Too often, figures are received and not checked on a regular basis to assess performance against objectives. For sports organizations, participation, attendance and income figures can be extremely important and are gauges, at the very least, of trends in organizational performance.

Quality procedures, appraisal of employees and management audits are other tools which can help ensure organizational effectiveness on a prolonged basis. Many other initiatives are examined and implemented but they tend to be spasmodic and not necessarily helpful or enduring. Employee appraisals are essential and can be extremely effective in controlling performance of individuals and organizations if the individuals involved are well briefed, and properly trained in how to make appraisals objective and ensure that appraisals are a genuine two-way process.

Practical finance control is essential for any organization, and monitoring of income and expenditure on a daily, weekly and monthly basis is essential to ensure cost-effective operation as well as to avoid any such major difficulties as liquidation problems and cash flow difficulties. This financial control starts at the very early stages of any organizational review or establishment in the setting up of accurate and appropriate budgeting techniques, with built-in monthly reviews of financial performance.

Organizational Change

In terms of change, structure always remains an important element but the values held by key people within organizations have a distinct effect on how organizations change. Change involves much more than just introducing or suggesting changes; it means that old beliefs and values have to be broken down and that new directions have to be charted. Individuals in sports organizations can have a major input to this, both positively and negatively. The structures have to be in place which allow this change to take place, but individuals, personalities and attitudes are just as fundamentally important in achieving any real change.

Management of Change

'The only thing that is constant is change.' This is an oft-quoted maxim, and it is true that things seem to change constantly throughout industry and, indeed, life in general. It is no less true in the sports business. In a new millennium people live in a turbulent world, and with the changes in technology; demography; the single European market; the disappearance of the Eastern Bloc; Best Value; political change and a vast array of other developments, there seems to be constant change facing the sports manager. There is no single answer to all these challenges, but if we are to be competitive and face up to potential threats then we must look to management procedures and practices—we must consider quality management and look for a Total Quality Management approach.

The recent past has seen enormous change in management circumstances and style, in both the public and private sectors. Some authors suggest that the 1970s was the last decade of the traditional order in management terms in the western world. Sports organizations in the private, public and voluntary sectors have to operate in a totally different situation to that which faced them previously. The political changes have been enormous and have resulted in Sports having to face the pressure of justifying itself in the face of spending cuts, rather than survive on the traditional ethos that Sports is worthwhile for its own sake. The advent of compulsory competitive tendering for the management of the vast majority of public sports facilities put different pressures on sports managers, and caused local authorities to look at the financial, rather than the service, priority in many situations. This was not always of benefit to Sports, and caused significant problems for the participants and organizers of Sports at a wide variety of levels, in relation to rising costs and reduced availability.

This has now been replaced by the Best Value policy—making it legally binding on local authorities to ensure they are delivering the most cost-effective provision on services. This presents new challenges and competitive and financial pressures on the sports managers involved. The changing structures of local authorities themselves, and fundamentally different philosophies, have caused problems for everyone in management in the local area. The various changes to management practices and structures have also caused significant challenge.

The sports manager must be able to foresee change developing in order to react appropriately, efficiently and effectively. Most changes, large or small, throw up opportunities as well as threats. It can be argued that the successful manager is the one who ignores or avoids the potential threats and seizes the opportunities unreservedly. This tends to be true in the wider commercial scene, but applies in Sports as well.The implementation of vocational qualifications is a good example of how sporting bodies could have seized the opportunity to push the standard of training of their staff and volunteers to a higher level, but many still ignore the opportunity and tend to regard such developments as threatening and too complex for them to undertake. It is often suggested in sports situations that 'we are very bad at marketing ourselves'. This can be seen as a result of the same intransigence—being set in our ways and failing to identify the potential opportunities and align Sports with them.

The marketing concept is not one which fits in easily to many sports situations as there is often no professional expertise, nor any appropriate enthusiasm to produce the increased participation or awareness that is desired. Reaction to change is the measure of the health of an organization, no matter how strong. Everyone has to be involved in the team effort to face the current challenges. Changes affecting sports in recent years have been many and their implications have often been very complex for the facilities, the staff, and the service offered. These changes can be internal, coming through the organization from the staff or customers, or external, coming from politicians (local or national) and other influential sources, such as the national sports agencies. Changes which have had a significant impact on sports managers and providers include:

- The formation of the Foundation for Sports and the Arts
- The reorganization of local government
- The advent of the National Lottery
- The restructuring of the sports councils in the UK
- Consideration of the national curriculum and its impact in Sports
- The need for drug-testing facilities at all major sporting events
- The abolition of minimum rates of pay
- The move towards more part-time and fewer full-time staff
- The increased demand for sports and leisure facilities
- The changing trend of sports demands (e.g. the growth of basketball due to massive television coverage).

Any change can be perceived as threatening by the personnel involved, but can also throw up opportunities which should be portrayed positively and taken advantage of as appropriate. A good manager will involve staff fully in facing up to changes affecting their operation. It is not adequate to tell staff that certain things have happened. Rather, it is necessary to inform them from a very early stage what exactly is going to happen and where they have a role to play in responding or leading the change, rather than being demotivated by factors which they perceive they cannot control. Team briefings are a key part of facing the challenge of change, and every sports organization should have well-briefed staff, whether paid or voluntary.

The old adage of knowledge being power can lead to managers not wishing to share their knowledge and understanding with staff. This is a sign of limited thinking and will lead to staid and restricted organizations which will not be able to respond well to the changes that face them. As mentioned above, the demands of participants in Sports tend to change in line with currently popular sports or trends in clothing or standards of equipment expected. Such change is almost constant, being driven by highly commercial agencies, and a key role of the manager is to attempt to foresee trends and patterns of participation and demand. As in any level of industry, the manager who gets in first with an initiative or reaction to changing trends will benefit both personally and organizationally.

In particular, in the public sector there has been a great deal of pressure to change the method of management and especially to make managers more accountable for their actions. This has led to the introduction of performance reviews and to tighter budget controls and cost examinations, as well as specific performance targets being set. In addition, the following advantages are intended to come from such accountable management and more localized spending of the budget:

- A lessening of bureaucracy, which allows better response to localized environmental factors and more adaptability towards customer care and consumerism
- Increased efficiency and effectiveness, which should bring about more economic working through localized setting of objectives

- The leaving of local operational management to lower-level staff while strategic planning is undertaken at a higher central level

This trend to local accountable management is closely related to constant consideration of whether public management should be aligning itself to business management practices. In the recent past, the Thatcherite agenda suggested that it should and that too much thought was given to the public aspect of the management rather than the management aspect of activity. There was a strong belief that moving public services to business operation and thinking would be beneficial. There is, however, a strongly held local (politician and officer) view that the delivery of public services is in essence different because of the differing ethos, which makes it quite distinct from the business community beliefs. The overall goal to provide service is quite different from the ultimate goal of providing profit.

In the 1990s, government began to set very specific targets for local service organizations to raise their management standards—this was the main thrust of the Citizens' Charter announced by the Prime Minister in 1991. The intention of this was to give quality customer satisfaction and care through a detailed set of expectations that the customer could see fulfilled on all occasions. This would be the standard that organizations would be judged against.

Decision-making

Interestingly, decision-making may be seen as a crucial factor in separating top-quality sports performers from the run-of-the-mill participant, and it is also a major distinguishing characteristic between top-level and mediocre management in the sports industry, as in many other industrial settings. It is vital that staff are given the power to make decisions, the support to carry them out, and that they are dealt with fairly if the result of these decisions is not all one would hope for—again, very similar to the response one would hope to get from top players, coaches and team managers. It appears that individuals tend to make decisions based on:

- Experience
- Judgement
- Creativity
- Innovation
- Personal skills.

As with so many other abilities required by the manager, if an organization wants good decision-making then it has to train and support its introduction and adoption. It is wrong to assume that decision-making ability will naturally exist in all potential sports managers, and even if it is latent it will only be reflected or enhanced through significant training and encouragement of individuals. Additionally, the organizational structure must allow for decisions to be made at the appropriate level by the appropriate individual without fear or favour and without constant worry about retribution for errors—we are all human and errors of judgement are inevitable, but fortune favours the brave and he who dares wins.

CHAPTER 9

In Practising Management

MANAGEMENT PROCESSES

Many people within sports organizations see themselves as administrators rather than managers. This assumption fails to recognize the major changes facing sports organizations, which require management that has to be provided by the top people in the organization, whether paid or voluntary. People with ability must be found—the ability to make the most effective use of the available resources, to search for new resources, to innovate and take risks in stretching the organization in pursuit of new horizons. Such change requires external awareness from everyone involved in the organization, beyond the very basic chalk-face operator. Effective officers must be oriented to working with people and drawing on their strengths, and be aware of the resources available outside their specific organization or limited role. Only by maximizing what is available internally and externally can progress be made in a time of seemingly constantly reducing resources.

Officers in any management role must be concerned with administering an ongoing effective service as well as being alert to the potential of collaborative problem-solving, which will ease funding through external sources. Such challenges demand two distinct areas of ability—a systematic approach to tasks and a creativity in developing opportunities.

Successful management depends on the ability to adapt management skills and organizational structures and practices to the demands of the agency's environment—both external and internal. It is important for sports organizations and their managers to be very aware of where the organization is functioning and to be active in the area in pursuing support for that activity. It is dangerous for any organization, especially sports organizations, to become insular and not to be responsive to external influences or at least be aware of any potential threats or opportunities. It is common in voluntary sports organizations to see people dig in their heels against local authority or sports council action when in actual fact they should be looking for opportunities to manage the situation to their advantage.

Financial Management

The raising, caring for, and spending of money is a constant battle for anyone involved in Sports. This is probably true in a wide variety of business settings, but in the sports industry, which is often strapped for cash, working on tight margins and operating in the voluntary sector, money becomes a major consideration. Two major concerns arise in particular about financial management in Sports.

- The individuals involved in Sports, whatever their role, are far more interested in sports participation than in looking after pounds and pennies. Financial management requires an attention to detail, and a regular and exact habit that to some extent is foreign to anyone involved in Sports.
- For the voluntary organization it is very often found that the individual who spends all their working life handling finance is reluctant to spend their spare time doing the

same; for example, the accountant would probably rather give their time to being a hockey umpire than being a treasurer. This reluctance to apply professional skills directly to the sports situation can give rise to some potential problems and can remove the highest level of professional skill to another role.

For sports organizations outside the private sector the first of these concerns is a real issue and should always be recognized. Within the private sector, the drive for a successful bottom line tends to ensure that finance is appropriately considered at all stages. There is also a major contradiction about money within many sports settings—people who bemoan the lack of money are not prepared to spend their time trying to raise it or control it, so ensuring that it is used to the best effect. Consequently they may have to restrict their activities even further. In short, money management is often seen as a restricting requirement rather than something which can enable activity and is a key part of any sound planning process.

Sourcing money is a key part of the work within sports administration, and looking after it once it is obtained is crucial to allow effective operation. The opposite situation is a lack of proper financial management impairing the functioning of the organization, reducing the opportunities it can provide, and ultimately restricting sports participation.

Failure to manage existing funds damages sports organization and individual opportunities, and can cause major damage to an organization's image. Such damage tends to multiply by creating a belief that money should not be directed to an organization because it previously failed to manage its existing finances properly. Sports organizations do not require treasurers or financial controllers who are overly restrictive in their expenditure and use their control over money to limit the development of the Sports, because they may have individual differences with general policy or they feel money is being spent wrongly. Equally, someone who is too lax with expenditure is not helpful, and such over-expenditure will return to haunt the organization in the future. The correct balance of secure financial control and ambitious development plans is crucial in a sports organization—a difficult, but essential debate to ensure progress based on a sound financial footing.

Often financial control in certain organizations is seen as something which is done for others, e.g. national governing bodies may feel that they undertake it for the Sports Council to justify the grant support from government funds. Such a belief is erroneous: financial control is key to any successful operation, and one only has to look at the major successful companies in the business world to see that financial considerations alongside strategic direction determine the ultimate success of the organization. This is equally true in the sports business—public, private or voluntary. Sports organizations must put in place systems and structures which ensure optimum use of finance to achieve organizational objectives. They should look upon finance as an opportunity rather than a threat, and realize that when money is available it is a major opportunity for enlargement of the scope of the business, and the obtaining of money is a vital part of allowing a Sports to develop. Financial controls are good business practice; they are not a threat to existence, rather an enablement for further progression and development.

The scope of this text does not allow detailed consideration of financial management—there are many specialist texts for those charged with the responsibility of looking after the money and, indeed, raising the money. The necessity for professionalism and meticulous care in handling these matters cannot be over-emphasized, as the potential problems are enormous for both the organization and the individuals involved. Apart from lost opportunities, ineffective control can cause significant difficulties and embarrassment all round.

Due to the vast array of locations in which Sports is delivered and practised, the requirements for financial control and management are extremely diverse. The following list indicates the difficulties in covering this completely, because many or most of these areas have to be considered in each case. The group or individual charged with controlling finances should perhaps look at the following list and identify the areas which concern them and seek appropriate further help or study sources. It is also advisable, where the sum of money is significant (as it is in many sports organizations) that professional help is sought at appropriate times in the establishment and monitoring of systems, as well as the assembly of end-of-year accounts and the auditing of these. Among the areas which might have to be considered are:

- Accounting
- Analysis
- Auditing
- Balance sheet
- Book keeping
- Budgeting
- Business plan
- Capital costs
- Cash control
- Cash flow
- Cash holding limit
- Cash summaries
- Costs
- Equipment purchases
- Estimating
- Expenditure
- Financial statements
- Financial targets
- Forecasting
- Income
- Information technology
- Inventory
- Investments
- Limited company

- Organizational structures
- Petty cash
- Point of sale records
- Pricing policies
- Profit
- Profit and loss account
- Profit margins
- Recording
- Revenue costs
- Risk
- Sales
- Security systems
- Span of control
- Staffing
- Stock control
- Stock recording
- Stock taking
- Subscriptions
- Tax.

This list may be intimidating, but it indicates the many areas to be examined and the potential for difficulties. It exemplifies the necessity to ensure that appropriate structures and systems are in place to guarantee financial propriety and effectiveness. Missing or ineffective coverage of any specific area will potentially cause enormous damage to the organization, by under-mining its practical efficiency.

> Sports is a business with a difference. The Board of Management usually do it for nothing and any surplus is usually reinvested in the Sports.
>
> —*Peter Lawson (formerly CCPR)*

Any sports organization, in whatever sector of the industry, must have a clearly laid out business plan and the financial targets to accompany it. Financial management is about assessing the success of the organization against these targets and monitoring its performance to ensure that any significant deviation is noted and acted upon. To produce effective figures for presentation in a business plan, careful estimating and budgeting of expected income and expenditure must be done. The necessary financial research must be undertaken to ensure that these budget figures are as accurate as possible. Once again, significant errors in this area are all too easy to make for lack of consideration at the appropriate point.

As in most situations, being conservative about income and pessimistic about expenditure is the best way for an organization to set its budget figures, while it is to be emphasized that they should be realistic and not artificially set. All too often, however, they are not based on past experience of the organization or the realistic situation the organization is currently in; or the figures don't reflect the practical situation for similar sports organizations in the country—this again is down to accurate research, which must be undertaken. It is a recipe for disaster to pluck figures out of the air which can then throw the organization off in the wrong direction. Beyond setting the correct targets, the key issue is to ensure that the organizational set-up can deliver these targets and that the structure formed can implement appropriate controls and systems to deliver on the items identified as necessary.

The key concepts about financial management in any sports organization are that:

- It addresses the issues that affect the business
- It is not ignored
- Everyone takes a positive attitude to what properly managed finance can do for the organization
- The dangers of not facing up to such matters in a professional manner are recognized.

There are no second chances: a pound once spent is gone, and if it is not used for the correct purpose then the Sports will suffer.

Legislation

A wide range of legislation affects the sports manager or administrator—it seems to increase almost daily. Areas such as health and safety, in the workplace in particular, increase in impact as Sports and legislation become more demanding. The operation of stadium and other sophisticated facilities entails more potential problems for managers. The frequency and volume of use can cause problems which are covered by legislation.

In general terms the professional sports manager/administrator should seek specialist advice from lawyers, health and safety experts, and others with specific expertise in areas in which they are unsure. The key point is that there are legal duties upon employers and organizers which must be met—failure to do so could lead to consequences which could permanently, or even fatally, damage the organization, and even have personal implications for management staff. Where appropriate, further reference will be made to specific items of legislation throughout the text, e.g. the arrangements and implications under legislation introducing Compulsory Competitive Tendering for sports managing contracts as a part of government legislation on leisure provision by local authorities. Some of the less direct Acts that need to be considered by sports organizers and administrators are:

- The Health and Safety at Work Act 1974
- Offices, Shops and Railway Premises Act 1963
- Employers' Liability (Compulsory Insurance) Act 1969
- The Sex Discrimination Act 1975
- The Race Relations Act 1976
- The Unfair Terms Act 1977
- The Fair Trading Act 1973
- The Consumer Safety Act 1978
- The Consumer Protection Act 1987
- The Supply of Goods and Services Act 1982
- The Public Health Acts of 1875, 1890, 1907, 1925, 1936, 1961
- The Open Services Act 1976
- The Town and Country Planning Act 1990
- The Water Resources Act 1991

- The National Parks and Access to Countryside Act 1949
- The Wildlife and Countryside Act 1981
- The Countryside Act 1986
- The Gaming Act 1968
- The Lotteries and Amusements Act 1976
- The Licensing Act 1990
- The Trade Union and Labour Relations Act 1974
- The Employment Protection Act 1975
- The Employment Protection (Consolidation) Act 1975
- The Wages Act 1986
- The Equal Pay Act 1970
- The Local Government/Miscellaneous Provisions Act 1976
- The Local Government Act 1972
- The Salmon and Fresh Water Fisheries Act 1975
- The Safety of Sports Grounds Act 1975
- The Fire and Safety of Places of Sports Act 1987
- Fire Precautions Act 1971
- The Football Spectators Act 1989
- Football (Offences) Act 1991
- The Children Act 1990
- The Data Protection Act 1998
- The Disability Discrimination Act 1995

All these, in addition to, for example the Home Office *Green Guide on the Provision and Layout of* Sports Grounds, and the enormously (and almost daily) increasing body of European legislation, are affecting many aspects of life. The impact of tax, in particular VAT, and the legal obligations of other relevant bodies with their appropriate legislation—the sports councils, National Trust, national heritage organizations, country parks and the Arts Council—can have an additional impact in the sports field where they are involved. Obviously it is extremely difficult for any one sports volunteer to be expert in all or many of these areas, and it is essential that advice be sought before definite action is taken. This list of statutes does not cover every relevant government edict, but does serve to illustrate and back up the point that consulting the experts is advisable when legal issues are involved—take proper advice.

A large number of other rules and regulations can apply, depending on the precise situation, e.g. the various licensing and food hygiene Acts, as well as various laws relating to local government. There may be an obvious need to consider issues such as public entertainment and to follow the right legislation in certain situations; it is all too easy for issues such as alcohol licences and street collection permits to be forgotten, but this can prove expensive and problematic. The sports manager/ administrator may fill a number of roles, such as facility manager, event organizer or scheme promoter, but in all cases will have responsibility for considering relevant pieces of legislation.

They must be aware of their detailed implications and try to keep up to date with the many changes that continually arise. It can be very difficult for the paid person to keep up to date; it is often verging on impossible for someone in the voluntary sector, but this does not make it any less essential. It must always be remembered that, on occasions, the very lives of participants or spectators may be under threat if proper procedures are not followed and organizers must keep their knowledge current with regard to relevant safe practice and legislation. There are, for example, recent publications covering the health and safety of individuals at public performances and those at pop concerts or other outdoor events.

This is in addition to the substantial legislation brought in as a result of the Taylor Report on the safety of stadia, after the tragedy at Hillsborough in Sheffield in 1989. Such legislation is designed to prevent any such disasters for spectators or participants in future, and is something that sports organizers should always be well aware of. In practical terms there are a lot of things that individuals can do to ensure that safety risks are minimal for event and sports participants. Sports organizers/ administrators should cover and be knowledgeable about measures which help ensure that there will be no difficulty, such as:

- Undertaking an appropriate risk assessment
- Ensuring that appropriate first aid cover is available
- Maintaining facilities to an appropriate and adequate standard ensuring that the rules of the competition specify a level of coaching qualification and constant coach presence during the competition or tournament
- Good planning of a competition—allowing adequate warm-up time to safeguard against injury
- Preparing participants to the appropriate level for the level of competition in which they are competing
- Raising awareness of participants and everyone involved in Sports about the inherent risks and the care that should be taken
- Seeking legal waivers such as appropriate permission slips where necessary and ensuring that parents and others understand the potential dangers of certain activities.

Also:

- It is the duty of the sports manager/administrator to provide a safe environment for participants—the facilities and equipment should be safe, appropriate and correctly maintained; where risks do exist they should be kept to a minimum; defective or improperly designed equipment should never be used.
- The organizers of the competition and certainly the facility manager, have a responsibility to ensure that maintenance and equipment are up to recognized international and national body standards, and that equipment is regularly inspected.
- This duty of care is shared by everyone involved in Sports—the facility manager, the sports organizer, the coach, the parent and indeed the participant.
- Coaches and officials should ensure that there are no mismatches in contact Sports in terms of different ages,

sizes, weights, skills or experiences being put in direct opposition, potentially causing significant damage to younger, weaker or less experienced participants (it is not the sole responsibility of the participants to ensure that they are not put in danger—everyone involved must take their share of the responsibility).

- Participants and officials have certain rights to be allowed to express themselves in an appropriate manner and have freedom against discrimination—they also have a right to a degree of confidentiality of information which they pass to the organizers and they should have protection from intentional injury caused by the opposition or by bad procedures on the part of the organizers; the organizers should have adequate and properly circulated safety rules to avoid damage to any of the participants and they should inform the athletes and officials of what is expected of them.
- Officials at games should be aware that they have a role in ensuring the safety of all participants through correct and fair interpretation of the rules and having a good knowledge of the rules; they also have the role of ensuring that equipment and procedures in any event or tournament are safely employed—this is in addition to the competition organizers and coaches and others involved.
- Spectators and bystanders at events have a right to expect fair treatment from event organizers, who in turn must ensure their safety; equally there should be some rules for spectators and they should be advised as to what procedures to follow, especially in the event of any emergency, e.g. an outbreak of fire or a failure of floodlighting.

As mentioned above, a significant part of the legal implications is the necessity for organizers to keep records to ensure that all necessary legal requirements have been met, and are checked on an ongoing basis. This is vitally important; if the worst comes to the worst it may be necessary for such evidence to be produced in court. Failure to keep such records will also probably mean that incorrect procedures are being followed in that no regular checks are being made.

Even if correct actions are being taken, it will be impossible to prove that this is happening (and that the staff are acting properly) if there is no record. For example, organizers should have a record or a checklist to be gone through when organizing an event so that they can brief all participants (and spectators) regarding fire and safety regulations. As mentioned above, in the area of legislation it is always better for an organizer or administrator to check with experts to ensure they have followed the correct procedures. Additionally, it is essential that individuals consider all areas involved, for example:

- Health and safety during the transportation of players and officials to and from a tournament or a facility
- Insurance for people involved in organizing and setting up the event.

Insurance is an area often forgotten by sports managers/ planning administrators. It relates to a wide variety of areas including personal liability, employee liability and employer liability, health and safety or health and accident insurance—another area well worth investigating. It is essential to understand that all sports managers/administrators need to consider all the legal obligations of the vast operation they are involved in. They should not be expected to be expert in all areas, but should seek appropriate advice on all occasions. Failure to do so is in itself negligent. A good sports manager/administrator will always learn from the experts how to do things in the correct way. It is never advisable to think that they know it all. This is not an area which can be left to chance—the consequences are too frightening and potentially damaging to all concerned.

Sometimes, also, sports organizations need to be aware of the rules and regulations involved in running local lotteries and raffles, and the many regulations concerning the use of facilities such as public areas, rivers and footpaths. Additionally, since many sports situations require catering on either a commercial or a voluntary basis, the Food Safety Act 1990 and the Food Hygiene Amendment (Amendment Regulations 1991) as well as the regulations of 1966 for market stalls and delivery vehicles have implications. The Lotteries and Amusements Act of 1976 is a key piece of information, and there are a significant number of additional considerations. The diversity of institutions causes all sorts of problems for sports managers, and they need to be aware and take appropriate advice while trying to get their thinking as wide as possible.

MANAGEMENT OF SAFETY

Safety management is a vital factor in Sports. There are a number of legislative considerations under this heading that affect everyone involved, and additional concerns that arise through participation in sports. A number of sports are hazardous and by their very nature are challenging. The participants seek danger, thrills and excitement, and this can cause the manager or administrator major headaches. The organizer must aim to provide a safe and controlled environment for staff and participants, as well as spectators and anyone involved in any other role. It may be thought that in relation to facility management, the management of safety is relatively straightforward, clear-cut and easily organized, but even there it can be difficult, and in some situations in the outdoors or the voluntary field it can be much more difficult to ensure. The organizer's role is to ensure that all the participants, customers and employees are, as far as reasonably practicable, in a safe situation and are not putting themselves or others in more danger than the Sports necessitates.

This may seem an obvious statement, but is often difficult to put into practice, largely because the people we are trying to protect are being protected from their own or others' stupidity. In many sports, challenge, to the level of risking life, is a part of the sporting activity itself. Legislation in this area is complex and manifold, and the advent of additional EU legislation has made it significantly more complicated for those involved in organizing sporting events.

Health and Safety at Work

It is essential for any event organizer to become familiar with the basics of health and safety legislation as they apply in such situations. There are a great number of items of legislation in the UK and the rest of Europe, all of which are designed to ensure the health and safety of participants and spectators in a variety of situations, with special emphasis on the workplace. Significant pieces of legislation include:

- The Health and Safety at Work Act
- Food Handling
- Manual Handling Operations Regulations
- Display Screen Equipment Regulations (Computer and Word Processing Operation).

This vast array of legislation has been enacted to make the workplace and places of public entertainment safer for everyone. These regulations can be seen as limiting a manager's activities, but, as has already been highlighted, where there is any element of danger, public controls are essential and inevitable and should be looked upon as part of the organizational process, since they are vital to public health and safety. All managers in Sports and recreation (as in other industries) must make correct health and safety arrangements, and undertake a risk assessment to ensure that there is no abnormal hazard or danger to anyone involved in the Sports itself or the facility in which the Sports is taking place. The Health and Safety at Work Act 1974 lays down a number of regulations, but first of all it suggests that each facility should have a health and safety policy and this policy should have five key elements:

- Planning
- Organization

- Control
- Monitoring
- Review.

The main focus of such legislation is that the manager of a sports facility, for example, has to ensure that to some extent individuals are protected against themselves and their own stupidity; for example, an unlocked door leading to a climbing wall might be seen as a chance for some individual to try their luck at this new and exciting Sports. Obviously, potentially the results are extremely serious and it is essential that facilities are locked and access is available only on a planned and agreed basis.

The Control of Substances Hazardous to Health (COSHH) Regulations are also a vital part of any sports facility staff guidance, because some of the chemicals used for cleaning could be extremely dangerous to individual and group health if incorrectly used. It is important that all staff are aware of their responsibilities and the nature of these regulations—ignorance is no defence in law or practicality. Any such hazardous materials should be properly stored for the benefit of customers and staff alike. The key items for consideration are that:

- A risk assessment must be undertaken on any work or participative area
- Potential activities must be given codings and rates against a frequency of risk—how often something is likely to happen based on past experience
- A safety audit related to all items of legislation should be carried out against the organization's current practice
- Regular review of such a policy and how the regulations are implemented should be in place

Another vital key issue in relation to health and safety is staff training—not just that it is done for their own and public protection, but also that it is logged and clear training records are kept showing the areas covered and when each individual member of staff attended any particular session. Staff should also be given updates, as sports facilities and equipment can change frequently as technology and techniques develop. It is essential that staff are aware of equipment, how it should be stored and set up, as well as practices in using that equipment which are seen to be potentially hazardous.

Examination of facilities, organizations and current practice by a new pair of eyes, from a safety point of view is an essential tool to minimize any possible risk through participation, and safe equipment and other such simple issues should be regularly attended to, maintained and an appropriate log kept. Individuals can now be held personally responsible where the health and safety legislation is broken, and can be liable for allowing incorrect practices to proceed in events or facilities under their jurisdiction. This may be a little intimidating for some, but it puts the onus on all managers to avoid the continuation or development of unsafe situations for participation in Sports. It also pressures individuals to assist in the formulation of the audits and procedures, necessary documentation and action frames for staff training.

It is difficult to exaggerate the absolute necessity for consistent quality safety management in all sports situations and for looking after participants (at all times, whatever their nature). This is because adverse publicity, apart from individual damage, can frighten people off certain sports and encourage the belief that these sports are in themselves dangerous and must be avoided. This could limit participation unnecessarily in a number of sports, such as gymnastics, diving and trampolining, and reduce individuals' enjoyment in these activities.

Coaches and organizers must also be aware of the increasing number of cases of litigation which have been seen in North America and in the UK. This may not necessarily be a constructive trend for the Sports in general, but it means that managers, coaches, administrators and everyone involved in any Sports must ensure that any duties they undertake are correctly carried out to ensure that there is no damage or potential damage to participants or others involved. Such a concentration on health and safety and ensuring that every possible step is taken to avoid ending up in litigation concentrates the mind of organizers to ensure that they think in a more decisive way about safe practice and carry out all steps necessary to guarantee, as far as humanly possible, the health and safety of all participant groups.

It is absolutely essential that all staff are adequately trained in appropriate procedures in terms of running an office or an event, including appropriate first aid knowledge, health and safety roles, emergency procedures and any facility regulations and roles laid down. In the sporting context there can be an added potential danger and the need, for example, for resuscitation to be applied in certain situations. The issue of health and safety is live, growing and will continue to grow, and needs to be closely considered in the establishment of any facility or any development scheme with Sports.

Not only local and national legislation are involved, but increasingly European legislation has to be considered due to the significant impact it can have in sporting situations. The Health and Safety Executive has been, and continues to be, extremely helpful in terms of educating individuals through providing educational booklets and pamphlets to everyone involved in situations where health and safety has a part to play, and certainly this is true of Sports. Sports coaches, managers and administrators are well advised to make use of all the information they can obtain from such sources, as ultimately, being well versed in this vital area will be beneficial to all the groups of participants in Sports. It is always worth remembering that ignorance is no defence in the eyes of the law.

MANAGING SUPPORT SERVICES

Often there is an erroneous concept in sports management that we are solely concerned with technical sports facilities, their provision and a high level of knowledge in their utilization. Realistically, nothing could be further from the truth—many of the organizational and motivational skills of the sports manager or administrator are common to managers in a variety of industrial spheres, especially in the wider area of leisure. Additionally, the role of the sports manager is often largely taken up by provision not seen, initially, to be directly Sports-related. The required back-up services for sports participants are an essential part of any manager's operation and must be seen as such—the typical facilities here are crèches, cafés, dressing rooms, toilet areas, meeting rooms, physiotherapy clinics, drug-testing facilities, etc. This list is extensive, but not exhaustive; it means the manager must be alert to the many requirements of supporting Sports.

The management of a crèche can be a complex issue with legal requirements and other needs which must be thoroughly examined before such a facility is established. It is, however, increasingly essential to any sports facility, and can be beneficial to participation levels in a wide variety of events, from half marathons to water aerobics. The complications of running a crèche are enormous and should be very carefully examined by management staff before embarking on this project.

There is a necessity to consider almost everything in this provision in terms of location, interior layout, windows, doors, storage, toilet provision, kitchen facilities, baby changing area, safety, overall space, specific equipment, both large and small. In addition, the staff and their training and abilities must be closely examined and checks undertaken with the criminal records office as to their suitability. A crèche is just one of the additional facilities that sports participation requires, and while it is one of the more complex, it just highlights the many other areas that the sports provider must know about.

Administration

Henri Fayol looked at administration and came up with a strategic view of the organization (Brodie, 1967). He argued that the administrative functions of any organization could be divided into:

- Forecasting
- Planning

- Commanding
- Co-ordinating
- Controlling.

He stressed the need for clear objectives, authorities, decisions and tasks, and for a unity of command from top to bottom. All personnel should be linked into a clear hierarchy and chain of command. The span of control of managers should be limited so that they supervise a limited number of subordinates to get things done. In practical sporting situations, administration is a hands-on delivery of sound procedures and systems to ensure that Sports in all its aspects happens as it should. Administration focuses on the organizational practices and procedures which ensure that the day-to-day competitions, tournaments and events happen as they should, as well as making the overall organization function as it should. The list of duties involved in this sort of administration is almost endless, but would include:

- Book-keeping
- Handling entries
- Arranging fixtures
- Organizing transport
- Keeping members informed
- Arranging venues
- Organizing meetings
- Applying for grants
- Keeping records
- Paying expenses
- Arranging events
- Organizing international events
- Supporting committees
- Preparing development plans
- Assisting coaches with training arrangements
- Liaising with the media
- Arranging team uniforms
- Selling tickets
- Inviting VIPs

- Liaising with sponsors
- Recruiting volunteer support
- Selling programmes.

It is about the practical, vital minutiae of Sports, and ensuring that it is organized. Participants in Sports need everything done for them (except to perform) or else they turn up at the wrong venue, at the wrong time, dressed wrongly. Careful attention to detail is the key to good administration, as is consistently applying quality standards in implementing the agreed policies of the organization.

Administration—delivering flawless organization—is every bit as crucial to the development of Sports as quality management or coachin. Top-class arrangements are needed for top-class Sports—poor administration will tend towards poor Sports in terms of performance and development. All too often the administrator is seen as the poor relation in the 'sports organization triangle', but this is quite, quite wrong—a good argument could be put that they are in fact the most important. Sound administration is the basis for all top performing sports organizations.

The Management of Sports as a Public Service

While change has been the constant theme of many aspects of industrial operation and has affected sports management as other industrial sectors, nowhere has it been more noticeable than in the management of Sports in the public sector. The public sector Sports is a major player through national organizations such as the Sports Council and the home nations sports councils, but also through the massive spend on sporting activity by local authorities.

The funding of sports activities, both local and national, has been dramatically affected by the limitations set on public expenditure by recent governments—a trend likely to continue well into the twenty-first century regardless of the political hue of the government concerned. The pressure on the public finances brought about by growing expenditure on the ageing population, social security and health payments has meant that all other sectors have had to take a significant cut. The effects of this have been seen in the leisure services generally and in Sports quite noticeably. While the lottery income has brought about a massive increase in the funds brought into Sports and sporting activity overall, this has been matched by a significant cut in the core funding of Sports at local and national level by local and national government.

The impact of Compulsory Competitive Tendering has also been marked in changing the focus of Sports from participation, enjoyment and community benefit towards the need to ensure that performance measures are met and that financial returns guaranteed by contracts are achieved. The impact of contract culture has been sizeable in both the short and medium terms, as well as potentially in the long term, but councils have begun to realize that the need to meet contract demands does not necessarily militate against developmental work in relation to Sports, and indeed effective contract tender specification can enhance sporting opportunity and development work rather than always being seen as damaging to it.

The efficient contractor will also see that being developmental and progressive can in fact lead to improved performance in contract terms. The drive for Best Value, and the need for continuous improvement to deliver it, is likely to place more strain on public sector managers. They need to provide services as part of councils' corporate objectives of social inclusion, but against a backdrop of ever-reducing resources.

In public provision, as in any other sphere of delivery of sports services, good leadership and effective planning will consider marketing and customer care issues as well as other more modern management techniques. These matters have often been thought to be solely private sector issues and not so clearly identified with public provision of sports services. It is essential, however, that these services are in fact delivered in a well planned, well managed and customer-focused way. The national government would maintain that all the initiatives it has identified in this area have been focused on encouraging such thoughtful planning and efficient delivery for the benefit of the consumer.

Some local government politicians, particularly those in an opposition party, would feel that many of the suggestions on how public leisure services should be provided have been imposed for reasons of governmental cost-cutting rather than for customer benefit. Recent years have seen public services inundated with a wide variety of measures aimed at improving the quality of service, and these have had an impact in sports management. Among others, these issues have included:

- Quality management
- Quality standards, e.g. ISO9001
- Investors in People
- Citizens' Charters
- Compulsory Competitive Tendering
- Best Value
- Vocational qualifications and other training initiatives.

CHAPTER 10

THE DIFFICULTIES AND CHALLENGES OF MANAGEMENT

Citizens' Charter

The main thrust of government thinking is that the management of public services in general, and Sports within them, needs to be improved. To achieve this it is seen as important that customers get a clear statement of what they can expect from any public organization. Such a clear statement or promise to customers means that the organization becomes much more accountable to the clients and will have to introduce control mechanisms to ensure that it delivers what it promises. Customer charters started with national organizations and organizations such as the Health Service, and have percolated down to local authorities, individual leisure departments, sports sections and individual sports facilities. It is not uncommon when entering a sports facility to see clearly listed a number of promises to customers in terms of a detailed charter of what they can expect within the facility, backed up by a brochure giving the full charter, and often by a defined complaints procedure so that any customer can raise an issue if they feel the customers' charter is not being fulfilled.

Competition

The 'threat of competitiveness' has also been used through Compulsory Competitive Tendering and market testing to give a more real challenge to the public service sector—especially at local government level. In practice a good deal of competition has come from the private sector through private clubs, hotel health suites and other such provision in the sporting area; however, research by the Centre for Leisure Research in Edinburgh has shown that competition for local authority sports and leisure management contracts in the first round of tenders in 1992-93 was extremely limited and very patchy indeed in its distribution. The private sector became more confident in the next round of tendering, although in many ways the context has changed. Many councils have become more aware of examining the methods of service delivery, and not just because the government has imposed Best Value procedures.

The biggest motivation for sports managers to change and develop facilities and services has been direct competition from the private, commercial and sometimes the voluntary sector for the finite number of customers in the market. The opening of new fitness suites with a very high standard of provision has meant that, to succeed and compete in the market, public facility managers and development officers must be able to provide something additional or at least of a similar standard to that which customers now expect. As with all provision in our modern society, customers' expectations are high and their experience through television, and other technological developments, is of a sophistication which many sports facilities have to struggle hard to match.

This drive to succeed in a competitive market has led to an improvement in the standard of many facilities, both new and refurbished, particularly in areas such as health suites and fitness training facilities where there is substantial commercial competition. The push for competitive success has led to the introduction of quality management techniques which were first seen in Japan and the USA. This has placed additional pressures on managers in all organizations to come up with quality practices and procedures.The movement towards quality operation and delivery has caused considerable additional work for the sports manager and administrator. While the end achievements of clearly understood working practices and correct procedures may be beneficial, the economic and social benefits have to be balanced to see whether the impact of the quality concept has been worth the time and effort it requires.

Best Value

The Labour Government, under pressure from its allies, the trade unions, devised a scheme to replace Compulsory Competitive Tendering (CCT) and its potentially punitive penalties. The unions felt that their members were losing out in terms and conditions of employment. The government placed a responsibility on local authorities to ensure Best Value in the delivery of all their services—meaning that the local authority had a duty to provide them in the most cost-effective manner available. It further insisted on a programme of continuous improvement to ensure that innovative and efficient ways are found of providing its services to its customers while not overcharging local council-tax payers. The government has continued its drive to enshrine this initiative in law, and in 2002 was in the process of finalizing its intentions and passing the necessary legislation through parliament in London and Edinburgh, and the assemblies in Northern Ireland and Wales.

Best Value is now clearly defined by all relevant government departments as 'a duty to deliver services to standards—covering both cost and quality—by the most effective, economic and efficient means available'. It will mean that local authorities will have to undertake fundamental performance reviews, set targets for sustained improvement in all their services and take into account the views of the local community and any nationally set government standards.

The government is also keen to establish a set of performance indicators that measure both output and outcome of local authority work, but this is complex and demanding and is taking some time to complete. As far as Sports is concerned, there are some real benefits to this drive to Best Value. Efficient and effective delivery of sports services must help everyone involved. The need to measure outcomes as well as outputs is also of potentially enormous benefit to Sports in the UK, especially because Sports has often been subject to short-term thinking and project delivery, whereas to produce significant change, development or improvement is usually a lengthy process. Very often, for example, in Sports the emphasis has been on qualifying coaches and the output statistics. It may seem a really great output to qualify 50 new assistant club coaches in a year—but what is the actual outcome?

- How many people do they coach and what age are they?
- Are they still coaching three years on?
- How do they progress up the coaching ladder?
- Do they undertake further training?
- How many new clubs are formed?
- How many were previously unemployed?
- What is the real impact on the Sports over a longer period, and in actual participation or performance?
- Was this a cost-effective use of the allocated monies?

Facing up to the demands of Best Value will be intimidating for some local authority officers, but, if positively and properly handled, could well enhance the long-term impact of the Sports services.

Financial Control

Central government has also used financial control to limit and dictate the activities of local authorities and other organizations such as the sports councils. This has been most effective in determining what activities these organizations will perform, and controlling staffing levels, otherwise central government funding, which is crucial, has been withheld. The claim of government has been that this will lessen the amount of, and the interference of, bureaucracy and get the money directly to the required areas—in truth, this requirement often tends to be what is perceived a priority at any given time by central government within financial limitations set by the Treasury.

National Standards

The government continues to seek more ways of reviewing of performance and delivery by the public sector, it has increased the activities of the Audit Commission and the role of the office of the Deputy Prime Minister to monitor the performance of public sector management in a number of spheres, as well as keeping tight control over local government spending. It has been keen to introduce a number of national tables or standards, which must be met or measured by local authorities laying down a national curriculum and examination and testing structure with league tables to show clearly how schools are performing, though obviously this is only one area of their performance.

This move is accompanied by the introduction of national performance indicators and public measures of the standards of provision. Designed to give the consumer more information on which to base choices, they are also intended to forge efficiency on public bodies and local authorities. Generally speaking, any rise in the standard of provision for participants and others involved in Sports must be welcomed and always aimed for, while there must be some type of real cost/benefit analysis to see whether the concept can actually work.

Pressure for Change

Perhaps the key issues in relation to the management of change in Sports, as in other settings, are:

- Who makes the change
- Whether it is imposed externally or brought about after a real consultation period
- Where the power to make the change actually rests.

One of the major areas of difference, and perhaps confusion, within Sports is the differences in working methods between the public, private and voluntary sectors. Change in the public sector is often imposed by national or local politicians, with officials left to carry it out and (where necessary) pick up the pieces, making the best use of limited resources in terms of cash or other requirements. They are sometimes left with little real power over the decisions made, so changes can be forced upon them.

This is the difficulty that some of these officials have in relating their situation to the private sector, where individual managers may well have significant power to make changes and to alter working practices. Managers must learn to recognize these differences, and perhaps be more tolerant of them when dealing with colleagues from other sectors. The voluntary sector, on the other hand, operates on a democratic basis and with committees and group decisions. This mechanism is not flexible enough to react quickly to change.

Voluntary Input and Management

Very often in voluntary bodies the power lies with committees rather than individuals, and even paid employees have very little real executive power in practice. One of the major changes being put in place by many governing bodies and being considered by others is in their management structure—aiming to make them more able to initiate changes they feel should be happening, rather than merely following sports participants into a change process.

This is a major consideration for governing bodies, which often react rather than lead sporting change, even in their own Sports. The consultation periods undertaken by bodies, such as the Sports Council are often too short to be practical for many of the voluntary groups involved in the sports industry, and this often leads to a reaction against new initiatives by sports bodies that struggle to keep up with the pace of change. True consultation with voluntary agencies is difficult because of their extended operational structures. This is a major issue since governing bodies really should be taking the lead in their Sports and yet, by their very organization and structure, often play the following role.

There is continuing government pressure to reduce the spending of money, through the sports councils, on governing bodies' general activities—the move is to eliminate as much bureaucracy as possible and fund to youth Sports and excellence directly, so that the money goes to other more general activities or administrative activities. This is a move that many in Sports support, while the long-term effects of such initiatives are not known.

There are also claims that too much money given to the sports councils is spent on bureaucracy—a view which may have some substance—but it is difficult to see how direct funding from central government to governing bodies, facilities or activities could function without an intermediary body such as the Sports Council. Also, the more money it has to allocate (e.g. through the lottery) the larger its bureaucracy must inevitably be. This issue is live and will continue to be so for the foreseeable future, especially if a government of a different political view comes along. Certainly, the government sees the Sports Council role as one of empowering other people to spend money to achieve Sports participation and performance. It is likely that this perceived role will not change significantly, especially as it is widely shared by those participating in Sports who do not like to see the Sports Council spending money on marketing itself.

Philosophical Challenges

Undoubtedly the key issue for Sports facing change is the need to ensure that its philosophy and concept are kept intact and that no damage is done to the fundamental belief in Sports which keeps sports managers, administrators and participants going.

This conviction that the provision of, and the participation in, Sports is vital to our health individually and culturally makes it worth facing up to challenge and change, making progress and leading the way for the benefit of all involved. With this positive philosophy in place, change will throw up many more opportunities than threats, because it will be met face to face by individuals with a commitment to the cause, taking positive steps, seizing the initiative and charting a way forward. Sports is all about ethics and philosophy linked to belief and commitment—anything that undermines such concepts has the potential to damage Sports, in the public or other sectors.

Investors in People

Investors in People (IIP) is a government scheme which aims to encourage organizations to take their people seriously as the key aspect for the improvement and development of the organization. The scheme sees a personnel development programme as key to improving industry quality delivery. The four principles are as follows.

1. An 'Investor in People' makes a public commitment from the top to develop all employees to achieve its business objectives.
2. An 'Investor in People' regularly reviews the training and development needs of all employees.
3. An 'Investor in People' takes action to train and develop individuals on recruitment and throughout their employment.
4. An 'Investor in People' evaluates the investment in training and development to assess achievement and improve future effectiveness.

A variety of sports organizations have become involved in IIP and have had either an initial, or in some cases, concluding assessments by the independent assessor provided by IIP. As in so many systems, the key issue is not the certification but the recognition of the crucial nature of staff and staff development to successful organizations. This initiative has, however, as in a number of other industrial settings, proved so onerous that the numbers coming forward are still small.

Leisure Trusts

Many local authorities have, in recent years, moved the management of their Sports and leisure facilities (and in some cases, services) into an independent (to a greater or lesser degree) leisure trust. This has largely been done to save money and to benefit from certain tax breaks, particularly in relation to VAT. The change is also intended to create more commercial opportunities and foster the adoption of good business practice to reduce over time any council grants. A number of smaller leisure trusts have also been formed to allow local communities to run their own sports facility or facilities. This has facilitated localized democratic control and input to the management process. The accountability to largely 'amateur' voluntary boards has become an issue under this sort of regime; again, different stresses and strains can appear and delivery can be affected.

Only time will tell whether the trust approach to sports provision has been successful, but the focus has been on saving money and necessarily improving service in the short term. The increase in commercialization may also mean that trusts will compete with the private sector for the better-off customers. In an attempt to maximize income, they may exclude some of the poorer members of society—the precise group local authorities are meant to be supporting and providing for. It does seem that there will continue to be a drive towards the leisure trust delivery mechanism in the foreseeable future—for better or worse.

Ageing Facilities

A major issue in UK Sports over the next decade will be the growing age of the facilities, particularly those under public control. The bulk of the facilities in the country are reaching their 'sell-by' age, supposed to be 30 and for many now approaching 50, and for some even passing this. This ageing process brings massive cost implications in terms of maintenance, refurbishment and replacement. Most public agencies simply can't finance these capital costs, even where lottery funding is available in support. There is a growing challenge in keeping these facilities operational, and there is a real possibility that some will close or at least start to offer reduced provision.

Performance Indication

In a number of settings, the levels of service delivery and their measurement have become increasingly important. Some believe that the public sector has become almost fixated by them. The government has imposed statutory performance indicators on local authority provision in leisure and recreation, including Sports. These are limited to basic percentages of the local population participating at the authority's facilities. Various initiatives have suggested ways of making these indicators more appropriate, but it is always difficult to identify ways of gathering the information on performance which we would like to know across the country. Sports England has recently produced a range of recommended performance indicators, of which local authorities can choose to adopt one or all. This leaves the situation somewhat *ad hoc,* but at least it gives a clear picture of what should be considered important in delivering local Sports services and what should be measured. The fundamental and difficult task is to make what is important measurable, and not just measure what we can—i.e. make the measurable important. Ultimately, the impact of the sports provision on the local community and its population is what is important.

CHAPTER 11

SPORTS MARKETING

'Brusque to the point of being businesslike.' This statement reflects a British viewpoint that being professional and businesslike means being curt and short with customers and clients. In a true customer-care focused business this is exactly the opposite of the truth; being businesslike is about spending time with clients, getting to know what they want and meeting their needs.

Business has only two functions: marketing and innovation.

—*Peter F. Drucker*

Marketing is a key area of operation for all modern-day businesses. It must be seen as a process, not a theoretical concept, and must be a shared concept for every one of the staff. Marketing should be seen as the responsibility not of one individual but of every person working in the business of Sports. It is often believed that marketing is the weakest part of some sports operations. This may well be due to the fact that the term is not understood by many and so is not implemented by everyone as it needs to be.

The definitions of marketing are many. However, all of them place the customer as 'king' and emphasize that the manager's job is to ensure that this is the case on every occasion, and in every circumstance. Sports administration is a client-led business. There can be little doubt that the function that people in sports management and administration do least well is marketing. As suggested above, the problem often originates from a misunderstanding of what marketing is, and this filters right through the organization to cause poor provision of the practical requirements in the implementation for sports management.

Marketing is a much abused word in many aspects of modern business and, indeed, some blame has been directed to the marketing professionals themselves for being seen as more interested in show and a 'razzmatazz' profile than in the delivery of a quality product. This misguided effort and the growth of the marketing industry, and all its spin-offs, have given some people a false impression of what is meant by, and what should be implemented under the heading of marketing. In any industry, marketing must be seen as a process and a practical approach to apply throughout the organization, and not just as a clever concept or 'the showy bits' of presenting a finished product.

It is as important for Sports to consider marketing, thinking back from the eventual product and the end client, as it is to consider sports policy. The analogy of genuine marketing starting on the factory floor where workers put bolts into cars is sound—marketing pervades the whole business. Everyone involved in the Sports, including (and sometimes especially) the performers, must see themselves as part of the marketing of the Sports and must make an effort to make the sports product attractive, if it is to be sold to potential supporters and customers.

Marketing is about the whole package, not just advertising. It is about the way everything is packaged and presented from idea to implementation. Part of marketing will be to produce an attractive product which is then sold to appropriate groups in an appropriate manner. Consideration must be given by everyone involved to their part in the whole marketing process.

The biggest task, then, in the area of marketing is to convince everyone that they have a role within marketing, and to get everyone working towards successful, genuine marketing of the Sports. This may sound easy, but for many traditionalists it is a whole new approach and a considerable amount of effort will be required to get any real movement in this direction. This change of thought process is absolutely essential for the marketing approach to work. To implement such a major change in thinking is very difficult with people who have often felt that participation in sports organization just happens for a small number of people who want to play the game, and there is no need to extend beyond the basic provision for the committed person.

In the mid-1990s, an official of the Rugby Football Union, speaking to a parliamentary committee, said that he saw no major problems for his Sports in terms of attracting sponsorship. It was a well supported game which was currently thriving. This type of complacent approach may mean that in a few years sports with such an attitude will not continue to thrive. This optimistic outlook can be justified in the periods of success, but to have genuine prolonged progress, Sports needs to have a firm foundation which can sustain its growth even through leaner periods. To be complacent because of what may be transient success in a specific Sports is to 'fiddle while Rome burns'.

The structures of Sports need to be able to withstand any fluctuations in success and to ensure lasting benefits in the future. Sports also have to recognize that good management practice will allow them to benefit from monies which may from time to time become available. If good practice is not in place then they may well suffer. A case in point could be said to be tennis in the UK. A lot of money has been available over a prolonged period, but the necessary marketing and the development of mass activity as well as the support structures for a number of talented individuals have not been properly in place to allow for the growth of standards or the production of quality players in the UK.

Money, while a major bonus, is not the sole contributor to sporting organizational success, nor is it a guard against external fluctuations. For example, it may be that rugby would suffer quite substantially if tennis were to get its act together in terms of producing quality in Britain and more public interest, or if one of the home nations were to be highly successful in the soccer World Cup then the interest in participating in rugby might fall dramatically, leading to a drop in standards possibly followed by a spiralling effect of continually reducing participation. This in turn could lead to less money and other support coming into the Sports. Coupled to the 'club versus area' professional team debate in Welsh rugby union, there is a serious threat from a successful soccer team tempting potential players and backers away from the game. Professional Sports needs to balance the books while maintaining longer-term interest for future investment.

A genuine marketing approach means that Sports will do its best to guard against fluctuations in performance and external factors to ensure the standard is consistent by targeting the Sports to attract new participants, satisfy existing ones, and develop the highest possible standards. There can be, especially, for the smaller sports, no opportunity for a 'sit back and watch' approach while the world is changing around them and other sports are growing. Clinging to the status quo is a recipe for death.

The aim must be to deliver a quality product in a form that is attractive to everyone involved. Even to participants, sports must be well presented and offered in a way that is attractive. This becomes increasingly important as demographic and economic movements mean that fewer people can afford to play more than one Sports seriously; or some choose a Sports for life or a range of sports for different levels of participation and commitment. An obvious example of how the product can be substantially changed is the many games that have introduced mini versions in order to please, suit and attract potential participants, especially young people, and tailor the product to the demands of these groups. Indoor bowls fundamentally changed its whole format and rules in order to attract television,

The Institute of Marketing has defined marketing as 'the management process responsible for identifying, anticipating and satisfying customer requirements profitably'. This concept has been widely accepted in private industry, but not so wholeheartedly in the public sector. A significant educational and motivational input would appear to be needed in both the public and voluntary sectors to get more effective marketing put in place for a number of activities, including that of sports management and administration. Marketing is ultimately about an organization, whether commercial or not, identifying exactly what it is trying to do and who it is doing it for, and then doing this efficiently and effectively. It is necessary for the end-product to be widely available, and to be seen to be available, whether it is a service or a manufactured product. The process of considering who the customers are and what they want will help focus the operation of the sports management service and will result in an improved product for the customers.

Effective marketing will also be very necessary for organizations in Sports, because they too are in a competitive environment and must compete for customers and clients, whether they will be paying or not. The demands on young people, for example, mean that governing bodies must effectively compete for their interest and participation if sports dealing primarily with young people are to survive and thrive. There is little doubt that marketing is the thing that sports organizations, particularly in the voluntary and public sectors, do worse than almost any other activity they undertake. This is not uncommon throughout industry, but Sports certainly must languish near the bottom of the pile in terms of marketing acumen in the UK. The problem is that the concept of marketing is not comprehended.

The process of marketing must pervade the whole organization at all levels and be seen as a total process rather than as an initiative taken by one individual, or a group of individuals. In order to embark on effective marketing one has to look at the current situation and consider users and non-users of the available sports facilities or services. This must be done by significant neutral market research. Research is essential, of both existing and potential customers, before goals and, more particularly, exact objectives are set for our organization. The whole group of managers in Sports must begin to see that marketing is an overall concept and relates to all aspects of the organization. They must begin to understand marketing in terms of the marketing mix and produce a marketing plan bearing all these factors in mind. In the traditional combination or marketing mix there are four 'p's:

- Product
- Price
- Place
- Promotion.

Modern thinking is that one or more 'p's should be added to this list, these new concepts being:

- People
- Physical evidence
- Process.

In Sports the following 'p's are also relevant:

- Programming
- Packaging
- Presentation.

In 'people' we are referring to the key marketing tool in terms of implementation and face-to-face contact. They are the number-one determinant for the quality of the individual customer's experience on visiting a facility or coming into contact with any service provision. The physical evidence is an area which is significant in sporting terms, because the physical experience will be a large part of what people see and experience and will affect their opinion as to whether they want to return in the future. The presentation of facilities, events and services is very important from a marketing point of view.

'Process' underpins service delivery in that the quality of the personnel and their delivery of the service in a helpful way is a major marketing bonus. If customers are to genuinely benefit and enjoy the experience then the process of staff involvement must be of prime importance. For certain areas of Sports and leisure facilities, the programming of facilities can become the eighth 'p' in the marketing mix, because the timing and presentation of a varied programme of activities for different levels of performer are key in increasing numbers and commitment of customers.

The balancing of a full and varied programme is a major factor in successful sports provision. Offering the right activities at the right time with the right leadership will determine substantially what type of uptake any provision obtains. Examining all these factors will lead organizations to produce a marketing plan which puts in place the approach that has to be taken to increase customer uptake, market share, or organizational image. There may be other aims depending on the specific situation, but these three are often shared by a variety of organizations.

Very simply, the marketing plan, having identified the aims and objectives to be achieved, will look at all the factors in the marketing mix and specify a strategy for achieving them. There are perhaps three key issues: staff training, involvement and understanding of the marketing process and the part they play in it; a SWOT (strengths, weaknesses, opportunities and threats) analysis of the situation as far as marketing is concerned; and the production of a promotion plan for the facility or service on offer. This is a very basic guide for the considerations in drawing together a marketing plan; it is a very specialized and challenging task, but one that should be undertaken by all sporting organizations, as with other industries.

There are many sources of further information on how this can be done, and the number of books on marketing is enormous. All managers should study this topic, make themselves more market-aware and understand fully how they may get involved in developing the market to its fullest extent. In practice, sports managers must first of all examine the location of their product or service, and where possible this should be made to be most suitable to potential customers. However, it has to be recognized that it may not always be possible to move this product. A sports centre cannot be moved to another part of town where customers might have different concepts and more money. It may be possible to open a new sports facility only in a limited space where there is enough land to make it viable. However, in terms of the internal place and finishes and furnishing, we should do everything we can to make it attractive and appealing to the consumer, present and potential.

One must realize that we are in a very competitive market and customer expectation is generally high. Many facilities in the public sector suffer because of a lack of refinement or polished finish when compared to high-spending, high-profile commercial facilities. In terms of product, Sports has to examine exactly what it is offering its customers, both present and potential. The quality of the product is often not considered, especially in terms of changing it. Rather it is presented to the potential user on a 'take it or leave it' basis.

At a very basic level, sports organizations have to consider whether their product is genuinely the type of thing that potential customers really want; is it the most suitable to the customers or is it the one that people tend to think of as most suitable? This would relate to things like mini games for under-twelve-year-old performers. Many sports see this as some type of extra rather than a total necessity if youngsters are to be attracted into their game. Children given the choice will not play games which they think too difficult or demanding with equipment which they cannot adequately handle.

The product, then, must be analysed and designed or altered, as appropriate to fit the customer's desires. The price of sports activities is, in many situations, outside the control of the facility manager or the individual closest to the shop floor. In some other sectors, such as the smaller commercial gyms or snooker clubs, the manager may play a key role in the setting of prices. The price factor is the key issue in making things appealing to people, and its importance should not be forgotten in terms of siting facilities and user patterns. People should not see pricing as separate from marketing, but should look at what monies can realistically be taken in at specific prices. Eli Callaway was a successful entrepreneur who turned his hand to golf-club production—starting famously with metal woods. He had an interesting belief as far as price was concerned: You cannot sell anything too expensively.

He thought that people valued and cherished expensive items and would pay for them. Cheap items were believed to be shoddy and undesirable: high price=high value=high quality. This proved an extremely successful strategy for him in selling golf clubs—probably quite cheap to produce—for a very high price. Perhaps giving tickets a low price, as many administrators do, indicates a low-quality product to strangers?

Promotion is another aspect of marketing, much talked about and very often done poorly. Indeed, it is what many people see as marketing, perhaps because it deals with the more visible aspects. Promotion is wide-ranging and includes publicity, media relations, press conferences and other areas. Much of promotion can be done on a high-spending commercial basis, or even substantial things can be done at minimal cost, especially by voluntary organizations. 'People' is the most important 'p', as mentioned above. It is not always added to the marketing mix, but it should be because ultimately, in sports terms people are the most important commodity both as customers and as clients, and indeed as factors attracting other people to take part in sports or in specific sports facilities. The way in which people react as management or frontline staff will determine very largely how well a facility is marketed or used.

We must always, always, always remember that we are operating in a people business where personalities can make or break impact in both a positive and a negative way. As mentioned above, when dealing with Sports there are three other 'p's which perhaps can be usefully considered. First, programming is important in how any particular Sports fits into the timetable of a facility or even the social life of participants. The timetabling of the busiest periods for the sports club or organization will be crucial—everyone wants to take part between 7p.m. and 9p.m., and creating programmes round these times is the secret to success, even if it is extremely difficult.

In terms of packaging Sports has often been criticized for not presenting itself well enough, for example, to be attractive to the family in user-friendly language and information targeted at that particular group. The presentation of Sports in terms of events and even publicity materials can be limited. It is unrealistic to believe that you will increase the participation levels if the presentation of Sports, both on paper and on the playing field, is not of the appropriate standard. It is often, and correctly, said that all consumers, including children, are becoming more and more sophisticated each year in the UK, and if Sports is not presented in a professional and attractive manner then it will not be taken up by many. This is particularly true as the number of young people to target is falling dramatically over the years.

MARKETING ETHICS

In recent years a number of considerations have become more important in terms of marketing. These are issues that have to be addressed now, for the first time in many cases. Ethics is certainly one. A specific prohibition, in most cases, is sponsorship advertising by tobacco and alcohol manufacturers. Only a few sports will escape severe criticism for becoming involved with such companies. In addition, the 'greenness' of products and the social image of sponsors is important to consider for sports getting involved with specific commercial interests.

Consumers are now worried and put off by high prices, deceptive practices, high-pressure selling or marketing, shoddy or unsafe products, planned obsolescence, cultural pollution, excessive political power, etc. There is a new marketing force in the air: marketing for the 'thinking customer'. A major concern is the image of Sports generally and of individual sports organizations. For all marketing activities—internal and external—image is all-important. The impact of 'drugs' on the public image of Sports has been considerable and can cause significant problems to individuals trying to promote Sports and the commercial benefits it can offer. As well as positive image, marketers must limit negative image and potential damage. There is something called bad publicity—just look at the Millennium Dome!

MARKETING PARTICIPATION

A lot of the time in Sports we talk about encouraging participation, and marketing and promoting this concept. It is interesting that many such campaigns, such as Sports for All, 50+ and other targeted groups have been relatively unsuccessful, because of the lack of effective reinforcing factors.

Ultimately, participation in Sports will be increased by potential participants seeing some greater benefit for participating—this may be in the form of health or fitness or some other reward which suits their purpose. They need to see that participation in Sports is supported by government, local and national, by public attitude and indeed by the public purse. It is pointless to ask people to take part in Sports if it is going to cost them too much for the initial participation.

Possible actions of positive reinforcement could be in the income tax system, or some other concrete method of encouraging participation not yet identified or practised in the UK. If taking part in Sports is genuinely good for health and this can be proved, perhaps participants should have a lower national health service contribution. Indeed, it may be that the government should encourage sports participation because such health benefits are a long-term saving for the public purse, and to encourage participation it should pass on these possible economic benefits to the individuals concerned.

This type of thinking may be radical but, until some such

change comes, it is difficult to anticipate further dramatic rises in baseline participation just for the sake of it. If the government truly wants us to take part in Sports and believes it is very important, then it must be positive about tax benefits or find some other basis of supporting this participation. Additionally, the whole issue of school Sports needs to be addressed with a view to encouraging schools, especially in this time of devolved school management, to consider school Sports as important and to fund such activity appropriately. The future of school Sports will be left in the hands of head teachers, and they must see some encouragement for this participation in terms of health and potential support funding.

Again, if the national government believes that Sports is important then it should be specified quite clearly within the national curriculum and enforced through government pressure in all possible ways. The benefits to the school system through reduced absenteeism, truancy and social misdemeanour could make any money spent in encouraging involvement in sports very well worthwhile, not just from a performance point of view. Marketing sports participation is not just about telling people; it is also about creating the correct environment and resource conditions in society.

IMPLEMENTING THE MARKETING PROCESS

It is important that the whole of the association or organization sees marketing as important and realizes that everyone within the organization must be involved if it is to be effective. In a sports centre, for example, the frontline staff (the reception and leisure attendant staff) are a key part of the organization marketing from the presentation and image point of view. Such staff must clearly see that they have a role in marketing the organization, and not feel it is an activity related only to advertising and promotion.

Obtaining such a positive belief on the part of all staff is extremely difficult, but should be undertaken since the benefits are considerable in terms of customer return; more intimidating is the prospect of negativity to all customers if this marketing role is not seen by all staff. The practical overt steps of marketing, such as market research, advertising and mailshots, should not be seen as the only marketing duties undertaken by any organization. The holistic approach, which involves all the staff in an ongoing process, is crucial to effective marketing.

Marketing Activities

The action dictated by marketing as an ethos and an organizational concept means that many additional activities have to be undertaken. It means that *ad hoc* decisions should not be taken in terms of organizational planning or action, but rather that significant research and analysis is necessary before any commitment is made which affects the whole marketing approach. It is essential that all the staff put marketing into practice and use their joint expertise to consider, and where necessary search, the market they are in.

There are a number of steps to be undertaken to put a more active marketing strategy in place. In particular it is important that the organization undertake a SWOT analysis. This means that the organization should examine its strengths, weaknesses, opportunities and threats. This analysis, if realistic, will help identify where exactly the organization is in terms of facing up to the competition and moving forward to capture more of its potential market. The typical strengths and weaknesses, opportunities and threats in a sports organization could be:

Strengths: Enthusiasm Commitment, Technical knowledge, Teamwork

Weaknesses: Lack of knowledge ,Poor co-ordination, Untrained staff, Lack of management

Opportunities: Public interest ,Positive image, Wide range of potential participants

Threats: Other attractions, Poor public image, Lack of understanding, Lack of direction Competition

It is important that, following on from the internal analysis, the surrounding environment that the organization operates in is examined, in particular identifying the competition which faces the sports organization. It is also essential that potential and existing customers are clearly identified to see who they are at present and who they may be in the future, and what may be done to service their needs. Overall the self-analysis process is to provide a better product for existing customers, and a more attractive one for potential customers. If this marketing analysis is correct then the number of participants in any given situation will probably increase, though if a significant mistake is made in terms of the presentation of the facility, operation or service on offer, then damage can be done and the proposed beneficial marketing could in turn become detrimental.

PUBLIC RELATIONS

Over many years Sports could be rightly criticized for having a generally poor image with the public, and this is something that it must work hard to improve. It is true in all sectors of the sports industry, and the poor image continues to the present day with the high public profile of the few athletes who take drugs as opposed to the millions who don't.

Sports organizations and institutions must work hard at their public image to minimize any negative effects. There is little doubt that this is one area of major failure of Sports in the UK. The arts appear to have a fair amount of public and political sympathy, though not necessarily money, whereas Sports tends to be the relatively poor relation in terms of such support and public awareness, and in fact government financial support—running at about 30% of that of the arts. This is particularly true of the amateur scene within Sports, but is also true of all but a very small minority of professional Sports teams or individuals.

Public relations (PR) is not just about publicity; it is to do with image, with comparing yourself to competitors; it is to do with public perception and is a process that should pervade the whole organization. It should start with an assessment of the current situation, and continue with production of a specialized public relations plan to improve image (and thinking) and the detailed consideration of how to implement this plan; there should be an evaluation at the end of the plan. Such a plan would have the clear goal of ensuring that a positive image for the sporting organization was established and maintained through many items of promotion and a full ongoing marketing overview.

For example, many clubs have worked hard to change their image to a multi-purpose family venue rather than the hard-nosed game only for the working men. Strangely, rugby league fought such a battle for many years before soccer, and has probably been more successful in its results. It is also arguable whether the family aspect of soccer is a real contributor to improving support or merely a cosmetic image frill. False imaging is long-term poor PR, as it will inevitably be found out. The need to change the general public attitude to Sports is well identified but is difficult to achieve, and certainly relates to a wide variety of issues including culture, family, religion, education, age, gender, social and ethnic groups, as well as socio-economic status. Public relations is a process that must be worked at; it is not an afterthought but an ongoing issue of considerable importance.

Fundraising

Sports and recreation are highly popular in the UK—many people take part, show tremendous commitment and derive enormous enjoyment from their activity. There is, however, something of a reluctance to subscribe to this participation or to support financially, both individually and organizationally. In comparison with many other countries, there is no large sum of public money pumped in by the government to support activity and development in Sports in the UK. This means that many, if not all, sports bodies seem to be constantly searching for money to enable participation, promote awareness and improve standards of performance.

Inevitably, this means that within any sporting organization someone or a group of people will have fundraising as their duty. Only in very few sports will money be easily found (relatively speaking) because of the high media image and the perception of it being good to be associated with that particular Sports, e.g. rugby and soccer. Some sports will have support at certain times when they have a high level of success or public image, but this may wane and the television exposure, for example, may be reduced significantly due to the rise of other sports, or the whim of TV programmers. For example, until recently athletics had a very high profile and successfully attracted sponsorship (even if not at the lower level of participation) but this has passed as the high standards of achievement were not maintained and its image was damaged by a perceived poor reputation for drug use. Sports such as darts and snooker have also reached a peak and then fallen away—every Sports must be wary of this and its financial and participation implications.

Regardless of the amount of sponsorship money coming into a Sports, there will be levels—very often the base level and early participation stages—which will require substantial amounts of money to function and yet will not benefit from major sponsorships. The largest part of any sponsorship in soccer, for example, goes to the professional game, not to the local amateur teams struggling to survive.

This means, as mentioned above, that fundraising will need to be undertaken by the sports body in order to continue to survive and, hopefully, to progress. There are many possible schemes of fundraising, but regardless of the scheme, the commitment of the fundraiser(s) and the novelty of the scheme will probably be the two key factors in obtaining any significant income for the organization.

It is also necessary, obviously, to get some commitment from the potential customers for the scheme, and it is important that club or association members themselves get involved and act as sponsors or supporters of the scheme. On the most basic level, there is no point in someone trying to sell local lottery tickets to friends and colleagues if the club members themselves are not willing to buy them and support the initiative. A united effort is essential to have any sustained success in fundraising, and to continue to keep the individual involved interested and not totally frus-trated by the lack of support and enthusiasm of others. In organizing any fundraising effort it is essential to consider the estimated net profit, assessing whether this is going to be worthwhile for all the effort expended.

The degree of difficulty in establishing the operation must also be considered, as what is desirable may be too difficult to achieve. It is not, for example, realistic for a single local club to organize a major national raffle or promotion without other partners or some significant base of support outside its own limited membership. The timing of the fundraising effort can be crucial, both from the organizational point of view in leaving enough time for success, and in relation to other competitors in the field. To launch a major promotion when everyone in the local area is about to go off on their annual holidays, or just before Christmas, when there is little spare money around, is not a recipe for success. Close consideration must be given to the actual ability of any organization to set up a fundraising scheme and the planning must allow sufficient time for success.

The fundraising resources needed, such as facilities and equipment, initial outlay, and publicity and promotion, must be closely considered. More particularly, the number of people required to support the initiative must be closely considered. If there is not going to be enough support from the relevant personnel, then the effort may well be doomed to failure. A surprising number of successful fundraising events, however, rely almost exclusively on one person; where this is all that is required, or there are relatively few demands on personnel, it may be possible to proceed. There must be detailed examination of the risks involved, i.e. any losses that may be incurred or any potential legal costs that could result from certain projects.

It is always worth considering the 'worst case scenario' that could arise before embarking on efforts to raise funds. Legal requirements mean that individuals or organizations should be aware of the permits and licences they may require, e.g. for a sportsman's dinner in a tent or a raffle. There are often more permissions required than realized at first glance. It is usually advisable to seek advice in this area. Generally, it is very useful to speak to others who have embarked on similar projects before or who are aware of some of the advantages and disadvantages of various fundraising projects. It is never sensible to 'reinvent the wheel'; it is always better to learn from their wisdom or their mistakes than from your own. Having examined some of the general rules and considerations, here is a list of the type of fundraising promotion that sports organizations might consider. These are based on personal experience and also some of the ideas listed by Stier (1994):

- Annual ball
- Bob-a-job
- Car boot sale
- Car wash
- Car raffle
- Celebrity autograph and photo session
- Celebrity sports dinner
- Deed of covenant scheme
- Donkey derby
- Race night
- Publishing a cook book
- Bring and buy sale
- Sale of work
- Merchandising
- Jumble sale
- Life insurance policy naming your organization as a beneficiary
- Pro-celebrity golf tournament
- Selling badges and pins
- Selling raffle tickets
- Selling programmes
- Sponsored walk, run or swim

- Lottery or raffle
- Wine tasting evening
- Swim marathon
- Celebrity coaching clinic
- Sponsored sales table
- Personality appearances.

These have varying degrees of staff input and complexity. Regardless of how we set about the process or which particular projects we choose, one key issue is identified by Stier (1994): 'many fundraising projects involve selling'. It is important that we teach relevant staff and volunteers how to sell successfully. Stier suggests the following guidelines:

- Identify potential customers
- Approach them
- Explain the product
- Emphasize the benefits to the purchaser
- Explain the nature of the non-profit sponsoring organization
- Clarify how the money will benefit young people and Sports or recreation programmes
- Handle objections
- Thank the prospect whether or not a purchase was made
- Maintain accurate records
- Over-aggressive hard-sell tactics should be strongly discouraged.

These guidelines are very helpful, as we often leave people to fundraise or to sell items on our behalf without giving them any indication of the type of thing they should do or not do, say or not say to potential customers. This often reflects badly on the individual and the organization, as well as damaging future prospects for fundraising. As in all sports administration, professionalism in fundraising will result in more success and be more beneficial to the organization's reputation.

Tax Relief for Voluntary Sports Clubs

In his budget speech in March 2001, the Chancellor of the Exchequer announced that the government would review the taxation of non-profit-making amateur sports clubs, with a view to giving them 'further support' and recognizing their 'contribution to community life'. This news followed months of concerted behind-the-scenes lobbying by (among others) Sports England, the Central Council of Physical Recreation and the National Playing Fields Association. The review is expected to consider whether 'community amateur sports clubs' should be exempted from a range of taxes (including income tax and VAT) to (1) help cut their tax bills and (2) increase their ability to attract voluntary donations from members of the public. At the time of writing, Sports England is working with the CCPR, NPFA and DCMS to help determine which clubs should qualify for any such exemptions, and recommend how a reformed tax system could be policed.

Sports Sponsorship

> Sponsorship is the hardest part of all.
>
> —*Robin Knox-Johnson*

Many people would think that sailing round the world single-handed was pretty difficult. Knox-Johnson, who did just that, suggested that his search for sponsorship was harder than that! Perhaps that sets the real hard work required in context.

> Sports is struggling for support; without sponsorship Sports would wither.
>
> —*Peter Lawson (formerly CCPR)*

McCarville and Copeland (1994) examine exchange theory in relation to sports sponsorship. They suggest that: 'Partners exchange to enjoy benefits that cannot be attained in isolation'. Their idea is that people seeking partners should discover exactly what the potential partners are looking for and how the sponsorship seeker can satisfy these desires. They further suggest that 'new sponsorship initiatives are likely to be undertaken when placed in the context of past successes and present priorities'. They continue that events should be aimed to meet a number of objects, including the success of the sponsorship and that outcomes should be realistically in line with what all concerned are hoping for. Ultimately, happy sponsorships are built on cooperation and mutual dependence: Those involved in sponsorship should offer a variety of benefits to their exchange partners'. McCarville and Copeland's conclusion is that 'it is important that those who seek sponsorship partners first discover those resources most valued by their potential partners'.

Much of this may seem straightforward and something we all know already, but there has been limited investigation into sports sponsorship especially in relating it to academic theories such as exchange theory. The lessons may be learned by experience, but it is better to learn from others' words and experiences than from your own misdemeanours. Many people have made mistakes in the field of sports sponsorship, and, unfortunately, some continue till today.

> Value for money! You bet. There is no other promotional area on which we can get such a bang for the buck.
>
> —*Leo Mehl*

> The sponsorship of Sports provides a service to the whole of Sports and to the community which Sports serves: in this respect therefore it also serves the public interest.
>
> —*The Central Council of Physical Recreation Committee of Inquiry into Sports Sponsorship (the Howell Report), 1993*

For most sponsors, sponsorship is part of the marketing budget. Sports organizations should also be aware of companies and their own marketing practices and targets in seeking and delivering sponsorship. It should be a highly publicized and high-profile relationship where the correct public image—of harmony and joint effort—is portrayed. Sponsorship is a mutually beneficial arrangement fuelled by publicity. There are many examples of quality sponsorship arrangements in Sports—some of great longevity. The ones which work best are those in which the partners both work very hard to deliver their joint objectives—the more they put into the sponsorship, the more each can hope to get out of it.

CHAPTER 12

SPORTS EVENT MANAGEMENT

Event Management means any service provided in relation to planning, promotion, organising and presentation of any arts, entertainment, business, sports or any other event and includes any consultation provided in this regard. It is the application of the management practice of project management to the creation and development of festivals and events. Event Management involves studying the intricacies of the brand, identifying the target audience, devising the event concept, planning the logistics and coordinating the technical aspects before actually executing the modalities of the proposed event.

The recent growth of festivals and events as an industry around the world means that the management can no longer be ad hoc. Events and festivals, such as the Asian Games or the Dubai Shopping Festival, have a large impact on their communities and, in some cases, the whole country. The industry now includes events of all sizes from the Olympics down to a breakfast meeting for ten business people. Every industry, charity, society and group will hold events of some type/size in order to market themselves, raise money or celebrate.

Event Feasibility

A crucial part of any sports organization's management operation will be its organization and administration of the sporting events that are part of its sphere of operation. It is sometimes assumed that sports people, almost automatically, know how to organize events. However, any casual visitor to most sporting events would identify some potential changes that would benefit the event and consequently the Sports itself. A large part of the public image of Sports is sporting events and their organization. Much of what we see on television or read in the newspapers relates to the special events—the showcases of Sports. This may be a slightly artificial picture of what is actually happening in Sports, but it is the shop window, so when looking at major national or international events, it is essential to ensure that they give the correct and, hopefully, favourable image of Sports.

As mentioned above, there can be a worrying impression that people who come into Sports automatically have the skills, knowledge and background to organize events—this is not necessarily the case and very seldom is project organization the business background which people come from. Certainly there is often an element of organizational ability inherent in the games player, and an element of teamwork is expressed in many sporting activities, but many people come into sports and sports administration through the involvement of their children, and their own sporting exposure may be quite limited. Additionally, it is always worth remembering that sound organizational skills are given to few, let alone the enormous amount of knowledge and commitment that is also required to do a sports event organization job effectively.

Another major difficulty for sports bodies is that very often the individuals concerned are not actually trained in organizing events, even after they have begun to work in the area of sports administration. Given an interest and some ability, potential organizers should still be supported and helped through appropriate training and support at relevant stages in their work in this area. It is difficult enough for somebody to be plunged into an area where they may not have enough knowledge or experience, but it is verging on the negligent not to give them some proper training and help ensure that they can fulfil the tasks better, so lessening the pressure on them. This is particularly true in the area of events because of the time and task pressures that can build up on individuals as they move towards event competition or embark on major projects, especially for the first time.

Trends

The growing recognition of the importance of events has been identified in a number of ways. Many local authorities, and not just the large cities, have appointed events officers. Even some of the UK's smallest local authorities have identified events organization as at least a part of the job role of one of their employees. This has happened as local authority managers have begun to realize that events are a big part of the work they do and key to the operation of the sports industry, in its widest sense.

They have begun to understand more fully that events are a major part of all aspects of the sports business in relation to marketing, promotion and public awareness, as well as being universal across the aspects of their department. If a department is going to start a new service then it will be necessary to have an opening launch for the facility, a press conference to let people know what is happening, a seminar for local councillors, or an open day for potential public users. All of these are events which require planning and implementation, even where they are going to be aimed at establishing, prolonging or publicizing a well-used service which will remain on an ongoing basis. Events can be used to set up services, to test the market, to create customer awareness, and can fulfil a host of other strategic purposes. One major trend in the UK over the past 15 years has been the recognition and use of events by politicians and others looking to urban regeneration in areas previously considered to be deprived in some way.

This has especially been noted in the larger cities of the UK, all of which have set out their stalls to attract major events because of the economic impact of attracting visitors and, it is suggested, some potential long-term investment. It is noticeable that major cities such as Glasgow, Manchester, Birmingham and Sheffield were among the first to set up events departments, and now go round Europe and the wider world trying to attract sizeable sports events to their cities. The most notable such effort recently was Manchester's (disappointingly, failed) bid for the Olympic Games in the year 2000. One could argue that, in itself, the effort to bid for the Olympics has been of immense benefit to the city, and the publicity gained can only benefit the north-west in general, by attracting media interest and public awareness worldwide. In addition, Manchester was selected as the host city for the Commonwealth Games in the year 2002. Sheffield, in bidding for and hosting the World Student Games in 1991, stated quite clearly the following objectives for the Games.

1. They would play an integral part in the economic regeneration of the area.
2. They would heighten Sheffield's profile nationally and internationally.
3. They would identify Sheffield's potential as a major sporting venue.
4. They would encourage local participation in Sports and collaboration in the Games themselves.
5. They would promote the concept of a relocation to Sheffield for seminars, conferences, etc.
6. They would leave the city with a legacy of world-class facilities as it headed into the twenty-first century.

There was therefore a clear set of objectives, most targeted at economic development, urban regeneration and long-term legacies rather than the short-term benefits of participation in the Games. For any incoming event, such as a major international tournament, it is likely that there will be a major short-term economic benefit for tourism through participant spending in the locality. This indicates that events may be worthwhile in themselves, regardless of any long-term benefit. The hope is that some of the sports people will later return with families for a holiday, again bringing money into the area.

This recognition of the importance of events is a significant and relatively new trend; while they have been used as a focus for attention on occasions such as the Olympic Games in London shortly after the Second World War, the real, localized benefits of such significant spends before, during and after events have only recently begun to be truly realized. In addition, the identification of events' importance has meant that quality event implementation and provision has become a more essential issue, partly because there is such competition between major cities to act as potential venues for almost every major event or international seminar.

Events—what are they?

One of the definitions of 'event' in the *Shorter Oxford English Dictionary* is 'something that happens'. While this is very wide, it has to be all embracing to allow for the innate universality referred to above. Events can range from a local competition to a ten-day international championship featuring teams from all parts of the world. Goldblatt (1990) notes that 'a special event recognises a unique moment in time with ceremony and ritual to satisfy specific needs'. The definition can be flexible to suit different situations, but exactly what is meant in terms of a special events department, or an events officer, or an organizing group must be defined before starting work on specific events. Events are important, and need to be planned and delivered with care and attention to detail.

The Purpose of the Event

Consideration of recent trends has identified quite clearly that the major cities, among others, have been able to identify specific purposes for holding events. This is the crucial point to all good events—having a genuine reason to hold them. Even a fairly small event will require a significant commitment by staff or volunteers. This is not going to happen for an event which is not seen as genuinely worthwhile, beneficial and serving some useful purpose within a wider scale of operation. According to Goldblatt (1990), 'there must be a clear purpose which is clearly understood by all participants'. This aim may be quite general and long-term, but it should be public and widely supported, for example:

- To encourage the identification of…as a venue for events in the sports field
- To encourage visitors to come to…
- To boost the participation levels of the local population in…

All these, and many others may be worthwhile aims in setting up sports events. The key point is that there must be a clearly stated aim, otherwise the event should not happen. Events demand a lot of concentrated effort and commitment. This commitment can only come out of a genuine belief, in all the participants, that they are worthwhile and they will be beneficial in the long term.

Event Objectives

As well as an overall purpose, any event must have its own set of objectives. They will number around three to five; they must be clear and be set down in a way which will allow us to judge the success of our event after completion. Objectives must be:

- Specific
- Measurable
- Agreed
- Understood
- Clear
- Achievable
- Realistic
- Simple
- Unambiguous
- Timed.

If we check this list, we will have objectives against which we can measure our event when everything is finished. This will be important to keep us working in a constructive planned manner, for effective evaluation after the event, and for better targeted events in the future. Examples of event objectives might include:

- To increase the numbers playing volleyball locally by 10 per cent in the next year
- To raise the venue's public profile through ten pieces of media coverage—one TV, three radio and six local newspapers
- To involve 100 local sports people as volunteer helpers.

Fundamentals

Basically, events need to be organized in exactly the same way as any other project in any business or industrial field. The same thought processes, planning and meticulous attention to detail are required to produce successful events as are evident in good project management in other commercial fields. Often, because of the voluntary nature of Sports, some of these principles are ignored, but when the suggestion of re-examining them is made most people are very positive and appreciate that extra thinking and planning are worthwhile in this demanding area. The key rule is that relevant principles, policies, practices and procedures should be identified, laid down and followed so there is no doubt about what course of action is to be followed. We must identify what has to be done to get the event achieved successfully, and then allocate roles and tasks to those who are going to do it properly.

The Basic Questions

Like so many other business (and life) activities, it is essential to approach the planning by asking some fundamental questions about what has to be done, why and how. The feasibility questions in sports event organization would begin with simple ones, moving on to the more complex ones which may only be applicable to the more complex events.

The questions to be asked include the following:

Why?: This is the fundamental issue when one is looking at events in sports or any other leisure area. If there is not a clear purpose and a set of parallel objectives, there should be no event. In particular, there should be a reluctance to hold any event just because it was held last year or because it is part of our annual calendar—this is not sufficient reason to hold a sporting event and takes up the organizers' much-valued time, which could perhaps be better spent. Events are a very important part of Sports, however, and if they are well thought through can be a major bonus—a development incentive to performers and, indeed, to sports organizations themselves, nationally or locally.

The potential impact for Malaysia or Manchester of holding the Commonwealth Games or any city going for the Olympic Games is enormous. As well as serving major national and economic purposes, such a major event will benefit Sports in the city, region and, indeed, country if successful. On a lower level, the running of a local tournament for badminton clubs or an inter-district championship for gymnastics may well be a major improvement in the competitive and development cycle for the Sports itself, helping give a focus and incentive to everyone involved.

Significant events give training targets and development milestones for individuals and organizations to develop to their own level of potential within a given Sports. Events are fundamental to Sports, but only beneficial if they are the right events for the right purpose and delivered in the right manner.

What?: Having decided that there is a purpose for an event, the next decision is what form exactly the event should take; should it be a championship, tournament, knock-out or festival type of event? Is it targeted at the appropriate age group and does it meet the purpose outlined? The precise details of the event should be specified and then followed through. Having the wrong type of event can be as bad as having an event with no purpose.

Where?: It is essential to ask whether the necessary facilities are present to host the chosen event. The obvious example here is that of Manchester, which had to provide, with government support, a velodrome and build other venues to improve its sporting facilities significantly in order to be taken seriously as a bidder for the Olympic or the Commonwealth Games. It is quite normal in the UK for people to want to hold events even though there are inadequate facilities, just to show that the UK can host major events. Realistically, until recently, there were very poor sports facilities and, even now, we lag considerably behind many other countries throughout the world. The notion of the UK—even London—hosting the Olympics seems fanciful, not just because of facilities but because of the lack of transport infrastructure.

It is essential also to ensure that all the facilities required to stage any event including ancillary rooms, medical facilities, training facilities, etc., are available. The requirements for many events are now enormous: for example, to hold the world gymnastics championships requires up to six adjacent training halls as well as a significant competition venue. Precise specification of facility needs must be clarified at early planning stages to ensure that these needs can be met.

When?: The timing of an event can be crucial, and is determined by many factors. The local, national and international sporting calendar will be a major factor in determining the timing, as will the availability of facilities and the general sporting calendar in the UK, if significant interest is to be generated and event clashes are to be avoided. For a large-scale event, perhaps the most important question is when it will fit in to the television or media programme, and close consultation must take place to see if dates are suitable for TV coverage if that is a major purpose of the event and will be key to attracting a sponsor. Indeed, this is where the organizers should start for any major event—with the broadcasting companies and their schedules.

Who for?: This is another fundamental question, because if no one is interested in participating in an event, is it worth trying to organize it? There may be a place for organizing an event to attract money into the Sports, or increased publicity, but generally speaking there has got to be some market of involvement that is satisfied, otherwise the effort will not be worthwhile and the event itself will be poorly attended. There can also be a tendency to organize events for the wrong people (in other words, the organizers rather than the participants) or to do it to keep a group of politicians happy though it is not the most appropriate development for the Sports at a specific time. To be worthwhile a sporting event needs a group of participating customers.

Who by?: This can be problematic in that an event can only be staged if there is a group of available and able organizers for it. Organizing events is demanding and needs some special characteristics in organizers, whether paid or voluntary. There is always a danger of a governing body of Sports, for example, offering to host an event when it does not truly have the necessary expertise or personnel available. It should never be assumed that because a group of people can organize the district or national championships they will automatically be able to organize the European or Commonwealth championships. It certainly will be possible to buy in event agencies' expertise or advice, but this can be expensive and certainly would have to be part of any initial budgeting exercise. If there is no one able to do the event, don't try.

Who Watches?: It is a common assumption among people involved in Sports that if they organize an event then lots of people will rush out to watch it—this is certainly not true. Apart from the major manifestations of Sports, such as the Six Nations Rugby Championship or the Premiership football matches, the numbers of people attending is not large. In fact, the number of people watching most sporting events would go a very small way towards meeting the cost of the event—this is even true of rugby or football in most cases, throughout the UK. Furthermore, because sports administrators are desperately interested in (to the point of being fanatical about) their activity, there is a natural tendency for them to find it much more interesting than almost anyone else. Because they have this interest and would be willing to pay to watch, they assume that others will; very often this is not the case.

Spectators usually only turn out at the very top, or the very bottom, of Sports since only supreme expertise or being a total novice tends to attract the interest of the non-expert or, particularly for the novice, all the family. As you develop up the excellence tree you will gradually find that fewer and fewer people will in fact come to watch you until you reach the very top in your chosen Sports, and even there only in a certain number of chosen sports. Added to this, certain sports, e.g. archery and shooting, by their very nature are not spectator events. The lack of people watching is not necessarily a major concern for the sports event as long as it is not relied upon to produce money to make the event viable, or assumed to attract sponsors on the basis of unrealistic spectator figures.

What will it Cost?: This is a fundamental issue which is sometimes not examined carefully enough. It is absolutely paramount that all the potential costs are identified and that potential sources of income are clearly matched against them. Failure to produce a detailed budget in advance is a recipe for worry and potential disaster. It is crucially important to be pessimistic about income and realistic about expenditure.

Who Leads?: Is there an individual or group who can lead the organization in the direction of achieving this significant commitment to organizing the event, carrying out the planning or implementing the event? The type of leadership required to build an effective team, which can work under the extraordinary pressure that it may be subjected to during an event, is not easy to find and should not be assumed, even in the natural environment of leadership which is Sports.

Who Pays?: The funding for sports events is often difficult, especially with larger events where it can be extremely difficult to find the necessary finance to make them viable. It is very important that, before embarking on any major project, a detailed budgeting exercise is carried out so that all the costs can be established accurately and precise methods identified as to how these costs will be met. Many events have come to grief in the past because realistic budgeting has not been undertaken in advance. It is common, for example, to assume that sponsorship can be found when this can be extremely difficult, and can end up being impossible. The nature of many sports events does not necessarily make them attractive to sponsors, and relying on such income can be a home-made recipe for disaster. There are people who may well support the event, such as local authorities, voluntary groups and other interests but the key step is that these potential sources of funding are identified clearly in advance. All these questions, then, need a positive and detailed answer before we embark on trying to set up what may be a significant commitment in time, money, staff time and resources. Sports resources tend to be limited—events may not be the best use for them.

EVENT PLANNING

Events are important to Sports, and they need a professional and thorough approach to planning. Earlier, we gave a somewhat simplistic view of events when defining them as something that happens. This is not all bad, but it suggests that they happen by themselves—nothing could be further from the truth. People will be required to make them happen. Additionally, perhaps, the crucial difference between what one might call 'routine' events and 'special' events is that the latter must always be planned or they will not end up being 'special'. This planning will fall into a variety of stages: it must be stressed that, regardless of the size of event, each of these stages must be gone through. Obviously, depending on the size of the event, the length of each planning stage will vary.

Event Planning Stages

1. Determine aims and objectives
2. Formulate policy
3. Carry out a feasibility study
4. Make decision to go ahead
5. Compile budget
6. Identify personnel
7. Identify resources
8. Identify event requirements
9. Identify tasks
10. Define structure
11. Communicate structure

12. Detail plan and time-scale
13. Establish control systems
14. Plan event—presentation, preparation, implementation and recovery
15. Finalize accounts
16. Hold debriefing
17. Compile and circulate final evaluation report.

Event Requirements

Having identified the overall planning progressions, it is necessary to be more specific and identify the precise process by detailing all the requirements for the event. This can be a time-consuming procedure, but should involve a number of people who can think in the widest possible way in an attempt to consider all the possible items which will be required to execute a successful event. This list, which can never be all-encompassing, is necessary to allow detailed planning and implementation to go ahead. The aim here is to identify every single heading that needs to be covered and, within it, every single item that will be required to produce an efficient, effective event of a quality appropriate to its level. This means going through a very precise thought process for every event, no matter how large or small, endeavouring to ensure that nothing is omitted which may ultimately be required. Having gone through this process, you will end up with a significant list of items that need to be considered and must then be double-checked against other events and/or by other people to ensure that nothing is omitted. Having identified the specific requirements for your run, you will have to:

- Analyse costs
- Identify necessary personnel
- Specify the timetable
- Construct the plan
- Implement the plan.

Implementation Plan

With the identification of requirements and the compilation of a time-scale to go alongside them, we are now in the business of producing a detailed implementation plan to get everything up and running. This will be our implementation plan, which, depending on the level of event, may be simple (one sheet of instructions to staff and volunteers) or, for a major international event, be extremely complex (many handbooks to VIP hosts, stewards, catering staff, etc). The possibilities are endless and, for an event like the Olympics, so too is the planning and the paperwork. For most events, however, it will be a fairly routine document, which may just be a checklist which shows who does what by when, etc.

Structure

This implementation plan can only be made to work within an appropriate structure for the event. This again may be very simple and straightforward, coming through an existing staff structure or voluntary committee. It could, however, be very complicated and be developed over a period of time for a major event. It will need to allow for individuals to work their best to get things done, while ensuring that everyone knows their role and how they relate to others within the structure.

Event Requirement	*Detail*	*Timescale*	*Undertaken by*
Bookvenue	Confirm suitability Fixdate	18 months ahead	Venue manager
Arrange main speaker	Sufficient standing in professionPencil in alternatives	12 months ahead	Conference director
Arrange venue layout	Space for working groupsas well as listening	3 months ahead	Venue manager
Confirm catering arrangement	Finalconfirmation after delegate numbers	1 month ahead	Catering manager

Fig: A simple implementation plan checklist

People

Probably the key factor in achieving successful events is getting the right people in the right positions to get things to happen in the best possible way. As every sports organizer is aware, the necessary commitment is considerable and cannot be limited to 9a.m. to 5p.m. The demands on personnel, whether paid or not, will be extraordinary and they must be willing to face up to these challenges. This is the type of person that events require—someone who is committed, who is willing to work very hard and who doesn't panic if anything goes wrong.

It is also important that everyone involved is fully aware of the objectives of the event and is clear about their role within the event achievement plan. Alternative event structures sure of their role and has a written job remit (or specification), clearly showing:

- Whom they are responsible to
- Whom they are responsible for
- What specific tasks they have to achieve.

It is to be emphasized that every individual involved in the event has this clearly specified job remit, regardless of their level. The job remit should not be dictated but should evolve in discussion with the individuals involved and then, when agreed, be made widely known, so that there is no doubt as to who undertakes what particular duties. This clear demarcation avoids confusion and staff conflict and gets things done. It is the best way forward for everyone involved. The personnel who will be the 'key performers' in event implementation must be clearly identified and it is important that there is a support system for them, giving training as well as rewards, in whatever way appropriate, to ensure that they are aware of all procedures and are well motivated (it's great what people in Sports will do for a T-shirt!). For example, 'front-of-house' personnel are the ones who will meet all the event participants, VIPs, officials and spectators and give the whole project its atmosphere. They must be trained in a way which will equip them to handle all the varied groups of customers properly during the event. It is wise to remember that money is not a major motivator for people involved in events; indeed, in many cases, money will not be available and the effort of many key personnel will be voluntary and amateur.

This means that they cannot be tied by definitive contracts and payments. A special effort must be made, then, to get cohesion and commitment, through good staff management and building on the interest that the volunteers have already shown. During any event tremendous demands will be put on volunteers and other staff in many situations. To be fair to them, there must always be a clear indication of what they are required to do and they should be consulted and involved on every possible occasion, to ensure that they always feel part of the event and its organizing team.

Funding

For many events finding the funding is the crucial item and the one which requires most work; it causes most headaches and worries leading up to any decisions to proceed with an event. Given the correct event, the correct aim, with the correct objectives, funding can be found. It must be a package and not an afterthought; there must be a clear mission and purpose to the whole operation from the start. Many agencies can have a significant interest in supporting events to ensure they happen successfully in a given location. The more obvious are local authorities and local tourist boards, but there are others, for example:

- Local enterprise agencies
- Tourist associations
- Hoteliers
- Local chambers of commerce
- National agencies, e.g. Arts Council, sports councils
- Major local employers.

Remember, sports events can have a significant effect on the local economy by promoting 'sports tourism'.

Sponsorship

There is a belief that sponsorship will easily be made available for events; sadly, this is not the case and only if it is handled in a professional and appropriate way will sponsorship be found in most cases; it will seldom be 'easy'. Many sponsorships are still found through personal contact and this should be exploited to the full, though obviously it cannot be relied on. Thereafter, preparing the necessary documentation for presentation to a sponsor, with follow-up phone calls, can sometimes produce sizeable amounts of money to support worthwhile projects. This must be targeted at sponsors that are generally likely to be interested in the particular project concerned. For example, a baby food manufacturer may be interested in crèche provision or the extension of an activity programme to cater for young children. This targeting is important as, ultimately, commercial firms will want to see some return for their investment—sponsorship is a business arrangement, not a charitable donation.

Perhaps the most crucial step in the area of sponsorship for events is to involve the potential sponsor from the very early days when the initial concept is suggested, and not to present them with a completed fixed package. There is little point in taking a totally inflexible finished package to a sponsor and saying 'take it or leave it'. If they are expected to put money into a project, then they are certainly entitled to make some comment on the construction and the detailed format. Throughout the event, successful sponsorship will be a partnership and this process, started at the conception, should continue in every aspect. This will produce the best benefit for everyone concerned in terms of a successful event for the organizers, and a good return on sponsorship investment for the sponsoring agency.

The next key is to establish exactly what each partner wishes to gain from the project, and how this can be done together. There may be occasions after initial discussion with the sponsor when it proves impossible to reconcile the partners' desires. This is the time for the relationship to stop, rather than trying to stumble through further problems that will inevitably arise with a lack of total commitment on both parts. Consistently throughout the projects, sponsors and organizers need to work closely together and to keep each other informed, especially of any problems that arise—there must be a full and close communication at all times. Ultimately, if we can deliver an event which becomes identified with the sponsor then we are beginning to get places. There are many famous examples of this in nationally covered events, e.g. the BBC's sponsorship of the Promenade Concerts, the Royal Bank of Scotland's sponsorship of rugby, Embassy's sponsorship of the World Darts Championship: the list is endless. Product identification and public awareness are the primary aims of most sponsors and, if the organizers wish to keep their support, these must become event objectives.

Characteristics of the Best Events

Good events have most, if not all, of the following:

- Definite purpose
- Market research
- Customer care
- Feasibility study
- Committed personnel
- Clear objectives
- Co-ordinated effort
- Quality leadership
- Appropriate structures
- Business planning
- Good communications
- Resources committed
- Appropriate management
- Political support
- Flexible systems
- Public support
- Accurate budgeting
- Financial control
- Detailed evaluation.

How, then, do we do it?

1. Have an aim and a set of specific objectives.
2. Examine all the event questions and issues.
3. Identify all the right requirements.
4. Recruit the personnel and take all the necessary steps to get these items carried out.

You need to obtain the appropriate:

- Funding
- People
- Structure
- Systems.

Event Evaluation

Many events struggle through lack of learning from previous mistakes due to insufficient evaluation, monitoring and feedback from past events. Event evaluation should be marked by the following characteristics.

- *Compulsory:* It should be done for every event, large or small.
- *Concise:* Should not be any longer than it needs to be.
- *Concurrent:* It should go on during the event as well as after it.
- *Constant:* How we are going to evaluate success (or explain failure!) should be a consideration throughout the event and even in the earlier planning stages.
- *Customized:* Even though we may have a specific checklist for evaluation, each event should have an additional set of criteria because the objectives were probably different from others in the past.
- *Consultation:* Evaluation involves seeking the opinions of as many relevant groups as possible: participants, officials, VIPs, sponsors, etc.
- *Canvass:* It is necessary to canvass opinion and not just wait for it.
- *Circulation:* It is necessary to circulate opinions gathered and also to circulate the debriefing document as widely as possible to help everyone involved build for the future.

- *Customers:* Whatever the nature of the customers for the event, they must all be asked for an evaluation through, for example, an exit survey, or questionnaires placed on seats.
- *Colleagues:* All staff, paid or voluntary, should be involved in the evaluation process for their part within the event.
- *Collected:* Care should be taken to collect confidentially appropriate information.
- *Catalogued:* It should be recorded in an appropriate way and filed for future reference, with due regard to the Data Protection Act.
- *Complete:* It should cover all aspects of the event from early arrival to departure.
- *Communicated:* It should be communicated to relevant parties during the debrief process and at the end of the debrief process.
- *Copied:* Successful evaluation methods should be reused in order to emulate their success in the future.

Event Management: Key Considerations

Remember, before embarking on an event it is going to be necessary to examine a number of key issues which will clarify whether the event is actually possible. This is best done by asking a series of questions. Some of these questions are as follows.

- Why do we need to hold an event in the first place?
- Is it the best way to achieve what we want to achieve?
- What will be the exact form of the event we are going to stage?

Is there a range of options, and, if so, which one will we choose?

- When is our event going to be held?
- Have we checked with all relevant people?
- Have we checked with television companies or the national arts calendar for the performers' agents?
- Where will our event be held?
- Do we really have suitable facilities for it?
- Would it be better being held in a more suitable facility that we can provide?

- Do we have everything that is required in the facility we intend to use?
- How can it be achieved?
- Is it possible for the mechanisms to be set up which will enable the event to be successfully completed?
- What will be the cost of running this event?
- Where will any monies come from?
- Who will organize?
- Who will attend?
- Who will watch?
- Who will participate?
- Who will pay?
- Will the media be interested?
- Will a sponsor be interested?
- Will the politicians (or superiors) like the event?
- Are there lots of events like this?
- Where do we go from here?
- How do we get started if we go ahead?

Event Preparation

We all turn up at large events and take the preparations for granted. For example, at the much publicized World Snooker Championships, the preparations start early. The World Championship was first staged at Sheffield's famous Crucible Theatre in 1977; the venue is now as famous for snooker as Wembley is for football, Wimbledon for tennis and Lord's for cricket. Six days before the championships start, the World Snooker Association moves into the theatre to prepare for the event. The theatre floor is lowered by three feet to install the set and a series of 16 jacks is installed under two tables which each weigh one and a half tonnes. The stage is carpeted, and the snooker arena is installed complete with press seating, boxes for the BBC commentator and photo-graphers and TV cameras. Meanwhile, behind the scenes, the rehearsal room is converted into the press room and the band room is transformed into an interview area.

CHAPTER 13

Management and Administration Oriented Education and Training

Apart from very specific organized coach training, there has been, until recent years, little significant input to the training of people who wanted to work in Sports as organizers and administrators. Thankfully, recent initiatives have seen a significant turnaround in this area, and the signs are that many more people working in Sports, including the voluntary sector, will be trained in the skills of sports administration.

The driving force for this movement towards better administrative and management training is difficult to identify precisely, but it relates to a movement in political thinking, the incorporation of colleges of further education, and a combination of sports' circumstances and the requirement for administrative professionalism, led by the professionalism of Sports itself. All of these factors are combining to produce a growth in courses and qualifications in Sports, recreation and related subjects which will prove to be of significant benefit to the management and administration of Sports. This has moved the profession from the days when all the managers came from the ranks of physical education teachers. A discrete new profession has developed, and a PE teacher would find it hard to break into the paid side of management and administration.

The arrival of vocational qualifications (now with a specific qualification in sports administration) has had an impact, but much less than the government had hoped for, although their influences on existing courses and training practices has been considerable. Vocational qualifications have been beset by many implementation problems, but the impact across the whole field of Sports and recreation has grown. When the issues of awareness and implementation are resolved, the proliferation of such competence-based qualifications will be helpful in all aspects of Sports. In particular, the assessment of ability to perform at present being able to lead to a qualification will be very appropriate for a number of Sports settings, where people have done the work before but have not been fully recognized for it, and often without possessing any specific qualifications.

The impact of training, qualification and recognition must be helpful to the individual, the organization and the whole industrial attitude towards sports management and administration. Hopefully, this combination of commitment and qualification will have a beneficial effect in producing improved organization for the sports participant, and regard from the sports participant for the sports organizer.

Coaching Awards

The UK has a long history of the training and certification of coaches. Most governing bodies of Sports have undertaken this role, with varying degrees of enthusiasm and commitment. There is a need to ensure the continual flow of suitable individuals to help produce their sports' performers for the future, as well as the need to introduce new participants to the benefit and joys of their particular Sports. There has also been a financial implication—charging people for courses and certification has been a significant income earner—while there has also been the concern (most importantly) to ensure that correct and safe techniques to educate participants and performers are followed, so ensuring correct and safe performance.

An element of coach education has been missing, in that many coaches have to take on administrative roles within Sports, in the voluntary sector in particular, but very often there has been no recognition of this in their training. In terms of club, district, regional and even national associations, coaches are expected to perform a number of important administrative tasks. This is inevitable and necessary, because Sports requires a degree of technical input to guide the direction of thinking of sports organization in administrative terms as well as in sports participation and performance terms. Such administrative requirements have, however, left coaches over-stretched, and to some extent individuals who have much to offer in the non-technical administrative areas have been underestimated and under-used by sports organizations.

While extensive coach education schemes have existed, there has been very little significant input from governing bodies to developing these coaches or any other volunteers into administrative or organizational skill enhancement. This has led to a great deal of coach wastage due to the pressure and stress of the issues surrounding the day-to-day coaching, and a feeling that the coach has to do everything while not necessarily being trained to perform organizational roles, or losing motivation since they are acting in areas in which they feel they have no special skills or knowledge. Someone who comes into Sports to work with a team or group of individuals to enhance their performance will not necessarily be highly motivated to spend a lot of time and pay attention to detail in delivering organizational and administrative roles with a sports body.

It is to be hoped that current developments in sports administration training can rub off onto coaches and give them some of the added skills they require, while not detracting from the quality of coach education and development directed specifically at the coaching tasks they have to perform. In this area, the impact of vocational qualifications is and will continue to be significant. Hopefully it will lead to higher and more equitable standards of coach education throughout Sports in the UK. It is to be hoped that a significant number of coaches will feel it appropriate to obtain vocational qualifications in coaching, and indeed will see it as relevant to encourage others to look for vocational qualifications in sports administration. Such an assessment of operational roles and the work to be done will be of significant benefit to Sports, and the whole process of working to national standards and competence assessment will benefit everyone concerned, making them think and become more aware of the needs and the necessities of the professional operation of Sports as a business.

It is also hoped that coaches will be able to spend less time on the administration side of Sports so they will be able to become more focused, while others take the pressure from them for organizing events and other duties. It is important to see that the administrator's job is in many ways to back up the coach, to support them rather than have conflict with them or endanger the coaching process. They are in fact enabling an effective coaching process in many cases. At no time should the strengthening of sports management and administration be seen as a threat rather than an assistance to coaches. It has been suggested that until recently many sports coaches probably needed administrative as well as technical training, because for many of them the administration is a sizeable part of their work, along with promotion and development. It often seems that the more organizational demands are put on sports coaches, the less coaching they do.

Education Versus Training

There is some debate about the difference and relationship between education and training, though few doubt the necessity for both. The actual differences can vary depending on the specific situation, but the most commonly perceived difference is that education is about the process, while training is about the product—the ability to perform is often seen as the end-product in terms of training, while knowledge can be seen as something accumulated through a learning process in education. Such differences should not be seen as derogatory comments on either side of the argument or as implying that one is better or more necessary than the other. It is essential that both occur in the area of sports management and administration because both have a part to play in guiding a professional approach to the industry and practice within in it.

The profession of sports management needs people who have come from a practical background with additional training, as well as those who could be perceived as academics who have come from an educational background. In many situations the difference may be seen as more to do with attitudes than with specific skill-based training—most industrial settings, and Sports and recreation is no different, would prefer an open-minded wider-thinking person whatever their background, so this is perceived to be one of the benefits of a more academic education.

Fundamentally it is much more important for people to have the enthusiasm and empathy for Sports and its participants than any written qualification, but it is important that they have the ability to think widely enough to consider everything that may impinge on the operation of Sports in their country as well as their specific situation in a club or national body. The width of education, perhaps from a degree or some other general management qualification, may well be effective for someone in sports administration if it is coupled with commitment and enthusiasm for the activity of Sports—the characteristic that distinguishes it from other management situations. Interpersonal skills and interest in Sports are, however, more important than any qualification or educational background.

The need for training is relevant regardless of whether a person already possesses a qualification, a degree or even a postgraduate award. Training can provide specific skills, knowledge and expertise that will not come from degree-level courses and will be essential for sports managers in the work situation. For example, a degree in sports management is never going to train one precisely how to handle volunteers in some of the situations that can arise in the day-to-day sports arena. Specific consideration has to be given to the practicalities that face people working in Sports and how they are going to cope with them—this is normally best achieved through a progressive and well-established training programme.

The training itself should be designed to allow the individual, group or team to better face up to the challenges around them at present and prepare them to face the future. It is vital that training is started by assessing the needs of everyone concerned both in a personal and an organizational way, then building on these identified needs and desires to produce an effective training programme which is self-managed by each individual as well as overseen by an appropriate supervisor or organizational leader. It is crucial that training is seen as an ongoing process which does not just relate to individual skills or short-term development through one-off courses, but rather is a full development process which leads to an effective organization through producing highly skilled and well motivated individuals.

An effective organization will come through individuals feeling that their personal development is valued and seen as crucial to the organization and the working of the staff team, including themselves. The staff must be seen as individuals worthy of education, training and development for their own benefit as well as that of the organization. Ultimately an organization is a set of individuals, and the development of their personal needs and skills will lead to an improved operational system.

It is often said, with some justification, that the UK has fallen down in industrial competitiveness due to its lack of attention to education and training. If this is true in industry then it must be especially true in sports management and administration, because training for full-time, part-time and voluntary personnel has, until recently, been limited to the point of being almost non-existent. Over the past few years, the UK sports councils have been actively developing a volunteer development programme called 'Running Sport', aimed at training volunteers who have been attracted into Sports and giving them a better idea of how to operate and perform the many roles they are required to meet within Sports in the UK. The existence of these courses reflects the importance of the volunteer and the need to support their actions rather than leave them feeling unwanted and unrewarded.

This programme is still relatively new, but it is an important initiative which should be a significant help to the operation of the voluntary sector in particular. This is a massive area in terms of Sports in the UK—between 1.5 and 2 million people according to 1995 figures. Too often in the past the training of these individuals has been ignored. Hopefully through courses such as Running Sports and related initiatives such as the Barclaycard Volunteer Investment Programme, the standard of support for these hard-working individuals will increase, so enhancing their skills and ultimately benefiting everyone involved in Sports. Training must not be seen as solely for leaders but is required for everyone involved in sports administration, even if they are working for only a few hours a week. It is certainly absolutely vital for the full-time sports administrator. For them it should really be compulsory and, however achieved, should be provided as a matter of routine operational practice.

Sports Management Education

US research by Masteralexis and McDonald (1997) has produced some significant recommendations on sports management education and suggested some key points: 'sports management educators must recognize that the opportunity exists for an international dimension to be included in sports management education'. The authors also quote Kelley *et al.* (1994) as noting the need for bold, assertive sports management programmes to go beyond departmental boundaries to enlist expertise of academics in other departments to create inter-disciplinary programmes. Sports management programmes could take this advice and encourage students to take language and cultural courses in liberal arts and international management in business schools to create international sports concentration.

Masteralexis and McDonald also note that in the USA the survey results indicate that there is interest from practitioners in enrolling in executive education programmes focusing on international issues in sports management. They further state that 'the international frontier will create challenges for sports managers; sports management programmes ought to be able to respond to the needs of these practitioners with training sessions specifically tailored to address the needs of individual sports managers'.

Such issues and research exist largely in North America, but as programmes develop in the UK and other parts of Western Europe there will be a need to take these issues on board, particularly in relation to the ever-expanding European sphere of management operation. Sports must react to the European dimension and the international opportunities in the more globalized world, just as any other industry has to.

Academic Qualifications

It is quite surprising, considering the relative size of the sports administration field, that relatively few academic courses are offered to provide for the needs of this occupation. There tends to be an assumption that administration is generic and that people with these skills and an interest in Sports are the suitable people to work in Sports. This is an interesting and ongoing discussion point.

Most people involved in Sports, whether they be coaches or development officers, need administrative and management skills to varying degrees—some to a very high degree—and it is surprising that Stirling University is one of the few that have put the two subjects together to any significant extent. There is some development at postgraduate level for those already practising, but at higher national or undergraduate level there is a slowly growing provision. This is a very interesting European situation when one looks across to North America, where courses in sports management are many and varied. There is obviously a gap in the market which will be filled as demand grows through increased expenditure, particularly from the lottery and the private sector, producing a need for more and more professional people with a knowledge of Sports, allied to high level management and administration techniques.

In the past decade, both higher and further education establishments in the UK have seen a massive increase in the number of people studying Sports. Particularly popular have been practical courses on sports coaching and sports science, but the study of sports management is growing as well (albeit more slowly). It is now possible to study sports organization in late secondary school right through areas such as sports development, to advanced strategic management at masters and postgraduate level. The numbers involved now are growing, and while relatively few may find jobs in Sports, their education and interest should benefit everyone in Sports.

Professional Institutes

The professional institutes in the Sports and leisure areas—particularly ILAM and ISRM—provide a variety of education and training opportunities, ranging from one-day specific skill sessions through to one- or two-year distance learning diplomas. They are all run under the banner of continuing professional development and/or professional qualification schemes. This work has proved immensely useful to, and popular with, the practising professional.

SPRITO

The most important and exciting development in the field of education and training in Sports in recent years in the UK has been the arrival of SPRITO—the National Training Organization for Sports, Recreation and Allied Industries. SPRITO is fundamentally about representing the views of industry on relevant education and training matters to government and other decision-makers so that the correct provision for practising industrialists at all levels is the underlying principle of policy-making. Having suitably influenced policy-making, SPRITO is now taking the lead in delivering appropriate mechanisms for overseeing, quality monitoring, and in some cases provision, of education and training opportunities for those working in the Sports and recreation profession throughout the UK. The organization is made up of a range of relevant industrial bodies: the professional institutes, the UK and national sports councils, the private sector (including the fitness industry and outdoor education), Sports Coach UK, the British Institute of Sports Administrators, the Institute of Groundsmanship and a range of other relevant bodies.

The purpose is to act as a genuine voice for people working in the Sports and recreation business. The importance of training has to be advocated, both within the industry and outside, and this role is also taken on actively by SPRITO, especially in terms of training support and resources internally and externally. It also encourages players in the business to join SPRITO, which is in essence a membership organization. Examples of the type of work in which SPRITO has become involved include:

- Investors in people in the Sports and recreation industry
- National traineeships
- Modern apprenticeships
- Graduate recruitment survey
- Review of vocational standards.

Occupational Standards and Vocational Qualifications

One of the major developments in training in all industries in recent years has been the development of occupational standards leading to vocational qualifications in a range of industrial sectors. Sports and recreation, previously through the industry lead body and now through SPRITO, has developed, is reviewing and will continue to develop appropriate occupational standards on behalf of the Sports and recreation profession. These standards should be seen as measures of competence at various levels for people working in the Sports and recreation industry. Over a considerable period of time a number of industrialists operating in various areas have produced occupational standards leading to vocational qualifications in a wide range of areas—sports coaching, sports development, facilities operation, spectator control, outdoor education, playwork, supervision and sports administration.

These vocational qualifications are offered at a variety of levels, starting at Level 1 for an introductory qualification, up to Level 5 for a course that could be judged to be around the standard of competence required to do a postgraduate qualification. In terms of sports administration, a large number of areas have been identified as units of competence for a sports administrator to gain a vocational qualification, as follows:

- Prepare a programme of activities
- Co-ordinate a programme of activities
- Contribute to the planning, monitoring and control of resources
- Maintain financial systems for an organization
- Contribute to the health and safety of others
- Provide information and advice for action towards organizational objectives
- Promote and evaluate services to maximize participation
- Contribute to the planning, organization, and evaluation of work
- Maintain services and operations to meet quality standards
- Contribute to the provision of personnel
- Contribute to the training and development of teams,individuals and self to enhance performance
- Establish and maintain relationships with organizations and individuals

- Create, maintain and enhance productive working relationships
- Service meetings
- Assist in regulating Sports
- Contribute to frameworks for participation and progression in Sports.
- Provide sports-related planning and co-ordination for a major sports event
- Recommend, monitor and control these resources
- Seek, evaluate and organize information for action
- Exchange information to solve problems and make decisions
- Promote and evaluate services to maximize participation
- Contribute to the implementation of change to services and systems
- Maintain and improve service operation
- Contribute to the recruitment and selection of personnel
- Develop teams, individuals and self to enhance performance
- Plan, allocate and evaluate work carried out by teams, individuals and self
- Create, maintain and enhance effective working relationships
- Enable committees to make decisions to further organizational aims
- Contribute to the formalization of policy
- Contribute to the implementation of policy
- Contribute to the regulation of Sports
- Develop a framework for participation and progression in Sports.

With each of these units containing an average of four elements, and each element in turn having around four performance criteria, these standards are extremely demanding and indicate the vast range of work that sports adninistrators undertake. Partly because they are so demanding, the uptake for this particular vocational qualification has been less than might have been anticipated judging by the number of people operating in the area.

Running Sports

The Running Sports programme is designed to improve the knowledge and skills of everybody working in Sports, both voluntary and professional. It is targeted at sports administrators at all levels, ranging from the local club treasurer to the chief executive of a large governing body. Many of the resource materials will also be appropriate for coaches, match officials and sports development officers. The Running Sports programme:

- Was originally a GB Sports Council initiative developed in partnership with the British Institute of Sports Administration, the British Olympic Association, the National Coaching Foundation, the National Sports Development Centres, the Sports Council for Wales, the Sports Council for Northern Ireland, the Scottish Sports Council and the respective sports associations
- Provides a series of publications, courses and workshops covering a range of sports-related management skills
- Is led by accredited, trained tutors who have been selected because of their strong sports administration background knowledge and their learning facilitation skills
- Is now forced forward largely by the resources of Sports England, although the other national sports councils are involved in some delivery and promotion.

Booklets

A series of short booklets has been written in a straigh-tforward, friendly and practical way. They are designed to cover a range of topics for those who need some basic help with the jobs that they have to carry out in Sports. The titles available include the following:

- *Running Meetings* acts as a guide to chairing a sports organization. It discusses issues relating to meetings, along with the role and skill required of a chairperson.

- *Running a Club* focuses on the role of the secretary in a sports organization, addressing aspects such as qualities needed, correspondence, agendas, AGMs and records.
- *Looking After the Money* focuses on the role of the treasurer in a sports organization, examining aspects such as paying the bills, accounting for the money, petty cash, budgets, income and expenditure and balance sheets.
- *Raising Money* acts as a guide to raising money for a sports organization, providing guidance on donations, grants, fundraising, marketing, promotion, publicity and sponsorship.
- *Managing Events* focuses on the basic requirements for putting together small-scale Sports tournaments, championships and events. It looks at some of the key planning issues and helps organizers plan more effectively and comprehensively.
- *Volunteering Matters* looks at volunteers in Sports—their importance and the roles they play. It considers how we find them, keep them interested and can encourage them.
- *Planning for Sports Development* looks at the sports development pathway—from getting started to being the best. It focuses on who can help, what is to be done, and planning principles and practice.

Resources for Club and People Management

Resource materials at this level have been developed to provide individuals with the opportunity to improve their knowledge and competency in specific areas. In some cases, courses have also been developed to support these resources. Courses will help people (especially administrators, coaches, officials, and development officers) to gain some of the underpinning knowledge and gather the necessary skills in a range of areas. *Personal Effectiveness.* This pack is intended for sports people who wish to run their Sports, business and home life more effectively and with greater enjoyment. It includes practical advice on communication, running meetings, office administration (or personal administration) and report writing. In particular, it will help you to:

- Deploy the principles of effective communication (oral and written) and appreciate its importance in fostering productive working relationships
- Assess strengths and weaknesses in written and oral communication, and identify strategies to develop these skills
- Assess personal administrative skills against recognized principles of good practice and devise action plans to increase work effectiveness and efficiency
- Understand how meetings should be run and how to contribute positively to meetings.

Time Management: Again, this pack is intended for sports people who wish to run their Sports, business and home life more effectively and with greater enjoyment. It includes practical advice on goal-setting, prioritizing and action-planning, and offers guidance on selecting strategies to reduce stress and gain greater satisfaction. In particular, it will help you to:

- Evaluate how you use your time
- Recognize where you are being less effective with your time
- Prioritize tasks and set achievable goals
- Set specific tasks to increase your work efficiency
- Plan, organize and evaluate your work better
- Identify strategies to improve your time management
- Manage your time-related stress better.

Leadership and Delegation: The pack is intended for sports people who need to get things done by managing, organizing or influencing others, or simply working effectively alongside others. It includes practical advice on leadership and management styles for employees, colleagues and volunteers; and strategies for making delegation both effective and rewarding. In particular, it will help you to:

- Understand a range of leadership/management styles
- Identify when to use different styles
- Appreciate the advantages and disadvantages of delegation
- Identify and plan how to delegate tasks to other people
- Plan and organize the distribution of tasks
- Monitor to ensure that delegates' tasks are achieved.

Motivation and Team Building: The pack is intended for sports people who need to get things done by managing, organizing, or influencing others, or simply working effectively alongside others. It includes practical advice on motivational strategies for employees, volunteers, and colleagues; and ways to make the team function more effectively and with greater satisfaction. In particular, it will help you to:

- Understand different theories of motivation
- Identify the strengths of colleagues, staff and volunteers
- Identify ways to develop more motivated colleagues, staff and volunteers
- Identify the characteristics of successful working teams
- Rate the effectiveness of any teams to which you belong
- Identify ways to improve the way in which their work teams function.

Balancing the Books: The pack is intended for sports people who have to handle money for their sports organization, handle their own finances or wish to understand financial accounts of their organization. It includes advice on book-keeping and accounting for revenue. In particular, it will help you to:

- Understand the importance of keeping accurate accounts and budgets
- Handle and account for cash transactions
- Prepare and analyse a receipts and payments account
- Maintain basic financial systems for an organization.

Managing the Money: Again, the pack is intended for sports people who have to handle money for their sports organizations, handle their own finances or wish to understand the financial accounts of their organization. It includes practical advice on budgeting, balance sheets and accounts. In particular, it will help you to:

- Calculate the accruals and prepayments relevant to each financial period
- Prepare detailed income and expenditure accounts and balance sheets
- Analyse an income and expenditure account and a balance sheet
- Prepare and adjust budgets and financial statements
- Operate stock control procedures
- Apply the taxation levels relevant to your situation.

New modules in various stages of development have been added to the range of courses available. Topics include the following. *Funding and Promoting Your Club.* This take-home study pack and possible accompanying course combine these important areas for sports clubs and their administrators. The idea is that the reader (or the tutor on a course) can 'pick and mix' the most appropriate lists for them and their club. Areas covered include:

- The meaning of promotion and marketing
- The importance of effective planning
- Assessing financial requirements
- Sourcing funds
- Completing appropriate forms
- Sponsorship proposals and grant applications
- Planning for promotion and fundraising.

Volunteer Management: This very important pack looks at ways of 'making the most of your Sports workforce'. It considers a number of vital issues about volunteers in Sports and suggests how they can best be managed—or at least co-ordinated and supported. The issues covered include:

- Recruitment
- Retention
- Rewarding
- Action plans for improvement

- Developing appropriate goals and targets
- Which structures and mechanisms can be used.

Other resources and home study packs are available covering:

- *Employment Matters*
- *Sports Development Planning*
- *Sports Facility Development—Planning a Building Project*
- *A Club for All*
- *Developing Sports Partnerships/Developing Junior Clubs*
- *Girlsport* (only with a workshop).

For most of these packs, a facilitated learning workshop exists or can be developed to assist in assimilating the topic and the materials. In addition, an accompanying suite of materials has been devised (in conjunction with Sportscoach UK) covering child protection—obviously an essential knowledge area for administrators as well as coaches. This includes:

- *Safe and Sound*—an introductory leaflet
- *Good Practice and Child Protection*—a workshop
- *Protecting Children*—a home study pack
- *Keeping Children Safe in Sports*—a distance learning pack.

In summary, Running Sports is about helping people, particularly volunteers, to help their Sports as effectively as possible by addressing key issues such as volunteer management, club finances and development planning. The focus is currently very much on supporting club development, recognizing the importance of this level of Sports and the need for helping volunteers at this level. Following up on Running Sports is easy—the best way to get involved is to contact your national sports council (addresses at the back of this text) and they will tell you more about resources or setting up courses.

Volunteering in Sports

Government Sports Strategy

In April 2000, the government published its strategy for the development of Sports in England over the next decade. An implementation group made up of leading figures from Sports education, local authorities and the national governing bodies (NGBs) of Sports was charged with agreeing practical ways of achieving the strategy recommendations. A subsequent action plan, *The Government's Plan for Sports,* was launched in March 2001. This action plan highlights the government's commitment to school Sports, developing a system for identifying and supporting top UK athletes, and to the training, development and recognition of volunteers. The action plan states that Sports relies heavily on an army of volunteers and that NGBs need to be supported to develop and implement volunteering strategies through which they can provide direction and support, and offer sound volunteer management. The government believed that Sports England should be the national advocate of volunteering across Sports in England. It asked Sports England to:

- Raise the profile of volunteering in Sports and highlight what Sports has to offer volunteers
- Develop a website that is effective in the promotion and support of volunteering in Sports
- Ensure that the strategic management of volunteers is integral to all relevant Sports England programmes
- Lead research, monitoring and evaluation of the effectiveness of volunteer management throughout Sports
- Advise and update NGBs on the impact of new and changing legislation on volunteer management
- Take the lead in researching and establishing links between Sports and volunteering organizations and initiatives at national and regional levels
- Identify and support effective pilot projects.

The action plan also states that 'Sports England will consult with all NGBs on a flexible, cross-Sports strategy for volunteering'. Key principles of this common strategy include the following:

- NGBs will be encouraged to identify and appoint a national volunteer manager to implement the strategy throughout Sports. That role will include the recruitment and management of volunteers' raising the profile of volunteering within the governing body and identifying training, support, recognition and reward need of volunteers through Sports.

- At regional level, volunteer management should be a key part of a Sports-specific development officer post. The key tasks of regional officers will be to co-ordinate the implementation of the volunteering strategy and support voluntary county and club co-ordinators.
- Volunteer co-ordinators should have key roles within county associations and clubs where they will raise the profile of volunteering and bring the strategy to life at grassroots level.
- All volunteer co-ordinators will be linked into the Volunteer Investment Programme network to be the first point of contact for volunteer management issues and advisory services and to play a key role in attracting volunteers into Sports from all sections of the community.

In order for all this to happen, adequate training is essential. The Department for Culture, Media and Sports (DCMS) allocated £4m to underpin training and support for young people aged 14-19 to develop leadership skills and to volunteer in their communities. The scheme, which is running from 2002 to 2004, builds on work already done by the Youth Sports Trust (YST) and Millennium Volunteers, and the Department for Education and Employment (DfEE) Citizenship and Sports programme linked to the Commonwealth Games in Manchester 2002. An additional £3m from the government's Active Community Fund will develop a nationwide implementation strategy, and train adult volunteers to mentor, lead, officiate and coach Sports locally.

Volunteer Investment Programme (VIP)

The Running Sports programme is now being supported by a programme called the Volunteer Investment Programme. It emphasizes the importance of volunteers to Sports, and suggests practical ways in which they can be recruited, retained and rewarded. Sports needs people who are skilled not only in the knowledge of the Sports itself, but also in the delivery of quality service to all the participants at whatever level. They will have to have the necessary job skills for the post and have them updated and enhanced through training on an ongoing basis. This will be true whatever post individuals occupy, and whether this post is voluntary or paid.

Training is one of the few areas where government ministers and trade unionists always agree there is a major priority. However, in the past, neither have put their money where their mouth is and promoted training in such a practical way. There is some evidence to suggest that the UK has one of the more poorly trained and underskilled workforces. We constantly face change, and a major push to upgrade skills is required in Sports and recreation as in other industries.

There must be a constant and consistent drive to get people trained, educated and qualified to the highest possible level to help keep their motivation high and increase their ability to perform the jobs they undertake. Investment in the education and training of administrators will ensure that everyone involved in Sports benefits. The benefits of good practice are not limited to the highly competitive business environment but can greatly enhance voluntary and public sports management and administration situations as well.

CHAPTER 14

Sports Administrator---Ability and Skill

Sports administration, like any other business, is about people and their performance. Improved performance comes through increased personal knowledge and skills, particularly the very practical skills of managing time, managing meetings and managing yourself. Sports administrators manage sports clubs or associations, undertaking activities such as promoting their Sports, obtaining corporate sponsorship and refining the rules and structure of their Sports.

A sports administrator may perform the following tasks:

- Talk to clients and conduct research to determine their needs
- Develop programs and services that meet client needs
- Consult widely to develop short- and long-term business plans for their Sports
- Supervise the design, planning and maintenance of Sports and recreation facilities

- Make sure facilities conform to fire and other safety standards
- Plan and organise sporting events
- Supervise office, facility and/or program staff
- Identify staff training needs
- Coordinate the business activities of the Sports, or of the club
- Report to various committees and/or government agencies
- Prepare, implement and monitor budgets.

Time Management

All managers in work situations feel stress and pressure due to perceived lack of time. This is particularly true in the sports industry, where one is dealing with many others' often conflicting demands on one's time, and with a range of very enthusiastic people coming at the manager or administrator from a wide variety of viewpoints, each demanding that their view be supported and that work be done for them. Additionally, the manager/administrator in the sports situation will be dealing with time during the unsocial hours, which many people see as their recreation hours—while for the sports manager it is probably paid work time. This necessity to work unsocial hours creates even more pressure for the manager/administrator and conflicts with other demands on their time such as home life. This means that effective use of time is particularly important—time lost between 9.00a.m. and 5.00p.m. cannot be caught up in slacker periods when people are not taking part in Sports, because there are no such periods.

Time Management Action Plan

In order to find more time, the manager must take some action to identify where time goes at present, set targets for its use, and the steps towards improvement. Having devised these targets, an action plan needs to be established to achieve them. In particular, steps must be taken to remove 'time wasters' and bring in 'time creating' moves. 'Time wasters' include:

- Stress and strain
- Crisis management
- Procrastination
- Poor prioritization
- Doing everything oneself
- Lengthy phone calls, meetings, face-to-face conversations
- Conflict
- Poor communication
- Lack of preparation
- Poor use of paper
- Taking work home
- Only doing easy tasks and allowing inadequate time for major tasks.

The following creative 'time makers' can assist in 'making' more time and compensate for the incorrect use of time, which is so common.

- Ranking task priority
- Setting appropriate deadlines
- Setting realistic schedules
- Saying no where appropriate
- Estimating time realistically
- Delegating appropriate tasks—with direction, authority, power and support
- Setting clear goals
- Identifying better working practices in terms of efficiency and operation
- Stopping procrastination
- Managing meetings properly
- Prioritizing phone calls and paperwork appropriately
- Using time, such as travel time to undertake suitable tasks
- Setting time aside each week for major project work
- Leaving spaces in the diary—daily, weekly, monthly, etc.
- Giving clear signals to colleagues as to when there is time available for them
- Using information technology.

There are countless books on the subject of time management, naturally of varying quality. It is a subject that should be studied in depth by the sports administrator due to the enormous pressures on their time. In particular, the sports administrator is plagued by this imbalance of the normal working period of 9.00a.m. to 5.00p.m. Monday to Friday, versus the desire of sports participants to see their administrators at work outside these hours. There will inevitably be work to be done by the sports administrator between the hours of 9.00a.m. and 5.00p.m. during the week, as they will have to deal with the suppliers and other routinely operating organizations, but they will also have to meet the 'spare time' demands of sports people who participate and attend meetings after 6.00p.m. and during weekends. To respond effectively to these conflicting demands, the sports administrator needs to prioritize tasks and manage their time effectively in completing them, otherwise they will crack under the strain of constant working hours and pressure from all angles.

Managing Meetings

There are some who believe that Sports survives on fitness and exercise, and numbers of participants—there are others who believe, more realistically, that Sports survives on meetings. This phenomenon of meetings, meetings, meetings is not unique to the sports business, nor indeed is it limited to the voluntary sector. There is a culture of meetings in business and industry, and the sports voluntary sector suffers from this as do many other organizations. There is a strong argument that a large number of meetings are important in areas of the voluntary sector because of their involving role—people come to meetings to be involved in the whole process of running their sports club or organizations. Inevitably, in the voluntary sector, there is a need to let people have their say and play a part in the actions of the organization, but this has to be moderated by some organizational practicalities and common sense on the part of the organization and the individual.

There is no doubt that many of the meetings held are necessary and, if conducted properly, can in fact be beneficial to the future development of projects and, indeed, the organization itself. The following general guidelines, however, are essential if real, effective progress is to be achieved. Theoretically, meetings on Sports, particularly in the voluntary sector, are about planning and achievement, but realistically they are often about social gatherings, discussions of current controversies and building informal interpersonal relationships which serve to keep the organizations going.

It is noticeable in the voluntary sector that people see meetings as their opportunity to express their strongly held views on issues affecting their Sports. It is perhaps a reflection of their profound commitment and enjoyment of their Sports that they attend many meetings, and so feel that there is the opportunity to consistently repeat their views on such occasions, whether they are relevant to the business of the meeting or not. Very often, such views are repeated constantly on a similar basis and do not lend anything new or significant to the proceedings. This may appear a somewhat cynical view, but it is often reflected in practice. Minimizing meetings and being more businesslike in the approach to procedures would considerably improve the achievement of many organizations and associations in the sporting world. Problems at sports meetings often arise because the first and fundamental consideration is often not examined closely enough, i.e. is the meeting necessary and what exactly is its purpose?

This is undoubtedly the most crucial issue and the one most often ignored by a wide range of organizations and individuals. If a meeting does not need to be held, and there are other ways of achieving certain tasks, then such other methods should be used first—there is absolutely no point in having unnecessary, time-consuming meetings which achieve nothing and tend to create resentment and frustration at having to attend, often during unsocial hours, with no relevant perceived outcome.

If there is a real purpose to the meeting then the correct procedures should be followed so that progress is made towards the necessary purpose and the agreed set of objectives. It is essential to ensure that the following points are implemented.

- All necessary preparation for the meeting is done by all those attending it.
- There is a clear pre-arranged agenda, a specified chair for the meeting and someone taking minutes or at least action notes.
- Notes taken for action are circulated to others as soon as possible after the meeting.
- Everyone present is given the opportunity to participate.
- All the people in attendance need to be there and have something to offer.
- The meeting is appropriately formal in terms of following the agenda, but not so formal as to limit meaningful discussion.
- All background papers are read before the meeting.
- Meetings are adequately planned and properly controlled.
- The chairperson prevents rambling discussion and keeps everyone focused on the correct agenda.

Sporting people at meetings tend to be quite fanatical about their activity, and apply this also to getting their own specific view across. This, coupled with informal meetings and a lack of respect for the chairperson (often known from another sporting situation on an informal basis), can be a recipe for chaos. Such almost inevitable informality creates its own problem for the chair of such meetings and they need a sufficiently strong personality to handle it sensitively, yet firmly, while allowing people to express their views, but not rambling on indefinitely on the same topic. In essence, in terms of such meetings it is vital that there is something that everyone wants to achieve from the meeting; that the group fits together well; that all the information required is to hand; that all the people around the table can get on well together or at least consider the views of others; and that each person listens as well as talks.

Sometimes sports meetings have the added pressure of poor or inappropriate facilities due to the lack of resources within the organization, and meetings having to be squeezed into the homes of individuals or inadequate back rooms of sports facilities. Such a situation puts an added pressure on everyone involved, even though initially it may be seen as a more convenient and cost-effective method of meeting. While meetings must be kept to a minimum, they are the lifeblood of the Sports in the organizational sense. Undoubtedly many are necessary, but equally many are not—the benefits can only accrue if they are appropriately planned, organized, arranged and chaired. When meetings fail it is generally due to a lack of:

- Preparation
- Purpose
- Communication
- Resource utilization
- Decision-making
- Implementation
- Clear objectives
- Time keeping
- Suitable physical environment
- Written agenda
- Strong chairing.

Most sports administrators complain that they have to attend too many meetings, and this is often justified. Often it can be beneficial to communicate in other ways. For example:

- By meeting people on an individual basis
- Through informal meetings
- By telephone, fax or e-mail
- By writing directly to an individual
- By issuing a memo to several people
- By getting involved in video conferencing or electronic conferencing.

However, there are still occasions when it is essential to have a more formal meeting, and these often prove useful mechanisms if used properly. Also, as mentioned above, the process of communication is often aided in the meeting situation. The necessity for a meeting, however, depends on its purpose and it involves concepts of control, communication, problem-solving and decision-making. It is often a useful exercise to think back to recent meetings and consider whether any of these processes are actually undertaken. Voluntary organizations can survive on meetings but they do not always achieve a great deal. Positive planning to get a more useful way forward will help everyone.

Meetings in Practice

Meticulous preparation for a meeting in terms of sending out papers etc. will help to make sure that everybody is there on time and understands what is going to happen. Additionally, however, it is vitally important that the chair or whoever will lead the meeting has all their planning done before the meeting in terms of paperwork and issues to be raised, that there is a definite purpose to the meeting and that everybody understands what it is. Meetings also have to be structured, and that structure needs to be followed.

It is essential that the agenda is circulated to all participants in advance and they are all made aware of any information which is required before the meeting; it is all too common for necessary information not to be made available to all parties sufficiently in advance of the meeting for it to be studied—this leads to people fumbling through unread papers at the meeting and causes an enormous waste of time. Additionally, it is important that only relevant points are placed on the agenda and discussed at the meeting.

This can be enforced by making sure that only current issues are covered in the pre-meeting papers, and that the chair prevents unnecessary items from being discussed—they should rule such irrelevancies out of order, as they can significantly delay the proceedings. It is essential also that agendas are not too long—having many more than ten items is asking for trouble, and indeed even this number may be too great. There are a number of formal agendas for annual general meetings etc. and these will be prescribed in the constitution of the organization; otherwise common sense should be used and only appropriate items included.

Every meeting should have some record of what took place and what is to happen after the meeting. This may be in the form of formal minutes written by someone, normally the secretary, and agreed by the chair of the meeting before circulation. Whatever form these minutes take, they should:

- Be accurate
- Be clear and unambiguous
- Be properly organized
- Be brief
- Be agreed
- Be non-personal
- Be a joint responsibility (e.g. chair and secretary)
- State clearly what has been decided
- State what has to happen as a result of the decisions
- Be circulated promptly.

There is a tendency in Sports for minutes to be too verbose and too person-alized. This causes a waste of time. To indicate the decisions of the group is helpful; to indicate who initiated such decisions can be disruptive and damaging. Decisions of committees once agreed must be acted upon in a unified manner; to cause divisions by allocating responsibility to one individual for any decision is not helpful and can in fact be quite detrimental to organizational efficiency. In order to get good organizational involvement it is important that the minutes of meetings wherever possible are widely circulated. They will not tell everyone an enormous amount, but they will make it clear what has been discussed and decided, thus fulfilling the need to keep everyone informed and involved. This will not allow anyone to make the usual plea of ignorance of what is going on within the organization.

There may be some occasions, e.g. in the case of disciplinary proceedings, when minutes should be very brief, and certain minutes may be confidential for legal purposes. Wide circulation will still be the general rule. In a sporting setting, especially where volunteers are involved, chairing the meeting can be quite a difficult task. Everyone will want to have their say, but the chair must push the meeting towards achieving its objectives and getting finished in a reasonable time. This is not to deny individuals the opportunity to put their point of view across, but this should only be done briefly and on a specific subject, rather than being a reiteration of long-held strong opinions. Ultimately, the chair takes the responsibility for structuring the meeting and ensuring it is carried out and recorded through the minutes in a proper way.

Chairing a meeting can be extremely difficult and requires special skills of personality and awareness, which can be sharpened up with practice and most importantly by preparation—it is vital that the chair is well informed about all the items likely to arise at any meeting and has thoroughly gone through any papers to be presented. Failure to do so will cause embarrassment to the chair and possibly others present, as well as significant delays in the proceedings of the meeting. It may be difficult to have a full knowledge or understanding of every topic on the agenda, but it is essential to know who will talk to a specific point and what should happen in relation to all the items on the agenda. The chair will benefit from some support, and indeed training, in performing this function as they need to have a considerable range of skills in order to be effective. Such skills include listening, questioning, encouraging and conciliating.

All too often in Sports these skills are expected to be present as soon as somebody is appointed, and we are not always very good at helping people once we have put them in such posts. Programmes such as Running Sports can be of significant assistance in giving individuals the basic skills required to take on such a role. The principle of training in meeting behaviour should be carried to all committee members as soon as they are appointed (or even to prospective committee members). Such action will mean that sporting organizations will function a great deal more effectively and, indeed, enjoyably for all concerned. Funda-mentally, successful meetings need:

- Minutes, with an action-by column
- Agenda and objectives
- Feedback and contributions
- To be well led
- Written reports
- A venue with all necessary equipment
- Appropriate atmosphere
- To be kept to time
- A timetable for each item and overall
- Clarity of expression and purpose
- Members with necessary skills and knowledge
- Decisions made leading to action.

Personal Management

The business of Sports requires managers in all sectors to be doing their work at a time when most other people are taking their recreation. As mentioned above, it is not a management role that can be confined to certain hours or shifts, but requires seven-days-a-week, 24-hours-a-day commitment and a considerable dedication if it is to be performed effectively and to the satisfaction of, at least, the majority of customers. This necessity to work long hours, coupled with the almost inevitably short time-scales and tight deadlines, exerts enormous pressure on managers and administrators, and their ability to respond successfully will depend largely on their own personal organization and management. To be personally effective in the sports business one has to be efficient in personal management.

This skill has a number of aspects, some of which are considered below. Some might argue that this section is the most important of the whole text. The issues considered here include time management, personal organization, managing meetings, and considering the job role and responsibilities.

It is a long-held belief that someone cannot be an organizer or an efficient administrator if they are unable to manage their own behaviour and organize themselves. Basically, to organize others one must be personally efficient and not continually have to rely on everyone else to do things or to find things or to arrange things or to know what is going on. This in essence must be the job of the administrator professionally, and therefore they must take steps to handle all the challenges that may face them individually. Sports administrators must be able to:

- Get control of their own time
- Avoid procrastination and take action promptly
- Manage interruptions to the work schedule and deal appropriately with inevitable social contacts
- Develop a telephone manner to shorten telephone calls
- Prepare for every meeting they attend
- Preserve personal time
- Devise appropriate methods of personal time management.

There is little doubt that there is a frequent tendency for individuals to get snowed under by a massive amount of paperwork, and this must be managed effectively if any progress is to be made individually. A paper-handling system must be developed, otherwise bits of paper will be handled countless times. Sports administrators should consider a number of items in dealing with the organizational and administrative tasks which face them. These include:

- Appropriate record-keeping systems
- Learning from others in similar situations
- Keeping appropriate diaries
- Organizing the desk appropriately
- Developing relevant filing systems
- Keeping appropriate records, such as health or absence records
- Recording incoming and outgoing mail
- Developing a file of resources and contacts.

The keeping of appropriate financial records is absolutely essential in terms of banking, invoice paying and issuing, extracting appropriate records from the financial statements for submission to the relevant committees, and dealing with potential investments and banking systems to the benefit of the sports club or organization. There is a wide variety of other personal, even domestic, arrangements that an efficient administrator could consider in the search for efficiency and ease of operation. The more that any individual can do to bring their personal time management into efficient operation, the more they, and ultimately the organization, will benefit.

As mentioned above, Covey (1992) lists seven guidelines to enhance personal effectiveness. These are as useful to the sports manager/administrator as in industrial situations, and the text is well worth reading by anybody who wants to increase their effectiveness. Covey suggests that people begin by being dependent, move to independence, and should ultimately move to a situation of interdependence. This reflects the fact that individuals can strengthen their own roles and actions, but ultimate success will rely on working happily with others—this is seen in sports administration in the networking situation mentioned elsewhere in the text. This is a vital part of sporting structures everywhere—working together for mutual benefit is very much what it is all about, and combining limited resources makes this most effective. Being personally effective is as much a case of who you know as what you know.

Covey's seven habits are listed at the beginning of this chapter, but are worth repeating:

1. Be proactive
2. Begin with the end in mind
3. Put first things first
4. Think win/win
5. Seek first to understand, then to be understood
6. Synergize
7. Sharpen the saw

Quick Tips for Managing Your Personal Life

This list may seem a little patronizing, but in the drive for time and organization to allow for sports involvement, it can be helpful.

- *Things others can do*—make a list of things it's better not to do yourself, but rather to pay others to do: car repairs, DIY jobs, etc.
- *Use the post*—why pay all bills in person? You can pay bills and indeed shop by using the post, the phone or the Internet.
- *Avoid peak hours*—do your shopping on a Monday morning. It is much quieter than a Saturday afternoon.
- *Organise your finances*—have a financial file at home. Keep all your money and related items in it. Make sure you have a bills-due folder and set definite times to pay them.
- *Don't get glued to the tube*—limit your television to a few shows of special merit each week; don't flop down and watch whatever comes on. Far better to use this recreation time to read something, do some exercise or just catch up on mental rest.
- *Keep a spare set of keys*—duplicate keys for home, car and office should be kept in safe, handy places. This is a real timesaver.
- *Forget perfection*—especially in household management, perfection is probably not possible so simply strive to make everything reasonably clean, comfortable and complete.
- *Keep in touch with the family*—make sure you keep a notice board or a phone message board at a suitable place in the home where everyone knows things will be posted.
- *Crowd your appointments*—make sure that you get all the appointments you can for yourself and your family as close together as possible, rather than having to go once a week for four weeks.
- *Have a master list*—put down items to buy at shops or work to do as they arise or come to mind.
- *Keep paperwork under control*—at the very least sort through your mail and other papers at least once a week, otherwise you will create a monster. A home filing system can be very worthwhile.

- ***Shop only twice a year for clothes***—this can be done at sale times and we can save money and a lot of inconvenience.
- ***Keep repairs under control***—make sure that clothing, equipment and home repairs are done as they arise. Don't put things away that need to be repaired, as they will be broken the next time you look for them.
- ***Keep an accurate professional and social diary***—everything must be on it. Perhaps a desk and pocket copy is the best system as long as they both say the same thing.
- ***Accept invitations or meetings selectively***—if you can't go or really don't want to go, be sure to say that your time is valuable.
- ***Make sure a holiday is a holiday***—don't take work away with you.
- ***Keep your eyes open for time management tips***—you can always learn from others on new improvements that are being made.

Sports Management A Futuristic Study

The future of Sports Management is bright but challenges are ahead. Now let us take a look at the future and ask a few questions about what might happen. At the time of writing it would probably help to be an astrologer to predict exactly where Sports will go over the next few years—there are so many questions in the air which will have a major impact on what happens.

1. Will the vast sums paid to some sports people continue?
2. What will be the impact of the National Lottery's declining revenue?
3. What will be the impact of the Institute of Sports?
4. Will pay-to-view television produce the anticipated sums?
5. What area will the private sector move into next?
6. What is the next boom Sports?
7. What will be the ongoing impact of the fashion houses and clothing manufacturers?

8. How will sports providers cope with the demographic changes in society?
9. How will education and training developments in the area of sports management and administration impact on sports provision?
10. How will the growing professionalization of sports administration impact on Sports?
11. What will be the impact of information technology, in particular virtual reality, on Sports,?
12. What additional environmental considerations will develop to encourage activities such as cycling and walking, but perhaps work against activities such as skiing and mountain biking?
13. What impact will the rapidly changing technological society have on Sports?
14. Will the change to home-based leisure activities continue?
15. What will be government's ongoing commitment to and views on Sports?

The answers to these and other such questions are not straightforward, and no-one knows any definitive answers at this point in time. However, a professional sports administrator must be keeping an eye on them and ensuring they are not caught out by changes of which they are unaware. For example, they should have foreseen the political step to remove tobacco company sponsorship from the sporting arena. This had been widely promoted in advance as party policy, and the professional administrator should have been looking to set in place replacement sponsorships long before any change of political power. Anticipation is essential for any professional manager and as society—politics and its technology—changes ever more rapidly, the need to take a forward-looking approach is all the more essential.

To assess what might happen in the future it is always wise to look to the past and examine how change has affected organizations: be a student of Sports and sports management.

This can be done through relevant journals and texts as well as the developing academic knowledge, but sports administrators can also learn from more general management thinkers and their potential view of the future. For example, Naisbitt (1995) gives useful insights into how our world and country may develop in the future. It is not necessary to accept everything that any management guru says, but it is certainly necessary to consider it. Getting it right is difficult, but getting it wrong, for Sports as well as for other businesses, can be fatal.

Handy (1997) suggests that we must look forward to uncertainty in the future and not seek the comfort of a sure and steady situation. We must make the best of the chaos and change that exists around about us, try to keep ahead, and recognize it rather than fight it. This concept is very pertinent to Sports since the old cosy clique is a thing of the past and traditionalists trying to cling to old methods and behaviours must step aside for innovative leaders who will be proactive in facing up to a changing future. There is a need to carve a positive direction for the future, with sports organizations being responsive to others' initiatives—to do otherwise could lead to withering on the vine and could cause fatal damage to some sports.

The future is not just going to be based on the past; change in society today works at a multiplier effect—as technology reinvents itself more rapidly than humans can extend it, computers double in power every two years. Having moved in 30 years from the first computer to computers appearing on every desk in industry, it has taken only two or three years for them to appear in many many households. Progress is extremely rapid in technology and related areas where we come to rely on such factors—this has a spin-off effect for all individuals and organizations, as well as society as a whole. Even to assess the work implications for such changes is difficult and has led to company downsizing, early retirement and major social impact. This has left the way open for more sports participation and made people more available to provide administrative support on a voluntary basis having given up their jobs relatively early.

As all these changes happen, the fundamental thing for a consumer business like Sports is that the needs, expectations and desires of the customers will change radically and these must be assessed and matched. Like society, our customers will change. It will become more important for sports administrators and everyone involved to be more aware of what is happening in other industrial settings. Industrial change has a massive impact on Sports, as indeed does, for example, the expansion of tourism, the development of the Internet, etc.—Sports must get in early, responding on its terms and leading the way where possible. Innovation that can be shown on the sports field needs to be shown in administrative terms as well.

The growth of the Internet throws up major opportunities for sports organizations to improve their communications network, improve public awareness, and sell their goods and services nationally and internationally. This opportunity will be exploited by others if it is not seized by Sports itself. There is a common phrase used by many management gurus at present: 'think globally, act locally'. This phrase is vitally important to Sports. It must take into account the wider picture while putting together the practicalities of Sports on a local basis where it has a real impact. The future then, as ever, provides opportunities and threats, necessitates action on the part of individuals and organizations who want to be truly successful and will be quite radically different from the past, even the recent past. Sports administrators and leaders of the twenty-first century must be more dynamic, forceful and proactive than in the past if they are to maintain and increase their share of an ever more challenging market place.

Like any area of management or business operation, learning—to improve performance—must be an ongoing process, and must be constantly updated and reviewed if genuine improvements are to be seen in the function of the organization and the effectiveness of individuals. The author has devised leisuretraining.com to help with this continual development on an ongoing basis. The general management concepts examined are valid in many contexts, and it is felt that the sports scene is no different in that respect. However, the author believes that there is a fundamental difference in the sports scene from that of the highly commercial, high-speed business scene and from most other areas of management operation—even other areas of leisure such as the arts.

Throughout the book an attempt has been made to apply theory and good commercial practice to situations which exist in Sports, but no attempt or intention has been laid out to lessen the 'specialness' of Sports and the unique nature of the situation and the staff operating in it. Anything that lessens the empathy of everyone involved for the special commitment (almost to the level of fanaticism) of those involved is damaging to Sports in the long term. So, while enthusiastically embracing management concepts and placing them in a context which is helpful to Sports, the author does not underestimate the special nature of Sports—quite the contrary, having spent my lifetime in its participation, administration and organization. It is to be hoped that this book will make that path easier for others in the future and that the thoughts contained in it will assist effective operation in a wide variety of sports situations.

There is always a danger of becoming a fanatic through involvement in Sports, in any role, simply because of the commitment it requires. This single-mindedness must not be allowed to let anyone in Sports ignore correct practices and procedures. The fact that the sports setting is unique should be a strength and not a weakness, but it can become a weakness if the difference is pushed to the level of believing that proper management practice is not appropriate in that unique situation. On the contrary, the special nature of the activity makes the need to link closely to 'good management and leadership' all the more important.

BIBLIOGRAPHY

Abdullah, M.S., Saad, J.M., Zakaria, A.A. and Selvaraj, O. *Sports Sciences into the 'Next Millennium: Bridging the Gap (Proceedings of the 11 th Commonwealth & International Scientific Congress)*, Kuala Lumpur: University of Malaya, 1998

Adair, J. *Effective Teambuilding: How to Make a Winning Team*, Aldershot: Gower, 1986

Adair, J. *Effective Leadership: a Modern Guide to Developing Leadership Skills*, London: Pan, 1988

Adams, I. *Leisure and Government*, Sunderland: Business Education Publishers, 1990

Allan, J. *How to Develop Your Personal Management Skills*, London: Kogan Page, 1990

Anon. *Management of Voluntary Organisations*, London: Croner, 1989

Anon. *The British Health and Fitness Club Guide 1993: The Definitive Management Guide to Commercial Health and Fitness Facilities in Clubs and Hotels*, Harlow: Longman, 1992

Argyle, M. *The Psychology of Interpersonal Behaviour*, Harmondsworth: Penguin, 1972

Armstrong, M. *The Management Process and Functions*, London: Institute of Personnel Management, 1990

Audit Commission. *Sports for Whom? Clarifying the Local Authority Role in Sports and Recreation*, London: HMSO, 1989

Audit Commission. *The Quality Exchange: Leisure Services, Sports and Recreation*, London: HMSO, 1993

Audit Commission for Local Authorities in England and Wales. *Local Authority Support for Sports: a Management Handbook*, London: HMSO, 1990

Badmin, P. *Leisure Operational Management, Volume 1 Facilities*, Harlow: Longman, 1992

Badmin, P. *Leisure Operational Management, Volume 2 People*, Harlow: Longman, 1993

Bale, J. *Sports Geography*, London: E & FN Spon, 1989

Bass, B.M. *Bass and Stogdill's Handbook of Leadership: Theory, Research and Managerial Implications*, New York: Free Press, 1990

Bennington, J. and White, J. *The Future of Leisure Services*, Harlow: Longman, 1988

Bischert, R., Taylor, J. and Fitzsimons, M. *A Practical Approach to the Administration of Leisure and Recreation Services*, 4th edn, London: Croner, 1992

Borrett, N. *Leisure Services UK*, London: Macmillan, 1991

British Quality Association Leisure Services Quality Committee. *Quality Assurance for Leisure Services*, London: British Quality Association, 1990

British Standards Institution. *Quality Assurance (BSI Handbook 22)*, London: British Standards Institution, 1987

Brodie, M.B. *Fayol on Administration*, London: Lyon, Grant & Green, 1967

Brown, P. and Hackett, F. *Managing Meetings*, London: Fontana, 1990

Bucher, C.A. and Krotee, M.L. *Management of Physical Education and Sports*, St Louis, MO: Mosby Year Book, 1992

Buswell, J. *Case Studies in Leisure Management Practice*, London: Pitman, 1993

Catterall, P. *Contemporary Britain: an Annual Review*, Oxford: Blackwell, 1994

Central Council of Physical Recreation. Wolfenden Committee on Sports. *Sports and the Community*, London: CCPR, 1960

Central Council of Physical Recreation. *Fair Play in Sports—a Charter*, London: CCPR, 1991

Central Office of Information. *Aspects of Britain: Sports and Leisure*, London: HMSO, 1994

Centre for Leisure Research. *Compulsory Competitive Tendering: Sports and Leisure Management—National Information Survey Report*, London: Sports Council, 1993

Chartered Institute of Public Finance and Accountancy. *Compulsory Competition for the Management of Sports and Leisure Facilities*, occasional paper, London: CIPFA, 1991

Chaudhry-Lawton, R., Lawton, R., Murphy, K., Terry, A. *Quality: Change Through Teamwork*, London: Century Business, 1993

Coakley, J. *Sports in Society: Issues and Controversies*, London: Mosby, 1994

Cochrane, A.J. *Science and Golf: Proceedings of the First World Scientific Congress of Golf*, London: E & F Spon, 1990

Collins, V. *Recreation and Law*, London: E & FN Spon, 1993

Cooke, A. *The Economics of Leisure and Sports*, London: International Thomson Business Press, 1994

Council of Europe. *European Sports for All Charter*, Strasbourg: Council of Europe, 1990

Council of Europe. *European Sports Charter*, Strasbourg: Council of Europe, 1992

Council of Europe Committee for the Development for Sports. *Workshops on Sports Management*, Strasbourg: Council of Europe, 1991

Covey, S.R. *The Seven Habits of Highly Effective People*, London: Simon & Schuster, 1992

Crowther, J. *Managing your Golf Club: the Facts and Skills of Golf Club Management*, Bakewell: Crowther, 1993

Dale, B.G. and Oakland, J.S. *British Standards Institution: Quality Improvement through Standards*, Cheltenham: Stanley Thornes, 1991

Davis, K.A. *Sports Management: Successful Private Sector Business Strategies*, Madison, WI: Brown & Benchmark, 1994

Department of Culture, Media and Sports. *A Sporting Future for All: the Government's Plan for Sports*, London: DCMS, 2001

Department of Education and Science. *Safety in Outdoor Education*, London: HMSO, 1989

Department of Education and Science. *Building on Ability: Sports for People with Disabilities*, available from Department of National Heritage, London, 1989

Department of Education and Science. *A Sporting Double: School and Community*, London: HMSO, 1991

Department of National Heritage. *Sports: Raising the Game*, London: DNH, 1995

Dickinson, J. *A Behavioural Analysis of Sports*, London: Lepus Books, 1976

Drowatzky, J. *Legal Issues in Sports and Physical Education Management*, Champaign, IL: Stipes, 1984

Druce, R. and Carter, S. *The Marketing Handbook: a Guide for Voluntary and Non-Profit Making Organisations*, Cambridge: National Extension College, 1988

Dumfries and Galloway Council. *A Leisure and Sports Strategy for Dumfries and Galloway, 2001-2005*, Dumfries: Dumfries and Galloway Council, 2001

Eady, J. *Practical Sports Development*, Harlow: Longman, 1993

Eastern Council for Sports and Recreation. *Sports Centre Design with Management in Mind*, Bedford: ECSR, 1979

East Midland Regional Council for Sports and Recreation. *Managing for Results: Report of the Sports Centre Management Seminar*, Nottingham: Sports Council, East Midland Region, 1979

Edwards, H. *Sociology of Sports*, Homewood, IL: Dorsey Press, 1973

Elvin, I.T. *Sports and Physical Recreation*, Harlow: Longman/ILAM Leisure and Management, 1993

Evans-Platt, C. *Health and Fitness Centres: a Guide to their Management and Operation*, Harlow: Longman in association with Baths and Recreation Management, 1992

Forbes, D., Hayes, R. and Reason, J. *Voluntary, but Not Amateur: a Guide to the Law for Voluntary Organisations and Community Groups*, London: London Voluntary Service Council, 1994

Fyfe, L. *Careers in Sports*, London: Kogan Page, 1994

Gerson, R.F. *Marketing Health/Fitness Services*, Champaign, IL: Human Kinetics, 1989

Gibson, R. *Rethinking the Future: Rethinking Business, Principles, Competition, Control & Complexity, Leadership, Markets and the World*, London: Nicholas Brealey, 1997

Gilson, C., Pratt, M., Roberts, K. and Weymes, E. *Peak Performance: Business Lessons from the World's Top Sports Organisations*, London: HarperCollins, 2000

Glatter, R., Preddey, M., Riches, C. and Masterson, M. *Understanding School Management*, Buckingham: Open University Press, 1989

Glyptis, S. *Leisure and Unemployment*, Buckingham: Open University Press, 1989

Goffman, E. *The Presentation of Self in Everyday Life*, Harmondsworth: Penguin, 1959

Goldblatt, J.J. *Special Events: the Art and Science of Celebration*, New York: Van Nostrand Reinhold, 1990

Goldblatt, J.J. *Special Events: Best Practices and Modern Event Management*, New York: Van Nostrand Reinhold, 1997

Goodale, T.L. and Godbey, G.C. *The Evolution of Leisure: Historical and Philosophical Perspectives*, State College, PA: Venture Publishing, 1988

Gratton, C. and Henry, I.P. *Sports in the City: the Role of Sports in Economic and Social Regeneration*, London: Routledge, 2001

Gratton, C. and Taylor, P. *The Economics of Sports and Recreation*, London: E & FN Spon, 2000

Grayson, E. *Sports and the Law*, London: Butterworth, 1994

Haggerty, T.R. and Paton, G.A. *Financial Management of Sports-Related Organisations*, Champaign, IL: Stipes, 1984

Hall, C.M. *Hallmark Tourist Events: Impacts, Management, and Planning*, London: Belhaven, 1992

Hammer, M. 'Beyond the end of management', in Gibson, R. (ed.) *Rethinking the Future: Rethinking Business, Principles, Competition, Control & Complexity, Leadership, Markets and the World*, London: Nicholas Brealey, 1997

Handy, C. *Understanding Organizations*, Harmondsworth: Penguin, 1985

Handy, C. *Understanding Voluntary Organizations*, Harmondsworth: Penguin, 1988

Handy, C. *Rethinking the Future: Rethinking Business, Principles, Competition, Control & Complexity, Leadership, Markets and the World*, London: Nicholas Brealey, 1997

Haywood, L. *Community Leisure and Recreation*, Oxford: Butterworth-Heinemann, 1994

Haywood, L., Kew, F. and Bramham, P. *Understanding Leisure*, London: Hutchinson, 1989

Health & Safety Executive. *The Essentials of Health and Safety at Work*, London: HMSO, 1988

Health & Safety Executive. *A Guide to Health, Safety and Welfare at Pop Concerts and Other Similar Events*, London: HMSO, 1993

Health & Safety Executive. *The Event Safety Guide*, London: The Health & Safety Executive, 1999

Heathcote, K. *The Gym Business*, Newton Abbot: David & Charles, 1988

Henry, I.P. *Management and Planning in the Leisure Industries*, London: Macmillan, 1990

Herzberg, F., Mausner, B. and Snyderman, B.B. *The Motivation to Work*, New Brunswick, NJ: Transaction Publishers, 1993

Hill, T. *The Essence of Operations Management*, Englewood Cliffs, NJ: Prentice Hall, 1993

Hodgkin, R.A. *Placing and Exploring: Education through the Discovery of Order*, London: Methuen, 1985

Hodgson, P. and Hodgson, J. *Effective Meetings*, London: Century Business Books, 1993

Hoggett, P. and Bishop, J. *The Social Organisation of Leisure: the Study of Groups in the Voluntary Sector Context*, London: The Sports Council/ESRC, 1985

Houlihan, B. *The Government of Politics and Sports*, London: Routledge, 1991

Hylton, K., Bramham, P. and Jackson, D. *Sports Development: Policy, Process and Practice*, London: Routledge, 2001

Institute of Baths and Recreation Management. *Practical Leisure Centre Management*, vols 1 and 2, Melton Mowbray: IBRM, 1992

Institute of Leisure and Amenity Management. *Competitive Tendering: Management of Sports and Leisure Facilities*, Harlow: Longman, 1989

Institute of Leisure and Amenity Management. *ILAM Guide to Good Practice in Leisure Services Management*, vol. 4, Harlow: Longman, 1995

Isaac-Henry, K. Painter, C. and Barnes, C. *Management in the Public Sector: Challenge and Change*, London: Chapman & Hall, 1993

James, S. *Chambers Sporting Quotations*, Edinburgh: Chambers, 1990

Jarman, C. *The Guinness Dictionary of Sports Quotations*, London: Guinness Publishing, 1990

Jarvie, G. (ed.) *Sports, Racism and Ethnicity*, London: Falmer, 1991

Jubenville, A., Twight, B.W. and Becker, R.H. *Outdoor Recreation Management: Theory and Application*, State College, PA: Venture Publishing, 1987

Koehler, R.W. *Law, Sports Activity and Risk Management*, Champaign, IL: Stipes, 1988

Langmuir, E. *Mountaincraft and Leadership: a Handbook for Mountaineers and Hillwalking Leaders in the British Isles*, Edinburgh: Sports Scotland; Manchester: Mountain Leader Training Board, 1995

Lee, M. (ed.) *Coaching Children in Sports: Principles and Practice*, London: E & FN Spon, 1993

Leisure Futures Ltd. *Marketing Leisure Services*, London: Leisure Futures, 1989

Leith, L.M. *Coaches Guide to Sports Administration*, Champaign, IL: Human Kinetics, 1990

Levant, J. and Cleeton, D. *Marketing the Training Function*, London: Kogan Page, 1993

Liddle, B. *Dictionary of Sports Quotations*, London: Routledge & Kegan Paul, 1987

Lock, D. *Project Management*, 5th edn, Aldershot: Gower, 1992

Lynam, D. and Teasdale, D. *The Sporting Word*, London: BBC Books, 1994

McCallum, C. *How to Raise Funds and Sponsorship*, Oxford: How To Books, 1995

McClelland, D.C. *Human Motivation*, Glenview, IL: Scott, Foresman & Co., 1985

McFee, G. and Tomlinson, A. *Education, Sports and Leisure: Connections and Controversies*, London: Chelsea School Research Centre, 1993

McPherson, B.D., Curtis, J.E. and Loy, J.W. *The Social Significance of Sports*, Champaign, IL: Human Kinetics, 1989

Manser, M.H. *Chambers Book of Business Quotations*, Edinburgh: Chambers, 1987

Marsden, A.K. *First Aid Manual: the Authorised Manual of St John's Ambulance, St Andrew's Ambulance Association and the British Red Cross*, London: Dorling Kindersley, 1992

Maslow, A. *Motivation and Personality*, New York: Harper, 1954

Mikalachki, A., Leyshon, G.A. and Zeigler, E.F. *Change Process in Sports and Physical Education Management*, Champaign, IL: Stipes, 1988

Mills, P. *Quality in the Leisure Industry*, Harlow: Longman, 1992

Mullin, B., Hardy, S. and Sutton, W.A. *Sports Marketing*, Champaign, IL: Human Kinetics, 1993

Naisbitt, J. *The Global Paradox*, London: Nicholas Brealey, 1995

Nygaard, G. and Boone, T.H. *Coaches Guide to Sports Law*, Champaign, IL: Human Kinetics, 1985

Ogilvie, K.C. *Leading and Managing Groups in the Outdoors*, Sheffield: National Association for Outdoor Education, 1993

Orlick T. *In Pursuit of Excellence*, Ottawa: Coaching Association of Canada, 1980

Outhart, T. and Taylor, L. *Leisure and Tourism for Intermediate GNVQ*, London: Collins, 2000

Parkhouse, B. *The Management of Sports: Its Foundation and Application*, St Louis, MO: Mosby Year Book, 1991

Parks, J.B. and Zanger, B.R.K. *Sports and Fitness Management: Career Strategies and Professional Content*, Champaign, IL: Human Kinetics, 1990

Parks, J.B., Zanger, B.R.K. and Quarterman, J. *Contemporary Sports Management*, Champaign, IL: Human Kinetics, 1998

Passingham, S. *Organising Local Events*, London: Directory of Social Change in association with the Institute of Charity Fundraising Managers, 1993

Public Administration Research Centre. *Supporting the Council: an Investigation into the Organisation, Charging and Costing of Professional Support Services in Local Authorities*, Bolton: PARC, 1988

Pugh, D.S. *Organisation Theory*, Harmondsworth: Penguin, 1971

Pyke, J. and Barners, R. *TQM in Action*, London: Chapman & Hall, 1994

Ray, R. *Management Strategies in Athletic Training*, Champaign, IL: Human Kinetics, 1994

Sayers, P. *Managing Sports and Leisure Facilities: a Guide to Competitive Tendering*, London: E & FN Spon, 1991

Sceats, A. *Sports and Leisure Club Management: a Handbook for Organisers*, Plymouth: Macdonald and Evans, 1985

Scott, J. and Rochester, A. *Effective Management Skills, Vol. 1—Managing Work*, London: Sphere in Association with the British Institute of Management, 1984

Scott, M. *Law and Leisure Service Management*, Harlow: Longman in conjunction with ILAM, 1993

Shaw, R. *Spread of Sponsorship in the Arts, Sports, Education, the Health Service and Broadcasting*, Newcastle upon Tyne: Bloodaxe Books, 1993

Shoebridge, M. *Information Sources in Sports and Leisure*, East Grinstead: Bowker-Saur, 1992

Slack, T. *Understanding Sports Organisations: the Application of Organization Theory*, London: Human Kinetics, 1997

Smithson, S. and Whitehead, J. *Customer Care in Leisure Organisations: Guide-lines for Managers and Staff*, Reading: ILAM in conjunction with Farnborough College of Technology, 1990

Sports England. *Getting it Right—Running Sports.* Wetherby: Sports England Publications, 1996

Sports England. *General Household Survey—Participation in Sports in Great Britain 1996*, Wetherby: Sports England Publications, 1999

Sports Council. *Managing Sports and Recreation under CCT: the Future Client Side Role*, London: Sports Council, 1990

Sports Council. *Recreation Management (Facilities—Fact File 1)*, London: Sports Council, 1994-5

Stayte, S. and Watt, D.C. *Events from Start to Finish*, London: Institute of Leisure and Amenity Management, 1998

Stier, W.F. *Fundraising for Sports and Recreation*, Champaign, IL: Human Kinetics, 1994

Tancred, B. and Tancred, G. *Leisure Management*, London: Hodder & Stoughton, 1992

Taylor, W.J. and Watling, T.F. *Basic Arts of Management*, London: Random House Business Books, 1988

Thomas, D.G. *Competitive Swimming Management*, London: Human Kinetics, 1988

Thomas, E. and Woods, M. *The Manager's Casebook*, London: Duncan Petersen, 1992

Thomson, I. *Alternative Approaches to Sports Development*, Stirling University, 1992

Tilling, R. Presentation at Scottish Athletics Conference, Glasgow, 2001

Torkildsen, G. *Torkildsen's Guides to Leisure Management*, Harlow: Longman, 1993

Torkildsen, G. *Leisure and Recreation Management*, 4th edn, London: E & FN Spon, 1999

Walker, M.L. and Seidler, T.L *Sports Equipment Management*, USA: Jones and Bartlet, 1992

Watt, D.C. *Event Management in Leisure and Tourism*, Harlow: Longman, 1992

White, A. *Managing for Performance: How to Get the Best out of Yourself and Your Team*, London: Piatkus, 1995

Wilson, N. *The Sports Business: The Men in the Money*, London: Piatkus, 1988

Wright, J. *Recreation and Leisure: City and Guilds Course 481, parts 1 and 2*, Kingston upon Thames: Croner, 1994

Yiannopoulos, C.T. *Sports and Management: in Search of Common Language*, Athens: Medoussa, 1996

Yule, W. and Gold, A. *Wise Before the Event*, London: Calouste Gulbenkian Foundation, 1993

Zeigler, E.F., Bowie, G. and Paris, R. *Competency Development in Sports and Physical Education Management: a Primer*, Champaign, IL: Stipes, 1988

ENCYCLOPEDIA OF SPORTS

Volume - 2

SPORTS MARKETING

ENCYCLOPEDIA OF SPORTS

Volume – 2

SPORTS MARKETING

Edited By:

Y.K.REDDY

SURESH PADMANAVIA

SRISHTI BOOK DISTRIBUTORS

New Delhi (India)

ISBN 978-81-89948-09-2 Vol-2
ISBN 978-81-89948-20-7 Set

Published by :
SRISHTI BOOK DISTRIBUTORS
4378/4-B-202, 2nd floor,
J.M.D. House, Ansari Road,
Daryaganj, New Delhi-110002
E-mail : srishtibookdistributors@yahoo.co.in
Ph. 011-23284904

***Edition* : 2011**

Rs. 1000 (Each Volume)

Typeset by :
Ambey Laser Printers
Delhi.-110046

Printed at
Shivani Art Press
Delhi-110032

Preface

The world of sports has changed radically over the recent years. What was once just a local Saturday afternoon activity for both participants and spectators now takes place on any night of the week, and can be intrastate or interstate, with the fan experience live or mediated. In increasing numbers, supporters are demonstrating their allegiance to sports via the merchandise they buy, the literature they read and the television they watch. Sports in the 2000s is a multifaceted, multimedia industry, with growing appeal to an ever-increasing number of stakeholders and supporters. What was once a clearly defined, stable activity is now a highly complex, constantly changing industry. This is the environment in which the current generation of sports marketing practitioners must operate.

The sports experience can present a host of problematic consumer preferences for the sports marketer to target—compounded by the fact that sports no longer faces competition merely from within its own ranks. With decreasing amounts of leisure time, and discretionary income being judiciously allocated, sports now has to compete for the consumer dollar with a vast array of both sports and non-sports activities. The various branches of the arts, the increasing proclivity towards short-term tourist activities and the growth of passive recreation all provide viable alternatives to the sports experience for the modern consumer. Sports is now just one component, albeit a very important one, of the entertainment milieu.

Given this cluttered environment, sports attracts consumers not through serendipity, but rather through carefully structured planning, creativity and perseverance. Successful sports marketing is the implementation of clearly defined strategies which are rooted in both perspiration and inspiration. The notion 'if we build it they will come' is no longer appropriate. Planning processes are now required that view, sports not merely as an athletic endeavour, but as an activity in which multiple individuals and groups can engage.

There is little doubt that sports is changing both on and off the field. While athletes have become fitter, stronger and faster to cope with the demands of the modern game, the management of sports has, at the same time, become a highly professional endeavour. To facilitate this process, and enhance the expertise of those charged with its effective management, education and training are now vital components of the sports environment. Increasingly, both the sports industry and educational institutions have realised that sports can no longer be managed by individuals or groups who do not come equipped with certain skills.

It is important to recognise the range of skills required to manage the modern sporting organisation when preparing the educational framework for future sports managers. The growth in sports marketing teaching and practice is accompanied by a growth in sports management education generally. Sports marketing remains a popular area of study, viewed as exciting and attractive to the next generation of sports managers. The challenge of preparing graduates and practitioners for the rigours of sports management lies in balancing the emotion and tribal character of sports with the need for an objective application of business principles. Modern management of sports is more than just a response to traditional actions or present realities. It encompasses a vision for the future and the strategies and implementations required for bringing about that vision.

This vision is based on a wellrounded curriculum cognisant of the need to integrate sports industry knowledge with the fundamentals of management, marketing, accounting and finance, and other business studies. Texts such as this one play an important part in assisting in this process. They are constructed by the profession who understands the sports experience and what it means to play, spectate and officiate, and who understands the meaning of management.

The ability to translate theory into effective strategic practice is the result of management education programs that utilise business practice to comprehend contemporary sports while simultaneously remaining cognisant of what sports means to the end consumer or fan. The modern consumer is discerning and needs to be treated as such. This text, through the provision of theory and example, will result in future generations of sports marketers having the skills critical to the successful promotion of their sports.

Sports Marketing is unique from two perspectives. It is the first sports marketing text to truly integrate international examples. Case studies, sportviews and examples from a myriad of national and international sports and events have been used to reinforce theoretical positions and key points. While this is important, more significant is the fact that there has been a conscious decision to place the text within a framework of strategic decision making.

Sports Marketing is aimed at undergraduates and entry-level graduate sports marketing students. It is also a useful resource for the practitioner engaged in sports marketing. While the case studies provide obvious examples of how the text can be used, we hope that this text will be used by sports marketing teachers and practitioners not only to stimulate the thought processes, but to engage with and improve the sports experience for the benefit of all concerned. Finally, it is hoped that the utility of this text will result in calls for ongoing literary contributions to the field of sports management.

CONTENTS

Introduction

According to the *Sports Business Journal,* an industry trade publication, today, sports marketing is a US$250-billion industry and includes sports-related advertising and venue signage, athlete endorsements, facility construction, sporting goods and licensed merchandise, event management and marketing services, sponsorship and ticket sales, media broadcast rights, and multimedia—including sports-related websites, magazines, books, and video games.

In the present time sports marketing has assumed an important place as the scope of sports related commercial markets are expanding everyday. In a broad sense sports marketing refers to the specific application of marketing principles and processes to sports products e.g., teams, leagues, events, etc. and the marketing of non-sports products e.g., cigarettes, beer, long-distance phone service, etc. through associations with sports. The first sports management firms, which managed endorsement deals and contract negotiations for professional coaches and athletes, began forming in the 1960s and early 1970s with Mark McCormack's International Management Group (IMG), Bob Woolf (Woolf Associates), and Donald Dell's ProServ.

Similarly, the first full-service sports marketing and sponsorship agencies were founded in the mid-1970s with Millsport LLC (now part of The Marketing Arm) and ProServ, which had expanded beyond athlete management into event production and sponsorship negotiations. The explosive growth of sports marketing came with the 1984 Summer Olympics in Los Angeles, when corporate sponsors used the Games as a platform to market their brands. New content distribution channels like the Web, email, voice messaging, streaming video and mobile are creating many new opportunities and challenges for sports marketers. Indeed it was the 1996 Summer Olympics at Atlanta where the big commercial break through was made, Coca-Cola were the main sponsors of the games, they had their headquarters in the city at the time.

This is currently a multi billion dollar industry. Players such as Tiger Woods, LeBron James, Peyton Manning, Sachin Tendulkar, M.S. Dhoni and many more are finding ways to make millions of dollars. They are getting outstanding deals to wear clothing during events, or do a commercial, or a photo shoot for and advertisement. Sports Marketing is becoming a current trend in business education now also. Many institutions and physical education colleges are offering this elective class and Sports Management classes. Many colleges are now offering Sports Management programmes to support the demands for employees in this industry.

The next decade will witness the most significant changes in the way we consume sports since the emergence of mass audience television and its growing popularity.The proliferation and fragmentation of media channels such as satellite and cable television, the Internet and mobile telephony has undermined the traditional free television model in every advanced economy. Well managed sports will remain valuable content and many will continue to prosper. Forward thinking governing bodies will grasp the opportunity by repackaging their sports to appeal to the new broadcast landscape. Others will not.

Brand marketers have seen the effectiveness TV advertising.The growth of sponsorship as a marketing tool is one consequence. However, sports must compete for the sponsor dollar with other forms of content such as music, the arts and culture and cause-related marketing, each of which offers a compelling alternative. At the same time some of sports biggest stakeholders, the soft drink, wine and fast food companies, will come under growing pressure from social and political pressure groups concerned about levels of obesity, binge drinking and anti social behaviour that have become such a part of modern life.

Companies such as McDonalds, Coca Cola and Budweiser face calls to cut its ties with sports, a bandwagon which will gain momentum over the next decade. Are we facing a ban on soft drink sponsorship similar to that of tobacco? Certainly, the removal of hundreds of millions of sponsorship dollars from the sports economy worldwide would have devastating consequences.*The Future of Sports Marketing* is a vital resource for marketing professionals within the sports business industry.

Defining Sports Market

Marketing, as defined by Kotler et al. is 'a social and managerial process by which individuals and groups obtain what they need and want through creating and exchanging products and value with others'. The identification of consumer needs and wants is a critical aspect of the marketer's role. Marketing strategies must be based on known consumer needs. In sports, it has been assumed that the original form of the game is naturally attractive and therefore satisfies consumer needs.

Many sports have modified rules to make their games more attractive, and in the case of cricket one-day matches have become an important part of the range of product offerings. One-day international matches played throughout an Australian summer have more readily satisfied consumer need for compressed entertainment and a quick result. At junior levels, many sports have been significantly modified to satisfy the desire of many more young people to participate in the game. Now T20 mathes creates tremendous scope in product promotion.

Inherent in this change has been the recognition that juniors wish to develop game skills through actual participation, to have fun, and in general to be with their friends through the sports setting. The sports marketer must identify what needs and wants are being satisfied through the exchange process. Kotler et al. (1994: 7) identify the process of exchange 'as the act of obtaining a desired object from someone by offering something in return'. What is offered in return for the sports consumer's membership fees or entry fee may include social interaction, physical activity, an avenue for competition, health and fitness, as well as entertainment. Identifying the needs of various segments of population is the challenge inherent in the early phase of the marketing process. Obtaining this information will allow the sports product benefits to be communicated in such a way as to define the sport's positioning. For example, the product attributes of one-day cricket matches and five-day Test match cricket are different, and are likely to attract different segments of the market.

Having established the range of product attributes in relation to needs and wants, the sports marketer embarks on the challenge of effecting the exchange. Sporting organisations must develop a mix of marketing strategies to influence consumers to buy their products, via either attendance or participation. Combined, the four variables of product, price, promotion and place are known as the traditional four Ps of marketing.

Sports Marketing Mix

The seven component strategies of the marketing mix, composed of the traditional 4Ps of marketing plus the 3Ps of service—process, people and physical evidence. These 7Ps form the nucleus of this book, and each will be described in more detail in later.

A brief description of the 7Ps is as follows:

- *Product*—ensures that product characteristics, provide benefits to the consumer (includes identifying the actual product).
- *Price*—ensures that the product is priced at a level that reflects consumer value.
- Place—distributes the product to the right place at the right time to allow ease of purchase.
- *Physical Evidence*—is the visual and/or tangible clues of the service product, such as the design and construction of the facility, and in general the aesthetic appeal.
- *Process*—represents the convergence of the marketing and operations functions and therefore affects real-time service delivery and quality.
- *People*—responsible for delivering the event and are a major distinguishing quality factor in the consumption process.
- *Promotion*—communicates the product's ability to satisfy the customer through advertising, personal selling, sales promotions, sponsorship, public relations and promotional licensing.

In sports, the combination and implementation of these marketing mix variables change due to the unique characteristics of the sports product. The most notable change from the traditional 4Ps of marketing is not only in its expansion to 7Ps, but in the order we recommend in determining marketing strategies for sporting organisations, particularly those reliant on facilities to host the sporting contest.

Characteristics Sports Marketing

In 1980 Mullin identified, for the first time, a series of characteristics of the sports product that affect the marketing process. Mullin argued that sports had progressed from a form of institution that was simply 'administered' to a form of organisation that required 'managing'.

In making this distinction, he noted that sports had reached a phase in its development where it was incumbent on the sports manager to be actively seeking ways to expand the revenue base of the organisation. Typically, the administrator is responsible for maintaining the status quo within the sporting organisation.

The manager, on the other hand, is responsible for assessing and evaluating environmental trends likely to affect the organisation's survival and, ultimately, its success. The modern sports marketer is charged with one simple responsibility: to increase the sources of revenue for the sports.

Sports Product

Sports is invariably intangible and subjective. It is inconsistent and unpredictable. Marketing emphasis must be placed on product extensions rather than the core product. Sports is generally publicly consumed, and consumer satisfaction is invariably affected by social facilitation. Sports is both a consumer and an industrial product. Sports evokes powerful personal identification and emotional attachment. It has almost universal appeal and pervades all elements of life, i.e. geographically, demographically and socioculturally.

Price of Sports

- The price of sports paid by the consumer is invariably quite small in comparison to the total cost.
- Indirect revenues (e.g. from television) are often greater than direct operating revenues (e.g. gate receipts).

- Sports programmes have rarely been required to operate on a for-profit basis.
- Pricing is often decided by what the consumer will bear rather than by full cost recovery.

Promotion of Sports

- Widespread exposure afforded to sports by the media has resulted in a low emphasis on sports marketing and, often, complacency.
- Due to the high visibility of sports, many businesses wish to associate with sports.

Sports Distribution System

Sports generally do not physically distribute their product. Most sports products are produced, delivered and consumed simultaneously at the one location. The exceptions are sporting goods and retail and broadcast sports. Almost every element of marketing requires significantly different approaches when the product being marketed is sports. Predictably, the critical differences lie in the unique aspects of the sports product, and the unusual market conditions facing sports marketers.

Consumer Involvement

Perhaps the most readily identifiable characteristic is the 'expertise' demonstrated by the sports consumer. On the one hand this is a disadvantage, as every move made by the sports manager and coaching staff is critically examined and dissected. The 'armchair selector' syndrome is an issue within sports. It is, however, one reason why sports is so popular. The pervasiveness and universal nature of sports, and the ease with which the consumer identifies with the sports product, compensate for the intensity with which the consumer follows sports. Very few businesses in the world are viewed with such simplicity and such personal identification by the consumer.

Unpredictability

As with most service products, the consumer's interpretation and enjoyment of the sports product are open to considerable subjectivity. Participation in, and attendance at, sporting contests allow the consumer to gain varying forms of gratification. For example, some spectators may enjoy the closeness of the game, others the entertainment surrounding the game, and yet others the inherent strategies of the contest. This makes it difficult for the sports marketer to ensure a high probability of satisfaction and hence repeat-attendance. The intangibility and subjective nature of sports spectating and sports attending clearly align sports with the service industry. No tangible product is taken from the sporting contest as opposed, for example, to the purchase of a washing machine or similar goods.

Equally unpredictable is the actual sporting contest, which varies week by week. This heterogeneity is a feature of sports. It is the unpredictability of the result, and the quality of the contest, that consumers find attractive. For the sports marketer this is problematic, as the quality of the contest cannot be guaranteed, no promises can be made in relation to the result, and no assurances can be given in respect of the performance of star players.

Unlike consumer products, sports cannot and does not display consistency as a key feature of marketing strategies. The sports marketer therefore must avoid marketing strategies based solely on winning, and must focus on developing product extensions rather than on the core product (i.e. the game itself). Product extensions include the facility, parking, merchandise, souvenirs, food and beverages—in general, anything that affects spectators' enjoyment of the event.

Cooperation and Competition

Another feature of the sportscape is the peculiar economy that dictates, in professional leagues at least, that clubs must both engage in fierce competition and at the same time co-operate. This is necessary to ensure that each club's contribution to the league enhances the strength of the league.

Sponsorship

Sponsorship of sports is also a unique feature of the sports economy. While not necessarily specific to sports, sponsorship has provided, and continues to provide, an opportunity for commercial advertising by corporations and businesses. Sponsorship represents the 'industrial' component of the sports product, and is manifested through commercial advertising of its industrial aspect.

Publicity

Complacency in developing adequate marketing strategies has resulted from an almost unlimited amount of media exposure for sporting clubs, leagues and associations. Sports has traditionally been able to rely on publicity as its principal form of marketing and promotion. The disadvantage of relying on publicity is the amount of negative press that occurs during a season or major event. More recently, major leagues, clubs and associations have become cognisant of the need to develop an effective public relations strategy to counter the issues that typically occur during a season or event.

Distribution

The final characteristic relates to the distribution system used by sports. As with most service providers, sports participation and spectating revolve around specific facilities for specific sports. To attend a sporting contest, spectators must travel to the venue, usually a major facility within a city. The actual facility becomes an integrated component of the marketing function, as the sports product is produced, consumed and delivered at the same time at the same venue.

Many facilities, such as the Melbourne Cricket Ground (MCG), the Royal Melbourne Golf Club, Fenway Park in Boston and Wembley Stadium in London, have developed an aura and mystique as a result of heroic performances on the ground over the years.

As a consequence of developments in television networks, the distribution system for sports has undergone radical change during the past decade. It is now possible to distribute a game to all parts of the country and the world via the networks. The introduction of pay-television in Australia has further enhanced the distribution network for sports, as well as increasing the number and levels of different sports competitions shown. In general, however, the televised sports product is different from the live event. The mix of benefits is slightly different in each mode of consumption.

Due to the relatively stable nature of distribution (i.e. one major stadium per sports per city), it is vitally important to locate teams and facilities so that they are able to compete effectively in the market. In Australia, product distribution has been the focus of intense debate during the past decade.

A comparison between the United States and Australia illustrates how important location of the product is in terms of developing appropriate marketing strategies, particularly in view of the substantial population differences between the two countries. The United States, for example, has a population in excess of 280 million, compared to Australia's 19 million. The US national competitions of basketball (National Basketball Association, NBA), football (National Football League, NFL), baseball (Major League Baseball, MLB) and ice hockey (National Hockey League, NHL) have evolved past the point of overcapacity in any one city.

Significantly, the three major markets of New York, Los Angeles and Chicago (all with a population of 10-14 million) all host professional franchises. However, not one of these markets hosts more than two teams of any one code. The importance of marketing as a revenue-generating activity for the clubs is important in this issue of location. Overcapacity intensifies competition and reduces the available income for each of the teams located in any one common market.

Significance of Marketing in Sports Management

As indicated earlier, marketing plays a key role in the sporting organisation's overall planning efforts. This has not always been the case. The professionalisation of sports during the past 20-30 years has raised the level of importance of the marketing function. For much of sports history, volunteers have administered organisations in the true spirit of amateur participation. As sports systems founded on club-based models evolved from amateur to professional clubs, leagues and associations, there was a lengthy transition period between what is described as 'kitchen table' administration and professional management. In Australia, this was the period pre-1970. During this period of voluntary administration the marketing function was non-existent. The predominant tasks were to ensure the ongoing operation of the club, league or association. Administrators adopted a very narrow view of their organisation, preferring to concentrate on internal operations. Typically, administrators dealt with only half of the accounting and budgetary process—the allocation and control of expenditures. Even as sporting organisations began to professionalise, the administrator 'culture' lingered for some years.

World Series Cricket (WSC) subsequently proved to be the catalyst that forced sporting organisations in Australia to embrace a greater range of business functions. This view is supported by Halbish (1995: 3), noting that 'looking back traditional cricket had grown out of touch with the fast emerging professionalism of sports in Australia'. By 1980,

WSC and the ACB had reconciled their differences; however, from that point marketing was to become an important element of business activity in sports.

Initially, marketing activities were outsourced by a number of sports. The ACB, for example, granted marketing rights to a company known as PEL Marketing. Taylor (1984: 13), managing director of PEL at the time, made the following observations about the status of marketing and sponsorship in sports following the reconciliation: Five years ago the Australian Cricket Board did not have a published programme... Last year more than 30,0000 copies of the ACB programme were sold and this year almost 20 publications will be on sale. Work has also been put into merchandising... it has taken five years to develop 29 licensees, but this season we expect cricket merchandise to top $5 million in retail turnover and to start producing a satisfactory level of return.

The importance that marketing has gained, despite a long period of resisting the need to promote and nurture new and fertile markets. For the first time, the identification and nurturing of new markets brought recognition that the customer is central to ongoing organisational survival. Sports had to find ways of generating revenue to sustain the growing costs of professional competitions. One-day cricket is an example of modifying the product to increase market share for the sports. Together with sports operations (i.e. all that surrounds the management of fielding a team), marketing is a sporting organisation's principal ground for identifying and creating a competitive advantage. Normal acquisitional strategies associated with for-profit firms are not so readily applicable to sports. Internal growth strategies tend to be the major ground on which sports competes.

Ethical Dilemmas

Increasingly, commercial pressures create tension for the sports marketer. That is, sportmarketing executives often find themselves caught between an opportunity to generate revenue for their sports and the consequences of changes that might accompany these revenues. Consider, for example, the staging of an Olympic marathon during the middle and hottest part of the day because a television network asks for it to be staged at that time to maximise ratings. What do you do? Clearly, scheduling the marathon at this time will not be in the best interests of the athletes. Alternatively, what do you do if you work with the NRL and the strategic goal is to reduce the number of clubs in the competition? This was a real-life dilemma, as the South Sydney Rugby League club was removed from the competition as part of a rationalisation strategy. The club subsequently won the right, through a protracted legal battle, for readmission to the NRL competition from 2002.

As a sportmarketing manager, with the goal of maximising revenues for the competition, how do you balance the commercial interests against social and community interests in the South Sydney club? These two examples illustrate ethical dilemmas, which are practical problems requiring solutions, often involving equally compelling reasons to act one way or the other. In essence, the sports manager must determine what is the right thing to do without a definitive 'rule book' available to guide decision making.

Although space precludes a detailed analysis of ethics and corporate social responsibility, sports managers must consider their actions within a broader societal framework. De Sensi and Rosenberg (1996:115) note that social responsibility 'involves a moral and legal accountability on the part of individuals for self and others... Questions regarding the nature of the complex relationship between society, sports and the formal organisations of sports are raised within social responsibility'. Given the significant standing of sports in Australian culture and as a social institution, community expectations in relation to the behaviour of sports managers are often high. There are many examples of sports-marketing decisions that create ethical tensions for individuals, and collectively for organisations, wishing to be good corporate citizens.

MARKETING THROUGH SPORTS

This refers to the use of marketing mix variables to communicate the benefits of sports participation and spectatorship to potential consumers. Ultimately, the goal is to ensure the ongoing survival of the sports in rapidly changing environmental circumstances. It is this aspect of marketing that has only recently developed in sporting organisations. Survival depends largely on the principal purpose of the sporting organisation. National sporting organisations predominantly associated with elite-level professional sporting competitions will be striving to develop their marketing mix to ensure that the sports product is attractive as a form of live entertainment and live television. Sports-governing bodies will also be responsible for ensuring that participation in their sports remains healthy. Participants are the lifeblood of sports, as they become the next generation of champions and spectators.

We do not make any notable distinctions in this book between marketing strategies specifically pursued for either spectator or participant sports. The theories posited are equally applicable, regardless of the principal objective of the marketing strategy. As with all marketing strategies, when the objectives change, the actions or strategies used to achieve the objectives also change. The application of the marketing mix does not, although various components of the mix may assume more importance in the two different scenarios. For example, the outlets used to advertise a junior sporting competition would be different from those used to advertise a major sporting event.

Students of sports marketing should adapt the concepts of sports marketing to either situation, because each is vital to the ongoing survival and financial wellbeing of individual sporting organisations. Sponsorship of sports by firms is an example of marketing 'through' sports. Large corporations use sports as a vehicle to promote and advertise their products, usually to specifically identifiable demographic markets known to follow a particular sports. Sports with significant television time are very attractive to firms seeking to promote their products through an association with sports. Developing licensing programmes is another example of marketing through sports. Typically, major companies such as Coca-Cola or Nike pay for the right to use a sports logo to place on their products to stimulate sales.

Given these perspectives, and information pertaining to marketing in general, the following definition of sports marketing is offered: Sports marketing is a social and managerial process by which the sports manager seeks to obtain what sporting organisations need and want through creating and exchanging products and value with others. The exchange of value with others recognises the importance of the sports consumer. The ability to recognise the needs and wants of consumers does not necessarily imply action. It is the action associated with the marketing process in sports that is the focus of this text. This is known as the marketing management process, which is described by Kotler et al. (1994: 9) as 'the analysis, planning, implementing and control of programmes designed to create, build and maintain beneficial exchanges with target buyers for the purpose of achieving organisational objectives'.

CHAPTER

Sports-marketing Planning Process

The strategic sports-marketing planning process is very important in deciding the critical aspects. It aims at to–

1. Analyse the external environment, the forces driving industry competition and the publics to be served.
2. Analyse the sporting organisation internally, to determine mission, goals and objectives, and to assess strengths, weaknesses, opportunities and threats (SWOT).
3. Examine market intelligence data in relation to the existing product range.
4. Determine the specific marketing mission and objectives for the prescribed period of the plan.
5. Determine the core marketing strategy using marketing mix variables, identifying and selecting the desired competitive position in relation to an identified sustainable competitive advantage.
6. Establish tactics to achieve objectives, and formulate benchmarks to measure progress.
7. Implement and operationalise the planned strategies.
8. Measure the success of core strategies, and adjust strategies where necessary.

A marketing programme is not delivered in isolation of the organisation-wide planning process. In normal circumstances, the marketing planning process must reflect the overall plans for the organisation. In sports, there is often little difference between organisation-wide planning and the marketing planning process. The ARU's overall direction and success are based solely on its major product offerings: Test match and club rugby. Determining the difference between organisation-wide planning and marketing planning requires careful attention by sports marketers. The first step of the SSMPP is equivalent to conducting an inventory. The data collected form the basis of decisions made later in the process.

External Forces

The environmental factors requiring consideration, are the forces that affect an organisation indirectly, they include government legislation, economic, climate, technology, political forces, and demographic and social trends. It is important for sporting organisations to monitor changes in each of these forces. Government legislation, for example, can alter the economic infrastructure of an industry through legislative changes. For instance, when pay-TV was introduced to Australia in the 1990s, government legislation dictated that pay-TV operators would not be able to sell advertising time for the first five years. This was designed to protect the free-to-air networks and, given the importance of sports programming to television revenues, this policy reduced pay-TV's capacity to generate revenue and, in turn, its capacity to pay for rights to broadcast sports. Technology can also change the way businesses operate. The Internet, through World Wide Web pages and e-mail, has altered the means through which organisations can communicate with members, players, coaches and officials. It is also an important source of information for fans.

Political forces, at a macro-level, might involve government policy directly affecting an industry. A change of government often leads to new policies. The most obvious and important policy for many sports is government policy in relation to funding support. Most national and state sporting organisations are non-profit, with limited sources of revenue. Government funding is critical for ongoing development. One simple example of government policy is the focus of funding and programmes for the elite or for mass participatory programmes. Demographic and social trends refer to the changing population makeup. For example, the increasingly multicultural composition of Australian communities will affect when, why and how sports marketers communicate with the community. It cannot be assumed that all sports consumers in a diversified society will respond in the same way to all marketing strategies, or that everyone will respond to the same sports. For many years, sporting organisations neglected to examine these forces and the impact that a changing environment might have on their sports.

Industry Competition

On a more direct level, sporting organisations need to monitor the industry in which they compete. Porter described five forces that managers should review when examining competition and the attractiveness of an industry:

1. The intensity of competition between existing firms within an industry;
2. The bargaining power of buyers;
3. The threat of substitute products;
4. The bargaining power of suppliers; and
5. The threat of new entrants.

The attractiveness of an industry is typically measured by profitability, which is not always the principal goal of non-profit and sporting organisations. Viability and winning games are important outcomes and become the primary measure of attractiveness for sporting organisations. In professional sports leagues, for example, the number and location of teams in respective markets require the league to assess the attractiveness of a market in terms of viability. Other questions indicative of industry attractiveness may include: Is the economic base of a city or region large enough to sustain just one or more than one team? How many other professional sports already exist in this market? What other recreation and leisure pursuits are potentially competing for disposable income?

POTER'S FIVE FORCES

Professional sports leagues for football will be used to illustrate the applicability of Porter's model. The model in this instance assumes that a professional sports league can be considered an industry, although this industry is subject to the broader market and competitive pressures of the entertainment and leisure sectors. The Australian Football League (AFL) and its member clubs, for example, turns over in excess of $300 million, making it a large and significant economic entity.

A brief review of Porter's five forces follows.

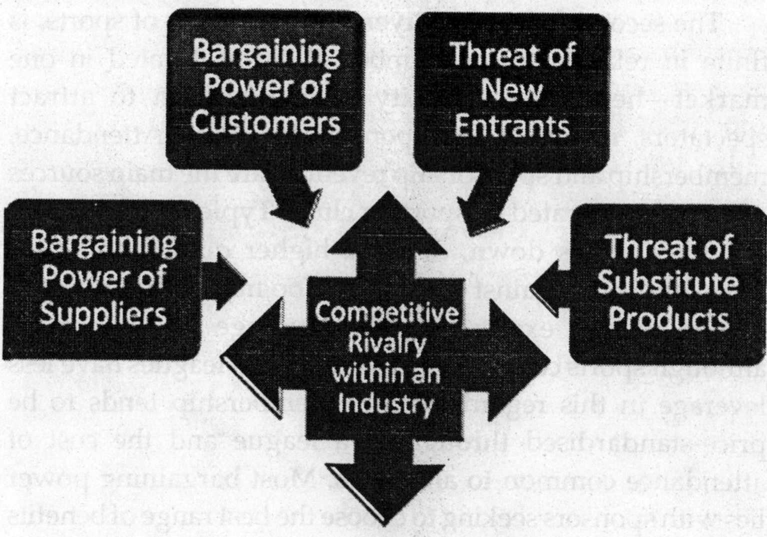

Fig: Porter's Five Forces

Intensity of Competition

The first force is the intensity of competition within the industry. In the case of a sports league, the number of teams and their location are the first indicators of the intensity of competition. Obviously, nine AFL clubs based in Melbourne and ten professional rugby league clubs based in Sydney intensify competition in these markets. This competition is further heightened by the presence of other sporting codes seeking sponsor dollars, spectators and members. In both codes, despite the large number of teams in each market, exit barriers have remained very high. This highlights the peculiar economics associated with sports leagues. Tradition, emotion and club loyalties often override the economic deficiencies experienced by some clubs, explaining why it has not been so easy to achieve a better geographical balance of teams competing in these national leagues.

Bargaining Power of Buyers

The second force, the buyers or consumers of sports, is finite in relation to the number of teams located in one market—hence the intensity of competition to attract spectators, members and sponsors by clubs. Attendance, membership and sponsorship revenues are the main sources of income generated by sporting clubs. Typically, customers can force prices down, demand higher quality and play competitors off against each other. Too many teams located in one market exacerbates the leverage of consumers, although sports consumers in some sports leagues have less leverage in this regard, as club membership tends to be price-standardised throughout a league and the cost of attendance common to all games. Most bargaining power lies with sponsors seeking to choose the best range of benefits from clubs. Sponsor bargaining power strengthens as the number of clubs based in a market grows.

Threat of Substitute Products

Another major force comes from the substitutability of products—that is, other recreation and leisure activities offering similar benefits to those provided by participation in sports. It is this force that provides the greatest range of competitive forces for a sports league. Under the broad heading of 'entertainment', a variety of products have the potential to attract the consumer's money normally available for leisure pursuits. These may include other sports, the movies, videos and the theatre. A major determinant of the strength of these potential substitutes is the switching cost associated with each product. Switching cost refers to the cost of changing brands or products. If the cost is low, both financially and psychologically, then consumers are more likely to switch, and a product becomes susceptible to substitution. This of course has the potential to erode profits. A major advantage possessed by various sports is that brand loyalty (to the sports or club) is very high. Psychological association with a sports or club is often far more important than economic considerations. In part, this explains the fanatical support for some sports and clubs, such as for soccer clubs worldwide and for AFL clubs in Australia.

Bargaining Power of Suppliers

Suppliers can exert bargaining power on participants in an industry by raising or reducing the quality of purchased goods and services. In a sports league the major supply required to operate successfully is the players. No one source has exclusive control over player supply and, with the exception of some sports like soccer.This is also the area that the sports marketer has least control over in terms of product quality. The bargaining power of the players has the potential to erode industry profits via their salary demands, rather than through what it costs to procure players from specific suppliers. In their quest for the ultimate prize, a premiership or championship, clubs often accede to the demands of high-priced athletes, explaining why the sports economy is often regulated by the use of salary caps.

Threat of New Entrants

New clubs or a new rival league can reduce industry profits and specific market share for the existing clubs and/or league. The commencement of the Superleague competition in rugby league is an example of a rival league's entry. Superleague, owned by News Ltd, was established to form a breakaway league, enticing existing clubs and players in the Australian Rugby League's (ARL) New South Wales competition to defect to Superleague. In the process, contractual obligations of both players and clubs were displaced, ultimately creating serious divisions within the league. In attempting to overcome the barriers to entry, the structure and product offerings of the ARL competition were seriously threatened. The gravity of this threat largely depended on the barriers to entry. The major barrier in this case was provided by the established and recognised keeper of the code—the ARL through the New South Wales Rugby League competition. Access to a supply of talented players is usually a major barrier to entry.

Publics

Examination of the external environment can be concluded by identifying the publics to which the sports is responsible. To an extent, some of these will have been identified from the competitive analysis conducted using the Porter framework. Kotler and Andreasen (1991: 89) define a public as 'a distinct group of people, organisations, or both whose actual or potential needs must in some sense be served'. The competitive forces model has already shown that diverse publics exist for a club competing in a professional league.

INTERNAL ORGANISATION CAPABILITIES

Sports managers gauge the significance of a sport's internal competencies on the basis of the opportunities and threats present in the sport's competitive environment. For example, the arrival of colour television in Australia in 1974 represented an opportunity for sports. The ACB,did not possess the internal capabilities at the time to capitalise on this development. Similarly, the globalisation of sporting competitions via the media has opened a window of opportunity for the professionalisation of rugby union.

SWOT Analysis

An important foundation for understanding the internal capabilities of a sports is the ability of the sports manager or marketer to match strengths and weaknesses with industry opportunities and threats. The international rugby union community clearly identified the threat of being overrun by the larger and more powerful professional football codes. The choice of the ARU to engage in an alliance with New Zealand and South Africa is evidence of a sports recognising an opportunity to share the production and professionalisation of rugby union, rather than be forced to expand the code in limited markets in each country. The strengths, weaknesses, opportunities and threats (SWOT) analysis is a commonly accepted tool used by managers to assess the current capabilities of their organisations. In essence, it provides a structure for their analysis:

- Strengths are resources, skills or other advantages relative to competitors.
- Weaknesses are limitations or deficiencies in resources, skills and capabilities that inhibit a sport's effectiveness in relation to competitors.
- Opportunities are major favourable situations in a sport's environment.
- Threats are major unfavourable situations in a sport's environment.

Mission, Objectives and Goals

Having established the internal capabilities, it is necessary to ascertain the mission of the organisation, followed by a review of the organisation's principal goals and objectives. The mission statement provides direction for the sports, defining and clarifying its meaning and reason for existence.

To be unambiguous, a mission statement should clearly answer 'What is our business?' For example, the Australian Sports Commission's mission statement is deceptively simple: 'To enrich the lives of all Australians through sport'. The key to defining a mission for a sporting organisation is to ensure that the mission statement is not so narrow that it limits its scope of operations or is simply a list of services provided.

In the context of sports, another factor impinges on formulating mission statements. Most sports are non-profit entities, and as such exist to achieve a common group of objectives by a relatively homogeneous group of people. Non-profits by definition exist to fight a cause. This cause becomes the operating charter, which is generally less flexible than the mission statement of a for-profit firm. If the cause ceases to exist, so too will the organisation. If profits cease to exist, the for-profit firm has the choice of redefining the business it wishes to be in and hence its range of product offerings. If, for instance, the ARU's alliance with other countries is not successful, professional rugby union could disappear and with it the Super 12s. Defining the mission implicitly defines the broad goals to be pursued by an organisation.

Organisational goals refer to the broad aims that organisations strive to achieve. In sports, these may include ensuring financial viability, increasing participation, raising the number of members, and stimulating public interest in the sports. Broad goals become the focus for devising more specific objectives, which are shown also for each key result area. Key result area, for example, is important, as the Australian Open in its own right is an important marketing and promotional tool used to lift the profile of tennis. These organisational objectives should provide the necessary detail to achieving key result areas. Objectives should be SMART, that is:

S—Specific M—Measurable A—Achievable R—Realistic T—Timebound

Key result area, for example, is specific in terms of competition players, non-registered players and participation frequency, and in each case a measurable target and time period are defined. Key result area, while a separate area, is in essence an aggregation of the other key result areas. The various products, including social and competitive tennis, major events and Grand Slam events for example, naturally promote and market the sports. The more successful these events and programmes, the greater the marketing-related benefits and the easier it will be to develop a coherent marketing strategy to promote and develop tennis at all levels.

USE OF INFORMATION SYSTEMS IN MARKET RESEARCH

The important phase of marketing research is undertaken to ensure that decisions made in relation to marketing missions and objectives are based on a sound understanding of the marketplace. Basically, market research in sporting organisations seeks to answer six questions about consumers in relation to their consumption of the product. Initially, sporting organisations need to know WHO their consumers are, but this is only the tip of the iceberg. WHY they choose the particular sports product and WHEN and WHERE that consumption takes place are equally important. WHAT that consumption entails in terms of pre-and post-event activities, and HOW the product is used also are critical in terms of establishing a complete consumer profile.

To make informed decisions, organisations need information, and lots of it. Yet the collection of this material is only a starting point for the construction of a management information system (MIS). Once compiled, this information must be integrated, analysed and used to guide the direction of the organisation. Stanton et al. (1995: 48) believe that an MIS is an 'ongoing, organised set of procedures and methods designed to generate, analyse, disseminate, store and later retrieve information for use in decision making'. Nevertheless, they also acknowledge that, for the MIS to be successful, the data should be not only of high quality but also used in a realistic manner and adopted as a source of decision making by the organisation. Information collated through market research and organised into meaningful data sets provides the foundation for sports marketers to determine marketing strategies. In other words, this information helps sports marketers refine and develop their sports, to know where and when to offer them and to what age groups and at what times. These are just a few examples of how this information underpins marketing strategy decisions.

MARKETING MISSION OBJECTIVE

Marketing must devise its own specific plans complementary to the organisation's overall mission, goals and objectives. The purpose of the planning process is to establish a competitive advantage over rival firms. The mission of marketing is to develop a range of product offerings that reflect a firm's organisation-wide mission statement. These products may be in the form of goods or services or both, depending on the nature of the business. In sports, the product offerings tend to be limited, although they are clearly in the service domain. Inherent in the challenge confronting the sports marketer is designing this portfolio of product offerings to achieve a competitive advantage.

Competitive Advantage

Porter (1985: 26) describes competitive advantage as 'the way a firm can choose and implement a generic strategy to achieve and sustain a competitive advantage'. This definition is specific to three generic strategies that he describes, which will be discussed later. The concept of competitive advantage, however, is broader than Porter's direct application to his theories. Implicit in this concept is the notion of sustainability. Without sustainability a competitive advantage becomes elusive. Coyne (1986: 55) posits three conditions that must be met for a firm to have achieved a sustainable competitive advantage:

- Customers perceive a consistent difference in important attributes between the producer's products or services and those of competitors.
- That difference is the direct consequence of a capability gap between the producer and competitors.
- Both the difference in important attributes and the capability gap can be expected to endure over time.

The key to sustainability is differentiation among competitor products. Coyne (1986: 55) further notes that: for a producer to enjoy a competitive advantage in a product/market segment, the difference or differences between him and his competitors must be felt in the marketplace: that is, they must be reflected in some product/delivery attribute that is the key buying criterion for the market. Each individual sports has its own unique set of product attributes, via the special nature of each sports. In this regard, some sports are inherently more appealing to some segments of the population.

For many years sports believed that these unique features of their game would remain popular forever. In Australian sports, this was proven not to be the case. The traditional sports of cricket, Australian rules football, netball and Softball suddenly found that their competitive advantage was being eroded by changing attitudes towards leisure options. Increasing diversity of recreational and sporting opportunities saw these sports struggling in the late 1970s and early 1980s, and as a consequence they had to re-examine their key buying criterion and look to repositioning themselves.

Product Market Expansion

Ansoff (1957) devised the product/market expansion grid, shown below, to help managers to balance their product offerings.

		Product: Present	Product: New
Mission or customer need	Present	Market Penetration	Product development
	New	Market development	Diversification

Fig: Product/market expansion grid

Market Penetration

Market penetration (or concentration) refers to making more sales to existing customers without changing the product. Typically, this involves intensifying the advertising and promotions campaign to attract consumer attention. Often this strategy involves also a price reduction aimed at moving consumers away from competitor products. The former New South Wales Rugby League (NSWRL) advertising and promotional campaign 'Simply the best', featuring Tina Turner, is an example of a market penetration strategy in sports. Although there were some minor adjustments to in terms of a crackdown on excessive on-field violence during the 1980s, the game itself remained unchanged. The NSWRL was successful in stimulating interest in the game, which translated into flourishing attendances and television viewership. The 'Simply the best' advertising campaign is considered to be one of the most sophisticated, inspiring, modern promotional campaigns seen in Australian sports.

Market Development

A market development strategy is a relatively inexpensive way of creating new markets for existing products. It typically involves few risks and requires only minor modification to the product. It depends on sound research indicating new segments of the population willing to buy the product.

Product Development

A product development strategy involves offering a modified or new product to current markets. Australian cricket's introduction of one-day cricket is an example of a sports exhibiting aspects of both market development and product development. One-day cricket can be considered to be the same product as four-and five-day cricket. Notably, the condensed version of the game has attracted a large following among women, which Test match cricket did not. On the other hand, one-day cricket can be considered to be a modified form of the game and better described as a product development strategy by the ACB. The weakness in this view is that one-day cricket has obviously had the capacity to expand the market interest in cricket. The traditional form of the game was not creating this expansion, although in recent times an exciting brand of cricket has been a feature of Test matches. This has largely been the result of rule changes that allow for extended hours to make up for time lost due to rain and the need to bowl a minimum number of overs in a day's play. Combined with an aggressive and relentless approach by the Australian cricket team, Test match cricket has undergone a resurgence of interest. It also illustrates the impact sports managers can have on the product through rule changes, such as those shown in cricket.

Regardless of the final distinction and product form responsible for growing cricket, it raises an interesting dilemma in sports marketing: namely, the point at which the game has been modified to such an extent that it is in effect a new product offering. In one-day cricket, for example, the basic elements of the game are still apparent: batting, bowling and fielding. The condensed version of the game forces more action, but whether this constitutes a new or different product is debatable, and illustrates the conflict that can exist between the 'purists' and those who prefer non-stop excitement in sports.

Another example of sports having to modify their range of product offerings has been seen in junior sports. For many years juniors played the adult form of the game, complete with all the rules and traditions associated with that particular sports. As research began to show that this was not providing a satisfactory sports environment for juniors, many sports were modified to make them more attractive to juniors. In essence, sports have been modified to encourage more success in game elements, increasing the likelihood of juniors continuing to participate. Although sports initially did not see this as a marketing related issue, this has now changed. The long-term fortunes of a sports, from both an elite performance and an ongoing interest and spectatorship perspective, are founded on the success of its junior programmes. Market development and product development strategies therefore assume a heightened level of importance, with sports carefully considering their range of sports offerings for juniors in various age groups.

Diversification of Product

The final category of product diversification requires a firm to develop an entirely new product for a new market. This can be achieved internally through a strong research and development function or via the external acquisition of a new firm with a new range of product offerings. In terms of the core sports product, this strategy is not common in sports. Sporting organisations in the main do not seek to buy other sporting organisations, although it remains an option, as demonstrated by the Western Bulldogs Football Club. In 1991 the Western Bulldogs (formerly Footscray Football Club) purchased a half-share in the Melbourne Monarch's Baseball Club. This is an example of product diversification in sports, in this case developing or acquiring a new but related (in terms of sports) product. The objective was to provide Western Bulldogs club members and supporters with added value via the provision of another sports, as well as to attract new consumers to the club and associated facilities.

The product/market expansion grid provides a framework for the sports marketer to consider the balance of product offerings. This balance of product offerings should reflect the marketing mission, which in turn should mirror the overall mission, goals and objectives of the organisation.

Generic strategies

Generic strategies as indicated earlier, Porter (1985) describes three generic strategies that firms can use as an alternative framework to achieve competitive advantage:

- Cost leadership;
- Differentiation; and
- Focus

Both the cost leadership and differentiation strategies aim to seek a competitive advantage in a broad range of markets. The focus strategy aims to seek a competitive advantage by using either a cost leadership or differentiation strategy in a narrow or niche market segment. Cost leadership is perhaps the simplest of the three options. The organisation's principal objective is to distribute its products to the widest possible market at a lower cost than competitors. Achieving lower cost may be the result of internal economies of scale, innovative technologies or lower distribution costs. In the end, it is the consumer who decides whether the cost differential is significant enough to warrant the purchase of one product over that of competitors.

Differentiation is typically more expensive. It involves an advantage based on distinctive product attributes. Products may, for instance, offer benefits that others do not, or they might be new and innovative products not currently available. Again, differentiation is seeking to establish its product prominence in as wide a market as possible. In sports, cost leadership strategies are difficult to achieve. In a sporting league, the clubs generally compete on equal terms in terms of cost. Standardised prices for attendance and membership reduce the significance of cost as a source of competitive advantage. For example, in 2002 AFL club memberships cost approximately $88, and ground entry to all matches was $16.50. If full cost recovery (in terms of covering event costs) were an objective, most sports would become too expensive for regular attendance.

Differentiation strategy provides scope for application in the sports setting. Although all the clubs in a league appear the same in terms of production, they do offer distinct brand images. These are of course the clubs themselves, with their distinctive colours, heritage and traditions, with which supporters identify with a good degree of emotional intensity. On a macro-level, each sports is a differentiated product in its own right, each offering similar benefits to consumers. The choice for consumers, in terms of physical activity, competing or spectating, is which of the myriad sports offer the best outlet to satisfy their needs and wants. This is equally applicable for juniors when choosing the sports in which to participate. Some sports, such as cricket, golf, Softball, swimming and netball, offer the challenge of special skill development without any excessive body contact. Football codes, basketball and wrestling offer a different range of skills, to be mastered in the context of body contact. The challenge for the sports marketer is to accentuate the differentiated product benefits to potential participants, and this sometimes means changing the fundamental rules and traditions of a sports. Although this is obviously an option, sports managers and marketers need to carefully consider the impact of proposed changes before implementation.

Organisation-wide data are required to place into context the role that marketing strategy plays in ensuring that a sports creates a sustainable competitive advantage. In the first instance, a sporting organisation needs to review the external environmental factors impinging on its existence. These factors are best described as the set of societal influences that encroach on all organisations, which include government legislation, economic environment, technology, political forces, and social and demographic trends. A more direct form of analysis involves a review of industry characteristics specific to a sports. Porter's five-forces model provides sports managers with a structured framework to scan the competitive environment, and is the precursor to a review of the internal capabilities of a sporting organisation.

Review of the external and internal environments is an important precursor to determining the best strategies to create a competitive advantage. In essence, marketing personnel are responsible for developing an array of product offerings that assist an organisation to achieve a competitive advantage. In predominantly single-product organisations such as sports, marketing's contribution to creating a competitive advantage is considerable. Sports and marketing, in many ways, are still becoming accustomed to each other. For many years most sports administrators did not believe that the role of marketing was important. However, as the sports landscape became increasingly competitive, sports managers began to adjust their thinking. Most large sporting entities have now created marketing departments, and many smaller sporting organisations are beginning to employ marketing specialists to manage the contribution of marketing.

CHAPTER

The Sports Consumer

CONSUMER BEHAVIOUR

Stage	Brief description	
Problem recognition	The consumer perceives a need and becomes motivated to solve a problem.	Motivation
Information search	The consumer searches for information required to make a purchase decision	Perception
Information evaluation	The consumer compares various brands and products	Attitude formation
Decision	The consumer decides which brand to purchase	Integration
Post-purchase evaluation	The consumer evaluates their purchase decision	Learning

Basic model of consumer decision making also referred to as EKB model (Engel, Kollat & Blackwell, 1969).

Mullin et al. (2000) suggest that models of consumer behaviour are a process rather than a prescriptive formula. To suggest that it is possible to construct a blueprint that is capable of determining behaviour is foolhardy, as the information sources for such models are both diverse and all-inclusive. The research on sports consumption is voluminous and in many instances emanates from disciplines beyond sports, although early works by Nowell (1995), Stotlar (1995) and Shoham and Kahle (1996), and more recently Hunt, Bristol and Bashaw (1999), Fink, Trail and Anderson (2002), Funk, Mahony and Ridinger (2002) and Mahony et al. (2002) indicate that it is being given increasing attention in the sports marketing literature. However, Kates (1998) suggested that while the fields of sports marketing, sociology and consumer research had much in common; the utilisation of each other's theories was minimal. He reasoned that by bringing such discourses together new marketing insights could result. Whatever the perception, there is little doubt that disciplines such as psychology, sociology, communication and anthropology have all contributed to our understanding of consumer behaviour.

The study of individual human behaviour is important and is the reason why the discipline of psychology has so much to offer our research efforts in understanding sports consumers. One important principle of psychology is that each individual is different and therefore each individual has a unique personality, different perceptions, life experiences, capabilities and interests, and importantly different attitudes, beliefs and values. Most but not all sports consumption is undertaken in groups, or with others. Many sports, for example, require a 'team' of people to compete against another team.

Attendance at professional sporting contests is always embedded in the context of large crowds, and the interactions between spectators are a large part of the sports experience. Sports sociologists are interested in determining how these group interactions shape the sports experience either through participation or as spectators. Anthropology is the study of mankind, in particular its societies and customs and the evolution of man as an animal. Sports has always been central to this form of analysis. The early origins of sports, for example, were embedded in the tribal instincts of primitive man whose skills required for survival, such as hunting, were practised and fine-tuned through sporting competitions. Viewed through the lens of anthropological analysis we can examine mankind's progress and its societies and customs through an institution such a sports. In other words, how does the conduct of contemporary sports explain mankind's evolution?

Funk, Haugtvedt and Howard (2000) explored the nexus between sports marketing and psychology. Delving into the social psychology literature, they determined that an understanding of attitude strength enabled the sports manager to better understand such factors as fan loyalty. In the process they suggested a framework for studying attitudes that enabled a greater understanding of fan allegiance to sports teams. Funk and James (2001) extended this analysis by establishing the Psychological Continuum Model (PCM), which was based on the four general boundaries of awareness, attraction, attachment and allegiance.

The vertical model characterised 'the various psychological connections that sports spectators and fans may form with specific sports and teams' (2001: 121). Models such as the PCM are important for the sports marketer as they allow for tracking, both upward and downward, of sports fans as well as determining the threshold limit. The authors argue that the PCM model is unique to sports in that it 'focuses on the psychological relationship an individual may form with a sports object' (2001: 122). Other models explaining consumer behaviour, such as Awareness, Interest, Desire, Action (AIDA), are premised on first being aware of the product, being interested enough to focus on product benefits and having a desire to purchase.

Funk and James (2001: 124) consider that the PCM 'concentrates on the internal psychological processes that account for different levels of psychological connection'. In other words, sports evokes interesting and varied levels of emotional attachment. Unquestionably, certain factors are germane to all consumer decision-making processes, and the integration of such provides a framework for understanding the consumer behaviour process. Consumer behaviour is invariably the product of what may be termed primary, secondary and tertiary factors.

Primary Factors

Primary factors are those elements that are internal to the purchaser or consumer. They are the set of beliefs that an individual holds in relation to the impact that the use of a particular product or service will have on their life. These elements are the intrinsic motivators to consume. They include issues such as the desire for health and wellbeing, and the opportunity to compete and test an individual's skills and capabilities against a variety of opposing forces, to establish new friendships or to escape 'reality'.

One theoretical example of this is Brooks' (1998) sports/exercise identity. She opined that a sports/exercise identity appears to be formed from comparisons between an individual's sports exercise self concept (a summary assessment of physique, physical condition, athleticism, socio-economic status, age and gender) and the stereotype the individual has of participants and attributes of movement encompassed by the sports or exercise' (1998: 38). While the backdrop for this specific research was the health industry and windsurfing clubs, it would be easy to extrapolate such a theory to a wide range of sports and physical activities.

An important consideration in the pursuit of any of the preceding activities is an individual's physical characteristics.

An individual weighing 65 kilograms may find contact or strength sports, especially those that do not have weight divisions, less enjoyable than sports or activities in which lightness is an attribute. Likewise, potential consumers whose centre of gravity is closer to the ground may be at an advantage where balance is a prerequisite, such as in gymnastics and skating.

Conversely, physically disadvantaged individuals may find particular sports and activities a challenge to be negotiated and overcome. The social aspect of sports has long been regarded as an important component of the consumer's decision-making process. Armstrong's (2001) study on the participation of black women in sports and fitness and its implication for sports marketing posited that, as a natural progression from the acknowledgement of women as viable sports consumers, ethnic consumers should be the focus of increased awareness. McCarthy (1998) had already examined marketing sports in the Hispanic community, but Armstrong's study was unique as she segmented it along the lines of both gender and ethnicity. Armstrong (2001: 18) concluded that 'marketing strategies designed for the mainstream market may not be effective in reaching ethnically diverse sections of the population'. Arguably, in a country as multicultural as Australia it makes sense to explore strategies for marketing to ethnically diverse groups.

Zhang et al. (2001) examined the relationship between five socio-motivational factors and attendance at sports events, in this case minor league hockey games. The five factors were: stress and entertainment, achievement-seeking, catharsis and aggression, salubrious effects, and community image. The authors suggested that three of these, stress and entertainment, achievement-seeking and salubrious effects, should be taken into account when constructing various marketing and promotional activities.

Secondary Factors

Secondary factors are those elements that are immediate influences on the decision-making process. Having recognised that a need exists, the individual explores potential solutions to the problem via avenues perceived to inject quality input into the process. In this instance, each opinion held by the individual is weighted by his/her degree of respect for the source of the information. Specifically, the most important secondary factor in the consumer behaviour model is the individual's prior exposure to the product or service. Past experience creates the evaluative mechanism on which future decisions to consume are based. Fans of the Collingwood Football Club, Arsenal, Canterbury Bulldogs or Chicago Cubs continue to watch their teams play because of their past experiences as fans of the particular club or code. If prior exposure had been less than satisfactory, spectators would have explored alternative avenues to fulfil their needs and expectations. However, in most cases fans of the above teams would be on the fourth or top tier of Funk's Psychological Continuum Model.

Resistance to change characterises the fourth or 'allegiance' tier and in such cases, especially for the long-suffering generations of Cubs fans who have not seen their team win a MLB World Series since 1908, past experience creates a loyalty bond that is rarely broken.

Family is another extremely influential secondary factor. In many instances successive generations follow the same codes, clubs and practices. Interestingly, however, in some instances gender differences may determine the importance of family variables. Dietz-Uhler and Harrick (2000) determined that women were more likely to think of themselves as sports fans if they attended events with family and friends, while men more usually considered themselves fans if they played the sports. Nevertheless, there is anecdotal evidence on every sports field and at every venue of the impact of family on the decision to be a sports participant or spectator.

If one family member plays golf, netball, soccer or volleyball, there is a higher possibility that children or siblings of the same gender (in gender-specific sports) will adopt that activity. In Australian V8 motor car racing, the Richards father-and-son combination is legendary. Similarly, while Tommy Smith is regarded as one of the greatest horse trainers Australia has produced, his daughter Gai Waterhouse has built a similar profile in this very competitive industry.

There is little doubt that if a parent is an avid fan of the National Rugby League (NRL) or the Australian Football League (AFL), it would be rare for a family member to support an alternative code of football. Even more significantly, a family divided by club loyalties— Carlton vs Collingwood, Manchester United vs Arsenal or Parramatta vs Canterbury—would be the source of interesting dinner conversations whenever the opposing teams met. Peers are also an important secondary factor. The behaviour and choices of companions often stimulate an individual to act. If a particular group is heavily involved in the consumption of basketball through playing, watching and reading, the pressure to conform to the group is strong. Individuals can either conform to the behaviour of the group or seek other groups whose interests are more in keeping with their own.

Other significant secondary factors may include clubs with which an individual is affiliated, schools or universities attended, or ethnic groups one is associated with. The values and beliefs of Scouts and Guides organisations, or the local Surf Lifesaving Club, will be incorporated into the individual's set of beliefs and influence the decision-making process. Similarly, a private school that provides a variety of extracurricular sports activities, such as rowing, skiing and mountain climbing, offers very different possibilities from a state-funded, inner-urban high school that is cramped for space and perhaps lacking the level of resources to purchase large-scale capital equipment. In such instances the academic focus may be on other areas of the curriculum, such as music, drama or visual arts, an environment providing a very different set of experiences. Moreover, a sports fan who is a recent immigrant to Australia will most probably follow a sports that resonates with his/her nationality before sampling more indigenous offerings. The ethnic association of many of the National Soccer League clubs provides an opportunity for the sports fan to bridge the gap between the old and the new sports experience. Geographical considerations are also important. The sports offerings of country or coastal schools and universities can be very different from those of their city cousins. Furthermore, climate cannot be ignored. Differences in sports consumption between Darwin and Hobart would be expected to exist, based on climatic differences.

Finally, although many Australians believe that they live in an egalitarian society, differences based on class, predominantly linked to economic considerations, do exist. While individual wealth will enable the purchase of the equipment to undertake a particular sports or activity, membership may be restricted for a variety of reasons. It may be easier to join a local golf club than the Royal Sydney or Royal Melbourne, even though the same equipment will serve at all venues. Moreover, unless you are a prime minister, the wait to join the Royal Canberra Golf Club may be very long indeed.

Tertiary Factors

Tertiary factors are those elements that are beyond the immediate sphere of influence, and should be recognised for what they are. In most instances they attempt to modify or construct individual behaviour, not just for the consumer's benefit but also for the benefit of the external group. Products, events and media provide information to the consumer in a manner that it is believed will encourage the consumer to buy. Occasionally, such groups may be at odds with each other. An incident on a sporting field may be downplayed by the organisation concerned as it does not want adverse publicity, which could result in reduced attendance or a lessening of participation.

Conversely, the media may play up the event, in the belief that graphic pictures or salacious commentary will sell additional newspapers or that television consumers will view other components of the host programme or indeed other programming. In most cases, media sources suggest that they are engaging in responsible journalism by presenting the product in toto. Equally, the ongoing discussion associated with an incident may prove a boon to talkback radio and discussion-type sports shows. Two examples from 2002 were the resignation of AFL Kangaroos captain Wayne Carey for personal, non-football reasons and the loss of all premiership points by the NRL's Canterbury Bulldogs for salary cap breaches.

In both instances the amount of media coverage devoted to these stories was arguably disproportionate to the nature of the events themselves. In the case of Carey, his private life was exposed in very public forums; in the case of Canterbury, it would be a brave sports fan or commentator that suggested that the Bulldogs were the only team in contravention of the salary cap. Nevertheless, various sections of the media capitalised on both incidents when there is no doubt that both the individual and club in question would have preferred a much lower profile.

Political, religious, cultural and service groups often use sports to place their organisation in a positive light or to piggyback on the popularity of a particular sports or activity. A local Rotary club's support of a community fun run is conceptually not very different from the entry of various church groups into a debate concerning the sporting use of religious holidays. In such instances, both groups are trying to establish a positive community profile. By linking themselves to sports and leisure they are endeavouring to position themselves as a similar product for consumption purposes.

Finally, an interesting trait on the part of our political leaders has been their willingness to be seen at a variety of sports events, to be photographed wearing a particular team's jersey or to stand in the winner's circle with the victors. It is an attempt on the part of politicians to be seen as just like 'the person in the street'. Here sports is being used as a fundamental link or lure to encourage the individual to consume a particular ideology. Although most senior politicians align themselves to one or other sports code or team, the connection has usually been ephemeral at best.

Decision-making Process and Sports Consumption

As previously mentioned, all the major steps in the sports consumption decision-making process are influenced by various elements. Person-specific factors (whether situational or demographic), psychological influences and social forces all play a part in constructing the context from which the decision to purchase is made.

Given that sports consumption is not unique to any one of the above, the potential starting point for a specific decision-making process is almost indiscernible. However, the following six steps represent the major components in the way the sports consumption process unfolds.

Step 1: Problem Recognition

Problem recognition is usually a result of the depletion of existing goods or services (...I *don't have much to do regarding entertainment late January...),* change in motivation (... I *always go to the movies but it does not allow me to have a chat with my friends...),* change in reference groups or family situation (... I *hang out a lot with my new friends from the physical education course I do at uni...* and new information, which may be interpersonal or the result of mass communication (*judging by the television and newspaper advertising, going to see outdoor events will be a lot of fun...).* Recognition of the problem (to find a new form of entertainment that will accommodate particular social needs) will lead to the search for information needed to make the decision.

Step 2: Information Search

The information search can take either of two forms: a recall of stored knowledge in the memory, or a seeking of additional information. Some goods and services are bought solely on the basis of an internal search (recalled memory) and are usually related to habitual or routine decision making. Here, the evaluation of alternatives is limited and based on what is remembered (... I *know there is a range of entertainment options available, such as the movies, going out to dinner, to see a show at the theatre or attend a sporting event...*).

With an external search the consumer is seeking information not contained in the memory. The adoption of an external search is usually a response to two factors: recognising that there is a risk involved in making the purchase (price and negative consequences of poor choice), and believing that this type of search will greatly increase the chances of making a correct choice (... *Perhaps I should find out the cost of the tickets, catering or the packages available, and see what some of my friends feel like doing...*). This leads to the consumer sourcing the information. At this stage, general information about the range of entertainment options available, complemented by more specific information about critical product characteristics *(Can I go with my friends? Can I have a chat during the event? etc.),* is collected.

Step 3: Information Source

Some sources of information are more powerful than others. For the sports marketer it is important to identify which information sources are most powerful when preaching the sales gospel. For example, a major source of information is via 'word of mouth' through family, friends and opinion leaders (... *My parents go to the theatre on regular occasions, so that might not be the coolest option for me and my friends...).* Another source of information is through general media forms, which include magazine and newspaper articles, new product reviews, and television coverage of events where the product is used.

In the sports industry, the wide media coverage received by most sports organisations allows for great opportunities to present sporting events as the preferred entertainment options to customers (... I *certainly see a lot of information about tennis in the papers since Hewitt retained his number 1 position in the rankings...).* Finally, information can be obtained through promotion media, which include myriad forms of advertising *(...If my memory serves me well there was an Australian Open insert in the last edition* of Inside Sports...). It can be seen that the information that is available combined with the source of the information will allow certain providers to position themselves favourably while the potential consumers are evaluating the alternatives available to them.

Step 4: Evaluation of Alternatives

An evaluation of alternatives is conducted according to a set of product selection criteria that may include the product benefits, the image of the product and/or the company, and the importance weighting of the range of product attributes according to the different groups of buyers (... *The theatre is for old people, during the movies we can't talk, going out for dinner is too expensive. Going to a sporting event offers scope on all those issues. But Melbourne can be very hot in January; it might be better to attend either indoor events or night matches at an outdoor venue...).* Only after evaluation does the decision to buy take place. e.

Step 5: Purchase

The decision to purchase a particular product or service can best be described as: Choice = Intention + Unanticipated circumstances.

Having made the decision to buy, consume or use, the individual proceeds with that intent in mind. However, at the last moment the individual may find that the store is out of stock, the stadium is full or the event has been postponed. Here a decision has to be made whether to consume an alternative offering or to wait for the selected item to become available (... *Everyone in the city must have turned up today, as all the ground passes are gone. However, it does not matter that much as I am on holidays. I will buy a ticket for tomorrow while I am here today just to be sure...).* Future product consumption is the result of post-purchase outcomes and evaluation.

Step 6: Post-purchase Outcomes/evaluation

Invariably there are three major outcomes possible during this stage:

(a) The consumer is entirely satisfied with the purchase and no further information is required (... *that was the most fun I have had at sporting event in quite a long time. Affordable, great action. I got to see some budding stars of the game, and I had a great time with my friends...).*

(b) The consumer is not entirely satisfied with the decision and may need to reappraise the alternatives gathered through the initial information search, or may indeed seek out new information (... *The day was OK but I do not know if I would rush back. Too many people, all the good matches were on Centre Court and the price of food and drinks was a bit over the top...).*

(c) The consumer is totally dissatisfied with the experience, may decide that the resolution to the initial problem may not be forthcoming from the sports/exercise experience, and may look outside this domain for satisfaction (... *That was no fun. Perhaps I should just spend my summers at the beach!!...*).

Establishment of the process by which individuals arrive at the decision to buy a particular product or service does not necessarily imply that each step in the process is always followed. Depending on the type and nature of the purchase, an individual may devote a significant amount of time and effort to the decision-making process, or may make a snap or 'spur-of-the-moment' decision. The latter usually occurs when the adverse consequence of a poor choice is minimal or the purchase has become habitual behaviour.

Involvement in the Decision-making Process

The amount of thought, and individual involvement, given to a decision to purchase can vary considerably. While the purchase of new laces for basketball shoes requires little involvement, the purchase of the initial footwear is often the result of a far more protracted process. The cost of a club membership often has to be weighed against a series of competing forces for disposable income, yet an individual may make the decision to attend a game at the last moment. The membership (or shoes) is a high involvement purchase; the single game (or laces) is a low involvement purchase.

High Involvement Purchases

High involvement purchases make full and extended use of the decision-making process. Expensive, complex and high-risk purchases fall into this category. In these cases the consumer will invariably undertake a thorough information search and carefully and selectively examine comparable services or products. The consumer may assess value for money, although cost may not be the major factor where special features, status or functionality are required. Finally, time will be allocated to the decision-making process and the positives and negatives of the purchase weighed. Once a tentative decision to buy has been made, affirmation may be sought from an expert in the field or from a significant other. Yachts, golf clubs, snow skis and club membership may fall into this category.

Sports-marketing strategies aimed at consumers involving a high involvement purchase process often relate to sponsor products, and include pointing out the specific or unique features of the sponsors' offering through the sports as a communication vehicle. This may include the provision of maximum technical or personal support for the service or product's use, and reinforcing the wisdom of the purchase choice. Advertising should be selective. It should target appropriate demographic-psychographic market segments as well as affirm lifestyle and connote quality and excellence. The following examples include high involvement product purchases such as cars, mobile phones and other commu-nications services (that require long-term commitment through contracts with the communications suppliers). Using sports in their sponsorship communications mix, the threshold of purchasing high involvement products, theoretically, should be lowered by offering attractiveness, recognisability and credibility.

In 2003 Kia used the Australian Tennis Open, while in 2002 Vodafone used the Australian Rugby Union and Skyy Vodka the 2002 Motorcycle Grand Prix at Phillip Island, to link their products to fans of tennis, rugby and motorcycle racing respectively. Likewise, in a historic move in July 2002, Telstra bought the naming rights to both the former Colonial Stadium (now Telstra Dome) in Melbourne and Stadium Australia (Telstra Stadium) in Sydney, which enabled the Telstra brand to be connected with two of the top, state-of-the art sports and entertainment facilities in the country.

However, it is not just products that use sports to reach potential clients. Financial services, bank organisations and private health funds all use sports to promote their services, believing that purchase involvement is invariably linked to that with which the consumer has some familiarity. In the early 1990s, QBE commenced a long-term sponsorship of the AFL's Sydney Swans in an attempt to penetrate the AFL-saturated state of Victoria. Whether it is insurance, cars or telephony, purchasers have a high involvement in the decision-making process. Sports selectively targets and segments audiences for sponsors, thus the connection between the sponsor's product and the sports creates a win-win situation.

Low Involvement Purchases

Evans and Herman (1987) define low involvement purchases as the decision-making process undertaken when the products or services to be consumed are socially or psychologically unimportant. In these cases information is acquired passively, the decision to act is made quickly, and the product is often evaluated when the purchase is made. The choice is usually routine or habitual; the level of prior experience with the product is high, as is the frequency of purchase; the pressure or time may be significant, but the consequences of poor choice are minimal. The purchase of a weekly sports magazine can be thought of as a low involvement decision. In establishing a strategy aimed at consumers exhibiting low involvement in the purchase process, sports marketers need to provide repetitive advertising and information, encourage familiarity, offer a variety of inducements, create attention-grabbing point-of-purchase (POP) displays and, if possible, distribute in multiple outlets.

The Sydney Olympic Ticket Policy

The Sydney Olympic Games provides an excellent vignette of the high/low involvement purchase strategy.

Potential spectators at the Olympic Games in Sydney 2000 were faced with numerous choices not only as to the events they could view but also as to the amount they could pay to see such events. The Sydney Organising Committee started its ticketing campaign in early 1998, with approximately 9.6 million tickets at its disposal. The key marketing messages of the campaign were that 88% of the tickets cost under $100 and 4 million tickets were directly available to the Australian public.

According to Thamnopoulos (2000), the criteria SOCOG set for the pricing of tickets were size of venue and seating availability; sports popularity; venue location and timing; the likelihood of Australian athletes performing well; the zoning of seats; and finally comparative prices at previous Games. Moreover, the prices were divided into four segments. The first segment, which focused on the finals and the most popular events, was titled 'super premium', with prices in excess of $350. 'Premium' tickets were generally between $100 and $200 and were for early rounds of popular activities and finals of less popular sports. Sports less popular in Australia but with international appeal (judo, handball, baseball, soccer, etc.) were priced at under $100, and the fourth segment, entitled 'the experience', sold for less than $60.

As Thamnopoulos readily demonstrates, for fans who simply wanted to be part of the Olympic experience, tickets were quite inexpensive, and the choice of sports was essentially a low involvement purchase, as being there was the important thing. For individuals who wanted to attend sports in which Australians might win medals, or who wanted to see the more highprofile Olympic sports, a higher involvement in the purchase was required. Interestingly, the Opening Ceremony could be seen for a round $1500 or less than $200, although the likelihood of getting tickets at the higher price was far greater than at the lower. Once again the relative importance of seeing the event brought into play the high/low involvement purchase paradigm.

Finally, fans who wanted a guaranteed seat at all events at the Olympic Stadium also had that option available. In 1996 Stadium Australia issued a prospectus offering 34400 golden memberships at $10000 each and 600 platinum memberships at $30000 each. As part of the membership package the purchaser was entitled to attend all Olympic events held in the stadium. There is no doubt that a resolution to purchase such a package was a high involvement decision.

A number of companies use sports to saturate the whole market with their message, as opposed to identifying a specific segment. Soft drinks and fast foods are examples of products that are omnipresent in the sports environment. It is hoped that the purchase of their products will become habitual. Furthermore, athletes are often used to promote basic everyday purchases. The Australian Cricket Team has promoted breakfast cereal, Kieran Perkins has promoted the virtues of milk and Grant Hackett has been seen chomping on Uncle Toby's muesli bars. Manufacturers believe that using athletes in marketing their products makes them stand out in a cluttered environment.

Characteristics of Consumer

Demographics

Demographics provide a statistical profile of a particular segment of a marketplace. Some of the more frequently recorded demographics include gender, age, marital status, household size and income, educational level and occupation. There may also be instances when information regarding an individual's religious or political affiliation, ethnicity and even class is required.

Lifestyle

Psychographics divides the market into segments or subgroups based on certain behaviours that relate to attitudes, lifestyles or values. Psychographics can be more important than demographics in the consumer decision-making process; however, they can be more difficult to quantify. For example, Lyons and Jackson (2001) examined factors that influenced African-American gen-Xers to buy Nikes and determined that this group placed importance on the style of the shoe, especially as it related to status. They argued: 'African-Americans tend to shop, purchase and consume apparel at a greater rate than do people of other races. The impetus for this above average consumption is the desire to "fit in" or look good.' (2001: 100) There is thus little doubt that such variables are lifestyle factors. However, while the variables 'to fit in' or 'to look good' are relatively easy to articulate, they are rather subjective, making formulation of marketing strategies around such concepts difficult. Here the use of focus groups is very important.

Personality

Hawkins et al. (1992: 307) suggested that 'consumers tend to purchase products that most closely match their own personality or that strengthen an area they feel deficient in'. In most cases personalities are individual, constant and enduring. They can change, of course, but this is usually due to the impact of a major life event. The two most common approaches to understanding personality are individual learning theories and social learning theories, more commonly referred to as trait vs state theories of personality.

Individual learning theory argues that personality traits are usually formed in the early stages of an individual's development and remain relatively constant into and through adulthood. Reserved, quiet, shy, extroverted, relaxed or confident are examples of this type of personality. It is easy to see why certain individuals prefer the cinema to day/night cricket, bushwalking to basketball, or golf to aerobics, based on their individual personality characteristics. *Social learning theory* argues that environment is an extremely important determinant of human behaviour. In such cases the personality of the individual may alter depending on the situation. An introvert in one instance can be an extrovert in the next, whereas an assertive, aggressive individual can very quickly become timid when faced with a particular fear or phobia. Bungy jumping is a good example: bravado and confidence disappear in the moments before the leap.

In *marketing sports and related activities it is necessary to cater for all personality types. For every fan* who wants to stand in the outer among 'like-minded supporters' and cheer him/herself hoarse for a favourite team or athlete, there is another fan who wants to watch the action unfold while seated and in a less emotionally charged environment. For every consumer who wants the latest, brightest and most expensive athletic apparel, there is another who is more than comfortable in a nondescript tracksuit and functional footwear. It is important that the product fit the consumer's personality and vice versa. An understanding of basic personality types ensures that as wide a range of consumers as possible is being catered for in the marketplace.

Environmental Factors

In the latter half of the 20th century environmental issues such as pollution in its various forms, rainforest destruction, overpopulation, urban sprawl, and the general degradation of land and ocean were pushed to the forefront of public consciousness. However, while society's relationship to the physical environment is usually viewed from a negative perspective, judiciously utilised changes in technology have the potential to provide the modern sports consumer with great benefits. Computer technologies and land management have allowed golf courses and resorts to exist side by side with rainforests and sensitive wetlands; sensible urban planning and council bylaws have allowed the establishment of new stadiums or facilities that are sympathetic to local architecture and demographics; and government legislation has been enacted to protect both the rights of individual consumers and the collective good. It is important that the views of all categories of consumers, whether long-term, new, emerging or potential, be taken into account when sports promotion takes place.

Understanding the sports consumer is not a simple task. The sports marketer needs to be aware not only of the primary, secondary and tertiary factors that influence consumer decision-making—he/she also needs to comprehend both the process and the level of involvement by which the decision to buy or consume is arrived at. Other important determinants that must be considered before establishing marketing strategies include the specific demographics and psychographics of the constituent group, along with germane environmental factors.

While comprehending the complexity of the sports consumer's decision-making process is one of the more intricate tasks facing the sports marketer, unquestionably it has become a critical part of marketing management strategy. Although it is not always possible to fully understand how this process takes place, assiduous attention to the unique characteristics of specific consumers, coupled with a broad awareness of how decisions are reached, will provide the sports marketer with a solid framework within which marketing strategies can be developed.

CHAPTER

The Importance of Market Research

MARKET RESEARCH AND STRATEGY

The most critical factor in marketing success is the marketers' ability to collect accurate and timely information about consumers and potential consumers and to use this data to create marketing plans that are specifically targeted to meet the needs of the specific consumer groups. There is little doubt that to make informed decisions organisations need information, and lots of it. However, the collection of this material is only a starting point for the construction of a Marketing Information System (MIS). Once compiled, this information must be integrated, analysed, and used to guide the direction of the organisation. Time spent on its assembly, maintenance and development can be the most effective marketing tool at an organisation's disposal.

DEVELOPING MARKETING INFORMATION SYSTEMS

Stanton et al. (1995: 48) suggest that an MIS is an ongoing, organised set of procedures and methods designed to generate, analyse, disseminate, store and later retrieve information for use in decision making. Nevertheless, they also acknowledge that for the MIS to be successful the data should be not only of high quality but also be used in a realistic manner and adopted as a source of decision making by the organisation. In this instance the population is divided into consumers and non-consumers, and relevant information is obtained using appropriate data-collection methods. The information is then collated and integrated. From this resource base marketing strategies can be formulated, along with mechanisms for monitoring effectiveness.

The current need for ongoing market research and the establishment of increasingly sophisticated MISs are the result of a dynamic, constantly changing sports environment. With less time for deliberation, increased accountability, growing consumer expectations and the ever-expanding scope of marketing activities, sporting organisations need rapid access to reliable information that will result in clear, appropriate decision making. Fortunately for sports, the quantity and quality of available information are constantly expanding.

General market data include all the information which relates to the broad environment in which the sports operates. Within its area of operation, most commonly referred to as its critical trading radius, the organisation needs to establish size, demographics, the consumer habits of residents and workers, the way such individuals choose to spend their leisure time, and any specific trends that will affect the sports positively or negatively. This information is particularly important for sports hoping to expand nationally and be successful. The profile of the specific sports fan needs to be well represented in the new market for the sports to have any hope of success.

Once *individual consumer* data have been collected and entered on the appropriate database, the sports marketer has a multitude of information available with which to establish marketing strategies. Name, address, phone number, gender, age, occupation or student type, purchase patterns and payment methods are a small representation of the type of information that can easily be collected by sporting organisations. Quick (1998, 1999) noted that the New South Wales Rugby Union Super 12 fan surveys in 1998 and 1999 offered inducements to fans to supply their names, addresses and phone numbers when responding.

A third source of information for sporting organisations relates to *competitors and their participants*. It is critical that sporting organisations not only be aware of who their competitors are but also know the consumers of a rival's products or services. A number of sports can sometimes successfully operate in the same area, when their fans are dissimilar. Basketball, tennis, soccer and netball appear to be quite different in their support bases.

So, apart from observing general promotional strategies, these sports would be best served by focusing on information that is internal to the organisation and sports-specific. Nevertheless, if a sports is jockeying for position in the marketplace, competitor pricing, promotion, and product breadth and depth need to be noted. This is particularly important when junior competitions and leagues are involved. Juniors will invariably gravitate to those sports which provide them with opportunities at the local level.

MARKETING INFORMATION SYSTEM DATA SOURCES

There are two major sources of data for any MIS—external and internal. External data may be primary or secondary and have been collected by the sporting organisation or an external agency. Internal data include all the information, such as basic enquiries, that the organisation collects during the day-to-day operation of its business.

External Secondary Data

There are numerous sources of secondary data that sporting organisations can use to assist in the formation of a strategic marketing plan. The most obvious starting point is government agencies, such as the Australian Bureau of Statistics (ABS). *Participation in Sports and Physical Activities, Australia* (2000a) and *Australians Less Active* (2000b) are two potential information sources.

ABS statistics (2000a) showed the numbers and demographic characteristics of persons involved in sports at some time during the 12 months 1999/2000. The data suggested that men had a higher participation rate in sports than women and that the Australian-born or those living in capital cities were more likely to engage in sports than their overseasborn or rural-domiciled fellow citizens. However ABS statistics also suggested (2000b) that participation rates in sports and physical activities decreased in all states and territories except Western Australia in 1999/2000. These are just two documents that provide basic information that is potentially useful for a number of sporting bodies.

Libraries and chambers of commerce are other useful sources of information, especially at the local level. Data relating to trends and uses of local events and facilities should be held there, as well as the various municipal rules and regulations governing the conduct of sports events. Larger community libraries, along with those attached to institutes of higher education, often contain much of the government or commercial data that have been collected in relation to sports. Chambers of commerce will hold data relating to the income and expenditure patterns of local industry, which can assist sports marketers in establishing profiles that may match their organisation.

An increasing amount of data is being gathered in various research units. While much of this information is proprietary, some of the findings are being presented at conferences and appearing in academic journals. Likewise, a growing number of sports-marketing academics are being used as market research consultants and are bringing an ever-increasing repository of skills and knowledge to their task. Advertising media are constantly engaged in the collection of secondary data. While it may not be specific to the focus of the sports marketer, information relating to demographics and psychographics may be useful for sponsorship or advertising. This is particularly the case when the characteristics of the media information match a particular sport's own data.

A final source of secondary data is private organisations. Hirons (2002) suggested that Uncle Toby was the best recognised sponsor, that swimming was still the most popular sports participation activity and that the Orange mobile phone carrier had 'made a spectacular entry into the sports sponsorship arena'. Similarly, Roy Morgan Research, most commonly associated with the Morgan Gallup Poll, has established a variety of services and products that can provide sporting organisations with significant data. The Roy Morgan *Monitor* covers areas such as tourism, entertainment and leisure, and the organisation annually conducts more than 60,000 personal interviews. The collection of such data provides wide-ranging information on consumer behaviour and media usage, and as such can be an invaluable secondary source for the sports marketer. For more specific data it is even possible in some instances for organisations to contract for an industry-related question to be included in a survey.

Primary Data

Primary data may be internal or external, and are a product of collection methods and purpose. The most common type of internal data are data collected from enquiries, letters and telephone calls. These may be in the form of complaints or praise. Accounts, credit card purchases and general sales can also provide a wealth of information, indicating consumer trends in relation to a sporting organisation's product or service. Other sources of internal information can include an organisation's employees, contractors, suppliers and sponsors. All can offer the sports marketer useful advice, and any such comments should be heeded. However, there is little doubt that the best data available to the sports marketer are those which are purpose-driven by the organisation. In this way direct answers to specific questions can be obtained about the habits and consumption patterns of sports participants and consumers. Moreover, the collection of primary data through market research is not difficult. All that is required is access to the information source, time, energy and good questions!

Sporting Organisations and Marketing Research

Basically, market research in sporting organisations seeks to answer six questions about consumers in relation to their consumption of the product. Initially, sporting organisations need to know WHO their consumers are, but this is only the tip of the iceberg. WHY they choose the particular sports product and WHEN and WHERE that consumption takes place are equally important. WHAT that consumption entails in terms of pre-and postevent activities, and HOW the product is used, are also critical in terms of establishing a complete consumer profile. In no particular order, the information requested generally falls into the categories of general and sports-specific.

General Information

Usually, the general information requested focuses on demographics such as gender, age, occupation, household size, place of residence and methods of transport. Similarly, information is often elicited regarding psychographic issues. Fundamentally, psychographic information conveys data on the what and how of consumer behaviour, such as how many times in a given period a person visits a particular establishment (e.g. restaurant, hotel or facility), the number and type of vehicles in the household, and the various electronic items they use. This last issue is becoming more and more important as sporting organisations endeavour to ascertain how many of their consumers not only use personal computers but also have access to the Internet. With many sporting organisations establishing interactive home pages, new opportunities for establishing enhanced databases are plentiful. The AFL's Sydney Swans is just one example of a professional sports franchise that communicates with its members on a regular basis via the Internet. Between 21 and 27 August 2002 the Swans were in touch with members via e-mail five times on matters as diverse as player retirements to 2002 final home and away game promotional activities.

An equally important general question relates to where consumers get their information. Frequency and type of newspapers read, radio stations listened to, television stations and programmes viewed, and magazines read, both general and specific, are crucial factors in determining promotional strategy. Results from a 1999 fan survey conducted for the New South Wales Rugby Union at Waratahs home matches indicated that 48% of all people listened to radio at breakfast time, Channel 9 was by far the most watched TV station, and 68% indicated that they read *The Sydney Morning Herald*. The most popular radio station for these rugby fans was the commercial-free, ABC's 2BL (Quick 1999). Research has generally indicated that television is the major source of event information, with radio rating poorly. The Waratahs scenario does little to disprove this belief. However, there are two other issues that need to be considered.

The word-of-mouth variable is a constant response, and a market research strategy needs to be developed to control this. Moreover, although general questions about magazines read almost invariably result in a sports-specific magazine response, magazines targeted at women often feature strongly. With the increasing female acceptance of and adherence to many sports and recreational activities, perhaps it is time that sports marketers allocated a portion of their advertising budget to this expanding market segment.

Sports-specific Information

Sports-or activity-specific questions often relate to attendance patterns, influences to buy or consume, and levels of satisfaction with various aspects of the event. In relation to attendance, organisations need to be aware of both the depth of product or service use and the breadth of use. Obviously, years of membership or season ticket holding is an example of depth, but the range of single-match buyback programmes, offering incentives to members who do not attend a particular match to place their seat/ticket back in the pool for general sale, is an increasingly popular example of the latter. Likewise, organisations need to know what influences the consumer's decision to buy this particular product when faced with the diverse and ever-expanding range of options in the sports or entertainment marketplace.

Finally, organisations need to be apprised of the customers' levels of satisfaction—that is, their perceptions of the range and quality of the merchandise and concessions sold, of the scope and type of services offered, and of the way in which the organisation conducts its business. By asking such questions of sports fans and consumers, organisations can establish comprehensive profiles of their customers, which in turn allows the organisation to strategically market its products or services in a diverse marketplace. As Huggins (1992: 40) notes: the principal focus of the marketing Function in sports is not so much to be skilful in making sports fans or participants do what suits the interest of sports as to be skilful in conceiving or doing what suits the interest of the fans or participants without changing the sports itself.

THE MARKETING MISSION

Before identifying the components of the market research process, it is useful to consider the benefit of determining the marketing mission. The mission of the whole organisation, in many ways, will also assist managers in setting direction for their respective departments, one of which can be the marketing department. Cheverton (2000) suggests that, rather than being platitudinous comments, good mission statements actually guide the organisation with some consistency through the decisionmaking process in a way that minimises conjecture or misunderstanding. Moreover, he argues that there are five key aspects to a mission statement.

These are: acknowledging the business the organisation is in; knowing the aspirational position; being aware of the core competencies that are needed to guide the organisation towards that vision; knowing which consumers or target market will best assist in reaching the position; and understanding how an organisation knows when it has arrived. In other words, what are the measurements of success? Baker (2000), however, concludes that the mission is more than just a strategic plan: it is the 'cultural glue' that enables a collective engagement in the marketing process, and it is this approach which is most appropriate to the sports-marketing environment. There is no doubting the importance of strategy in sports marketing, but given that sports organisations are eclectic organisations, the overarching mission or vision is the focal point around which such diverse units can congregate.

Inherent in such strategic plans, stated visions or marketing missions are the objectives by which the desired outcomes might be realised. Once again in keeping with this text, such objectives are strategic in that they carefully elucidate the manner in which the organisation reaches its stated goal. There are numerous types of organisational objectives, but in the main they fall into either of two major categories: sales or communication. Furthermore, there are a number of acronyms in existence (e.g. SMART = Smart, Measurable, Achievable, Realistic, and Timely) that guide the objectives construction process. But the fundamental underpinning in the selection and creation of strategic objectives remains their evaluative benefit.

The success or otherwise of the marketing mission is determined via the ongoing monitoring and evaluation of the stated objectives. The ongoing scrutiny of results against the framework of organisational objectives is necessary because of their basically organic nature. Organisational objectives will change as intermediate goals are obtained, or with the realisation that a structured strategy is not delivering the desired results, or if an external trigger necessitates an internal change. Quality market research further enables the sports organisation to collect the information that is necessary to keep the organisation on the right strategic course.

The Process of Market Research

The days are gone when sporting organisations could rely on general sports market research to inform their decision making. It is not difficult for sporting organisations to conduct their own market research, to engage a specialist to assist in part of the research, whether it be questionnaire construction, data analysis or interpretation, or to contract a consultant to deliver product-specific information. Organisational decisions should be based on the needs and expectations of the consumer, and the only way this can be ascertained is to ask. While the phrase 'use it or lose it' is a sports cliche, when applied to market research there is not a more appropriate sentiment.

The market research process principally consists of five distinct phases. In order to guide the complete process, and to achieve maximum results with limited resources, the first step in the process is to clearly define the research problem and set a number of measurable objectives. The research problem and objectives often are a direct derivative of the marketing mission of the organisation. The second step in the process is to develop a research methodology—that is, to determine which data sources are needed (primary or secondary), and which methods of data collection are best used in the context of the research. The third step then involves the research planning and data collection, who collects the data, when and where. When all data are collected they need to be analysed. Data analysis, as the fourth step in the process, can involve the crunching of quantitative data with the help of statistical analysis software programmes or the interpretation of more qualitative (e.g. interviews) research data. The final step in the research process is the presentation of the findings so that the research objectives are achieved and the research problem is best answered.

Data-collection Methods

Surveys

The personal survey is still potentially the most useful of all research methods, as it allows the sports marketer to source first-hand information on the purchase and consumption patterns of sports fans. These data can be collected at the event, by going door to door in a defined geographical area, at a shopping centre (mall intercepts) or via the telephone (telemarketing). Most sports organisations that are serious about providing services to their constituency regularly engage in this type of research. Moreover, a serious sports organisation is not just a professional or semi-professional franchise. Local clubs and groups can often use the survey format to gain consumer or participant feedback. Obviously, the more professional an organisation is and the larger its stakeholder base, the more sophisticated the survey and its accompanying tools of analysis will become. Nevertheless, the underlying philosophy remains constant, and that is the collection of quality information that will assist in decision making and guide the running of a successful club.

Focus Groups

A focus group is a small group of interested individuals gathered to talk about the issues that an organisation and its consumers believe are important. Usually the size of the focus group is less than ten, which provides everyone present with an opportunity to contribute. This method encourages individuals to engage freely in dialogue with each other, with the data collector in this instance prompting, guiding and recording. Trends and issues emanating from focus groups are often the catalyst for more structured, follow-up research.

Observation

Although not always undertaken in a formal manner, the observation technique should be used by the sports marketer on an ongoing basis. From Bill Veeck with baseball during the 1940s, to Kerry Packer and World Series Cricket in the 1970s, to Michael Wrubleski and the National Basketball League (NBL) in the 1990s, good sports promoters have recognised the value of getting out and both talking to the fans and watching their behaviour. This simple act can inform sports marketers about which aspects of their market strategies are having the desired result and which need some work. Ideally, the observation will lead to the focus group, which could lead to the structured survey, which should then lead to action based on rigorous data collection.

Experimentation

Experimentation can be useful to the sports marketer in specific circumstances. Here the researcher or promoter manipulates one variable while holding all others constant. Changing the venue, time or day of event, or altering uniforms, are just a few of the variables that professional sports clubs manipulate during a pre-season competition in order to gauge reaction to such changes. If the changes prove popular, they may be adopted for the regular season. If not, the previous modus operandi is utilised.

RESEARCH DESIGN

Although types of research design are as varied as the sports products and services being researched, there are a number of basic principles that should be adhered to:

- Sports marketers should ask only questions they need to know the answer to. If responses to perceived personal questions, such as income levels, are not needed, they should not be asked for, as incorrect responses can bias results.
- For ease of analysis, questions should be closed, mutually exclusive and free of ambiguity.
- While questions should be thematically linked, each response should provide a unique piece of information. This approach means that a questionnaire or survey can be reduced to sections, which can then be used and manipulated as a stand-alone instrument.
- The research design should be of sufficient scope to provide all necessary information, but short enough to encourage broad-based participation in the process.
- Mullin et al. (2000) suggest that the sports marketer needs to have a feel for the kind of answers expected. While it could be argued that this may introduce bias

into the project design, most research is initiated through some type of intuitive process.

Potential Uses of Marketing Research

Sports-marketing research generally can have numerous outcomes, although the following are the most common uses:

- It can enhance the flow of communication between the organisation and the customer.
- It may facilitate the creation of promotional strategies or the development of sponsorship proposals.
- It should assist in general decision making and programming.

SEGMENTING THE SPORTS MARKET

On any given weekend, sports attracts millions of spectators and participants who participate for myriad reasons. Moreover, members of the same family or household may witness or participate in a particular activity for a variety of motives. In an attempt to encourage such groups to initiate or maintain their involvement in the sports or activity, different marketing strategies must be developed that are specifically aimed or targeted at such groups or market segments.

What is Market Segmentation?

Stanton et al. (1995) suggest that market segmentation is the process of dividing the total, heterogeneous market for a product or service into several segments, each of which tends to be homogeneous in all similar aspects. The advantage of market segmentation is that it is a consumer-oriented philosophy and as a result endeavours to satisfy as many needs and wants in the marketplace as possible. Moreover, by segmenting the marketplace promoters can more judiciously allocate marketing resources, and this should result in greater returns on the investment, or 'more bang for the bucks'.

Mullin et al. (2000) further suggest that segmentation is central to an understanding of consumers, as it recognises differences in consumer behaviour, which directly informs marketing strategies. Consequently, the task facing sports promoters is first to determine how consumers use sports products or services to meet individual needs, and then to determine which factors are common. This allows the sports marketer to categorise or group customers according to the type of people they are, the way they use the product or service, and finally their expectations of it. Although the segmentation possibilities are endless, there are a number of broad-based variables that provide an effective starting point for segmentation strategy. Commonly, consumers are segmented on the basis of demographics, psychographics and behaviour towards the product.

The Market Segmentation Process Demographic Segmentation

Demographic segmentation is the most common form of segmentation, with the most important demographic determinants being gender, age, religion, income, occupation, level of education, marital status, geography, and stage in the family life cycle. Social class is another important consumer demographic but is usually an amalgam of other variables. Although all demographic variables are potentially important, stage in the family life *cycle* has the greatest impact on sports consumption. Traditional life cycle stages include singles, married couples with and without children, 'empty nesters' and elderly singles. However, single parents, older childless couples and divorced individuals are increasingly representing alternative stages in the family life cycle. Stages in the family life cycle directly affect consumer behaviour, and it is essential for sports marketers to provide mechanisms that encourage customers to remain loyal from childhood to senior years.

Geographic issues such as regions, city size, the urban-rural dichotomy and even climate can also influence strategic sports marketing. While it may appear safe to assume that spectator expectations in country and regional areas are quite different from expectations in the city, even the cities cannot be treated as homogeneous for the sports marketer. While ease of event access, parking and travel time are often important to the suburban commuter, public transport and additional entertainment possibilities may be far more important to the inner-city dweller.

Psychographic Segmentation

While demographic information can inform the sports marketer who the consumers are, this information alone does not tell why they consume. To partially answer this question, consumers need to be further categorised according to psychographics. Psychographic segmentation is based on variables that are associated with personality types or lifestyles. This approach attempts to explain consumer behaviour in terms of the reasons for purchase and the needs it meets. In the process, categories of values and lifestyles are established, such as outer-directed, inner-directed and need-driven (Mullin et al. 2000) or socially aware, visible achievement, traditional family life, young and optimistic (Stanton et al. 1995).

However, while the nomenclature may differ, basically the sports marketer must cater not only for the consumer who is confident and assertive, believes that there are advantages in being associated with the sports product and wishes to be seen to be involved with it, but also for the consumer who wishes to satisfy intrinsic as opposed to extrinsic needs. Such intrinsic needs may vary from personal development to pure escapism. Hence individuals may buy a snowboard because they can, or because they like the scene associated with snowboarding and want to fit in or belong. Likewise, they may see the purchase as an opportunity for individual growth through the development of new skills. Irrespective of the reasons for consumption, all individuals must be catered for if possible.

Behavioural Segmentation

Behavioural segmentation refers to the benefits and usages attributed to the consumption of the product. Stotlar (1993) comments that benefit segmentation is based on the unique benefits of a product or service that motivate a consumer to purchase—that is, on the different benefits that the consumer expects from the product or service. An important feature of this concept is that the consumer is purchasing the benefit, not the product. For example, athletes may buy an electrolyte-replacement drink not because they are thirsty or like the taste but because they believe that it will replace essential elements the body has lost during intensive exercise. Hence the athlete is purchasing the benefit, a more rapid recovery, rather than the product, a sports drink. However, the most obvious case of benefit segmentation in sports relates to the purchase of athletic shoes. Correct pronation or supination, arch support and cushioning or a glow in the dark are just a some of the potential benefits of athletic footwear.

Benefit segmentation is not applicable to only sports products. A person may choose to attend a basketball game not because he/she has an innate love of the sports, but because a friend is going. Here the benefit inherent in going to the game is the opportunity for social interaction. If the friend were going to the zoo, the idea of attending the basketball game would be moot. In this instance the chance for social interaction is just one benefit that the sports promoter provides. Similar benefit segmentation strategies can focus on the entertainment aspect of the event or the opportunity to escape from the rigours of the daily grind and indulge in recreative activity, to be involved in the production and presentation of an event or activity, or simply to be seen at an event. The volunteers for the Sydney 2000 Olympic Games became involved in the event for many and varied reasons.

Volunteer Attrition

The key reasons why potential volunteers chose not to continue included poor communication, inadequate training sessions, a failure to be appointed to the venue of preference, reporting to multiple supervisors, and the apparent perception that the environment was less than caring and supportive. Other reasons included a less than demanding position, the inability to actually see events, an inability to interact with athletes, an apparent lack of a comfortable uniform, a perception that the food was lacking in variety and quality, an inability to make new friends and, finally, plain boredom. This is an expansive and wide-ranging list of apparent grievances.

However, Gritsi's (2000) study demonstrates the variety of seemingly inconsequential reasons that influence the consumer decision-making process as it relates to expected benefits. Usage segmentation focuses on the amount of the product or service consumed by the customer. The usage pattern for a product or service is especially applicable to spectator sports. In attempting to define the consumer in respect to usage patterns, broad categories including non-user, light user, medium user and heavy user are established.

While it is often desirable to encourage consumers to elevate their level of consumption, this is not always possible or even desirable. For example, Spolestra (1991) believes that in terms of the consumption of professional sports, the season ticket or membership is not for everyone. Whether it is due to lack of finance, time or even interest, consumers often find that attending every game is not possible. Hence he argues that the concept of seat sharing, whether corporate or with friends, results in maximum use of a particular seat. By adopting an approach called full-menu marketing, the organisation provides numerous packages that allow fans to consume at a level with which they are comfortable. Here the market has been segmented based on usage.

Multiple Segmentation

The establishment of a segmentation strategy depends on a number of features such as size, reachability and receptiveness of the target market. As such, multiple segment strategies are often developed, which enable the sports marketer to construct different yet coordinated strategies for delivering a product or service. The establishment, maintenance and ongoing addition to an organisation's MIS will assist sporting organisations to become increasingly discerning and creative in their target market segmentation strategies.

Examples of Sports Spectator Segments

In 1995 Graham Halbish, former chief executive officer of the Australian Cricket Board (ACB), identified four target audiences that had developed since the World Series Cricket era:

- The purist, who understood the nuances of the game and often had a history of active participation in the sports;
- The sports enthusiast, who followed a wider range of activities;
- The follower, who, while unlikely to attend matches, avidly followed the game via the media; and
- The entertainment seeker, who sought action and excitement.

Each segment was important for distinct reasons. While purists were perceived as essential for Test match cricket longevity, enthusiasts were important for their current level of interest. Similarly, while followers were important because of their desire for cricket information, entertainment-seekers provided for an important segue into the female and youth market. Smith and Stewart (1999:174) devised a classification of team-sports spectator behaviour and developed five spectator categories and motivations for adoption of such categories:

- The passionate partisan, who displays undiminished loyalty to a team over time and identifies closely with winning and losing;
- The champ follower, whose loyalty is essentially a function of team success;
- The reclusive partisan, who displays strong identification, which does not necessarily translate into actual support;
- The theatregoer, who seeks a close encounter and wishes to be entertained; and
- The aficionado, whose loyalty is to the game rather than the team.

In many instances, especially related to sports consumer behaviour in the context of seasonal sports competitions, the passionate partisan is an important target market. Each of the other target markets requires different marketing strategies aimed at the specific orientation of potential consumers held by the market. When we decide that a particular market segment is going to be the focus of a sports organisation, we have selected a target market.

Target Market Selection

The selection of the appropriate target market follows the process of segmentation. Having identified the segmentation variables and developed profiles of the different segments, the next step is to identify the attractiveness of each of the segments. To enable the sports marketer to identify attractiveness, market segments must be substantial enough to justify consideration, their size and attractiveness must be measurable, the sports organisation must have access to the segment, and must have the resources enabling the organisation to approach the segment, and the segments must enable differentiation from other segments. When these criteria are fulfilled, the sports marketer can assess the segment's size and growth potential, the segment's structural attractiveness (this can be identified by applying Porter's five forces analysis), and whether the segment offers scope to achieve the organisation's strategic objectives and generate vital resources.

Based on this information the sports marketer is in a position to select a (number of) target markets. Target market selection strategies include the selection of a single segment, a number of unrelated segments, a number of segments that are selected on the ability of the sports organisation to deliver a particular product (e.g. football spectator services), a number of segments that are based on the ability of the sports organisation to serve a particular market (e.g. the Melbourne metropolitan football market) very well, or a full market coverage strategy, targeting the market as a whole.

The growth of snowboarding since the 1980s may serve as an interesting example. Capitalising on the popularity of skateboarding and surfing and the growth in extreme sports, snowboard promoters identified a target market that was young, had discretionary income, eschewed the normal alpine skiing activities of their parents, and wanted to be seen at the leading edge of a new recreational activity. While initially the alpine industry examined ways to ban the sports from many resort areas, snowboarding quickly gained a foothold and debuted as an Olympic sports in 1998. A sports once considered fringe is now at the forefront of winter activity. Moreover, resorts that had previously turned their back on this particular segment now aggressively market to this cohort and establish areas on the slopes where they can pursue their sports to the full. Some resorts even try to position their location as the place for snowboarding.

Positioning

Before we move into marketing 'action'—that is, the application of the marketing mix—the final piece in the puzzle of preparing for action is the identification of positioning strategies for each of the segments that we have chosen to target. In this process it is important to remember that the key to successful positioning lies in the sports marketer's ability to differentiate the product offering from segment competitors. Whatever is different in the offering of the sports organisation needs to be important and distinctive for the consumers to consider the (alternative) offering. For example, positioning can focus on the benefits that consumers seek in consuming the product; quality or price can be used to set the offering apart from others; or the image of the product or organisation can sway consumers to purchase a trendy 'brand' rather than a non-branded product.

In their far-reaching text, Ries and Trout (1986: 5) suggest: 'the basic approach of positioning is not to create something new and different, but to manipulate what's already in the mind'. In other words, positioning is really about what the marketer does in the mind of the consumer. In reality, there are probably two ways in which sports can be positioned in the mind of the consumer. As Ries and Trout indicate, the best option is to be first; but if you can't be first, be different. When it comes to sports, marketers and promoters constantly try to effectively position their product or service in the mind of an increasingly discerning consumer. Furthermore, given that consumer preferences are in a constant state of flux, the positioning process demands creativity, responsiveness and perspicacity.

For example, Teutsch (2002) refers to the September release by the president of the Australian Medical Association of the results of a national health survey. This survey quizzed more than 1000 people about their sports and exercise habits. While former trendy sports such as rollerblading and aerobics were considered passe, activities such as yoga, Pilates, 'boxing-type' classes, personal training, and adventure activities such as snowboarding, climbing and sailing were considered to be growth areas. While it is hard to argue against snowboarding being a sports of the future given its current Olympic standing, there is little doubt that it is rapidly moving from cult to mainstream status. Darby (2002), writing in the travel section of the *Herald Sun* (Melbourne), discussed skiing in the Rocky Mountains and suggested Canada as a valuable destination for skiers and snowboarders. Of the ski area Fernie, he noted that cult skiers were drawn there 'by the five big bowls, the stunning features, the great skiing and the naturally good snowboarding terrain' (2002: T06).

However, he also indicated that the area was fast making the transition from cult to consumer destination. Hence, it can be reasonably concluded that snowboarding, initially positioned as a cult activity with a clearly defined non-mainstream target market, rapidly progressed through stages of development (which included alpine resorts endeavouring to position themselves as snowboard-friendly) to a point where it is positioned as a mainstream sports of the future.

Given that the sports marketplace is so dynamic and constantly in a state of change, sports marketers must not only recognise change but be strategically ready to respond to it quickly. Moreover, the speed at which change occurs will only increase in the future, and sporting organisations, already sensitive to market share (if mergers and franchise relocations are any indication) will need to be increasingly creative in their segmentation strategy.

In the 21st century, ongoing data collection is essential for the adaptation of an organisation to a volatile and changing marketplace. Moreover, such data need to be collected in a systematic ongoing manner and stored in a marketing information system (MIS). The MIS should not only allow for ready accessibility but also enable ongoing decision making and strategy selection. The major sources of information for an MIS include both external and internal data. External data may be classified as primary or secondary, and includes data that have been collected by the sporting organisation or an external agency. It should be understood, however, that while some general market and sports market research may have universal applicability, the sporting organisation cannot do better than collect its own data.

Market research in sporting organisations seeks to answer the questions of who, when, where, what, how and why. While the survey is the most popular mechanism for gathering sports-related data, mall or shopping centre intercepts, focus groups, observation and even experimentation are becoming increasingly popular. Collected data should explore general market conditions, individual consumers and competitors. Internal data consist of information that the organisation collects during the conduct of its business.

A major advantage of solid market research is that it allows the sports marketer to divide the total market into several segments. Commonly, consumers are segmented on the basis of demographics, psychographics and behaviour. This latter category is further divided into the benefits wanted from the product and product usage. Finally, it should be remembered that the sports marketplace is in a constant state of change.

CHAPTER

Sports Service Product

A product is anything that satisfies a want or need in terms of use, consumption or acquisition. Moreover, a product is a problem solver in that it is purchased because of the benefits provided. Essentially, consumers buy benefits, not the product. Quality is another feature of perceived product benefits. McCarthy and Perreault (1990: 219) define quality, from a marketing perspective, as 'the ability of a product to satisfy a consumer's needs or requirements'. As the authors point out, this definition focuses on the consumer's view of what quality may mean, or of a product's suitability for some specific purpose. In sports, the product is easily discernible; however, the quality of the core product is something over which the sports marketer has no control. This is a distinctly unique aspect of sports and sports marketing. For this reason, it is important to recognise a broader definition of the product than simply the game.

Mullin (1985) identifies the playing of the game as the core product and all the related activities, such as food and beverage, merchandise, half-time entertainment, video screens and the facility itself, as product extensions. For example, the Australian Tennis Open and the Melbourne

Park facility and all the services provided within and during the tournament are crucial in measuring the overall success of the event. Ultimately, once players have agreed to play in the Australian Open there is little organisers can do to ensure quality matches. Even matches receiving 'top billing' such as Hewitt vs Agassi or Williams vs Hingis do not always guarantee quality contests.

The quality of the supporting product extensions, however, can be guaranteed. It is at this point that similarities are observed between the importance of quality service provision and quality product extensions. Often, most product extensions possess an element of service provision, and hence quality is important. As a consequence, product extensions have the capacity of ensuring that spectators at the tennis have an enjoyable day despite on-court results.

Branch (1992: 25) supports the need to broaden sports product position and programme concept, observing that: Forward-thinking professional sports marketers realise that the game, sport's 'core' or primary product, is not the organisation's only or most important product... diversifying sport's programme concept in this manner, the core product accrues substantial Value added' qualities.

In other words, the event becomes a more consistent buy for sports consumers. The Hornets entered the NBA as a new franchise in 1988, primarily comprising cast-offs from other teams. On-court success was not realistic, so attention to detail and customer satisfaction with the experience of the event became benchmarks for the Hornets' marketing efforts (Macnow 1990).

The Charlotte Hornets' 43rd consecutive sold-out home game belied the team's on-court record. Having won less than a quarter of their games since joining the NBA, they seem to have proven the sports traditionalists wrong. Conventional theory has it that teams must win games to consistently play in front of sell-out crowds. Not so in

Charlotte, with the 23388 fans filling the stadium. The Hornets may be the most thoroughly packaged franchise in sports, with everything from half-time shows to players' uniforms designed down to the most minute detail. How well does it work? Consider the following:

- In their inaugural season, the Hornets led the NBA in attendance, drawing more than 950000 fans despite losing 62 of 82 games.
- The franchise turned a larger profit than any other NBA team.
- The club's fans spend money not just on tickets but also on ancillary products. In 1989, fans spent an average of 39 cents per person at every game on shirts, mugs, key rings and other licensed souvenirs.

Attention to detail and total customer satisfaction with the experience of the event are benchmarks for the Hornets' marketing efforts. 'We've borrowed the philosophy from Disney that the small things count,' says general manager Scheer: To us, taking the fans for granted is the ulti- mate sin. What plays in Charlotte now is the Hornets. And though they've lost more than they've won so far, they are playing to great reviews.

The Charlotte Hornets illustrate another important concept in product planning—branding: 'Branding means the use of a name, term, symbol, or design—or a combination of these—to identify a product.' (McCarthy & Perreault 1990: 235) The Hornets represent a brand within the NBA competition. Brands are important to their owners, as they help consumers to recognise a company's products; and if brand recognition and acceptance are high, there exists the potential for high brand loyalty. In sports, teams and clubs such as the Hornets are examples of a brand, and it is through team and club loyalty that prominent brand recognition is achieved.

Developing highly recognisable brands as trademarks and logos is an important source of revenue and promotion for sporting organisations and athletes. These trademarks form the basis of merchandise and licensing programmes, an important form of product extensions. This section has stressed the importance of quality service provision in the product extensions, so it is appropriate now to consider in more detail how and why sports is a service product.

Sports as a Service

Services marketing has grown in importance across a wide range of industries during the past decade. In Australia, the Department of Industry, Science and Resources in collaboration with the Australian Services Network (2000: 2-3) has noted that: The Australian service sector makes up the largest proportion of the Australian economy in output terms. In fact, for the 12 months to June 1998, output of the sector contributed to over 76 per cent of total output of the Australian economy (excludes ownership of dwellings).

Similarly, the sector also dominates employment, employing over four of every five Australian workers (just under 82 per cent)… Between February 1990 and May 1999, a net total of 913,700 jobs were added to the Australian economy, of which the service sector contributed 1,057,800. The difference arose due to a decline in the number of non-service sector jobs of the period of 144,100… the service sector was the main driver of economic growth, averaging annual real output growth of 3.2 per cent per annum compared with 2 per cent per annum for the non-service sector, and 3 per cent for the economy as a whole.

Sports is an important contributor to the service economy. Unfortunately, sport's contribution is contained within the broader classification of 'Cultural and Recreational Services', which consists of motion pictures, radio and television services, libraries, museums and the arts, sports and recreation, and gambling services. It is not possible to be specific about sport's contribution, but the 'real output of the Cultural and Recreational Services group grew by an average 3.3 per cent in the eight years leading up to 1997-98' (DISR 2000: 48). The industry's share of service sector output grew from 2.5% to 2.9% and employment rose from a low of 145000 in 1990 to 217000 in May 1999 (DISR 2000). Major sporting events such as the Ford Australian Open and Formula 1 Grand Prix have the capacity to add to the strong performances indicated in the tourism-related, cultural and recreational service activities. The number and magnitude of sporting events in Australia have seen the evolution of sports tourism as a niche classification within tourism, which ultimately contributes to service sector output across a number of areas, including accommodation, cafes, restaurants and transport.

Service Defined

Why is sports considered a service? This section will answer this question by discussing the characteristics that distinguish a good from a service. A common theme of authors writing on sports marketing (Mullin 1980, 1985; Mullin et al. 2000; Shilbury 1989, 1991; Sutton & Parrett 1992) has been their agreement on how the unique characteristics of sports as a product require marketing personnel to adopt different strategies from those traditionally espoused.

Although many of these writings are devoid of specific references to services marketing, the discussions pertaining to these unique characteristics align sports to the attributes of a service. Zeithaml et al. (1985) summarise the characteristics distinguishing a good from a service. This summary helps in describing sports as a service:

- ***Intangibility:*** Services cannot be seen, tasted, felt or smelled before they are bought. Services are performances rather than objects. For example, is it possible to describe what product benefits people take home with them after playing sports? Or the benefits derived from watching a game of basketball? There is no tangible take-home product in this example.

- ***Inseparability of Production and Consumption:*** Services are simultaneously produced and consumed. The product cannot be put on the shelf and bought by the consumer. The consumer must be present during production. For example, consider getting a haircut, attending a sporting contest or visiting a physiotherapist. You need to attend during the process.
- ***Heterogeneity:*** Services are potentially variable in their performance. Services can vary greatly depending on who performs them. Many different employees can come into contact with the consumer; therefore, consistency becomes an issue. Few sporting contests are the same from one week to the next, and the consistency of service delivery by people working at such an event can also vary.
- ***Perishability:*** Services cannot be stored. Hotel rooms not occupied, airline seats not purchased or tickets to a sporting contest not sold cannot be reclaimed. Simply, it is lost revenue and indicates the importance of understanding that services are time dependent.

Perhaps the most significant difference between a good and a service is the simultaneous production and consumption of a product. A *service,* then, is predominantly any activity or benefit that is intangible and does not result in ownership. Both spectators and participants take from the game a series of experiences, none of which is physically tangible. Students of sports marketing should be careful not to confuse some of the tangible products that can be bought as a consequence of the game or sports (product extensions) with the game or sports itself (core product). Without the sports, the merchandise would not exist.

Classification of Services

When classifying services we need to determine the extent to which the customer must be present. To assist in making this determination, Lovelock (1991) uses a four-way classification scheme, involving:

- Tangible actions to people's bodies;
- Tangible actions to goods and other physical possessions;
- Intangible actions directed at people's minds; and
- Intangible actions directed at intangible assets.

Physical participation could be classified as a people-based service directed at people's bodies. Attendance at sporting events could more accurately be classified as a people-based service directed at people's minds. The context of participation in sports is important in framing marketing strategies. The most obvious example is the formation of marketing strategies aimed at attracting players to participate in a competition or sports and the marketing strategies required to attract people to attend a sporting event.

In either case, it is necessary to ask why such a classification scheme is important. Lovelock (1991: 27) notes the following, which helps to answer this question:

1. Does the customer need to be physically present:
    a. throughout the service?
    b. only to initiate or terminate the service transaction?
    c. not at all?
2. Does the customer need to be mentally present during service delivery? Can mental presence be maintained across physical distances through mail or electronic communications?
3. In what way is the target of the service act 'modified' by receipt of the service? And how does the customer benefit from these 'modifications'?

If, as is the case in sports, customers need to be present to play or watch a live event, they must enter the service factory, returning us to the importance of simultaneous production and consumption. When spectators or participants enter the sports factory, this has an obvious implication for the sports marketer. In sports, it is hard to overcome the winning (I had a good day/night) or losing (I had a bad day/night) syndrome. Although this special range of emotions will never be removed from the sports product, their importance can be diminished by ensuring that the quality of service is very good. Again, the importance of the product extensions through quality service provision is highlighted. Slowly, sporting organisations are beginning to recognise the need to plan for service quality.

Service Quality

Service quality research has become prominent in the marketing literature during the past decade. Much work has been conducted to identify the key attributes of quality service. These attributes have been developed from the perspective of the consumer. Extensive research using focus group interviews, conducted by Parasuraman, Zeithaml and Berry during the 1980s, identified the ten dimensions of service quality. Parasuraman et al. (1985: 46) note that, 'regardless of the type of service, consumers used basically similar criteria in evaluating service quality'. The lack of tangible clues creates difficulties for consumers in making decisions about service product purchase. In relation to purchasing a good, it is often possible to try out the product before purchase, or at least to see it in action. This would be the case with the purchase of a car or computer.

As services are time-dependent, it is often not possible to try out the product before purchase. Consumer recommendation about a service is a powerful influence in pre-purchase decisions. Similarly, past experience with a service provides the same opportunity to develop perceptions about the quality of the service being considered. Finally, external communications, via advertising, create levels of expectations about service quality.

The gap that ultimately exists between 'expected' service and 'perceived' service is a result of the four factors consumers bring to product consumption. Companies should ensure that they do not promise more than they can actually deliver, as unrealistic expectations created by a company can negatively affect the level of perceived quality, when in reality the level of service quality was good. By implication, a firm needs to understand customer expectations as well as to have an intimate knowledge of the product attributes, which are the genesis of the expected service levels and product positioning.

Positioning the Sports Product

Positioning the sports product in the marketplace is strategically important, as it plays a pivotal role in marketing strategy. In essence, positioning is the perceived fit between a particular product and the target market. To a large extent, the success of a product within a chosen market depends on how effectively it has been positioned. The sports product, like any other product, is subject to the same range of preferences and perceptions by consumers.

Establishing Position

Establishment of a desired position in the marketplace is a priority for the sports marketer. This can be achieved in two ways: by physical design, and through advertising. Physical design refers to the rule changes and modifications that can be made to render a sports more attractive to certain segments of the market. Cricket is the best example of this. Establishing a product position through advertising is being used more and more by sports marketers. The most notable campaign aimed at repositioning a sports was the former NSW Rugby League's (NSWRL) advertisements featuring Tina Turner. In 1989 the NSWRL embarked on an advertising campaign aimed at presenting rugby league as a glamorous, racy and exciting game.

This was necessary, as the league was emerging from a period where the game was beset by image problems such as excessive on-field violence and a struggling image at both club and league level. The 'What you get is what you see' and 'Simply the best' campaigns were extremely effective in creating a new and different image for the game. In effect, the game was being repositioned to broaden its appeal, which had been predominantly to the blue-collar male market. Between 1983 and 1990, when the league embarked on its turnaround strategy, attendances doubled and television ratings rose by 70%, indicating some success in broadening the appeal of the game. This is also indicative of the phases through which products pass in varying stages of their life cycle.

Product Development

Kotler et al. (1989: 354) note that 'a company has to be good at developing new products. It also has to be good at managing them in the face of changing tastes, technologies and competition. Every product, including sports products, seems to pass through a life cycle. Typically, this follows a consistent pattern: the product is conceived or born, and develops through several phases of maturity before dying as new and improved products emerge. In sports, it is also true that various sports oscillate within this described life cycle. There are some differences, however.

In general, it is unusual for a sports to die. It is possible to trace the history of many sports worldwide and to note how the majority have stood the test of time. Not all sports have always been successful, but they have continued to exist and experience varying levels of success.

Rather than the actual sports dying, sporting competitions, events, tournaments and clubs or teams tend to disappear or require marketing strategies designed to extend their life cycle. Relocation of teams, rule changes, mergers and the provision of new facilities all constitute ways in which various forms of the sports product endeavour to avoid decline. The other major difference is that sporting organisations do not often release new products in the way that the car and computer industries do. The sports product is again seen to be reasonably stable.

The NRL, like the AFL, is an example of a sports that has had to rejuvenate its products. Expanding to form national competitions was one way in which this was achieved. In rugby league, the previously described Tina Turner adver-tising campaign was an integral part of relaunching a sports that was losing market share or, in product life cycle terms, was in decline. Other strategies included expanding the competition to Queensland, the ACT, Victoria and, for a brief period, Western Australia. Within Sydney itself, some clubs were closed or relocated to overcome changing or declining inner-city populations.

For example, the Balmain Tigers survived 87 years on the dedication of its fans and working-class traditions. As the demographic profile of the Balmain region changed, the club was forced to look elsewhere to maintain the necessary financial infrastructure to continue participating in the league. The club's name was changed to the Sydney Tigers, broadening its appeal, and it relocated to a new facility in Parramatta.

The product life cycle curve

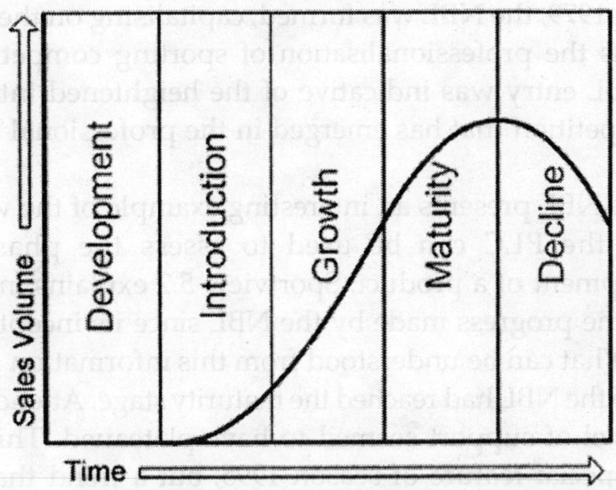

The typical PLC curve is S-shaped and characterised by four different phases:

1. Introduction is a period of slow sales growth. Profits are non-existent at this stage because of the heavy expenses of introducing the product to the market.
2. Growth is a period of rapid market acceptance and increasing profits.
3. Maturity is a slow period of sales growth because the product has been accepted by most potential buyers. Profits stabilise or decline because of increased marketing designed to defend the product against competition.
4. Decline is the period when sales show a strong downward drift and profits erode.

In the late 1970s and early 1980s a number of traditional Australian sports entered the decline phase of the PLC. Cricket, the Victorian Football League (VFL) and NSWRL all struggled as Australians' appetite for sports and leisure options began to diversify. A subsequent surge in interest for individual sports and recreational activities such as jogging, triathlon, aerobics and cycling saw the profits and previous market dominance of these sports begin to erode. Also in 1979, the NBL was formed, capitalising on the trend towards the professionalisation of sporting competitions. The NBL entry was indicative of the heightened intensity of competition that has emerged in the professional sports sector.

The NBL presents an interesting example of the way in which the PLC can be used to assess the phases of development of a product. Sportview 5.2 explains in more detail the progress made by the NBL since its inception in 1979. What can be understood from this information is that by 1995 the NBL had reached the maturity stage. Attendances and level of support seemed to have plateaued. This was not a special feature of season 1995, but a trend that had become apparent during the 1993 and 1994 seasons. Attendances had peaked at about 80% of stadium capacity, sponsor interest had levelled, and the NBL was still experiencing problems in attracting good television ratings.

The challenge for the NBL was what to do to arrest the decline. One solution examined during 1996 was to change the playing season, moving it to the summer. Not only would this provide the impetus to relaunch the NBL as a summer game—it would, as shown in the perceptual map, have the capacity to alter its direct competitors, including the capacity to obtain more television time. Moving to summer would see the intense competition provided by the AFL, NRL and Super 12s reduced, at the risk of moving into cricket's competitive space.

The National Soccer League (NSL) would become relevant competitors, but the NSL does not have the same product intensity as the AFL, NRL or Super 12s. Cricket, in particular one-day cricket, does have the competitive intensity to create difficulties for the NBL. Programming of cricket is not as intense or as weekend-oriented as that of the AFL and NRL. In winter, the AFL often schedules matches on Friday night, Saturday afternoon, Saturday night and Sunday afternoon. This creates difficulties for basketball in terms of both television and live attendance. Cricket has fewer matches, and these tend to be concentrated in one major city on any given weekend. The opportunity to rejuvenate the NBL was therefore presented through the season change that ultimately took effect in the summer of 1998.

The NBL—Product Development

A substantial drop in attendance figures forced the NBL to review its marketing strategies, in a bid to generate more excitement and momentum in the early part of the 1993 season. After ten rounds, the NBL—which trumpeted a sensational growth in attendances throughout the 1980s and early 1990s—was down by almost 270,000 fans. (Brown 1993:6) The ten-team NBL competition commenced in 1979 as an outlet to provide a regular opportunity for its elite players to play top-line basketball. It also quickly became the promotional vehicle for basketball in Australia. The gate for the first season was 196,000 for all home and away games. By 1995, as is shown in the table, attendances had risen to 1,097,678 from 201 games played across the country. An average of 5461 fans attended games in 1995. From 1979 to 1984 attendances grew 82%, to 355 828 spectators; but in the five years to 1988 they jumped 130%, clearly demonstrating the sport's appeal, and in the five years to 1993 they rose to just over 1 million. Seasons 1993-95 show that growth then slowed and that the NBL in terms of attendances had plateaued.

The success of the NBL in capturing the public's imagination in the 1980s can be traced to several reasons. It was a highly entertaining game, played in a comfortable, warm stadium, enjoyed by men and women, and revered by children. Hype generated by the NBL was also fostered by enormous goodwill from the print media and radio media. There was no question that this most American of sports had taken off in Australia, but to continue to grow it needed television to play a more significant role (Brown 1992). The Seven network, which held the rights to televise basketball in Sydney and Melbourne prior to 1992, was reluctant to give basketball a greater profile. Channel Ten took up the rights to televise the NBL in 1992 on the promise that the NBL would be shown in prime time. As season 1992 unfolded the Ten network realised that NBL programming was suffering from low ratings. The only exception to this was Perth. Following the break for the 1992 Olympic Games, the Ten network removed the NBL from prime time television.

Television remains a source of frustration for the NBL. In 1995, the NBL made the following observations in relatior to television and its impact on product development: With television we found ourselves in a difficult situation. In order to make television work, the NBL will have to become much more flexible in its scheduling (playing in noncompetitive days and times), consider changing the time of year we play, clean up the court clutter (to increase NBL branding and strengthen television advertising). All of these strategies may have a cost to the clubs.

This cost will not be initially met by television rights revenue. But without making some or all of these changes, television rights revenue may never reach the level to be able to finance the changes. Almost every aspect of the NBL/Club business now comes back to creating success on television. Marketing, merchandising, attendance, rights money and sponsorship levels all point to television needing improving. The television ratings are a mystery. Our worst rating performance in recent history comes at a time when a new ARM Quantum survey shows that basketball has increased its stranglehold on the youth in this country.

Basketball ranks as the top sports played by boys (10-17) at 59%, 12 points above the next team sports, cricket (47%). For girls, basketball ranks third at 31%, behind swimming (52%) and netball (36%).

There are more mysteries in the result of the survey that indicates what the youth market are watching on television. Basketball is way out in front at 50%, ahead of cricket at 38%—significantly improving its position since the last youth monitor three years ago. Finally, in the 10-17-year group, basketball is the best attended sports at 22%, ahead of rugby league at 17% (NBL 1995).

In 1996 the NBL made the decision to move the NBL season from its traditional winter season to a summer season. This necessitated a transition, or interim season, from January to July 1998. The new summer season commenced in October 1998. The rationale for the change according to the NBL (2000) was (a) to improve television arrangements, (b) increase media coverage through reduced clutter (i.e. less AFL media), (c) maintenance of sponsorship, although it was recognised that reduced attendance might result from the change. Although the interim season had a negative impact in terms of club mergers and further erosion of the fan supporter base, television coverage improved, albeit mainly through pay-TV Fox Sports supported by ABC coverage.

Attendances grew 8% in the first full summer season, compared to a 5% decline in the interim season. The second summer season allowed the NBL to experiment with innovative fixturing, such as the pre-season blitz, double-headers, an open-airgame at Rod Laver Arena, Melbourne Park, as well as promoting local derbies. Attendances also rose by approximately 14%, with average weekly television audiences of about 580000.

By season 2002, however, the NBL and its teams were experiencing difficulties. Dampney (2002:101) noted that 'two clubs appointing administrators, no naming rights sponsor, no free to air television rights—no national basketball League?' Both the Victorian Titans and Sydney Kings appointed administrators in 2002, although a consortium—including former Australian boomer Shane Heal and Bob Turner, a founding member of the NBL in Australia—eventually bought the Sydney Kings. The Victorian Titans' future was less certain mid-2002. Leading into season 2002/03, the 11 teams in the NBL competition were facing a series of collective challenges. As Dampney (2002) asks: 'Is all hope lost for a game once labelled the world's fastest growing participation sports?' Product development is again a major issue confronting the NBL.

Stages of the Product Life Cycle

The introductory stage is characterised by the need to communicate the existence of the product to potential consumers. This can be very expensive, and accounts for the high start-up costs for a new product. The principal objective in this stage is to build awareness. Returning to the NBL example, building awareness of the new competition in 1979 was the primary objective for competition organisers. Successfully achieving this goal was inhibited, as basketball was not a traditional sports in Australia. Typically during the introductory stage, profitability is low or negative and sales near zero. Attracting 190000 spectators in the first year of the NBL competition compared to just over 1 million in 1995 illustrates the initial difficulties of developing a market segment for basketball.

The other important consideration in this introductory stage is identifying the channels through which the NBL is distributed. Each club in the league was based in a major capital city or regional centre, with the intention of developing product awareness in that city or region. The most difficult phase of developing product awareness was trying to build team loyalty and team rivalry.

Growth

As product awareness began to build for basketball it moved into the next stage of the PLC: the growth stage. The NBL attendances grew to 242022 by 1984 and to just over 800000 by 1990. In this period considerable growth was achieved as many clubs moved to larger playing facilities. During the growth stage, the range of product offerings tends to widen, and refinements are made to the way in which the product is offered. The NBL found it necessary to provide large comfortable facilities as well as quality product extensions. It was through product extensions that the NBL made its greatest change to product offerings.

Merchandise and licensing programmes emerged, associated television programming appeared, and basketball began to identify and open up new market segments. To overcome the high cost of enticing new consumers to NBL games, the clubs began to recognise the importance of retaining their members and loyal supporters. This marked the transition from the growth to the maturity stage. The clubs themselves became the most important marketing vehicles for basketball. Brand loyalty via individual clubs became important, and club memberships began to stabilise post-1990.

Maturity and Revitalisation

The mature stage is characterised by a plateau in sales—in the NBL's case, sales in the form of attendance, memberships, sponsorships and merchandise. As has already been discussed in this section, action needs to be taken to extend the PLC. This returns us to the reasons why the NBL is considering a change of season, to recycle or extend the capacity of the NBL to capture market share. Given that the NBL is a relatively new sports product in Australia, it will be worth seeing what other action the NBL takes to extend the PLC of basketball.

VARIATIONS FROM THE PLC CURVE

The PLC is a useful tool for the sports marketer to assist in strategy development for sports and sporting league and associations. The S-curve however, can be misleading. Not all products progress incrementally through the stages of the life cycle described, making it harder to discern at what stage of the PLC a product can be classified. Another complication is the time taken to progress through the stages of the PLC. It is very hard to predict how long it will take a product to move from an introductory stage to maturity. Indeed, the NBL has been caught in this situation of taking at least two years to identify maturity, and a subsequent levelling off of interest.

SPORTS AND TELEVISION

Earlier in this chapter we discussed the benefits provided by a product as being vital to the consumer's decision to purchase. In sports, television has emerged as an important substitute for attendance at the live event. Another question is whether sports on television is the same product as the live event. At issue also has been the revenue aspect of televising sporting contests versus the live game. That is, consumers have the choice either to attend the event or stay at home and watch it on television. For sports where consumers may decide to stay home and watch the event on television, this choice represents direct lost revenue.

It is, however, also revenue that may find its way back to the sports indirectly in the form of television rights as a consequence of high programme ratings. Alternatively, the short-term lost revenue may result in a long-term revenue gain as the consumer is enticed to attend future games because the televised game was entertaining and enjoyable. The relationship between television and sports has always been prickly, as the balance between live coverage, delayed coverage and 'blacking out' home markets has created tension between respective sports and the television networks. Other tensions are observed in the form of scheduling, as television looks to the most favourable programming options to maximise its investment via television rights.

In relation to sports, two important concepts have implications for sports marketing. The first is the core product, defined as the actual game, over which the sports marketer has no control. The sports marketer must be very careful not to overpromise in terms of how good the game will be or how well specific athletes may perform. The second concept is the importance of product extensions to the overall marketing effort. It is here that the marketer can ensure that acceptable levels of quality are achieved. Discussion in this chapter also focused on the importance of delivering quality service. The dimensions of quality service were discussed and the areas requiring attention in the delivery of product extensions indicated. These include anything that affects spectators' attendance and enjoyment of an event.

Issues of strategy were also considered when discussing product positioning and the product life cycle. In both cases these techniques allow the marketer to assess the relative standing of a product in relation to competitors and the phases of product growth. The perceptual map was used to illustrate the concept of product space and the way in which this defines direct and indirect competitors. Perceptual mapping also highlights the importance of key product attributes and their ability to entice consumers to purchase or attend games. Level of excitement was used as an example of a key product attribute. In this example, it was possible to determine the direct competitors of the NBL and other sports.

The NBL was also used to illustrate the application of product life cycle analysis, which revealed some interesting challenges confronting the NBL in its quest to arrest the plateau in the fortunes of its competition. -

Finally, the importance of television to sports was noted. A distinction was made between the television product and the live product. It was posited that televised sports is a different product from the one viewed live. Different benefits are offered, so a different range of options is considered in the pre-purchase process.

CHAPTER

The Strategic Pricing Process in Sports

PRICING STRATEGIES

Cost of production, however, is only one of the variables to take into consideration when setting or adjusting price. The strategic pricing process incorporates both internal characteristics of the organisation and its products (e.g. goals and objectives) and external characteristics (e.g. competitors' pricing behaviour). This will enable the marketer to create a pricing strategy beyond the short-term future of the organisation.

Step 1: Determine Pricing Goals

Although there exists a subtle difference between introducing a product then setting a price and adjusting the price of an existing product, the pricing goal must be determined for both. It is vital to recognise the influence that price has on customers' perceptions of the product. A relatively high-priced product will often be perceived as a high-quality product. Pricing, in other words, has a strong impact on the positioning of the product.

Determining the pricing goals should be a direct derivative of the organisation's reason for being (i.e. its mission) and the resulting marketing goals. Marketing goals of different organisations and derived pricing goals are shown below.

- Determine pricing goals
- Determine market sensitivity to price
- Estimate the cost-volume-profit relationship
- Determine pricing strategies of major competitors
- Determine constraints on pricing behaviour
- Determine constraints by other marketing mix variables
- Determine time dependence
- Determine final price

Maximum Shareholder Value

Private enterprises and privately owned sports franchises often pursue goals designed to maximise shareholder value. In order to achieve maximum shareholder value, pricing goals would include maximising profit, maximising sales growth or maximising revenue. *Maximising profit* is often seen as a short-term goal concentrating on current financial performance, assuming little influence from competitors (i.e. to undercut the set price). *Maximising sales growth* is a long-term pricing goal. Although profits could be higher, the organisation aims to sell its products at a lower price to as many customers as possible. The goal is to obtain a large share of the market and reap the subsequent long-term benefits. *Maximising revenue* can be the pricing goal of, for example, the organisers of Wimbledon. With an infrastructure (buildings, equipment and personnel) in place, every extra customer adds to the revenue of the organisation. The organisation itself is incurring little extra cost by providing services to that one extra visitor, and this makes selling the extra tickets, such as ground passes, extremely attractive.

Most Innovation

If an organisation aims to be an innovative company, the pricing goal may be to skim the market. Nike, as an athletic footwear manufacturer, establishes a price high enough for a small segment of the market to buy its products. As soon as competitors introduce similar products, Nike lowers the price to sell to the segment below the 'early adopters'. Nike skims the market by receiving the maximum price from the different segments in the market. Nike can adopt this strategy because it ensures that it is the first to introduce a new, trendy, high-quality product.

Highest-quality Products

If an organisation aims to deliver the highest-quality products, a premium pricing strategy may be an alternative pricing goal. In order to communicate the high quality of the product (e.g. a world title boxing contest), a correspondingly high price is set. Customers, valuing the high-quality features of the product, will pay the premium price, and the organisation will achieve an above-average return.

Community Accessibility

Not-for-profit organisations, government organisations and many sporting organisations often set pricing goals such as partial cost recovery or full cost recovery. Public hospitals, for example, may set prices in order to recover their costs because they do not need to make a profit, their main goal being to serve the community. National sports-governing bodies can price their products in order to break even, incorporating funding from the federal government (partial cost recovery). Setting or adjusting the price depends not only on the goals of the organisation but also on the other elements of the pricing process. This will become clear in the following sections.

Step 2: Determine Market Sensitivity to Price

How sensitive customers are to a change in price is important in determining a range in which the final price may be set. It is also vital to know the estimated size of the market and how the market is segmented. The concepts of demand and supply, price elasticity and non-price factors are important in determining market sensitivity to price. Given the marketing focus of this book, we start by discussing the concept of demand.

Demand

The quantity demanded of the product by potential customers depends on the price assigned to the product. In general terms, the higher the price of a product, the lower the quantity demanded. The quantity demanded also depends on the prices of other factors, such as product (substitutes and complements), income of customers, expectations of future prices and the size of the population. *Substitutes* are products that can be used in place of another product (e.g. spectator tickets to a football match and to a basketball match). If the price of a product (football tickets) rises, the quantity demanded of the substitute (basketball tickets) is likely to rise as well because consumers will elect to purchase the cheaper substitute. *Complements* are products used in conjunction with another product (e.g. golf clubs and a golf course membership). If the price of a product (golf course membership) falls, the quantity demanded of this product and its complement (golf clubs) will rise. Generally, when the income of customers rises, demand for most goods will also rise.

Expectations of higher prices in the future may prompt customers to buy now, and hence demand will rise. In general, the larger the population, the greater the demand will be for products.

Supply

When a product is providing attractive returns to producers, more organisations will be inclined to supply the product to the market than when the price is relatively low. In general terms, the higher the price of a product, the greater the quantity supplied. The quantity supplied also depends on resource prices, technology, the number of sellers and the expectations about future prices. In general, when resource prices rise, the quantity supplied will fall. Similarly, technological improvements and increasing efficiency will result in a rise in the quantity supplied because a greater quantity can be produced at the same cost. The more sellers there are, the greater the quantity supplied. Expectations about future prices are a more complicated issue. When a sporting goods firm expects prices of tennis racquets to rise after the final at Wimbledon, it may choose to hold back the racquets in stock in order to sell them at a higher price. Racquet manufacturers, however, may decide to increase production and supply more racquets to the market.

Market Equilibrium

If the demand for tennis racquets after the Wimbledon final rises, the demand curve will move to the right. This will result in a rise in the quantity supplied (i.e. a movement along the supply curve) because the price will go up to establish a new equilibrium. Let us assume that people keep demanding the new quantity. With this increase in demand, new producers will be lured to the market because of the higher price, supply will go up, and the supply curve will move to the right. This again will result in a fall in price. Equilibrium will return to the point where it is not attractive enough for new suppliers to enter the market. At the end of this process the only change will be that the total quantity supplied has risen.

PRICE ELASTICITY OF DEMAND

We have now explored the influence that price can have on the quantity of products supplied and demanded. What we do not know is how sensitive a customer is to a change in price. Will a rise or fall in the price of a product result in a great or small change in the quantity traded? Price elasticity of demand is a measure projecting this relationship. It is calculated as the absolute value of the change (%) in the quantity demanded, divided by the change (%) in price. The absolute value can range between 0 and infinity. A value between 0 and 1 represents inelastic demand; a value greater than 1 represents elastic demand; a value of exactly 1 is called unit elastic demand: In other words, the organisation will benefit from raising price because the number of customers lost will be less than the gain in revenue. For example, the number of customers will not vary greatly when the price of tickets for the World Championship Soccer Final is raised.

Factors Determining Elasticity

The size of the elasticity of demand is mainly determined by three variables:

- The substitutability of the product;
- The amount of time since the price change; and
- The proportion of customer income spent on the product.

The more substitutes there are available for a product, the easier it is for a customer to replace one product with another when price rises, hence the higher the price elasticity. A range of professional sports are playing in the metropolitan area of Melbourne less than 1 kilometre apart. A rise in the admission price for one sports will force customers to search for cheaper alternatives. A substantial price rise will result in an even more substantial loss of customers. However, existing customers of a basketball club, for example, will not immediately be able to go to a football club because they may have purchased longterm memberships. The longer the time since the price change, the more opportunities customers will have had to find alternatives, and hence the greater the elasticity of demand.

The higher the proportion of customer income spent on club membership, the higher the elasticity of demand. If expenditure represents a large part of an individual's income, every extra dollar on top of that expenditure will be scrutinised and can make him/her decide not to purchase. If, however, a very rich person has to make the same decision, money spent on membership represents only a small portion of total income, and a price rise will not greatly affect the decision to buy. This last example shows that price elasticity of demand can differ not only between products but also between consumer groups, and provides the marketer with the opportunity to differentiate between customer segments.

AFL Kicks a Goal on Marketing Strategy

The AFL's marketing strategy since the early 1980s has boosted football and helped to reverse the game's long-run decline in attendance, say two Melbourne economists. Research conducted by Mr Peter Fuller and Mr Mark Stewart at RMIT has rejected the belief widely held among football fans "that the AFL is conspiring against the best interests of the game. To the extent that increased attendance at football matches is deemed the yardstick by which football administrators are judged, we can only endorse their recent actions," Mr Fuller and Mr Stewart have concluded.

The AFL's decision to hold down ticket price rises in the late 1980s, the construction of the new Great Southern Stand at the Melbourne Cricket Ground, the closer competition, the player draft from 1986, and the continued programme of ground rationalisation were major factors in boosting game attendances. But Fuller and Stewart have found that the AFL could now push prices up further without suffering any loss in gate takings. In both Victoria and South Australia, attendance was in decline from 1948, "indicating football was becoming proportionately a less popular from of entertainment," the economists have found, using an analysis based on attendances as a proportion of each State's population.

Crowds hit rock bottom in Victoria in 1987 and in South Australia in 1989. However, some of the game's popularity has been restored since those low points. According to Fuller and Stewart, this is partly because the real cost of admission has been held down in the minor round games, and partly because of improvements in administration. "Increased competitiveness allowing people the opportunity to attend games at different times, ground rationalisation and the move to the National competition (especially in South Australia) seem to have played a part in this, " they said. The research has suggested that the player draft and the salary cap have helped by making games more even.

'Analysis of the impact of price changes on crowd size shows that a 10% increase in ticket prices (adjusted for inflation) eventually reduces attendances by around 6%. This means "the AFL could increase gate receipts by charging higher prices. The implication is that in terms of revenue derived from attendance, both the AFL and the SANFL are under-charging, according to Fuller and Stewart".

Non-price Factors

Non-price factors influence buying situations and reduce the importance of price in the buying process. Non-price factors include an intangible perception of a product, resulting in a perceived value. In other words, some customers may be willing to pay a higher-than average market price (premium price) to receive product benefits. Other customers may be willing to forgo these benefits in return for a lower-than-average market price. For marketers, it is therefore important to understand key product attributes in order to enhance the perceived value and hence charge a premium price.

In the sports industry, non-price factors are very important. The rules of demand and supply and price elasticity can be applied to sport's core product and extensions. In addition, different combinations of core and extensions can enhance the perceived value of the total product, justifying extra expenditure for customers. The core product cannot be remixed, but in combination with different product extensions the perceived value of the total package can be increased. Also, the more important the product is to the consumer, the less important price will become.

For example, a $100 repair on a bicycle of $2000 will enable the owner to ride the bicycle again. The perceived value of the $100 expenditure is likely to be higher than that of another $100 expenditure on something less important (e.g. a television repair) to the bike-rider. If the marketer is able to enhance the perceived value of the product, customers will become less sensitive to price (i.e. elasticity will decrease), and the organisation will benefit from raising price.

This applies also to the reverse situation. If the marketer is able to filter out the product attributes less valued by customers (e.g. cushioned seats or undercover seats in a sports stadium), customers will become more sensitive to price (i.e. elasticity will increase), and the organisation will benefit from lowering price. It is clear from these examples that different segments of customers are targeted as part of the pricing strategy.

Step 3: Estimate the Cost-volume-profit Relationship

Cost-volume-profit analysis, also called break-even analysis, examines the interaction of factors influencing the level of profits. These factors, as identified by Anderson and Sollenberger (1992), are:

- Selling prices;
- Volume of sales;
- Unit variable cost;
- Total fixed cost; and
- Sales mix.

The first four factors are discussed in this section, with sales mix left to the section on constraints by other marketing mix variables (product mix). In general terms, the total costs of production represent the minimum financial figure (i.e. break-even point) that needs to be recovered from sales in order to at least break even (total costs = total revenue). Total costs are made up of a fixed cost and a variable cost component. Fixed costs are the costs that an organisation has to incur in order to operate (e.g. costs of plant and equipment, taxes, insurance) regardless of the level of production. Variable costs fluctuate in direct proportion to changes in the activity of the organisation.

The cost of direct materials like leather for shoes is a good example. Pertaining to the goals of the organisation, the break-even point may vary. For an organisation with a partial cost recovery goal, this point is relatively lower than for a full cost recovery organisation. Both organisations, however, need to be able to ascertain their cost of production, enabling the organisation to arrive at a minimum price for its products by dividing the cost of production by the (estimated) number of products sold.

For a large athletic footwear manufacturer, total costs are made up of a fixed and variable component. In order to produce 10000 pairs a day, for example, a certain infrastructure needs to be evident. Plant, equipment and labour are needed in order to start operations and represent the fixed costs of operations, which are independent of the output level. Raw material to manufacture the shoes is the major component of the variable costs, which vary with the output of the plant. Although certain levels of production will be more efficient, in this example it is assumed that the variable cost per unit of production is the same.

In other words, the fixed cost component will decrease with volume of production. If a factory with building costs of $10 million produces 100 million pairs of shoes over its productive lifetime (e.g. ten years), the fixed cost component in every pair of shoes is $0.10. When we turn our attention to service products, and many sports products are service products, the unit variable costs in the break-even formula are much harder to determine.

Many costs are both fixed and shared across different services. In a large stadium, the building, its equipment (e.g. indoor courts, tennis nets, computers) and labour (a majority is often multiskilled in order to deliver different services) are all needed to provide the total mix of services offered by the facility. The variable costs per unit are hard to determine. What, for example, are the variable costs of providing basketball spectator services when one extra ticket is sold? Most costs have to be incurred, irrespective of the number of customers on the day or over a longer period.

We can state that most costs are fixed. This is why it is very attractive to entice that one extra customer: with little to no extra (variable) cost, the revenue from one extra customer is almost pure profit. This explains why, in the health and fitness industry, competition is based primarily on price. An organisation has to incur little extra cost in order to gain a substantial increase in revenues. This also indicates the importance of managing the non-price factors in the sports industry. Because we know that most costs are fixed, it becomes a matter of sophisticated marketing in order to enhance the perceived value of the sports product. This should lead to sufficient and sustainable market share to at least cover the costs of operation.

Step 4: Determine Pricing Strategies of Major Competitors

As in any strategic-planning effort of an organisation, it is important to monitor competitor behaviour and adjust actions accordingly. The first questions that need to be answered are: Who are the major (potential) competitors? Do they operate in the same market (e.g. an amateur soccer team and a professional basketball team) or even in the same segment of the market (e.g. a central-business-district golf course and a working-class-suburb golf course)? Organisations can then determine when to respond to price changes by competitors.

The next step is to determine how competitors are positioned in terms of their relative prices, providing an organisation with an indication of the competitive price range for which the product is on offer. It would also be very useful to know which strategies of competing firms are successful. Finally, if an organisation is able to find out what the probable responses of competitors would be to a price change, different pricing scenarios can be developed in order to make the appropriate choice.

Step 5: Determine Constraints on Pricing Behaviour

Laws and regulations are the most obvious constraints on pricing behaviour. Most of these are a direct result of government intervention in regulating the market behaviour of organisations. Some cases of price fixing (i.e. agreement between organisations about price) can be regarded as disadvantageous for the public and are therefore forbidden by law. In order to keep government-owned facilities accessible to all members of the community, local gove-rnment can set a maximum price level (ceiling). Even when a management company is hired to manage the local pool, local government can constrain it in its pricing strategies. Regulatory organisations, like national sports orga-nisations, can set membership fees for members, clubs and associations in order to optimise participation levels.

Social responsibility constraints can also affect the pricing behaviour of organisations. If, for example, the local professional soccer club feels that disabled members of the local community should be able to enjoy a game of soccer, it will have to adjust its facility in terms of access and seating arrangements. This will have a direct impact on the fixed cost component of the total costs of the club, and it may decide to set different unit (i.e. admission) prices to recover those costs. The pricing strategy of this club will be different from that of a club focusing solely on profit maximisation. Legal and social responsibility constraints therefore limit the pricing range for the product.

Step 6: Determine Constraints by Other Marketing Mix Variables

The variables of the marketing mix—product (mix), place (dependence) and promotion (mix)—all affect each other.

Product Mix

Prices in supermarkets are based on the overall mix of products rather than the individual products. Some products are priced at an attractive level (e.g. soft drinks during summer) in order to entice customers to do the rest of their shopping in the same supermarket. The AFL's admission prices are low compared to other sporting codes. These prices attract larger crowds, enhancing the atmosphere for attractive television coverage and as a consequence the attractiveness of the total product for television sponsors. The AFL can offset the loss of income from gate receipts against the increase in income from television, sponsor contracts and other in-stadium purchases.

Place Dependence

A majority of sports products are produced and consumed in a facility specifically designed to produce those sports products. The capacity of the facility limits the number of customers that can be serviced at a certain point in time and consequently the maximum total income.

The location of the facility determines the catchment area of potential customers and hence partly determines the profile of the customer. In general terms, dependence on the place of distribution further limits the possible pricing range of the products of the organisation. The commercial turning point for hallmark sporting events occurred over a decade and a half ago. It has been widely recognised that the 1984 Los Angeles Olympic Games created a turnaround in attitudes towards embarking on the colossal task of organising mega-events such as the Olympics and soccer's World Cup and Euro Championships. The LA Games demonstrated that when astute business ideas are applied to selling spectator sports products, money can be made.

Over the past two decades, it has been the vast injections of money that have made the world of big events go round. It is the positive economic impact of events on the hosting communities that has been the critical (political) justification for investing heavily in bidding and building for the event. Hallmark events have the propensity to deliver immense economic development to a region as an outcome of the combined encouragement of government, business and visitor spending.

The economic benefits of hallmark events are typically expected to outweigh their costs. In economic terms, this is because large-scale events have a high cost-benefit ratio. In other words, their capacity to generate exports, stimulate domestic spending, improve capital utilisation, develop and regenerate infrastructure, mobilise government involvement, marshal commercial sponsorship, assemble community supporters and drive consumable manufacturing are irreplaceable, and seldom achieved via any other programme or activity.

Nevertheless, despite the anticipated benefits of hosting hallmark sports events, the exponential increase in their funding, and often the need for underwriting by the local government, has driven the need for more rigorous justification of investments. As government authorities provide the lynchpin infrastructure for the events, they also assume the burden for justifying the community rewards in expending public monies.

Thus, to invest in hallmark events for communal benefits, there has been a greater need to validate spending by measuring the event's contribution to the economy. For example, research (Diopter/ Meerwaarde 2000) commissioned by the Dutch government identified that the Euro 2000 tournament contributed 248.2 million guilders (US$110 million) to the Dutch economy. Of this sum, 238.2 million came from foreign visitors while the Dutch spent an additional 10 million, on top of their 'normal' expenditure. This 'extra' money flowed to the four Dutch host cities of the event: Amsterdam (112.1 million), Rotterdam (71.8 million), Eindhoven (41.1 million) and Arnhem (27.6 million), ironically leading to a net loss for the rest of the country of 4.4 million. On top of visitor expenditure, the Stichting Euro 2000 spent an additional 72 million (sponsor and UEFA contribution) on the organisation of the tournament, resulting in a total positive economic impact of 320 million guilders.

PROMOTION MIX

The promotion mix (i.e. the means through which communication with the target markets will take place) can be constructed after product, price and place information is available. A low price strategy often needs an intensive promotional effort in order to sell as many units as possible. If the tools for intensive promotion are not available due to limited funds, the organisation will be limited in pursuing a low price strategy. The promotion mix is constraining the pricing strategy. A pricing strategy never stands on its own, as it needs to be backed by adequate promotional efforts. One of the characteristics of services is that they cannot be stored, as services are timedependent.

The LA Games demonstrated that when astute business ideas are applied to selling spectator sports products, money can be made. Over the past two decades, it has been the vast injections of money that have made the world of big events go round.

It is the positive economic impact of events on the hosting communities that has been the critical (political) justification for investing heavily in bidding and building for the event. Hallmark events have the propensity to deliver immense economic development to a region as an outcome of the combined encouragement of government, business and visitor spending.

The economic benefits of hallmark events are typically expected to outweigh their costs. In economic terms, this is because large-scale events have a high cost-benefit ratio. In other words, their capacity to generate exports, stimulate domestic spending, improve capital utilisation, develop and regenerate infrastructure, mobilise government involvement, marshal commercial sponsorship, assemble community supporters and drive consumable manufacturing are irreplaceable, and seldom achieved via any other programme or activity.

Nevertheless, despite the anticipated benefits of hosting hallmark sports events, the exponential increase in their funding, and often the need for underwriting by the local government, has driven the need for more rigorous justification of investments.

As government authorities provide the lynchpin infrastructure for the events, they also assume the burden for justifying the community rewards in expending public monies. Thus, to invest in hallmark events for communal benefits, there has been a greater need to validate spending by measuring the event's contribution to the economy.

For example, research (Diopter/ Meerwaarde 2000) commissioned by the Dutch government identified that the Euro 2000 tournament contributed 248.2 million guilders (US$110 million) to the Dutch economy. Of this sum, 238.2 million came from foreign visitors while the Dutch spent an additional 10 million, on top of their 'normal' expenditure.

This 'extra' money flowed to the four Dutch host cities of the event: Amsterdam (112.1 million), Rotterdam (71.8 million), Eindhoven (41.1 million) and Arnhem (27.6 million), ironically leading to a net loss for the rest of the country of 4.4 million. On top of visitor expenditure, the Stichting Euro 2000 spent an additional 72 million (sponsor and UEFA contribution) on the organisation of the tournament, resulting in a total positive economic impact of 320 million guilders.

Final price determination is based on cost, competition, demand or a combination of the three. Most of the time, one method provides the basis for decision-making, although the others often contribute. The break-even analysis has been presented as a cost-based approach. Many providers in the health and fitness industry will base their pricing on competition. In this industry it is important to fill the capacity of the facility and thus to attract those few extra customers from the direct competitors. It is likely that the larger spectator sports organisations base their pricing on demand. In this method, the value of the product to the buyer is estimated.

Westerbeek and Turner (1996: 394) found that: together with an increase in televisual appeal and hence income, the AFL was able to devise strategies in which demand characteristics of their markets (like elasticity of demand) could be used to optimise net income. Mass attendance at games was deemed more important than maximum profit from gate receipts. By undercharging at the gate it was found that demand was inelastic at the current pricing level, income from TV and sponsorship could be raised, leading to greater total income rather than maximising gate receipts.

It can be concluded that, ultimately, the AFL based its pricing strategy on the perceived value of its total product mix and, along similar lines, the price charged by the Grand Prix organisers for tickets makes up only a small component of the overall pricing equation.

The final price charged by Grand Prix organisers includes a significant tax contribution by the local residents of Melbourne and Victoria, not to mention a range of environmental costs. Overall, the 'final price' paid for the right to host the event is a function of the range of benefits, both tangible (economic) and intangible (social and cultural), that the event is able to generate.

To enable the sports marketer to set appropriate prices, it is important to set pricing goals in concert with the overall organisational and marketing goals. Then the sensitivity of markets to changes in price can be determined and, as a consequence, the elasticity of demand. This information, combined with marketing data such as the size of the market and the number of competitors, is used to estimate costvolume-profit relationships, leading to the creation of a break-even chart with an emphasis on a cost-based pricing strategy.

When the organisation is able to base its pricing on the demand in the market—in other words, powerful enough to lead the way in setting price—the emphasis will be on demand-based pricing. It may, however, be more important to find out about the pricing strategies of competitors and to determine constraints (legal, social, other marketing mix variables) on pricing behaviour in the industry. This can lead to a competitorbased pricing strategy. When taking into consideration the time dependence of many sports products, a combination of cost-based, demand-based and competitor-based pricing will often be exercised in setting the final price or adjusting the current price.

CHAPTER

Sports Facility Planning

Planning of facilities for mega-events like the Olympic Games, or facilities for a professional basketball club, or facilities for the local sports clubs, all should involve a long-term perspective in terms of the prospective usage of the facility. With production and consumption of the sports products taking place in the facility, both current and future provision need to be taken into consideration. It is extremely costly to redevelop and redesign existing facilities.

In that regard, does the sports facility as it is significantly determine opportunities and limitations for sports product provision? The Olympic Park soccer stadium in Melbourne, for example, due to its size and design, is not able to host a cricket or Australian Rules football match. Soccer matches cannot be played at Olympic Park during excessive rainfall, which, due to poor drainage, floods the field. The Amsterdam Arena in the Netherlands, on the other hand, can host soccer matches at any time of the year. Opened in 1996, it is the world's first 'real grass' soccer stadium with a retractable roof. Excessive rainfall, in this case, is not a potential limitation.

Since the opening of the Arena, other sports providers have followed suit. For example, the Telstra Dome in Melbourne has a retractable roof, allowing for soccer, 'indoor' cricket and Australian Rules football matches through its unique Australian design. It must be noted that the Amsterdam Arena in particular has had problems ensuring that the 'real grass' playing surface is of sufficient quality (due to limited daylight exposure) to play premier league soccer matches. This just shows that when you plan to solve one problem, another may arise.

Many sporting arenas around the world were originally developed and built to host sporting events and enable a certain number of spectators to watch the game. Few of the older arenas, however, were built to host guests in corporate boxes. With many sporting organisations dependent on corporate dollars, an old stadium can become a severe competitive disadvantage. In other words, the ability to cater for a range of sports products is highly dependent on the planning and design of the sports facility.

Servicescape for Sports Consumers

In the case of leisure services, it is more than just the perceived quality of the service rendered (e.g. whether a meal was delivered in a timely fashion) that influences whether consumers are satisfied with the service experience. For example, the purpose of going to an amusement park, a theatre, or a sporting event would seem to be for the excitement and stimulation of the experience. This kind of situation differs from a trip to the dry-cleaner, in which the customer is not likely to have any expectation of emotional arousal.

Because the sports product is generally purchased and consumed simultaneously, and typically requires direct human contact, customers and employees interact with each other within the organisation's physical facility. Ideally, therefore, the organisation's environment should support the needs and preferences of both service employees and customers simultaneously. Even before purchase, consumers commonly look for cues about the organisation's capabilities and quality. The physical environment is rich in such cues and may be very influential in communication the organisation's image and purpose to its customers.

Bitner (1992) found that the facility itself, or the *servicescape,* may have a substantial effect on the customer's satisfaction with the service experience, and hence will play an important role in determining whether the customer will repatronise the service-providing sporting organisation. The important aspects of the servicescape are the spatial layout and functionality of the facility and the elements related to aesthetic appeal. Wakefieldand Blodgett (1994) tested the importance of the servicescape on Major League Baseball (MLB) consumers.

The effect of the servicescape has been gaining increased attention by owners of MLB teams, as rising attendance and increased fan satisfaction have accompanied new stadiums in Baltimore, Cleveland, Texas, Toronto and Chicago. MLB stadiums provide a good setting in which to explore both the layout and functionality aspects of the servicescape, as well as the aesthetic appeal.

The ways in which seats, aisles, hallways and walkways, food service lines, restrooms, and entrances and exits are designed and arranged influence fan comfort, while the external environment, the architectural design, facility upkeep and cleanliness, use of decorative banners and signs, and personnel appearance all influence the ambience of the place. Wakefieldand Blodgett (1994) exposed potential customers to two different servicescapes: one old, low quality servicescape stadium and one new, high quality servicescape stadium. They found that the old stadium was being perceived as a significantly lower quality servicescape compared to the new one.

Respondents who perceived the servicescape to be of high quality reported higher levels of satisfaction with the servicescape, and hence were more willing to attend future games. Respondents who perceived the servicescape to be of high quality also experienced greater levels of excitement, and hence satisfaction with the servicescape. It was also found that respondents who felt crowded were less excited about the servicescape and perceived the servicescape to be of lower quality. The results of the study may have direct implications for those who have investments in stadium projects. A return in increased gate receipts might be expected owing to new stadiums or renovations. Spectators are likely to be more excited and more satisfied when in a high quality stadium and therefore more likely to come back.

Consistently fielding a winning team is increasingly expensive and difficult owing to uncontrollables such as player injuries and changes in competitors' performances. Thus another basic recommendation coming from this study is that owners/managers should be sure that the controllable aspects of the servicescape are properly managed to maximise stadium capacity. Based on extensive market research, economic trend analysis and environmental scanning, the sports marketer can determine current demand and predict future customer needs.

This should lead to market information on which specialists such as the architect and the engineer can base their sports facility planning and construction. If the sports marketer can influence facility location, design and construction decisions, the place variable will be optimised in terms of facility opportunities. It should be noted though that many sports marketers have to work with existing sports facilities. Nevertheless, identification of the service provision opportunities and limitations of the facility remains a task to be performed by the sports marketer in order to move on to the next step: supplying physical evidence.

Physical Evidence

Legg and Baker (1987) identify three major areas of concern that customers face when purchasing services:

- Understanding the service offering;
- Identifying the evoked set of potential service providers; and
- Evaluating the service before, during and after purchase.

Stated differently, it is hard for the customer to judge the quality of the product, and compare it with other products (providers) to arrive at a final purchase decision. If the sports marketer is able to make the sports product more tangible for the customer prior to purchase, the customer is more likely to buy it. The sports marketer has to lend the sports product physical evidence.

Physical evidence should support the quality characteristics of the product, because the majority of customers will judge the product on its quality. Physical evidence can be enhanced by optimising:

- Sports facility design;
- Promotion material and advertising; and
- Service provision.

The third factor, service provision, is discussed below:

Sports Facility: The sports facility is the most tangible and visible physical evidence sports marketers can have for their products. The name of the facility can be displayed and marketed as the place where exciting events occur. The FA Cup at Wembley, the Australian Football League (AFL) Grand Final at the Melbourne Cricket Ground and the National Basketball Association (NBA) playoffs at Madison Square Garden are all examples of events growing in their perceived quality in combination with the respective venues. Who would get excited about the FA Cup at Queenstown football ground, the AFL Grand Final at Bendigo football oval or the NBA playoffs at Pinola basketball stadium?

High-tech scoreboards showing instant replays and the provision of sports trivia enhance the tangibility of the event. In addition, banners, photographs or statues of sporting heroes can decorate the outside and inner walkways of the facility. All past Australian Open tennis champions decorate the inside walkways of Melbourne Park. Video or television screens and trophy exhibitions can show the famous moments of success of the teams playing in the facility. The museum at Barcelona Football Club's Nou Camp stadium in Spain has a continuous video display of Ronald Koeman's winning goal in the final of the 1992 European Club championships at Wembley football stadium. To add impact, the European Cup stands next to the video display.

Promotion: Because of the intangibility of the sports product, promotion is another way to add to the physical evidence. Adding this physical evidence is not specific to distribution through the facility, and examples are therefore not necessarily facility-linked. Through either advertising or promotions, distributed among potential customers or distributed by direct mail to selected markets, the quality image and brand name of a sporting organisation can be enhanced.

Legg and Baker (1987) suggest that advertisements should be vivid, using relevant tangible objects, concrete language and/or dramatisations. Photographs of past events, listings of services and explanations of different product offerings will materialise intangible services offered by the organisation. Media channels are another important consideration. Satisfied customers prepared to participate in these promotions can be used to endorse the different products, communicating their satisfaction. Celebrities, or even athlete celebrities, can also be used in this process as an influential and forceful communication channel.

Irrespective of the media channel used, the sporting organisation should try to link pictorial (posters, merchandise, advertisements) and written (brochures, flyers, advertisements) physical evidence to the name of the organisation. Licensing strategies (team merchandise) used by the LA Lakers, the Australian Cricket Board (ACB) and Manchester United Football Club are excellent examples of sporting organisations adding to their physical evidence and making money with their marketing promotions. These organisations also show that the fit between the name of the organisation and physical evidence is very important when considering a licensing and merchandising strategy.

Process: So far only the variables that can be manipulated when preparing for the customer to come to the facility to buy and consume the product have been discussed. Purchase and consumption involve the process by which the sporting organisation actually distributes the product to the customer. Sports marketers heavily involved in this sports service delivery process can influence and optimise the contacts between the customer and the sporting organisation. Shilbury (1994: 31) notes that 'the facility is of paramount importance because it represents the convergence of the marketing and operations functions'.

The Marketing Function

Gronroos (1990) distinguishes between the marketing department and the marketing function of an organisation. In traditional consumer goods marketing, the marketing department is the unit responsible for planning and implementing marketing activities. How to market a can of beans is almost the sole responsibility of the marketing department of the manufacturer; the retailer has only to put it on the shelf and sell it. In an emerging service economy, however, marketing activities (delivering the service as opposed to selling the beans) cannot be taken care of solely by the marketing department. Contacts between the service provider (e.g. the basketball club) and the customer are so important in overall customer satisfaction that marketing activities have to be carried out by the whole organisation, not only the marketing department. Ushers and food and beverage sellers are producing and delivering parts of the overall service package and can be identified as 'part-time marketers'.

They belong to what Gronroos (1990: 177) defines as the marketing function, 'including all resources and activities that have a direct or even indirect impact on the establishment, maintenance, and strengthening of customer relationships, irrespective of where in the organisation they are'.

Sports Servuction Model

The process of how the overall package of services is planned, produced and delivered to the customer can best be explained with the help of the sports servuction model. This model will be further explained by using service delivery at a basketball match as an example. The term 'servuction' refers to the visible production and delivery of the service experience. The sports servuction system model portrays the invisible and visible parts of the organisation.

In the invisible part, facility management and the two basketball clubs' managements combine to organise and plan for game night. This can be classified as the traditional marketing department role. The visible part of the organisation consists of the facility itself, the inanimate environment (physical evidence) and the service providers (contact people). Contact people, like ticket sellers, ushers and food and beverage sellers, but also the basketball players, provide the different services to the customers. This accumulation of services represents the customer's overall perception of their interaction with other customers, facility staff and players.

It is in the invisible part of the organisation that managers put together the service delivery process. Questions like where do we locate merchandising stands, how many ticket sellers and ushers do we need, how do we want ticket sellers and ushers to approach customers, and how many food and beverage stands will we operate are asked in the cause of optimising the service delivery process.

People

Staff are responsible for the delivery of the product, and as a consequence are the main distinguishing quality factor in the consumption process. The outcome of the basketball game cannot be guaranteed; therefore, consistency in service delivery is of the utmost importance in determining the customer's overall perception of the quality of the sports product. These are:

- Tangibles;
- Reliability;
- Responsiveness;
- Assurance; and
- Empathy.

These five criteria show the importance of marketing function personnel in the delivery of quality service. Apart from tangibles (partly personnel) and security, all the criteria are fully dependent on the training, skills and abilities of people in delivering high levels of service quality. The selection and training of human resources for service delivery in sports are tasks in which the sports marketer should have strong involvement. The level of training, skills and abilities of potential employees of the sporting organisation become 'people variables' that will make the difference between mediocre and excellent service provision.

Blueprinting the Sports Service Delivery System

Having identified the four variable components of the marketing mix element place, and knowing how one component can be varied independently from the other components, the sports marketer can start looking at how to combine the different components in an integrated fashion. By identifying operations (service preparation and service delivery) within the physical design of the sports facility, it is possible to make an overview or blueprint of the sports service delivery system. The blueprinted sports service delivery system will incorporate the four variable components of place. It now is up to the sports marketer to create the right mix of what is to be produced and consumed in the system.

The accumulation of these interactions contributes to the overall service experience of the customer. Facility planning and physical evidence directly affect all visible operations. The design of the facility determines how easy it is for customers to move between their seats, restrooms, and food and beverage stands. Physical evidence such as signage not only tells customers where to go and what is going on in the facility during their visit, but can also be used to advertise or communicate upcoming events. Poster and video displays of past events can increase the customers' perception of being in a place where the product is basketball entertainment. Facility planning has an equally important influence on invisible operations. How monitoring, maintenance and television operations take place is highly dependent on provisions made in the design and construction of the facility.

This involved process and people issues such as how to approach customers, how to supply them with information or food, how many employees will be needed on game night and in which functions (ushers, food and beverage sellers, ticket sellers), and how often and when to clean restrooms. With larger crowds, parking issues and crowd flow to and from the facility become important. The blueprint tracks the customer from entering the facility to exiting the facility and maps all possible interactions with the sporting organisation and its personnel. The blueprint identifies where the sports marketer can influence and vary the different components of place. A blueprint therefore is a vital instrument for the sports marketer in optimising the service experience. It is, however, only a start. As described at the beginning of this chapter, the actual delivery of service is the key to success. In the final section of this chapter, traditional marketing channels are discussed, using the basketball example again to relate these channels to the distribution of sports products.

Sporting Goods and Services Marketing Channels

It was noted earlier that most sports service providers deliver the sports product to the customer directly. The organisations involved in the process of making the product available for consumption or use are jointly called a marketing channel. The marketing channel performs different functions in order to enable producer and customer to exchange goods or services. Boyd et al. (1995) identify the following functions of marketing channels:

- Transportation and storage;
- Communication of information via advertising;
- Personal selling;
- Sales promotion;
- Feedback (marketing research);
- Financing; and
- Services such as installation and repair.

In the headline story, the organising committee of the Sydney Olympic Games has used all described marketing channels to distribute the variety of sports products. Olympic sports events were distributed through newly built facilities or existing/renovated government owned facilities. Some events were not shown on television. The majority of events, however, were broadcast throughout the world on television.

Huge amounts of Sydney 2000 Olympics licensed merchandise were produced by many different manufacturers around the world. Both before and during the distribution process, facility planning, physical evidence, process and people are all place variables to consider in the short and long term. Quality service delivery both during and after the Games was and will be of the utmost importance to ensure that the Sydney Games are remembered as the best of the 21st century.

Identifying sports products primarily as service products, it was explained how layout accessibility, facility aesthetics, seating comfort, electronic equipment and displays and facility cleanliness all have a significant influence on how sports fans perceive the quality of the stadium. In turn, the perceived quality of the sportscape affects the sports fan's satisfaction with the sportscape. And if sports fans are more satisfied, they are likely to stay in the stadium for a longer period, spend more money, and return to the stadium more often.

Sports product delivery can be enhanced by planning and designing the facility to suit customer and management needs. Providing physical evidence to the intangible sports service product can enhance distribution of the sports product and the actual service delivery process, and the people involved in this process are crucial for the success of the sporting organisation. Where and when to intervene, and how to influence the service delivery process, were highlighted by introducing the blueprint, or an overview of the sports service delivery system.

The Multipurpose Requirement

Most modern-day stadia cannot afford to be built for single-sports usage. According to Rod Sheard, senior principal at sports architects HOK, stadia need to be future proofed by building a critical mass of other facilities that will ensure the project's economic survival in another 20 years' time' (Menary 2001: 46). As a result of the changing functionality of sporting arenas, the current (fourth) generation of stadia incorporate facilities such as office space, hotels, restaurants, retail arcades, exhibition pavilions, television studios, business centres health and fitness areas, and late-night activity options such as bars and nightclubs.

The Corporate Push

The cost structure of building new stadia has traditionally been based on the standard 'cost per seat'. Dependent on the standard of quality required—and this largely relates to the type of league the club is playing in, and the type of customers it wants to target—stadium construction costs start as low as US$700 per seat.

According to Colin Fearns, director of Birse, the contractor building Leicester City's new stadium, you can get a nice stadium, including executive suites, for about US$1120 per seat (Menary 2001), which is very reasonable compared to the US$1750 per seat costs of the Bolton Wanderers Reebok stadium. The fact is that average income from corporate seats can amount to US$4200 per season, whereas the average income from a regular attendee will probably not exceed US$1000 per seat (per season). This explains why so many sports organisations devote more space to developing their corporate facilities. With this increased preoccupation with building, and hence catering for corporate hospitality, comes the impact on attendance (patterns) at matches. Not only is the corporate dollar an increasingly important source of revenue for facility operators, the space in the stadium devoted to corporate facilities, the architectural building style and multiple relati-onships with other stadium stakeholders also requires a reassessment of the facility's positioning strategies. In other words, the facility operators need to reassess their target markets.

Service Quality and Customer Satisfaction

In addition to spectator and participant retention, there are many positive consequences associated with service quality and customer satisfaction, including fewer complaints, more positive word-of-mouth, the buying of additional products, less attention paid to competitors, reduced transaction costs, and reduced marketing expenses. Together, these positive outcomes contribute to profitability, or, in the case of not-for-profit organisations such as community sports centres and clubs, longevity.

Despite the many positive outcomes for sports organisations that provide high-quality and subsequently satisfying products, sports marketers and scholars have only recently turned their attention to service quality and customer satisfaction. This lag in sports marketing knowledge is surprising given the growing sports-business nexus and the failure of many sports organisations, whether for-profit or not, to operate at optimal capacity. Consider for just a moment the number of empty seats at many professional sports events, or the numerous community clubs confronting financial stress due to declining membership.

Sports, perhaps more than many other industries, should demonstrate additional concern for its customers' evaluations of satisfaction and service quality. This is because the sports product is discretionary and substitutable (Martin 1990). The sports product is discretionary in that it is not essential in the same way that products such as food, petrol and medical services are. That is, no one has to play netball or attend a basketball game. The sports product is substitutable in that there are many other organisations outside the sporting arena that can cater to the leisure and recreation needs of the would-be sports consumer. That is, the competitive market in which the sports organisation is but one player contains also the arts, cinemas and cultural organisations. Many of the needs satisfied by the sports product (e.g. excitement, escape, social facilitation) can be satisfied by products from other industries. Today, most sports marketers recognise the importance of satisfying spectators and participants and providing them with service experiences of high quality. Moreover, there is a growing acknowledgement in the sports industry that service quality and customer satisfaction can provide a competitive advantage in the quest for the sports customer's dollar.

Definitions

So what are service quality and customer satisfaction? To begin with, service quality and customer satisfaction are both a type of evaluation, and they can both mean different things to different people and in different contexts. For the purposes of this book, service quality is defined in terms of excellence in accord with Parasuraman, Zeithaml and Berry (1988) and, more recently, Lovelock, Patterson and Walker (2001). That is, service quality is the spectator's or participant's judgement about how excellent a sports service or service component is. The more closely the spectator's or participant's perception approximates excellence, the higher his or her evaluation of service quality will be.

Customer satisfaction, on the other hand, is defined in terms of pleasurable fulfilment in accordance with Oliver (1997). That is, customer satisfaction is a judgement that a sports service, or service component, has provided a pleasurable level of consumption-related fulfilment. Like service quality, customer satisfaction is a matter of degree: that is, the greater the degree of pleasurable fulfilment, the greater the spectator's or participant's satisfaction.

Service quality and customer satisfaction are sometimes referred to interchangeably, but they are distinct, albeit-related constructs. The most readily agreed on and perhaps key point of differentiation between the two types of evaluation is that whereas satisfaction is experience-dependent, service quality is not. That is, a person must experience a sports product to be either satisfied or dissatisfied with it, but no experience is necessary to form perceptions of quality. For example, a general admission ticket holder of a sports stadium may never have experienced the spectator experience from a corporate suite but still have perceptions of the quality of that service.

Evaluations of What?

Thus far, service quality and customer satisfaction have both been referred to as evaluations. But exactly *what* do spectators and participants evaluate? In addition to the overall sports service, research demonstrates that sports customers evaluate a virtual plethora of service components, with the customers' summary satisfaction and perception of quality being a function of many different, 'smaller' evaluations. The sheer breadth of the sports service, and thus the likelihood of multiple evaluations for the one sports product, is evident in the sports servuction model. The model illustrates the factors that influence the sports service experience. The visible part of the model has three components: the inanimate environment, or the facility itself;

the contact personnel, such as ushers; and the customers. The model's invisible part consists of the invisible organisation and systems such as the marketing department. An astute sports marketer recognises that customers can and do form evaluations of the sports product pertaining to each of these components.

For example, a spectator at a professional sports event might evaluate the cleanliness of the stadium's restrooms (inanimate environment), the courtesy and helpfulness of service staff (contact personnel), the management of unruly and annoying co-spectators (customers), and the ticketing (invisible organisation). An understanding of the sports servuction model helps the marketer comprehend the sheer scope of the sports service and many aspects of the sports service, which contributes to a customer receiving a high-quality and satisfying experience. Furthermore, the model reminds us that things other than those which spectators and participants can see for themselves (i.e. the invisible component) have considerable propensity to influence customer satisfaction and service quality.

The Core Product and Product Extensions

In mainstream marketing it has long been realised that customer satisfaction and service quality arise from both dimensions, with many arguing that, in the context of services, these evaluations are most strongly influenced by the non-core components. While sports marketers acknowledge the importance of both dimensions, until recently it was not known which dimension most strongly influenced customer evaluations. A sports-specific service quality study that simultaneously addresses the differential effects of the core product and the product extensions has yet to be conducted.

The dominant role played by the product extensions in a spectator's satisfaction is good news for sports organisations because it is the product extensions and not the game that fall under the control of sports marketers. That is, the sports marketer can more readily ensure the quality and hence manipulate customer satisfaction arising from such service aspects as merchandise and half-time entertainment than from the game itself. Up to this point service quality and satisfaction have been discussed together. The next section will focus specifically on customer satisfaction, addressing the measurement of satisfaction, as well as its determinants and the process by which it arises. The latter half of the chapter will focus on service quality.

MEASURING CUSTOMER SATISFACTION

Given that customer satisfaction is so important, it is critical that the sports organisation is able to identify exactly how satisfied spectators and participants are with the overall service as well as with its individual components. Sports organisations can assess customer satisfaction levels both directly and indirectly, as described by Hoffman and Bateson (1997). Indirect methods of customer satisfaction measurement include tracking and monitoring customer complaints, sales records, profits and customer retention. Although these indirect measures are useful, they should not be used in isolation. There are many other factors, external to customer satisfaction, that affect the number of complaints an organisation receives, its sales, profits and number of customers retained. Therefore, indirect measures should be combined with direct measures.

Direct measures of customer satisfaction vary. One of the most popular is the very satisfied-very dissatisfied approach typically conducted via personal interviews or selfadministered questionnaires. Customers are asked to indicate the extent to which they are satisfied or dissatisfied on typically a five-or seven-point scale, where 1 = very dissatisfied and 5 or 7 = very satisfied. This approach can be used for: (a) specific service aspects such as ticketing, staff courtesy and skilfulness of players; (b) broader service dimensions, such as the core product and product extensions; and (c) the entire sports experience, such as the season ticket or club membership.

For additional insight, the very satisfied-very dissatisfied rating scale approach should be accompanied by a mechanism to identify why customers are either satisfied or dissatisfied. This can be achieved by simply requesting spectators and participants to identify exactly what was particularly satisfying or dissatisfying about their sports experience. This method has great diagnostic potential, as it enables the organisation both to pinpoint problems and seek ways to remedy them and to identify where the organisation is performing exceptionally well so as to ensure continued good performance. Spectators and participants can also be asked for their opinion on how improvements could be made to the organisation and its services. Sports customers are often highly identified and emotionally involved with the products they consume and are thus likely to be more forthcoming than most in providing customer satisfaction researchers with this sort of valuable information.

How Satisfied should Customers be?

Having conducted a satisfaction study, a sports organisation might identify that 83% of customers surveyed reported being satisfied or very satisfied. The sports organisation will probably give itself a pat on the back for having only 17% of customers less than satisfied. Another sports organisation may be equally self-congratulatory on identifying the average satisfaction rating for its customers as 5.5 out of a possible maximum of 7. However, according to Jones and Sasser (1995), the results for both of these organisations are not as good as you might initially think.

First, given suitable alternatives, less-than-satisfied customers, particularly participants and spectators who are not avid fans, are highly likely to defect to competing organisations. How many sports organisations can afford to lose 17% of their customer base (remembering the concept of customer lifetime value)? Also, customer satisfaction is a matter of degree, with customers ranging from being just satisfied through to very satisfied (perhaps even delighted). Jones and Sasser (1995) report that, in most circumstances, favourable outcomes such as loyalty and improved financial performance result only from the very highest levels of customer satisfaction. Finally, most customer satisfaction research, at least for studies involving a self-reporting methodology, reveals that the majority of respondents are satisfied (Peterson & Wilson 1992). That is, there appears to be a propensity among respondents to indicate higher than actual satisfaction levels. In other words, a sports organisation's spectators or participants may not really be as satisfied as its research indicates they are.

Sports organisations need to identify spectators and participants who are not completely satisfied in order to identify the cause of the less-than-optimal satisfaction and remedy it. Apart from asking survey respondents to identify these reasons via a customer satisfaction study, management can do this through complaint inducement mechanisms. Two strategies to encourage customer complaints described by Oliver (1997) and suitable for most sports organisations are: (a) free-to-the-customer communication channels such as toll-free numbers and postage-paid feedback cards; and (b) contacts instigated by the organisation, generally by telephone, asking customers if their sports service has been satisfactory.

The identification and successful handling of complaints has positive implications for sports organisations and the satisfaction of their customers. The work of Bitner, Booms and Tetrault (1990), for example, indicates that a well-handled complaint can alter the sports customer's evaluation of the product in a positive way. In other words, successful complaint resolution can result in what Lapidus and Pinkerton (1995) refer to as second-order satisfaction. The spectator or participant who was initially dissatisfied with some aspect of the sports service can experience satisfaction with the remainder of the service. Essentially, sports organisations should recognise the value of customer complaints. Complaints provide the organisation with an opportunity to identify and fix problems and consequently satisfy and retain their customers.

Customer Satisfaction Determinants

As noted earlier, it is not important merely to understand *how* satisfied a sports organisation's customers are, it is important also to understand *why* they are satisfied. Therefore a valuable body of research addresses the factors that contribute to, or determine, the satisfaction of customers. The three determinants that appear most regularly in the literature are expectations, perceived performance and disconfirmation. Together with customer satisfaction, these three determinants form the 'disconfirmation of expectations model' (DEM).

The DEM is based on the premise that customers form certain expectations of product performance, observe or experience the performance and form perceptions of the performance. It is proposed that these perceptions of performance will be compared to the customers' originally held expectations (Churchill & Surprenant 1982; Oliver 1997). This comparison can result in one of three outcomes—negative disconfirmation, zero disconfirmation (i.e. confirmation), or positive disconfirmation—which in turn influence the extent to which the customer is satisfied.

Negative disconfirmation results when performance falls short of expectations. The original and simplest interpretation of the outcomes of the three different types of disconfirmation described previously is that satisfaction results from expectations being met or exceeded (with some arguing that delight, as opposed to mere satisfaction, arises when positive disconfirmation is extreme) and dissatisfaction results from expectations not being met. However, as will be outlined later, the outcomes of disconfirmation can vary with the expectation type used (Miller 1977; Swan & Trawick 1980).

Although the DEM and various extended versions of it appear regularly in the marketing literature, the model has not made inroads into the sports marketing literature. Nonetheless, some models of sports customer satisfaction have been developed. In the context of spectator sports, Madrigal (1995) found that the affective components of basking in reflected glory (BIRGing), or an individual's inclination to 'share the glory of a successful other with whom they are in some way associated' (Cialdini et al. 1976: 366), together with enjoyment, disconfirmation of expectations, team identification and quality of opponent, contributed to customer satisfaction with university women's basketball games. Also in the context of spectator sports, Wakefield and Blodgett (1994) identified that the quality of the sportscape (i.e. sports facility) as well as crowding, excitement and involvement influenced spectator satisfaction with the facility.

Perhaps the most comprehensive study of spectator satisfaction thus far is Van Leeuwen's (2001) research using a sample of season ticket holders from an Australian professional sports league. She accounted for the uniqueness of the spectator product when testing a model of customer satisfaction based on the DEM. Her model accounted for both the core product and product extensions of the spectator sports service, as well as the win-lose phenomenon of sports and the extent to which season ticket holders personally identify with a sports club (i.e. club identification). The results revealed the importance of considering the uniqueness of the sports service in sports-specific customer satisfaction research. That is, the spectator's club identification, as well as the win-lose phenomenon, was shown to greatly influence the amount of satisfaction season ticket holders experienced. The more highly identified the spectator and the more games won, the greater the season ticket holder's satisfaction. It is worth noting that the season ticket holders' identification with their club actually had the greatest influence on determining their satisfaction.

Service Quality

Quality in this book pertains to the perceived excellence of the sports product. The concept of quality in services such as sports is somewhat different from quality in the manufacturing sector. However, it was in the manufacturing sector that the concern for quality was born, and a basic understanding of quality as it pertains to manufactured goods provides a starting point for understanding service quality.

Goods Quality versus Service Quality

The 1980s were marked by a quality revolution in terms of manufactured goods. Traditionally, quality had been determined by an end-of-production checking process whereby inspectors checked final products for defects. Inspectors sorted out the good from the bad, placing the defective products on the organisation's 'scrap heap'.

The quality revolution of the 1980s involved a shift in focus from checking the end product to maximising the effectiveness and efficiency of the process resulting in the end product. Thus the first principle of the new quality era was doing it right the first time (Chase & Stewart 1994), with the ultimate aim being the production of zero defects.

The new way of ensuring quality was attributed to W. Edwards Deming, and is now commonly known as Total Quality Management (TQM). Deming introduced manufacturers to methods of statistical analysis that helped them to identify and reduce the variability in their production processes, thus enabling them to produce goods of consistent quality. Although consistent quality is central to TQM, the zero-defects quality model of the manufacturing sector does not work well for service organisations. This is largely due to the unique nature of the service product—especially its characteristic of inseparable production and consumption, whereby the customer becomes part of the production process. For example, the NRL spectator experiences the game as it is produced, as does the netballer or golfer. The involvement of the customer in the production process inevitably results in some degree of variation in the production of the service, and where there is variation there is room for error or, in TQM terminology, a 'defective' service experience.

Moreover, even if the quality of the service is without variation, service quality is a matter of perception (i.e. the customer's perception), and two people who experience the same service may thus have very different perceptions of its quality. This is particularly so in the context of sports, where two customers, whether players or spectators, are barracking or playing for opposing teams. Further, an individual's perception of service quality may vary from one experience to the next due to myriad factors often beyond the organisation's control, such as his or her mood.

All in all, service quality is more complex and more difficult to achieve than quality in manufacturing. However, sports organisations find it even more challenging to ensure the quality of their products than do other organisations. This is due to the sports organisation's inability to control the core sports product—that is, the game itself. As mentioned earlier controllability of the core sports product has resulted in marketers focusing on the product extensions. Whereas the game itself is beyond the marketer's sphere of influence, he or she can do much to influence the quality of the product extensions of the service, including the half-time entertainment, ticketing processes, merchandise, and design and cleanliness of the facility.

Modelling Service Quality

Sports marketers can improve the quality of their services by first understanding how service quality is determined. The service quality process can be understood in terms of a number of gaps, as described by Parasuraman, Zeithaml and Berry (1985). These are gaps between the expectations and perceptions of three different groups: customers, management, and employees. The most important gap, the service gap, is the difference between what customers expect from the service and what they perceive they have actually got. The service gap is a function of four other gaps, including the knowledge gap, standards gap, delivery gap and communications gap.

The Knowledge Gap: The gap between customer expectations of service and management perceptions of these expectations. This gap occurs when what management believes customers expect is different from what customers really expect. For example, the programme manager of a community sports centre might believe that players expect hour-long games of netball when they would instead prefer the opportunity to play shorter but additional games.

The Standards Gap: The gap between management's perceptions of customer expectations and the organisation's service quality specifications. This gap occurs when the organisation does not have the resources to deliver what the customer expects, or when management is indifferent to providing the expected levels of service. For example, the marketing manager of a professional basketball team may be aware that season ticket holders expect opportunities for more interaction with players but not see this as a priority. Alternatively, the marketer may be fully cognisant of the season ticket holders expectations but have difficulty meeting them given the numerous other commitments of the players.

The Delivery Gap: The gap between the organisation's service quality specifications and actual service delivery. This gap occurs when quality specifications are not met, and is typically due to a lack of willingness or ability of the service personnel. For example, even though an aquatic centre's service charter may stipulate that its service staff be friendly, courteous and helpful to customers at all times, its staff may be either unwilling to go this extra distance for customers or simply not have the customer service and interpersonal skills enabling them to do so.

The Communications Gap: The gap between actual service delivery and external communications about the service. This gap occurs when the organisation promises more in its advertising and other communications than it can actually deliver. A classic example would be a professional sports club's advertisements promising its supporters a win at the next home game. (A basic premise of sports marketing is that winning is one thing that you can never guarantee and that you therefore shouldn't promise!).

In summary, sports marketers need to be cognisant of each of these gaps and how they contribute to spectators and participants getting what they expected and consequently their evaluations of service quality. Sports marketers will be able to improve the quality of their services by identifying and then closing each of the knowledge, standards, delivery and communication gaps. Just as Parasuraman et al. (1985) developed the original gap model, depicted in a modified to enable us to better conceptualise the service quality process, they also later developed the most popular measure of service quality.The service quality instrument is based on the disconfirmation of expectations paradigm and the five service quality dimensions of tangibles, reliability, responsiveness, assurance and empathy (Parasuraman et al. 1988: 23):

- *Tangibles:* Physical facilities, equipment, and appearance of personnel;
- *Reliability:* Ability to perform the promised service dependably and accurately;
- *Responsiveness:* Willingness to help customers and provide prompt services;
- *Assurance:* Knowledge and courtesy of employees and their ability to inspire trust and confidence;
- *Empathy:* Caring, individualised attention that the firm provides its customers.

The SERVQUAL instrument comprises two sections. The first is an expectations section, containing 22 statements to measure customer expectations of excellent firms in a specific service industry (e.g. the professional sports industry). Each of these statements pertains to one of the five dimensions mentioned previously (i.e. tangibles, reliability, responsiveness, assurance, empathy). The second is a perceptions section, containing a matching set of 22 statements to measure customer perceptions of the particular organisation within the service industry being evaluated (e.g. Collingwood Football Club).

Customer expectations are measured on a seven-point scale, anchored by the labels of 'not at all essential' and 'absolutely essential'. Customer perceptions are also measured on a seven-point scale, anchored by 'strongly agree' and 'strongly disagree'. The results of the expectations and perceived performance sections are then compared to determine the 'gap scores' for each of the five dimensions. Large gaps indicate poorer than expected service and hence low service quality. The smaller the gap, the higher the evaluation of service quality and therefore the better. As with the 'very satisfied-very dissatisfied' approach to customer satisfaction measurement, the SERVQUAL approach enables researchers to assess service quality at the micro-level (e.g. ticketing procedures), the broader dimension level (e.g. tangibles) and the macro-level (e.g. the entire sports product).

Although SERVQUAL is the most popular service quality measure, it has attracted some criticism. The most common criticism is that the instrument's five dimensions (tangibles, reliability, responsiveness, assurance, empathy) can often not be replicated in different industries. In other words, the dimensions are relevant to some industries but not others. However, most researchers accept that SERVQUAL remains an important diagnostic tool for evaluating an organisation's service quality performance. Furthermore, and as indicated by its developers, SERVQUAL is an instrument that can help service organisations improve their service by better understanding the expectations and perceptions of its customers. As when measuring customer satisfaction, when using SERVQUAL sports marketers are advised to seek additional qualitative information from spectators and participants, including why they evaluate the service the way that they do and how the service might be improved.

Measuring Sports Service Quality: TEAMQUAL and QUESC

Given the generic nature of SERVQUAL, its developers readily acknowledged that it should be modified to accommodate the peculiarities of certain industries. Examples of modifications of SERVQUAL in the context of sports are many and varied, including McDonald, Sutton and Milne's (1995) TEAMQUAL instrument for spectator sports and Kim and Kim's (1995) QUESC instrument for sports centres. These studies provide evidence of how SERVQUAL, although not perfect, is a good starting point for sports organisations wishing to evaluate service quality.

McDonald et al. (1995) modified SERVQUAL to accommodate the professional team sports spectator service. Specifically, they incorporated additional items into the instrument to account for the multiple-encounter nature of the spectator service (e.g. encounters with ticketing staff, concessionaires and merchandisers). Examples of some of the items pertaining to ticketing staff included ushers giving prompt service, ushers being consistently courteous, and ushers having the knowledge to answer questions. Developed in the United States in the context of professional basketball, their final instrument, TEAMQUAL, comprised 39 items grounded in the five SERVQUAL dimensions.

Kim and Kim (1995) developed their 33-item service quality instrument, the QUESC, in the context of Korean sports centres. Although they used the five SERVQUAL dimensions as a starting point for their research, their final results identified eleven distinct service quality dimensions (i.e. ambiance, employee attitude, employee reliability, information available, programmes offered, personal considerations, price, privilege, ease of mind, stimulation and convenience). The dimensions they identified support the industry-specific nature of the service quality construct and should serve to remind sports managers of the necessity of accommodating the uniqueness of their particular service in service quality evaluations and research. Some of the items comprising the QUESC pertained to the variety of sports on offer, instructions for accessing or using facilities, and privacy.

EXPECTATIONS: A BETTER UNDERSTANDING

Having read the previous sections of this chapter, you should now realise that a sports customer's expectations play an important role in his or her evaluations of quality and satisfaction. The centrality of expectations to both constructs merits further discussion. Just as it is accepted that expectations are the standards customers use to compare product performance in order to arrive at a level of satisfaction, so is it accepted that the disconfirmation of expectations process is key to determining perceptions of service quality. What is believed to differentiate the service quality process from the customer satisfaction process, though, is the type of expectation used.

Miller (1977) acknowledged four different types of customer expectations in his research. These included ideal (can be) expectations, expected (will be) expectations, minimum tolerable (must be) expectations, and deserved (should be) expectations. Ideal expectations operate at a wished-for level (e.g. *I expect my tennis coach to help me perfect my serve in one lesson).* Expected levels of performance are much more realistic, and reflect the probable or most likely performance (e.g. */expect my tennis coach to help me improve my serve after several lessons)*. Minimum tolerable expectations reflect the minimal level of performance that will be tolerated or considered acceptable (e.g. */ expect my tennis coach to improve my serve to the point where I can at least get the ball over the net on most attempts)*. Finally, deserved expectations reflect the performance to which customers believe they are entitled given their inputs or investments (e.g. */ expect my tennis coach to help me greatly improve my serve after several lessons as long as I put in plenty of practice by myself too)*. Another type of expectation falling somewhere between ideal and deserved expectations is what the customer desires.

Service quality studies in accord with the conceptualisation of quality in terms of excellence typically use ideal expectations. Customer satisfaction studies traditionally utilised predictive (will be) expectations (Oliver 1993; Parasuraman et al. 1988), although studies employing higher-level expectations such as deserved expectations (e.g. Patterson 1993) and desired expectations (e.g. Swan & Trawick 1980; Swan, Trawick & Carroll 1982) are increasingly common. This trend towards higher-level expectations was necessary because the DEM posits customer satisfaction as the outcome of confirmation and positive disconfirmation but fails to account for the possibility of very low expectations. Yet it is possible that dissatisfaction as opposed to satisfaction.

It does not make sense that customers would be satisfied if they anticipated a poor service experience and received exactly that. Consider the example of a spectator who watched her favoured team lose the National netball grand final by 27 goals when she had already anticipated that such a loss was likely (i.e. confirmation of low 'will be' expectations). Nor does it make sense that customers would be satisfied if they received only a slightly poor service.

Consider the case of the lap swimmer who arrived at the aquatic centre on Boxing Day to find his favourite lane crowded but not quite to the extent he'd imagined (i.e. positive disconfirmation of low 'will be' expectations). In these examples, irrespective of the service being equal to or better than expected, it was still nothing to be really satisfied with. In brief, the use of higher-level expectations diminishes the possibility of dissatisfaction arising from confirmation or positive disconfirmation.

Irrespective of the type of expectations spectators and participants hold and the relationship of each to service quality and customer satisfaction, it is important for sports marketers to understand the influence they have over what their customers expect. Expectations are influenced by many factors, several of which are under the control of the sports organisation, including (a) promises made by the sports organisation, for example through advertising and other communications; (b) tangible cues in the physical environment, predominantly the sports facility itself; and (c) pricing.

Given the centrality of expectations to service quality and customer satisfaction and the influence that sports organisations can exert on their customers' expectations, it is essential that sports marketers learn to manage what it is that their customers expect from them. Sports marketers must not promise more than their organisations can realistically deliver. They should ensure that the physical environment with which their customers interact is of the highest possible standard in terms of aesthetic appeal and cleanliness. Likewise, they should ensure that product prices are commensurate with product quality.

The provision of high-quality and subsequently satisfying sports services was linked to organisational success through a number of positive consequences for the sports organisation, one of the most important being customer retention. Customer satisfaction and service quality were described as types of evaluations. It was noted that these evaluations can be of the overall spectator or participant service, as well as individual aspects of each service.

Given the sheer breadth of the sports service, it is necessary for myriad factors to be successfully managed in order for customers to enjoy the sports experience and thus evaluate it positively. Due to the uncontrollability of the core product, though, sports marketers must realise that they have minimal influence over perceptions of quality and feelings of satisfaction arising from the game itself. As such, sports organisations must focus on ensuring that the product extensions are of the highest possible standard.

It is recommended that sports marketers ask their customers not only how satisfied they are and how high they perceive the quality of the spectator or participant service to be but also why they perceive the service the way they do. This combined approach enables sports marketers to identify things their organisation is doing particularly well, together with those things that need improving. When measuring customer satisfaction and service quality it is important to note that sports marketers should not be complacent about less-than-excellent levels of customer satisfaction and service quality. Suboptimal evaluations often present opportunities for competitors, especially when the sports customer is not an avid fan.

In addition to emphasising the importance of identifying the extent to which customers are satisfied and perceive the service to be of high quality, the section described the processes by which customers arrive at their satisfaction and quality judgements. Customer satisfaction was shown to arise from disconfirmed expectations of the sports service in accordance with the DEM, with the customer's disconfirmation being the key influence on whether he or she was satisfied or dissatisfied. Alternatively, service quality was modelled in accord with Parasuraman et al. (1985), who conceptualised it in terms of a number of 'gaps' (i.e. service, knowledge, standards, delivery, communications) between the expectations and perceptions of customers, management and employees.

Sports marketers need to acknowledge that customers can hold several different types of expectation and that evaluations of satisfaction and quality will vary with the expectation type used. More importantly though, sports marketers must understand those factors that influence the expectations held by spectators and participants and learn to manage them successfully. Through identifying, understanding and managing expectations, sports organisations will be better placed to provide high-quality and thus satisfying sports services which in turn may provide them with a competitive advantage in the quest for the sports customer's dollar.

CHAPTER

Sports Promotion Mix

Your marketing plan will be executed by using the tactical elements of the Marketing Communications, or Promotions Mix. The Marketing Communications Mix is the specific mix of advertising, personal selling, sales promotion, public relations, and direct marketing a company uses to pursue its advertising and marketing objectives.There are four main aspects of a promotional mix (or *communication mix*). These are:

1. *Advertising:* Any paid presentation and promotion of ideas, goods, or services by an identified sponsor. *Examples: Print ads, radio, television, billboard, direct mail, brochures and catalogs, signs, in-store displays, posters, motion pictures, Web pages, banner ads, and emails.*
2. *Personal Selling:* A process of helping and persuading one or more prospects to purchase a good or service or to act on any idea through the use of an oral presentation. *Examples: Sales presentations, sales meetings, sales training and incentive programmes for intermediary salespeople, samples, and telemarketing. Can be face-to-face or via telephone.*

3. *Sales Promotion:* Incentives designed to stimulate the purchase or sale of a product, usually in the short term.
   Examples: *Coupons, sweepstakes, contests, product samples, rebates, tie-ins, self-liquidating premiums, trade shows, trade-ins, and exhibitions.*
4. *Public Relations:* Non-paid non-personal stimulation of demand for a product, service, or business unit by planting significant news about it or a favourable presentation of it in the media.
   Examples: *Newspaper and magazine articles/reports, TVs and radio presentations, charitable contributions, speeches, issue advertising, and seminars.* Sponsorship is sometimes added as a fifth aspect.

DEFINING PROMOTION STRATEGY

Broadly, a promotion strategy is a controlled, integrated programme of communication designed to present an organisation and its products or services clearly to prospective customers. Furthermore, it communicates needs-satisfying attributes in order to facilitate sales. This in turn contributes to long-term profits. Underpinning promotional strategies is the communication process, and an understanding of such processes is required to enable the formulation of relevant strategies. Communication occurs when an individual attends to a message and attributes importance to it. Once information processing occurs, communication is said to have taken place (Cravens 1994).

Conceptually, communication involves the message context and source, the intended receivers, the encoding and decoding processes, message pathway and interference (or noise), and the outcomes. However, as these variables are broken down the true complex nature of communication is realised. Devito (1999: 9) suggests that 'there are four contexts for communication and they are the physical, cultural, socio-psychological and temporal'. Significantly, all are relevant to the sports experience. The physical context refers to the space in which the communication takes place. An example of this is the difference in crowd behaviour at various sporting contests. The spectators at a Super 12s game at Aussie Stadium in Sydney will be far more vocal during the play than a tennis crowd in Melbourne during a final of the Australian Open. While it is perfectly acceptable to abuse the referee, albeit in a witty manner, at a football match, the same cannot be said for tennis. Similarly, different cultural groups may require, and exhibit, different communication processes.

Witness the differences between the motorcycle fan at Phillip Island and the polo spectator at Werribee. In both instances the communication process may alter according to other variables, such as the closeness of the score, injury or even changes in the weather. This exemplifies the social-psychological context. Finally, the temporal context relates to the position of the message in time and space. A winning performance is likely to result in other patterns of communication than losing. A favourite team or athlete winning would be the cause for celebration, whereas a loss, especially an unexpected one, could result in sadness and a desire to be alone.

Once the context has been established, any resultant message is both encoded by its source and decoded by its receiver. Messages do not always need to be verbal, as nonverbal cues are often more powerful. The use of a previous elite performance to promote an upcoming event is an example of this. In the lead-up to the Commonwealth Games in Manchester in 2002 the Seven Network highlighted the earliest performances of contemporary elite athletes, which conveyed the message that the Games might be the birthplace of new Australian champions—hence their viewing should not be missed. However, it is important when messages are encoded, whatever the medium, that they are not so abstruse as to confound the intended receiver.

Reebok's clever yet somewhat mystifying television ad in the late 1980s which featured the slogan UBU left many viewers scratching their heads.

This advertisement was eventually pulled, as the message of individuality, non-conformity and independence was lost on the intended audience. DeVito (1999: 9-11) suggests that 'understanding how communication works (communication competence); cultural specificity, acquired knowledge and previous experience are all critical to an appropriate encoding/decoding process'.

The greatest inhibitor to successful message conveyance is 'noise'. Noise can be physical, psychological, or simply an unintended interpretation or decoding of a message. The effective sports promotion uses a simple, non-confronting, unambiguous message to highlight a service or product. Nike's 'Just Do It' is probably the most obvious example of this. Finally, the intended consequence of the communication process is to produce a change in behaviour. In most instances it is to predispose the intended recipient towards the product or service featured in the message. Ultimately, the desired outcome is usually the consumption of the product or service.

A Response Model

As well as understanding the communication process, it has become increasingly apparent that there is a need to comprehend the buyer readiness model that essentially drives the communication process. Whereas communication models are generally driven from the producer, buyer readiness models are end user-driven. According to Belch and Belch (2001), there are three main categories of response models: traditional response hierarchy models, alternative response models, and integrated information response models. Within each category there are a numbers of subcategories. This section focuses on the AIDA model, which is one of the four traditional response hierarchy models. All four models comprise a cognitive, affective and behavioural stage, with AIDA an acronym for attention, interest, desire, action. In this instance the promotion aims at getting the consumer's attention, creating an interest in and a desire to purchase the product or service, and finally engaging in an exchange process, which usually involves the actual purchase. In 2002 Foxtel added a dedicated Australian Rules football channel to its cable network. The Network cleverly adopted an AIDA-type model in encouraging uptake by potential subscribers.

Well before the channel actually appeared on the screen, other cable stations promoted the day on which the new channel would become live, hence generating *attention.* During the initial phase broadcast was provided free to existing cable subscribers, thus generating *interest*. In this initial telecast, phase highlights packages were shown which demonstrated the more sensational aspects of the game.

Moreover, promises were made that each week every game would be telecast. Consequently, it did not matter which team was supported, the fan would get to see that team's game on television. The result was that a *desire* was created. Finally, to encourage the fan to take up the package, special financial inducements were offered for early *action* relating to subscription to the service. The AIDA model was clearly in effect in this instance.

Promotion and Product Demand

As previously indicated, the ultimate goal of promotion strategy is to stimulate demand for a particular product. However, before strategies are developed there is a need to understand the type of demand that exists, which may be:

- Generic; or
- Brand; and
- Direct or indirect.

Generic demand is the demand for a particular product category. At a national level, a government policy may promote sports and recreation as a means of raising health and fitness levels among the population at large. In this case tennis clubs, fitness centres, sports stores, and recreational and tourist accommodation can all benefit from the generic campaign. Occasionally a market leader unilaterally engages in generic advertising when industry sales are down. At a league, competition or association level, sports marketers engage in promoting the sports or competition while leaving clubs to their own marketing devices.

For example, during the Australian Open, Tennis Australia will create a generic demand for tennis by promoting the sports in general. It is then up to local clubs and associations to establish localised promotion strategies allowing them to tap into the generic demand.

Most consumer promotion is directed towards boosting brand demand. The Sydney Swifts, the Adelaide Thunderbirds and the Queensland Firebirds of the National Netball League (2002 Commonwealth Bank Trophy) all adopt specific promotion strategies in an attempt to encourage consumption and support of their particular teams—the brands. In the process, the demand for the generic product (i.e. the national league) is increased. Occasionally brand switching may occur when for example a Melbourne Phoenix fan becomes a Melbourne Kestrels fan, but in the main the promotion strategy results in better industry (i.e. national league) sales, or in this case an increase in the number of fans attending women's netball games.

The majority of consumer promotion is an attempt to stimulate direct demand for a specific product. Sporadically, a manufacturer may promote an element of a product, which may stimulate demand for that component, which in turn may directly stimulate indirect demand for a particular brand. For example, lycra manufacturers promote the attributes of lycra, which indirectly stimulates demand for products made using the substance, such as fitness and cycling apparel.

Irrespective of the type of demand, the audience targeted by the promotion strategy invariably remains the same. Current and future customers, stockholders, the public at large and special-interest groups are all existing or potential consumers. However, responses to promotion strategies will vary based on myriad consumer behaviour factors and models of response such as AIDA. Acknowledging such differences, sports promoters need to tailor marketing strategies in order to attract specific consumer groups. This is done by fully comprehending the stages in promotion strategy development and then manipulating the promotion mix.

Stages in Promotion Strategy Development

In establishing promotion strategy development, an organisation needs to undertake the following steps. First an initial analysis of the specific situation is required, when the following questions should be addressed: What is the general direction of the firm in the prevailing social and economic climate? What are the product or service's strengths and weaknesses compared with those of the competition? Are there legal, technological or distribution issues that need to be factored into the decision making?

Once an analysis of the situation has been undertaken, objectives need to be developed. Consideration here should the composition of the target market, what the sales objectives are and, equally importantly, the message to be communicated. Once the objectives are known, programmes need to be established that will enable the objectives to be accomplished. These may include the creative and media strategies to be employed, the sales promotion to be utilised, reseller support programmes, and the budget that underpins the breadth and scope of the programmes.

Concurrently with programme execution, a system of evaluation, or for monitoring the effectiveness of such strategies, needs to be rigorously implemented.

These evaluative mechanisms need to be specifically linked to the stated objectives. By clearly defining the stages in promotion strategy development, an organisation not only establishes a framework for future activities but also, by constantly using it as a reference source, creates an excellent evaluative mechanism.

DEFINING THE PROMOTION MIX

The growth of World Series Cricket in the late 1970s provides one example of the multifaceted nature of the promotion mix. In the late 1970s, the establishment of World Series Cricket was an excellent example of a controlled promotion strategy. During the period 1977-79, the World Series was positioned as an alternative to the traditional game. In the process, it not only used the best athletes the sports had to offer, it also radically altered the tone of cricket by creating stylistic changes in the game's production and presentation. In numerous ways the sports was repackaged as a television spectacle to captivate the home viewer. Multiple camera angles, coloured uniforms, on-screen gra-phics and various auditory devices were introduced, which elevated the entertainment level of the game. Sports and entertainment fans in general, not only cricket devotees, were captivated.

Simultaneously, other promotion strategies were implemented—at the ground, on television, on radio, in newspapers and magazines, and in department stores and supermarkets across the country—which resulted in multiple layers of cricket consumption. World Series Cricket sold books, fruit, paint and even lunchboxes, as well as cricket apparel. Furthermore the catchy song used to promote World Series Cricket ('C'mon Aussie, C'mon') became one of the most popular songs on Australian radio. Commenting on the song, Haigh (1993: 220) indicated 'top rating [Sydney] radio station 2SM played "C'mon Aussie C'mon" until its needles were blunt'.

The message World Series Cricket communicated through its promotional strategy was one tinged with excitement, glamour, aggression, superstars and non-stop entertainment. Judging by the numbers that turned up to see World Series Cricket limited overs games, it is obvious in hindsight that the successful promotion strategy adopted by the organisation for cricket worldwide also marked a watershed in sports marketing in Australia. The promotion mix consists of advertising, public relations and publicity, sales promotion, promotional licensing and personal selling, which includes sponsorship and telemarketing. How these elements are combined, and in what measure, depends on the target market, the organisational objectives and the promotion strategy that is to be utilised.

Advertising

Advertising is a non-personal communication by an identified sponsor. This is the most obvious form of sports and event promotion. On a regular basis, sports producers such as the NRL, the NBL and the ARU advertise their products on television and/or radio, as well as in the daily newspapers, with the intent of informing potential consumers and shaping their choices. In regard to events this information would contain the names of the sponsoring organisation and the organisation paying for the advertisement, the time and place of the event, the featured acts, sports or athletes, perhaps cost and, invariably, a telephone number for further information. Advertisements for a fitness centre could include information as to the range of services offered. Advertisements for sports equipment such as tennis racquets could include the particular facts of the equipment and also, for specific versions, technical specifications. The major advantage of advertising is that the advertiser can control the time, placement and content of the advertisement. The major disadvantage is cost per exposure per consumer, especially with mass advertising.

PUBLIC RELATIONS AND PUBLICITY

Two other forms of communication are public relations (both proactive and reactive) and publicity. *Publicity* is a non-personal communication that is neither paid for nor sponsored by a promoting organisation. The best example of this is the amount of copy, space and time given to sports and related activities in the media. The various football codes dominate the back pages of newspapers during the winter, while cricket predominates during the summer. Less regular publicity is given to sports like basketball, netball, motor racing, hockey and bowls. Activities such as golf, tennis and horseracing may attract significant publicity at specific times of the year. The tennis Grand Slams, major international golf tournaments and the Melbourne Cup all feature heavily at the appropriate time. Moreover, similar scenarios occur whether on television or radio or in the newspapers.

The major advantage of publicity is that it is free. However, the disadvantages can be numerous. The relevant sporting body cannot control the time and placement of the story, nor can it control the slant a particular journalist or writer will place on a story. Undoubtedly, publicity can be either positive or negative, and it is thus up to sports to promote the former and minimise the latter. Similarly, it is incumbent on sports promoters to have a public relations strategy in place to negate the effects of adverse publicity.

Sales Promotion

Sales promotion is the set of promotion activities that stimulate and support advertising, personal selling and publicity. Usually such activities are temporary in nature and may involve price or non-price strategies.

What if you held a promotion and nobody came?

One of the more bizarre sports promotions was reported in the *Sydney Morning Herald on* 10 July 2002 and featured a minor league team from Charleston, South Carolina—the Charleston Riverdogs. Apparently the organisation took the unprecedented step of locking everybody out of the stadium in an effort to record the lowest attendance at a professional baseball game on record. The gates were padlocked and only organisation employees, scouts and media representatives were permitted inside Joe Riley Stadium. So what of the hundreds of fans that turned up to see the game? They were kept outside the stadium until the game was recorded as official (after the fifth inning) and only then were they let into the park. In the meantime they were provided with food and beer at a party thrown by the organisation.

For the record books, the attendance was recorded as zero and the Columbus Red Stix beat the Charleston Riverdogs 4-2. Unfortunately for the fans, all the runs were scored before they were admitted to the venue. Sales promotion based on price invariably involves 'two-for-one' deals, group discounts or, in some circumstances, 'half-price tickets', which is a popular concept in the theatre industry. In July 2002 the NRL reduced game ticket prices for the remainder of the season in an effort to swell crowds at rugby league games. Promoted on the basis of making the game more affordable for the family, by illustrating pricing comparisons with its major competitors, the promotion was an instant success, with bigger crowds for the ensuing games. The use of give-aways, such as caps, drink bottles, posters or sports memorabilia, is an example of non-price promotion.

Although such promotion can occasionally offer an adult premium, more often than not it is directed towards children, which in turn influences family attendance and consumption. Spolestra (1991: 12) contends that: for a premium to excite fans enough for them to buy tickets, the premium needs to have a perceived value equal to the price of the tickets. Irrespective of whether the sports marketer chooses to run with a price or non-price promotion, Spolestra also argues that energies should be directed not to increasing average attendances but to increasing the number of sold-out games, which will boost average attendances.

Personal Selling

Personal selling is paid personal communication by an identified sponsor. It uses oral presentation to prospective consumers or purchasers. Evans and Berman (1987) suggest that the key features of personal selling are:

1. Identifying prospects;
2. Determining the customer's needs;
3. Selecting a sales strategy;
4. Communicating with the buyer; and
5. Evaluating the sales strategy.

The two most obvious varieties of personal selling are the 'face-to-face' presentation and the increasingly common telemarketing.

Face-to-face Presentation

Face-to-face presentation is most closely related to sponsorship, and the growth of this component of the promotion mix in the sports marketplace was exponential over the latter half of the 20th century. This is evidenced by corporations such as McDonald's, Coca-Cola, Qantas or Telstra, which are prepared to invest a significant part of their marketing budget in direct sports sponsorship. The fundamental underpinning of this position is the belief that sports, especially on television, delivers a captive audience to the company. As a result, organisations are prepared to pay large sums in an effort to connect with clearly segmented consumer markets.

Telemarketing

Telemarketing is not as advanced in sports in Australia as it is in North America, but the concept is well known.

Insurance companies, credit card organisations, banks, telecommunications agencies, the tourism industry and general market research firms are constantly in phone contact with Australian homes, day and night.

By accessing existing databanks the telemarketer usually has some knowledge about the potential client's consumption patterns. In North America the selling of season tickets and requests for alumni contributions to universities are clear examples of telemarketing. There, representatives of the respective organisations phone previous or current consumers (i.e. fans or students) in an attempt to either initiate or elevate patterns of consumption. Relevant information is held in existing databanks.

In the case of university students, alumni are asked to recall their positive experiences with the university and then requested to pledge a donation, either one-off or continuing, to one or a number of universities. At the forefront of many such requests are college athletic programmes. Such donations may assist capital works programmes, student athlete scholarships, or ongoing awards and honours. Whatever the case, the donation, gift or commitment is usually solicited by telephone and relies on known information about the client.

Similarly, with season tickets, at the end of one season an organisation's telemarketers quickly need to swing into action for the next. Existing season ticket holders are quizzed as to their future intentions, and lapsed members and season ticket holders can once again be reminded of membership benefits. Both current and previous consumers should be well known to the organisation through in-house databases. By pre-selling a large percentage of seats, merchandise and services, an organisation establishes its product as a premium article, which assists not only in sponsorship development but also in future pricing strategies.

While the former are examples of telemarketing at a macro-level, this promotional tool also has strong relevance to community sports. Local recreation centres can canvass former clients as to the reasons for their failure to continue to use the facility's services and, in the process, discern how their needs are currently being met.

The benefits of doing this are numerous: the centre can be made aware of service shortfalls, and it may also be apprised of changing demographics or psychographics within the catchment area. Conversely, it may stimulate reconsideration of facility use, and useful information may be provided to frame future marketing strategies. Likewise, information regarding the facility's services can be provided to local industry with the intention of assisting the latter to conduct its business. This can take the form of offering group or corporate rates for specific programmes or services, conducting 'contra' arrangements where relevant expertise or products are exchanged, or even providing onsite consultancy and health, fitness and wellbeing services. In many cases it is the function of the telemarketer to initiate interest and, if appropriate, instigate some action.

Finally, the local junior sporting club engages in a form of telemarketing when it contacts parents and interested individuals to assist in the operation and organisation of the club's affairs. Money is not always the focal point of the request: more often than not it is labour, time and expertise. Nevertheless, conceptually it is the same as telemarketing for season tickets, for alumni support, or for tracking information on fitness centre defection. In each case there is an exchange process taking place with the intention of creating a win-win situation. The exchange may not always involve physical goods, as feelings, perceptions or beliefs can form part of this process. Nevertheless, benefits and costs are clearly established and comprehended by both parties to the agreement. If this happens, the telemarketer has done his/her job well.

According to Irwin, Sutton and McCarthy (2002: 242), promotional licensing 'is the act of granting a second party permission to use a mark, name, symbol or likeness'.

Interestingly, the authors believe, and provide evidence, that 'promotional licensing as a promotion strategy may have reached its zenith in the mid 1990s with a 100% increase in sales of major US sports merchandise between 1990 and 1994 but with only 5% increase in sales in the ensuing 5 years' (2002: 242-3). Nevertheless, officials of the Atlanta organising committee for the 1996 Olympic Games suggested that corporations paid as much as US$50.7 million to have an official association with the Games.

Licensing can involve the use of a logo, an association, the right to designations such as 'official', the right of service, or the privilege to conduct promotion activities. Merchandise examples of sports promotional licensing are numerous. Caps, shirts, windcheaters, jackets, scarves and keyrings are merely the tip of the iceberg in licensed goods. Products on supermarket shelves, in service stations and in hardware stores often carry the name of a sports, team or athlete, which on sale will return a percentage to the licensing agent. There is no doubt that the growth in promotional licensing over the past decade has been prolific. However, in some instances it has created dissent as to use of trademarks, images and logos.

Selecting the Promotion Mix

Selecting the correct promotion mix is potentially one of the more difficult decisions facing the sports promoter. As is the case when selecting the appropriate marketing mix, the blend of promotion activities engaged in to entice the consumer must reflect the type and nature of the product or service and the specific characteristics of the consumer. Not only would a billboard on a major freeway for a marginal sports or niche product be inappropriately placed, the expense involved would be disproportionate to the 'cost per exposure'. A combination of selected advertising in a sports-specific magazine, publicity in local or community news-papers, and telemarketing using in-house databases would be a more appropriate way of connecting with potential consumers.

Conversely, national sporting organisations employ promotion strategies such as national advertising on radio, television and newspapers; they promote sports-specific magazines; they are the beneficiaries of a colossal amount of publicity across all media; and they engage in telemarketing and personal selling to boost attendances at events. Here the use of billboards on major arterial routes would be most appropriate, especially if a significant event in the sports were about to occur, such as a final, a playoff, a State-of-Origin or a blockbuster match-up. Yet it is equally important for local, community and regional clubs and organisations to establish an appropriate promotion mix. Moreover, while the scope and size of their mixes may be vastly different from those experienced at national or professional level, conceptually they are very similar.

Sales Promotion, Ticketing and Participation

In 1995, the Sydney Swans chief executive officer undertook a series of research projects that enabled the organisation to formulate a promotion strategy aimed at 'selling' the team to what the chief believed to be a potential AFL spectator base in Sydney of 650000. In June 1996, Smith reported that (1996a: B6, 1996b: 42): from this research the club launched a series of acquisition, retention and cross selling programmes that led to a 50% increase in membership, the development of a solid database, a strategic alliance with East's Rugby League Club, Swan-link—a transport joint venture with the NSW Department of Transport, and a four-fold increase in the sale of Swans merchandise.

The impact of the promotional activities undertaken by the Sydney Swans on match attendance and club membership is one of the success stories in Australian sports. In 1997 a record crowd of 46168 witnessed the last home game of that season, and in 1999 the club had an unprecedented 31000 members. By undertaking this research and implementing a number of key recommendations, the Swans management demonstrated a fundamental knowledge of the attendance frequency escalator principle discussed below, and instigated programmes and techniques to boost sales.

The Attendance Frequency Escalator

One of the key issues facing the sports industry is how to encourage existing consumers to elevate their levels of involvement at the same time as introducing new consumers to sports products and services. This is as true for recreational activities and merchandise as it is for professional sports. The consumption of sports was initially thought to be analogous to a staircase. Consumers would make an initial foray into the product by purchasing a single game ticket or buying a single piece of apparel or merchandise. The consequences of an incorrect choice would not be great. Once the consumer was happy that the right decision had been made, they would increase their level of consumption to a degree with which they were comfortable: in other words, they would take a number of steps up the sports consumption staircase. Marketing was focused on the new consumer, ignoring the contribution that an existing member, fan or participant could make to the sports or organisation. (Potentially, the satisfied customer is an organisation's best salesperson.)

While the staircase analogy may have had initial applicability to the sports industry, the sheer complexity of potential sports consumption choices created the need for a framework that exhibited greater flexibility and fluidity. Furthermore, the initial staircase structure did not allow for non-direct consumers or non-consumers. The frequency escalator provides a mechanism for tackling such shortcomings. Mullin (1985) contends that the distribution of existing consumers 'is a continuous series of steps on an escalator that runs from one through to the number of games in a season'. Conceptually, this can be applied not just to the sports spectator but also to the snow skier, fitness centre member, tennis player or golfer, who may indulge in their activity of choice from infrequently to daily. When these are combined with pre-consumers, who are divided into non-consumers and indirect consumers, the possible levels of consumption are vast. Hence the escalator principle recognises both the fluid nature of consumption and the increasing levels at which consumption is possible.

Non -consumers

While non-consumers may be divided into aware and non-aware categories, establishing promotion strategies aimed at such groups is problematic. The sports promoter either does not know the constituency of the group or realises that a conscious decision not to consume the sports offerings has been made. While advertising campaigns that both inform and educate may have some success in introducing new consumers to a product, such strategies are little more than one part of an extensive promotion campaign. Nevertheless, non-consumers are now a significant part of the sports consumption process and need to be acknowledged accordingly.

Indirect Consumers

Indirect consumers listen to sports on the radio, watch it on television, read about it in the newspapers, and discuss it with friends and colleagues. In all respects this group is extremely important. If fans refused to listen to or watch the game, buy the merchandise, or associate the sports with a particular manufacturer, the potential for corporate involvement in sports would be severely limited. Only 16000 tennis fans can watch the ladies' and men's final of the Australian Tennis Open live, but many millions can be transfixed by the event on television.

Here it is the task of the sports marketer to attempt to convert the indirect consumer to one who purchases the live or actual experience or commodity. Given that in most instances such consumers are predisposed towards the sports product, the inducements that can be utilised to offer the one-off experience are numerous.

Moreover, if such inducements are tied to an appropriate advertising campaign, the potential to add to the direct consumer base is enhanced. Nevertheless, it should be recognised that indirect consumers are an integral part of any attendance or participation act, and as such their level of commitment must be appreciated and acknowledged. Moreover, strategies should be implemented that ensure their ongoing support at the level with which they are comfortable. Junior supporters' clubs on television, sports-specific magazines and home pages on the World Wide Web all provide for a specific level of sports consumption.

Direct Consumers

Direct consumers are categorised into light, medium and heavy users, and promotions should be designed to encourage consumers to move towards the heavy end. Shilbury (1994) suggests that sports marketers should initially aim for a 60% heavy, 10% medium, 30% light combination of consumers, and this idea has merit. The selling of 60% of tickets pre-season enables early financial strategy and fiscal planning, while the 10% allocated to medium users, or mini-season ticket holders, provides a mechanism for light users to elevate their level of consumption without making the leap to a full season ticket. This is especially important in sports such as basketball, where the season is invariably long and many games are played. By reserving 30% for the walk-up crowd the sports marketer ensures access to infrequent game attenders, first-timers and fans who want to see an individual game due to a strong match-up, star players or game promotion.

The advantage of this ticketing strategy is that it allows for fluidity in fan movement. The suggestion inherent in the sports attendance frequency escalator is that the consumer is moved by the sports or organisation towards higher levels of consumption. It also argues that, given the variety in light, medium or heavy use, the movement from one category to the next is rather seamless, with a relatively ill-defined transition phase. This is in contrast to the sports participation staircase, where the consumer makes a conscious decision to move to the next consumption level. In this case, stages are discrete and may be mutually exclusive.

The key issue related to the sports attendance frequency escalator is: How do sports encourage higher consumption levels? Strategies and programmes need to be developed that will not only enhance awareness of the benefits resulting from additional investment on the part of the consumer but also result in increased sales. By encouraging different levels of participation and hence segmenting the market, the sports marketer strives to ensure maximum consumption of the event—the sellout. It should not be forgotten that the first objective of sports attendance is to sell out the stadium.

The second objective is to repeat the first as often as possible. Spolestra (1991) argues that it is much more fun to go to a sold-out event than one that is only half-sold. Sellouts create premium tickets, which in turn elevate the profile of the event. This in turn enhances the desirability of the product, which itself leads to increased sales. Once an event has been sold out, the sports marketer can focus attention on providing excellent service to the fans on hand.

However, the sports marketer should not create a perception of a sellout merely in an attempt to create premium tickets. In the early 1990s the Sydney Kings organisation had to work assiduously to combat the notion that their basketball games were always sold out. Although this was not the case, basketball fans, believing this to be true, often stayed away from games when excellent seats were still available.

Programmes and Techniques to Boost Sales

The four major areas that need to be concentrated on with respect to sales are:

- Indirect consumers;
- Light users;
- Medium users; and
- Heavy users.

While the first three groups are encouraged to elevate their usage level, anti-defection programmes need to be implemented for the heavy usage category in an attempt to prevent them from falling off the escalator.

Indirect to Light

Converting indirect consumers to light users is not so difficult and is best accomplished using advertising and sales promotion. These consumers have already shown a predisposition towards the product by being media fans or purchasing related merchandise. What needs to be done is to provide them with an incentive to walk into an arena and see firsthand what has previously been mediated for them. The number of possibilities here are endless. The most obvious is providing a tangible connection between the products consumed at home and the event itself. Media competitions, game-redeemable coupons and event-associated product purchases all provide an attractive entry into the initial consumption experience.

Light to Medium

Moving the light user to the medium user category can be achieved through sales promotion and personal selling. Consumers at this stage are still predominantly price-sensitive, so offering reduced prices for bulk purchases and discounts on selected associated goods will often encourage light users of the product. Given that there are various levels of medium usage, designated seating, newsletters and invitations to pre-or post-game functions and special events may be appropriate incentives.

Medium to Heavy

Encouraging the medium user to become a heavy user is rather more difficult than the previous scenarios, as more often than not medium users have reached saturation level in terms of their personal consumption. This may not be a problem if the season is not excessively long or expensive. To encourage heavy usage, organisations need to make this individual feel very special. Here the emphasis should be on personal selling and premium sales promotion. While group-specific deals and give-aways can be negotiated for this group, these may be only the start of the service offered. Sports promoters need to think about the range of value-added extensions that can extend the heavy user's enjoyment of the product, such as valet parking, special dining, boxes and access to play-off or finals tickets.

They also need to be aware of those club resources which may facilitate the heavy users 'or members' conduct of their own business. These may include the use of athletes to promote facets of the members' business, the use of organisational space and expertise to conduct business seminars and workshops, or even the provision of net-working opportunities across this category of membership. All participants should be working towards a win-win situation.

ANTI-DEFECTION PROGRAMMES

Although all products and services have natural attrition rates, this does not mean that defection should be meekly accepted. Programmes aimed at minimising defection should be firmly entrenched and constantly evaluated in any promotion strategy. By being aware of the client's purchase and usage habits through constant monitoring of databanks, changes in patterns of behaviour may quickly be noticed. Immediately a decline in usage is evident, sales staff or other appropriate individuals need to contact the client quickly to discern the reasons for consumption fall-off. By responding to consumer issues and concern in a prompt manner, organisations are more likely to maintain their heavy usage consumers.

Establishing promotion strategies is a complex yet exciting task. Advertising, public relations and publicity, sales promotion, personal selling, including sponsorship and telemarketing, and promotional licensing are crucial to the success of any sports product, event or service, and as such are vital to the promotion mix. Furthermore, the sports marketer not only needs to be fully conversant with the components of the promotion mix but also needs appropriate application skills for any given situation. Once the promotion strategy has been established, it is incumbent on sports marketers to analyse consumers within the framework of the frequency escalator to monitor ongoing consumer behaviour. Programmes and techniques to boost sales and prevent defection need to be established and implemented, to ensure continued consumption of the product and to extract maximal gain from the specific promotion activity. Contemporary sports marketers also need to be able to offer the 'money-back guarantee'.

CHAPTER

Role of Advertising

Advertising and Product Life Cycle

Entertainment products have short life-cycles; their demand is usually greatest at the time of launch and declines very quickly in subsequent weeks. Hence marketers have to decide on advertising levels for such products even before the product is launched.

Before making decisions as to the appropriate media to be used, sports marketers need to understand the relationship between advertising and the phases of the product life cycle. During the goods or services introductory phase, advertising should be informative. Here the advertisement should provide all the salient information about the product. This may include special features, relevant technical speci-fications, pictorial or illustrative representations, place of purchase and/or consumption, and even price. Basically, the sports promoter is stating what the goods or services are and where they can be obtained. During the growth and maturity phases, advertising should be persuasive in nature. Consumers should be reminded of the benefits and/or the desirable attributes that can be gained by consuming the product.

During the decline phase, reminder advertising should be used. The intent behind this is to provide impetus for consumers to reconsider purchase options or, if the event is cyclical, to remind past consumers that the event will return at some stage in the future and to keep that time free. Annual events such as the various motor vehicle grand prix are a good example of this process. Initial advertising emphasises information as to event location, date, ticket options and purchase sites, and promoter. As the day of the event approaches, advertising promotes the participants or stars, becomes more subjective and develops emotional overtones. The 2001 Qantas Australian Motorcycle Grand Prix used the advertising slogan 'You can't beat the world's best', while the 2002 Skyy Vodka Australian Motorcycle Grand Prix used the advertising slogan 'You can't beat 317kpm'. The Australian Formula 1 Grand Prix held in Melbourne during March 2002 simply proclaimed 'The World According to Formula One'. Intermittent advertising takes place through the year, usually associated with similar events, providing fans with broad details of the next race.

PURPOSE OF ADVERTISING

Stanton et al. (1995) state that advertising is the activities associated with presenting a paid, sponsor-identified, non-personal message about an organisation and/or its products, services or ideas. While advertising can take many forms, it is basically constructed around a message that is designed to build audiences and promote sales. Joel Hochberg, president of DDE Needham Worldwide, believes that (Marketing News 1988: 3): an ad that doesn't sell product has no purpose. To work in the marketplace it must have relevance, originality and impact. If it is not relevant it has no purpose, if it is not original it will not attract attention and if it does not have impact it will leave no lasting impression. Hence it can be argued that, irrespective of context, the foundation of successful advertising is the ability to communicate.

The philosophy behind this methodology is that if people can remember a commercial, its intended message and the brand name, there is a better chance that persuasion will occur and the brand will sell. The most common recall-testing method used in television is the day-afterrecall (DAR) interview, which is conducted within 24 hours of the advertisement's display. This interview establishes respondent type, programmes viewed, whether or not the respondent recalls the advertisement and the components recalled.

With respect to the print media, the Starch Readership Test also examines recall. Less than 17% related recall is regarded as low and anything above 32% as high. It should be ascertained through additional questioning what respondents were doing during the advertising period and what media they were attending to. To perform well in a test of recall, a commercial must cut through the clutter of the medium and the apathy of viewers and gain attention, which in turn maximises the audience for the message to follow. This has tended to lead to loud and flamboyant commercials. The ARU, the National Basketball League (NBL) and World Series Cricket have adopted stunning visuals, usually augmented by rock'nroll, to advertise their respective products. Although there is no guaranteed formula for success, effective advertisements usually exhibit the following traits:

- They identify the brand early.
- They are simple, yet interesting and involving.
- They adopt audio and visual reinforcement.
- They link the brand to the image created.

Once an advertising campaign has been tested, the results obtained can give rise to different courses of action. An organisation may:

- Give an unreserved green light to the campaign;
- Alter the media mix;

- Alter timing based on demographic information; or
- If the advertisement is not communicating the intended message to the correct demographics, decide to start the process again.

Sports advertising is now a multi-billion-dollar industry and has as its prime purpose the influencing of consumers to respond positively to products or services. The foundation of successful advertising is the ability to communicate, and this can be conducted through various media using vastly different strategies.

Newspapers are current and relatively inexpensive and reach a mass audience, while magazines invite leisure readership. Radio can bring the imagination into play, while television unquestionably reaches the largest possible audience. Outdoor advertising involves the presentation of an uncomplicated message, while brochures, flyers and posters effectively segment the market. The Internet is increasingly being used to provide information and links to sponsors' home pages and to conduct sports business. Two additional factors that need to be considered, irrespective of the media alternatives, are timing and cost.

Media selection depends on elements such as objectives, whether they be sales or communication, budget and target audience. However, there are a number of qualitative and quantitative media factors that need to be considered. The successful advertising campaign must not only be clear and objective and aid in the decision-making process—it must also offer good value, be valid and reliable as well as practical and defensible, and produce understandable results. Advertising services is different from advertising goods.

However, through advertising to employees, realising the value of word-of-mouth, providing tangible clues, making the service comprehensible, ensuring continuity in advertising themes and images and, most importantly, promising only that which can be delivered with total certainty, the potential impact of intangibles on service can be reduced and, to a lesser extent, controlled.

Recognising that creativity in advertising is very much a matter of individual choice and perception, this chapter has focused on the strategies that can be adopted to inform the creative underpinnings of sports advertising. A thorough understanding of the objectives of, and the budget allocated to, a sports advertising campaign will in part dictate the type of campaign to be run and the media to be used. Once these decisions have been made, the creative component can be established within a well-defined structure. A clear indication of the effectiveness of the strategies can be obtained through ongoing monitoring of the advertising campaign.

CHAPTER

Sports Marketing and Television

SPORTS AND TELEVISION

For many sports, including the National Basketball Association (NBA) and National Football League (NFL) in the United States, cricket and the Australian Football League (AFL) in Australia, and soccer, golf and tennis worldwide, television rights provide a substantial source of revenue. Television networks now demand more from their right to broadcast than in their previous passive business partnerships with various sports. To ensure that networks maximise their revenue and profits, programme directors and television executives are increasingly influencing the scheduling of games and events. The balance between playing at times conducive to optimum athletic performance and playing at times best suited to optimum ratings is one aspect of the sports-television relationship that creates tension. This tension has the potential to upset the mutually beneficial relationship currently in existence.

Fundamentally, the business of the commercial television industry is the sale of airtime to advertisers. The price at which commercial TV airtime is sold is a function of a number of factors, the most important of which are the number of television viewers, and the price and availability of advertising space on suitable alternative media. Commercial television uses programming to influence the size and profile of its viewing audience, which is measured by independent ratings (ANZ McCaughan 1993: 9): The principal profit equation for commercial television is to ensure that the revenue generating capacity of a schedule of programming sufficiently exceeds both its cost of production or acquisition as well as associated overheads, to produce a reasonable return on investment for the broadcaster.

In general, advertising agencies form buying groups, allowing them to obtain discounts on advertising rates from the networks. These discounts are obtained due to the high volume of advertising inventory purchased by the advertising agency, a volume that corporations individually cannot match. Corporate clients at times also negotiate directly with networks, although this is less common because of the ability of the advertising agency to negotiate more favourable rates due to the volume of inventory being purchased.

The Sportbusiness-television Relationship

Advertising agencies also offer expertise in recommending the most efficient forms of advertising or media buys for a particular product. A media buy refers to the range of advertising spots purchased across a variety of networks and programmes. In its broadest sense, a media buy also includes other avenues for advertising, such as radio, newspapers, magazines and outdoor billboards. A spot refers to the purchase of advertising inventory on television, usually in the form of a 15-, 30-or 60-second placement of an advertisement during a programme.

Sports Programming

The importance and significance of the sports-television relationship are indicated by the rapid increase in sports programming in Australia since the inception of television in 1956. In Sydney in 1958, just over twelve hours of sports programming went to air during the week commencing 1 September. Ten years later during the week commencing 31 August, four stations showed a total of 22 hours of sports programming. Channels Seven and Nine covered Australian Rules and rugby league, with ten one-hour boxing and wrestling programmes also shown.

By 1978, in the week commencing 2 September, 33 hours of sports programming were shown in Sydney, and by 1988 five channels showed 43 hours of sports during the week beginning 15 August (Jarratt 1988). In Melbourne during the week beginning 26 May 1996, free-to-air sports programming had escalated to 79 hours. By 2002 in the week commencing 16 June, the five free-to-air networks showed just under 100 hours of sports programmes. In addition, pay-television providers offer three channels dedicated to 24 hours of sports programming. The increase from 1996 is largely, but not solely, attributable to the extended period of major sports events noted in the headline story. During 2002 Australian pay-television services underwent a rationalisation, with Optus Vision withdrawing its sports content channels, and opting to develop an alliance with Fox Sports to deliver Fox Sports channels.

These results suggest, as did the headline story, that sports programming is a ratings winner. Networks would not schedule so much sports programming if it were not profitable to do so. Why then is sports programming so attractive? Klattell and Marcus (1988: 4) summarise the intrinsic value of sports programming to television: At its best, television sports is the finest programming television can offer. In many respects, sports may be the quintessential television programme format, taking fullest advantage of the role TV plays in our daily lives. Sports on TV have visually attractive elements—splashy colours, attractive locations, motion and movement galore. They have expansive vistas, exquisite details, and larger-than-life images ... There is drama, tension, suspense, raw emotion, real anger, unvarnished joy, and a host of other responses. Most of all you are watching real people compete for real, as unsure of the outcome as the viewer. In sports TV the 'bad guy' of the script often wins, unexpected things happen, virtue doesn't necessarily triumph, and goodness is not always rewarded.

The features of sports programming described by Klattell and Marcus underpin the reasons why sports is so attractive to television. They also explain why the networks are prepared to pay large fees to obtain the exclusive rights to broadcast a competition such as the AFL or cricket, or a major event such as the Olympic Games. How is the IOC able to command these fees, and how do sports such as cricket, rugby union and tennis command significant revenues from the sale of these exclusive rights? Calculation of fees is based on the projected advertising sales and profit derived from the exclusive broadcasting of an event such as the Olympic Games. The value of advertising is determined by the system of measurement used to determine the popularity of programmes or, more specifically, how many people watch.

Measuring the Television Audience

The size and composition of television audiences are measured by ratings services. Ratings are collected by using the 'people meter', an electronic measuring device that records what programmes are being watched. This device also has the capacity to record who is watching, which provides important demographic information to networks and advertisers.

Measurements Made

The following terminology is used in relation to measuring television audiences.

Homes Using Television

Homes using television (HUT) is the number of homes where at least one television set is switched on at any point in time. For example, in 2002 there were 1.47 million households (HH) in Sydney with a television and 1.37 households in Melbourne. In excess of 4.75 million households use a television in Sydney, Melbourne, Brisbane, Adelaide and Perth (OzTAM 2002a). In relation to households with pay-television, OzTAM (2002a) estimates show 412000 in Sydney and 316000 in Melbourne, with a five-city aggregate of just over 1 million households.

Programme Ratings

Programme ratings are the percentage of households that are tuned to a particular station at a particular time. OzTAM and the television networks are interested in the specific rating points for those programmes, which are derived using the following formula:

Rating = HH tuned to programme + Total HH

Audience Share

Audience share is the percentage of the total viewing audience in a given period tuned to a particular station. This is an important figure, because it considers the number of televisions actually in use and the total size of the potential audience. The number of televisions in use is likely to be fewer than the total number of households with televisions. Audience share is calculated by dividing the number of households watching a programme by the number of households using televisions:

Share = HH tuned to programme HUT

Gross Rating Points

Gross rating points (GRPs) are another cumulative measure representing the sum of TARPs for a given schedule, often referred to as total TARPs. Cumulative ratings such as GRPs and TARPs are usually calculated for a week or month and, as noted by Buzzard (1992: 40), are often 'used as a comparison to circulation figures in the print media.

It measures the station's overall effectiveness, or the total number of different people who saw a programme or commercial'. Reach is a measure of the number of different people watching, and frequency is the number of times a person or household watches the same programme, commercial or station.

Average Audience

Average audience is the estimated audience over a stated period, usually 15 minutes. This figure is usually expressed in thousands.

People Meters

The method used to collect ratings data has changed during the past fifteen years. Up until 1991 the diary was used. This required randomly selected households to fill in their viewing patterns during a two-week period, usually referred to as the ratings period. At the end of the two weeks, the diaries were collected and analysed to determine programme ratings. The method by which this information was collected, collated and interpreted was rather slow and cumbersome, compared to thè use of the people meter.

In 1989 the first trials began with ACNielsen's people meter. The most significant change as a result of using the people meter was that data could be collected for 52 weeks of the year, thereby removing the tendency of networks to schedule major programmes during known ratings periods. A major advantage of the people meter technology is its capacity to download the results of the previous day's viewing by nine o'clock the next morning, providing television executives with immediate feedback on the success of their programmes. In 2002 ACNielsen's people meter service was replaced in the metropolitan area by OzTAM, which is a joint venture between the three main commercial broadcasters in Australia. OzTAM subsequently appointed Advanced Television Research (ATR) as the ratings provider, or in other words the agency responsible for data collection. What then is the people meter, and how does it work?

The people meter is a small eight-button unit placed on top of the television set. Each member of the household is assigned a button number, and their names are printed above their assigned button number. There is a set of red and green lights on the front of the unit to indicate whether selected people are in the viewing audience. Green indicates viewing; red indicates no viewing. Household members indicate their viewing by pushing their assigned button on either the people meter or the remote control, changing their light from red to green. There is a button labelled OK that must be pressed when all viewing entries have been made. When a household member leaves the room, he/she must again press a button to indicate no viewing and press the OK button to signify a change in audience. When visitors come into the room, they must indicate their presence by pushing a visitor button on the unit placed on the television. Visitors will be asked their sex and age.

Data collected from people meters are downloaded to a central computer, and it is from here that the various rating figures are generated. As can be seen from the need for visitors to input their basic demographic information, detailed reports are possible for every programme. Indeed, detailed reports are possible for every minute of the day for every programme. Typically, data are reported in 15-minute blocks. People meters are an improvement on the diary system, where the accuracy of data reported by households was often suspect. Household members often forgot to complete the diary daily, relying on their memory to fill it in at a later date. Of course, people meters rely on household members diligently turning their green and red lights on and off as they cycle in and out of watching television.

The other major weakness of the people meter is that it cannot detect whether household members are actually watching television, even though they are recorded as being in the room. Remember, this is important because the advertisers assume that people recorded as being in the room actually watch the programme and register or acknowledge the advertisements shown.

Audience Sampling

People meters are not installed in every house using a television. This would be too costly and time-consuming. To obtain reliable data a random sample of the population is taken. The objective of the sample is to install meters in a random, representative and projectable sample of households for the defined market.

At present OzTam uses a sample of 3000 metropolitan households randomly selected, including 750 from Sydney, 700 from Melbourne, 600 from Brisbane, and 475 each from Adelaide and Perth. These 3000 homes determine the success and failure of television programmes and in turn the value of advertising. Regional and pay-television ratings data are collected by ACNielsen. To ensure a valid sample, there must be a genuine representation of the population within each city or regional area. Factors taken into account include postcode, size of household, number of television sets, age of the grocery buyer, presence of children and claimed reception of TV stations (OzTAM 2002a). Households not eligible for the sample include:

- Non-private dwellings—hospitals, prisons, schools etc.;
- Households without a television;
- Households of people working in the television, market research or advertising industries;
- Households moving within the next three months; and
- Households occupied for less than nine months a year.

Advertising during Sports Programming

Super Bowl XXXVII (2003) advertising inventory is expected to sell at just over US$2 million per 30-second spot. Friedman (2002: 3) notes that 'Walt Disney Co. has taken the unusual step of selling Super Bowl inventory much earlier than usual, making the game broadcast on ABC part of an unprecedented deal with OMD USA, New York that exceeds $1 billion. OMD has agreed to buy about one third of the inventory in the Super Bowl—around 20 30-second commercials. Although OMD will probably secure these spots for less than the anticipated US$2 million due to volume purchase, it nevertheless is still a significant sum of money to pay for advertising during sports programming. The Ten Network, broadcasters of the 2002 AFL Grand Final, one of the biggest TV-watching days of the year in Australia, were hoping to attract advertisers nationally across the network at $60 000.

Individual markets ranged from $30000 per 30-second spot in Melbourne to $6000 in Brisbane. In the 2001/02 summer of cricket, advertising rates peaked at $16000 for the first and second one-day finals played in Sydney and Melbourne. Test Matches played against New Zealand in 2001/02 attracted advertising rates of $2900, rising to $4800 for Test matches against South Africa. Interestingly, 30-second spot rates for the Perth Test match televised in the eastern states during prime time (three-hour time difference) rose to $10000. National sponsorships of such sporting events usually offer more to the corporation than traditional spot advertising. In this example, television sponsorship benefits included:

- Specially produced opening and closing and internal billboards;
- Promotion—sponsor will receive logo association with telecast promotion;
- Ten 30-second spots spread through all telecasts on all Nine Network stations;
- Placement—4 x 30 seconds on Saturday and 6 x 30 seconds on Sunday.

Television Sponsorship

National sponsorship of the telecasts of the Melbourne Grand Prix is available and provides association with this unique sporting event. Sponsoring an event like the Grand Prix is obviously more expensive than simply purchasing a series of 30-second spots. Most coverage of major sporting events includes television sponsorship opportunities. Sales of advertising time and television sponsorships are the precursors to determining the worth of television rights purchased by networks. It is important for sports managers to value the potential revenue to networks from televising their sports.

Calculating the Worth of AFL Television Rights

The first live telecast of Australian football occured in 1957. The popularity of these broadcasts resulted in the Victorian Football League (VFL) charging £500 per station to televise football in 1958. The television station that has remained most closely aligned with football is the Seven Network. In 1976, Channel Seven paid $3 million over five years. Channel Seven has retained the rights until 2002 except season 1987. In 1988, the Seven Network paid $30 million for the seasons 1988 to 1992. In 1991, the Seven Network renegotiated the rights for $47 million for three years to the end of the 1995 season. A further $10 million in free advertising was also negotiated during rights deal with the Seven Network for a figure reported to be $90 million for the three years 1996 to 1998. Another new contract was established for the period 1999 to 2001 and was negotiated in 1995. This latest deal also included an agreement between the Seven Network and pay-television operator Optus Vision to telecast all AFL games during the 1996 season. Mostly, these games were replays, with a handful shown live.

Data collected during the 1995 season showed how much revenue advertising during AFL programming on the Seven Network generated. The information shown in this sports view was collected during telecasts of Rounds 21 and 22 and the first final round of the 1995 season.

Content analysis of the sports programming shown in Melbourne revealed 860 minutes of AFL programming shown during Round 21,870 minutes in Round 22 and 570 minutes during the first week of the finals. The purpose of this investigation was to determine the worth of advertising during these matches to the Seven Network. On average, 81.6% of telecast time was devoted to football. The remaining 18.4% of the telecast featured non-programme material of which 15.9% was devoted to advertising and 2.5% to Seven Network promotions. The total potential revenue generated through sale of advertising was determined by multiplying the rate for a 30-second commercial by the number of advertisements that appeared throughout the telecast. A 60-second advertisement was simply credited with two commercial placements and a 15-second advertisement with half a commercial placement. The cost to advertise (30-second spot) ranged from $1500 for Sunday game day to $4000 for Saturday night replay, Saturday and Sunday night live, and $4800 for Friday night.

From calculating the worth of time dedicated to advertising, revenue to the Seven Network during each weekend of the broadcasts was worth in excess of $1.2 million. Over the three weekends $3854000 of advertising inventory was available. Actual revenue generated was $3307850, which represents inventory available minus Seven Network promotions. The Seven Network paid approximately $13.5 million for the rights to the 1995 season. Based on a 22-week home and away season, and three rounds of finals (total 25 weeks), there was a capacity to generate advertising revenue in excess of $32 million (averaged over 25 weeks at $1 284700 per week) in the Melbourne market. Other special events during the season included State-of-Origin, the Brown low Medal count and the Grand Final, which would generate significantly more advertising revenue and value to the advertiser.

Numerous methods exist enabling advertisers to measure the cost efficiency of their advertising in terms of number of people reached. These methods utilise the value of gross rating points, total audience rating points, cost per rating point and cost per thousand. To obtain a measure reflecting the needs of advertisers, the cost per thousand (CPM) was used to determine advertising effectiveness (i.e. homes reached). CPM is defined as 'how much it costs to advertise to reach 1000 homes or viewers' (Buzzard 1992:42).

The formula for determining CPM is the cost of the buy divided by the average households or persons reached, per average minute or quarter-hour, multiplied by 1000. Average household ratings for each segment were obtained for each telecast and converted into the total number of Melbourne households (1118000) tuned into the telecast. The cost to reach 1000 Melbourne homes ranged from $14to $29 over the review period of the telecast.

The range in Round 21 was $15 to $22, in Round 22 , $14 to $19 and in the first week of the finals $14 to $ 29. Using the Friday night Round 21 fixture as an example, the calculation of the CPM is obtained by taking the advertising rate of $ 4800 and dividing by the average homes viewing (220000, rating 18.9). This figure is then divided by 1000, providing a resultant figure of 22, indicating that it cost the advertisers $22 to reach every 1000 Melbourne homes during Round 21 Friday night game. These figures indicate a good return on investment to advertisers in terms of audience reach. In essence it cost advertisers 22 cents per home. Results achieved from this study indicate that the Seven network seems to be performing extremely well in recouping its investment in football. Revenue exceeding $1 million each weekend for 10-15 hours of telecast equates to in excess of $27 million for the season, solely from the Melbourne market. These figures are achieved despite the Seven network forgoing $4.5 million of potential revenue each season in order to promote its own programmes.

The Seven network incurs production costs as well as its outlay to the AFL for the rights, and these production costs reduce the revenue generated from sale of advertising time. Production costs usually assume approximately 20% of the network's total outlay. Considering the cost of the rights paid to the AFL ($500000 per weekend) and including costs of production (assuming costs in the region of $100000 per weekend), the revenue obtained from the Melbourne market appears to indicate a very healthy return on investment. Income exceeding $1.1 million each weekend, minus expenditures of $600000 for production and station promotions, provides a weekly profit in excess of $500000. Over a 25-week period this represents profits exceeding $25 million.

Lawrence (1995) indicates that in 1994 the rights fees were worth between $15 million and $17 million and the revenue generated from sales of a advertising was worth $35 million. Based on the figures obtained from the analysis of three rounds of AFL extrapolated over 25 weeks, it would seem that a large proportion of this $35 million would be generated through the Melbourne market alone, highlighting the strategic significance of the Melbourne television audience to both the AFL and the Seven Network.

Advertising Effectiveness

Nakra (1991: 217) notes that: commercial avoidance and audience erosion are two interrelated problems that marketing executives and media planners have been aware of for more than 30 years. With the rapid advancement of technology the problem of 'zapping' has become even more predominant. Zapping involves viewers rapidly changing channels in order to avoid commercials. It also involves video-recorded programmes, where viewers simply fast-forward past the advertisements. Zapping therefore represents a fundamental challenge to the basis of the television advertising formula, which assumes, as indicated earlier in this chapter, that viewers recorded as watching a programme also watch and acknowledge advertisements.

A difference can exist between exposure to the programme and exposure to the commercial messages. It is likely that further advances in technology will improve the ability of the viewer to zap commercials. Central to this issue of zapping is the cost-effectiveness of advertising. The best-known method for establishing the cost-efficiencies between programme buys is cost per thousand (CPM). Lloyd and Clancy posit three questions in relation to their suggestion for the use of a measure known as cost per thousand involved (CPMI):

1. Do individual programmes differ in their ability to involve viewers?
2. Just how closely related are CPM and CPMI for the same set of programmes?
3. In other words, would media planners and buyers make the same or different media buys if the decision were based on CPM versus CPMI?

The answers to these questions are based on the extent to which the media environment affects, tempers or moderates the nature of the advertising response. Two hypotheses have emerged from research investigating these questions. The first asserts that the more involved viewers are in a programme and the more they like it and are engaged by it, the weaker will be the advertising response. Proponents of this hypothesis maintain that commercial breaks represent an unnecessarily intrusive element in an otherwise enjoyable viewing experience. As a consequence, the advertisements are filtered out, perceived negatively or simply avoided. The second hypothesis adopts the opposite view. It suggests that characteristics of the programme, as subjectively perceived by the involved viewer, produce efforts to minimise surrounding distractions and cause an enhanced orientation towards the programme and source of the stimulus (Lloyd & Clancy 1991). Enhanced involvement prompts the viewer to remain activated, producing a more positive impact on advertising effectiveness. Implications of these hypotheses are:

- To develop appropriate ratings indexes to determine programme involvement; and
- To factor these indexes into CPMI measures.

At present, no research is available indicating the level of involvement that sports programming generates. However, sports programming for cricket, for example, where only one short commercial can be shown between overs, may have an advantage in ensuring that viewers watch and acknowledge the commercial (i.e. do not zap). Australian Rules football may also have a similar advantage, as commercials are shown after a goal is scored and are typically last just 30 seconds before play recommences. Sports such as golf, basketball and car racing may provide viewers with the opportunity to leave the room, knowing that a series of four to five commercials will be shown.

This also raises the question of advertisement placing in programmes. Typically, first-in and last-out commercials are considered more valuable, as viewers see the first before leaving the room and the last when returning after the commercial break. Interestingly, networks often use the first or last advertisement for their own station programme promotion purposes. All of these factors impinge on the effectiveness of advertising during sports programming. Little research has been conducted on sports programming to shed more light on the answers to the questions raised in this section. There is little doubt, however, that these issues form the basis on which networks set advertising rates and, as a consequence, the amount in television rights they are prepared to pay sporting organisations.

Pay-television

Another player has recently entered the sports-business-television relationship. Pay television was introduced to Australia in *1995*. It is slowly becoming available worldwide, contributing to the globalised economy and in particular the familiarity of sports. The business basis on which pay-

TV is predicated is fundamentally different from that of the free-to-air networks described in this chapter. So far we have described how free-to air networks rely on advertising as their primary source of revenue and profit.

Free-to-air networks are in the business of reaching the widest possible audience, hence the term broadcasting. Free-to-air television is popular and generally taken for granted as an everyday part of life. Pay-television, on the other hand, requires the payment of subscription fees to receive programming. The basic operating premise on which pay-TV exists is known as narrowcasting, and its revenue base is sourced from subscription fees. Unlike with the free-to-air networks, advertising is not the predominant revenue source. In terms of extracting rights revenue from pay-TV operators, the same principle applies as for free-to-air operators: to determine how much revenue the sports contributes to the network. The difference is that it is not so easy to calculate this contribution. Free-to-air networks, as shown earlier in this chapter, can simply calculate the total advertising time in dollar terms, thereby determining how much direct value sports programming represents.

It is more difficult to determine how many subscribers subscribe solely or predominantly because a specific sports is shown on a pay-TV channel. In some cases, major sports such as cricket, the AFL and rugby league clearly add to the likelihood that subscriptions will grow due to their availability on a pay-TV channel. The AFL, for example, has a dedicated channel on Fox Sports at an extra cost of approximately $8 per month. Rugby league is also shown extensively on Fox Sports, exemplifying the impact of the major sports as a strategic source of programming.

Fundamentally, sports not already receiving extensive free-to-air coverage will want to obtain exposure on pay-television. In the end, for some of these sports, the benefits may be the exposure via programming rather than any financial gains via television rights for exclusive coverage. This highlights the important role of television in the overall marketing and promotion of sports. Some sports, as demonstrated in this chapter, have the capacity to gain financially from television broadcasts; others do not have this capacity. For some sports, the opportunity to gain exposure through programming without receiving any financial incentive is another important consideration when developing promotion mix decisions. It is also possible that some sports will have to pay to have their sports shown on either payTV or free-to-air television. In this case, the decision to spend money will come from the promotion mix budget. Television therefore is an important consideration when framing promotion mix decisions.

Another question that arises is what sports managers need to do to enhance the attractiveness of a sports for television. There is no easy answer to this question. Some sports have used rule changes to make the game more attractive; other sports have changed the uniforms worn by players to make them more appealing; still other sports have simply paid for airtime until their sports has become well recognised and people want to watch it on a regular basis. Whether it is pay-TV or free-to-air television, the formula does not change. Television executives will want to know how much revenue and subsequent profit the sports will attract for the network before they agree to show it on television. It is possible that pay-TV offers slightly greater opportunities in the early years, as there will be pressure to fill programming, particularly on all-sports channels. One thing is certain: the complexity of the sports-business-television relationship is intensifying in terms of attracting revenue sources and viewers. What has not changed is that programming is designed to capture a market of viewers, to either expose them to advertising or to get them to subscribe to a pay-TV operator's range of channels.

Digital Television

Fancy using your television to order a pizza, enter a competition or change the narration on a documentary? Digital television promises such features, but Australians are far from being able to take up the advantages. Not so in Britain, where 39% of the population has access to interactive TV—compared with 35% who use the Internet—allowing them to control which court they watch during Wimbledon, for example, or to order food while watching a Pizza Hut ad (Hickman 2002: 6). This is the brave new world confronting the television executive and ultimately the sports consumer and sports marketer. Imagine being able to choose your preferred match and court at Wimbledon, or the golf hole or players you, the sports fan, would actually like to watch during a golf tournament. This may be possible with the onset of digital television during the next decade. The implications for sports broadcasting are significant. Nevertheless, during the next decade high-definition television services will become available with the potential for interactivity.

Although pay-TV has brought a greater number of channels to consumers worldwide, this is nothing compared to the capacity of digital television, which has the potential to unblock the content bottleneck through the provisions of hundreds and hundreds of channels. In the traditional analogue format, delivery was restricted by television's large usage of spectra or frequencies available to broadcast. Digital transmission is expected to improve quality and allow interactivity and consequently, greater control by sports consumers of the type of programmes watched, and the cameras and angles used. At the heart of this technological revolution is bandwidth: 'Bandwidth refers to the capacity to distribute content... Digitized information can be made to take up much less space than analog signals. In a process known as compression, unnecessary information can be removed from video signals.' (Todreas 1999: 79)

The opportunities to arise from technological developments such as digital television need to be carefully considered by sports-marketing managers. The implications extend beyond the value of television rights to sporting organisations, but also to where the control starts and stops for the provision of services to sports consumers. Recent issues surrounding virtual advertising, essentially made possible by digital technology, highlight the complexities new technologies create for sports managers and television executives. For example, virtual advertising can be incorporated in a telecast without disrupting the view to the spectators. However, these images can be set to block out existing ground signage, which would cause some obvious problems (individual corporations pay for the right to display ground signs knowing that television will pick up these signs as part of the broadcast).

Di3: Sky Gamestar Invests in Interactive TV Software for World Cup 2002

Sky digital viewers can join in this year's biggest sporting event and manage their own international football team in a new interactive World Cup fantasy football game, using software developed by Di3. The game allows budding Sven Goran Erikssons to pit their sporting wits and select and manage a team of international players from the 32 football World Cup squads. Di3's back-end database management and scheduling technology does all the maths, allowing players to monitor their team's performance from the comfort of their armchair as the tournament unfolds.

Di3's interactive games engine was first used by Sky for Sky Sports Super Manager—the UK's first cross-platform fantasy football game. The existing software has now been enhanced by Di3 to handle transfers throughout the FIFA World Cup competition and prompt swapping of eliminated players after knockout phases. Registered users of Sky Super Manager will be able to transfer their existing username and password to the World Cup competition. Adrian Pilkington, Head of Games at BSkyB, commented: 'Fantasy Football has been a tremendous success so far with over 70,000 Sky Gamestar teams registered since launch in November. The Sky World Manager version lets players compete nationally for the glory of becoming the ultimate Manager—all through their Sky remote control'. Mark Hughes, managing director, Di3, explained: 'Sports has already proved to be an extremely popular genre for contextual interactive TV services. For the sports fan, iTV enhances the viewing experience by adding a new entertainment dimension. For the content provider, it attracts increased revenues and generates viewer loyalty'. Di3 designs game engines and other iTV software that can be extended to serve a number of platforms and a variety of payment mechanisms. For example, online players pay a registration fee via a secure server while set top box players pay via a premium rate telephone number. New games and genres can also be added cost-effectively.

Television rights to sporting events are one of the most visible and talked-about components of sports marketing. The networks of the world pay exorbitant sums for the exclusive rights to broadcast sporting events such as the Olympic Games and World Cup soccer. These sums merely recognise the number of people watching such events. Sporting events at varying levels some worldwide, some nationally—deliver audiences to advertisers via programming, which in turn delivers revenues to sports in the form of rights fees and profits to television networks via the sale of advertising inventory. The people meter is the electronic device used to measure the success of television programmes.

The people meter collects ratings, which measure how many people with televisions are watching a particular programme. Audience share and TARPs also measure the success of television programmes, providing detailed and specific information about who is watching. It is not enough simply to identify how many people with televisions are watching a programme: it is also important to know the demographic profile of these viewers. Advertising rates are based on ratings figures, and the income derived from advertising determines what rights fees can be paid for the exclusive broadcast rights to sporting events.

Some sporting organisations have been slow to awaken to the value of their product. In marketing terms, many sports have not maximised their revenue opportunities through television, primarily through not understanding how the worth of television rights is calculated. As the sports sector professionalises, this is changing, as evidenced in the escalation of rights fees during the past decade. The other major marketing benefit to be gained from television is exposure. Indirectly, televised sports has the potential to attract viewers to the live event, thereby contributing to the revenue generated via gate receipts. In many ways this is a vicious circle. Televised sporting events can contribute to reduced attendances, explaining why sports programming is often 'blacked out' in the city where the event is being staged. Television therefore is an important consideration when framing marketing and promotion mix decisions.

Pay-television contributes to the exposure sporting organisations may gain from television. The relatively recent introduction of pay-TV to Australia has meant exposure for sports not normally shown on television. Pay-TV is beginning to offer reasonable exposure because the subscriber base is steadily growing. Therefore, only the major professional sports have demonstrated the capacity to attract revenue from pay-TV providers. Over a period of time, however, it might also offer some revenue-generating potential for smaller sports.

This chapter showed that the principal source of revenue for pay-TV operators comes from individual household subscriptions; however, pay-TV operators are also allowed to show advertisements, thereby diversifying sources of revenue. This revenue source is not anticipated to be large in the short term, but will create some discomfort for the free-to-air networks. The various business relationships described in this chapter are neither mysterious nor surprising once the commercial basis on which television operates is understood. What is interesting is the complex set of relationships developing between sports and television as both endeavour to maximise the revenues and profits from their respective product offerings.

CHAPTER

Role of Internet in Sports

The Internet be considered in a holistic manner by organisations. These theories can be generally described as IT 'assimilation theory'. Assimilation theorists include Armstrong and Sambamurthy (1999), El Sawy, Malhotra, Gosain and Young (1999), and Raghunathan and Raghunathan (1994). They conclude that the greatest benefits to organisations via the Internet occur when merging IT strategies with the overall strategic thrust of the firm (Raghunathan & Raghunathan 1994) and incorporating IT into the entire spectrum of organisational activities. In other words, the emergence of the electronic economy has provided a business environment in which the Internet permeates every aspect of an organisation. This understanding affects the Internet strategies employed by sports organisations.

Although generating revenue is rightly the key consideration in Internet strategies, value can be created in a number of other ways. Cutting costs and improving customer service are not as noticeable as large rights deals, but are important elements of a holistic Internet strategy.

Similarly, keeping stakeholders informed is important in a professional business environment, and can be achieved readily via the Internet. In fact, IT assimilation refers to the myriad ways that the Internet can be incorporated into an organisation, with the sum of these applications representing potential competitive advantage. There are countless other IT applications that fall under assimilation theory.

E-mail, for example, has revolutionised many business activities, and intranets allow staff and stakeholders to access internal information. The opportunity for staff to work from outside the office as 'outworkers' has also been facilitated. In short, assimilation theorists call for organisations to examine their entire operation in search of opportunities for improved performance via the Internet. Three such opportunities are:

- Disintermediation;
- Knowledge management; and
- Customer service.

Each of these examples of assimilation opportunities is now reviewed.

DISINTERMEDIATION

Standing (2000:4) describes disintermediation as encompassing the process by which 'middlemen' companies are being 'bypassed by the Internet revolution as more companies that create the goods and services interact directly with the consumer without the aid of intermediaries'. The three functionality opportunities stemming from the 'distributors' stakeholder branch—ticketing, netcasting and merchandising—all offer disintermediation opportunities. Both ticketing and merchandising can be performed through a virtual store, and represent disintermediation prospects. For example, an organisation's ability to sell match tickets online, and subsequently to reduce or eliminate the commissions paid to ticketing agencies, represents a disintermediation possibility. Such opportunities are related to revenue-generating strategies, and clearly affect bottom-line profits through cost-cutting. Virtual stores provide a similar example of potential disintermediation benefits, with the elimination of the need to pay commissions to merchandise wholesalers improving profits above and beyond the revenue associated with additional merchandise sales.

The growing use of the Internet for audio and visual game broadcasts represents a further, significant opportunity for disintermediation. Clubs may be able to bypass traditional broadcasters altogether, and package their own product for advertisers. The potential of such netcasts is explored more fully later in this chapter, but in terms of disintermediation, each of these three examples has presented opportunities for sports organisations to use the Internet to eliminate 'middlemen' and their margins and to interact directly with their customers.

Knowledge Management

According to the *Harvard Business Review on Knowledge Management* (1998), the way companies generate, communicate, and leverage their intellectual assets is an important source of competitive advantage. The Internet is a dynamic tool that has created a number of ways for sports organisations to improve organisational learning. In terms of knowledge generation, the compilation and electronic storage of information on athletes, business activities, and in particular supporters, is growing. A key component of strategies to generate supporter information is the development of online communities. The communication and leveraging of this knowledge can be facilitated by intranets, the importance of which is evidenced by their inclusion as a functional element of several stakeholder branches.

Internally, knowledge management techniques include intranets for the 'employee' stakeholder, which allows them access to job-relevant data. For example, coaches, doctors and nutritionists could have remote access to the ever-growing athlete files, recruiting data and relevant reports in order to improve on-field strategy and performance. Similarly, management-related information that accumulates over time can be made available to off-field employees such as marketers.

Externally, the relationships with 'sponsors', 'league/ central body', 'venue' and 'strategic partner' stakeholders can all be leveraged with strategic intranets based on knowledge. For example, the ability to grow, access and utilise market information over time, and across geographical boundaries, is a significant resource that will generally be extremely appealing to sponsors, leagues and strategic alliance partners. The marketability of such databases as a revenue source is also considered later, as part of online community development. For 'venue' stakeholders, the ability to access 'to the minute' ticket sales information, for example, can assist in timely seating configurations that maximise prearranged capacity, proximity, safety and functionality trade-offs. In short, effective knowledge management is a significant source of competitive advantage that can enhance numerous aspects of operations for sports organisations.

Customer Service

A website can provide customers with timely and accurate information and results, and the ability to conduct transactions online. These types of services are essential to maintain high-level customer service, and ultimately affect the organisational bottom line. Creative, value-added services like club screen savers and links to other useful sites are also part of improved customer service. In addition, sports organisations are increasingly offering highservice Internet memberships that provide customers with 'gold service packages', including privileged news releases. Sports organisations can conduct market research to assess each of the activities their customers engage in, and identify where they can assist via the Internet or improve the overall customer experience. These services can be particularly helpful in the case of international sports where geography restricts customers, and their implementation helps to build community feeling among supporters, the latter another essential component of Internet strategy.

The implementation of IT assimilation strategies offers numerous competitive advantage opportunities for sports organisations. Before considering the impact of the Internet on the four stages of buyer readiness, we look at the concept of online communities. A critical element of online success in any industry, sports has an inherent advantage in the creation of this valuable commodity.

Online Communities

According to Martin (1997: 44), 'digital communities are the future lifeblood of the net'. They are the Internet version of the loyal audiences eagerly sought after by newspapers, trade publications, interest-based magazines and television stations. The ability to hold an audience is crucial to success in these businesses, with product sales and advertising revenue inexplicably tied to consumer numbers. Online communities in the sporting environment are simply those customers who regularly visit the organisational website. These customers may seek information, interaction or services and, if they can be fostered, provide enormous opportunities for organisations.

While the Internet does indeed alter the way organisations and marketers reach their customers, it is also demonstrating its ability to provide new channels for achieving this objective. Online communities are a natural evolution from a medium built on networks, both technical and human. Simeon (1999: 298) observes that 'many commercial Web sites have moved from providing basic company and product information to becoming an integral part of product and service launch strategies'. She goes on to identify some of the dynamic website features capable of developing online communities, including bulletin boards, chat rooms and audio and video capabilities.

The 'culture' of sports provides its businesses with an arguably unequalled head start in this element of online success. Providing customers with a forum to 'meet' like-minded individuals, and encouraging and supporting conversation, is crucial in the development of an online community that, according to Judson and Kelly (1999: 154), 'may spur sales of high-margin peripheral items related to the product'. This process is somewhat easier when the product around which the community is being built is highly involved. In this respect the sports industry makes the leap into cyber community building, with a product arguably generating higher levels of consumer passion and desire to be associated with the product than any other. Online communities are difficult to manufacture for fast food or whitegoods. They are, however, a natural progression for the sports product and its traditional membership base.

Manchester United, the Los Angeles Lakers, the New Zealand All-Blacks and the Collingwood Football Club are all in a commanding position to manufacture an online community, because for many consumers their product is highly involved. The ability to provide access to chat rooms, regular feedback, interesting competitions, up-to-date information, as well as tickets, merchandise and broadcasts, makes customers want to return to a place they feel part of. The website also provides an opportunity for clubs to promote athlete-supporter interaction in a safe environment via chat rooms, which clubs can ultimately leverage. Sports organisations can use these types of strategies to build a large, loyal, online community, unrestricted by geographical boundaries.

In some cases the online community is also evolving into a Virtual home'. For NBL club the Melbourne Tigers, the closure of the historic Albert Park home base to make way for a golf course created something of an identity crisis—a situation familiar to a growing number of 'homeless' sporting organisations. The Internet has presented a cost-effective meeting point for the organisation and its supporters and other stakeholders.

The advantages of a large and loyal online community for a sports organisation are substantial, and can be both assimilation-and revenue-related. Customer service can be drastically improved, and increases in revenue occur through primary and associated products: for example, the emergence of a new demographic attractive to sponsors and the development of a group of human advertisements for a business are significant benefits associated with online communities. Bishop (1998: 77) concurs with this evaluation, promoting organisational strategy that both expands and enhances the richness of customer databases. Bishop adds: 'as it becomes larger and more useful, [a customer database] will help increase sales and, if appropriate, can become an asset you can sell or rent to other organisations'.

Having constructed an online community, sports organisations are in a position to move these cyber consumers through the different stages of buyer readiness, and ultimately into buyer action!

Buyer Readiness and the Internet

Like the process of building an online community, customers can be systematically moved through the buying process of AIDA (attention, interest, desire, action). Sports marketers can utilise a number of Internet features to facilitate this process and ultimately improve revenue streams. Each of the four elements of buyer readiness is now reviewed in relation to Internet marketing strategy.

Attention

The promotion of a web address and its features through traditional media or sales promotions is an important part of the promotional mix, and plays a vital role in generating attention for the site. Indeed, a cursory review of sports advertising on television and in newspapers demonstrates the increasing importance of promoting websites. However, using the Internet as an independent communication channel, sports organisations can be proactive in grabbing the attention of sports consumers through such strategies as the manipulation of search engines and databases.

Sports organisations need initially to consider their actual web address, the key words they link to their site, and the search engines they register with. These decisions affect traffic to the site. In addition, strategically identified databases can be targeted for e-mail advertising and promotions. Tactical alliances with related organisations that provide mutually beneficial web links can also increase traffic where strategic links are identified as important functional components for three stakeholders: 'sponsors', 'league/central body' and 'strategic partners'. By maximising the likelihood that web users will find their site, and electronically promoting the site through appropriate databases and the strategic use of web links, sports organisations can draw significant attention to their website.

Interest

Having got the customer's attention, Internet sites must generate an interest in staying. This important element of buyer readiness requires the high involvement of the sports-marketing department. Websites should be clear and well designed, and convey as closely as possible the culture of the organisation. This can be achieved through consistent use of corporate colours and logos for example, and here the input of professional graphic designers is as critical to websites as any other communication channel. Ease of navigation and speed are as important as 'look and feel' in retaining customer interest, and should be a priority for web designers. This phase of buyer readiness is also an integral part of community building, in that it influences a customer's inclination to return.

Desire

At this point a successful Internet strategy will have attracted potential customers to the site, and sparked their interest with a speedy, easy-to-navigate site that has a unique 'look and feel'. The next step is to stimulate a desire to become more highly involved. Sports marketers are now limited only by their imagination. The Internet can facilitate all of the traditional sales promotions, trials and giveaways associated with arousing purchase desire, and the unique features of the Internet make it suitable to any number of novel marketing strategies. Promotions can be both truly global and interactive. Again, as with community building, the highly involved nature of the sports product places it in an enviable position. Sports marketers are well placed to leverage the 'sexiness' of their athletes and the public desire to associate with their success and athleticism, via both traditional and innovative online sales promotions.

Action

Online purchasing by consumers is the ultimate aim of a well-executed Internet strategy from the sports organisation's point of view. The ability to facilitate action is what the buyerreadiness sequence is all about, and revenues being generated online are already significant. Church (2000) reported that 1999 revenues from advertising on sports sites amounted to US $612 million.

This figure, however, pales in comparison to her projections of US$ 6.27 billion for advertising through the same channels by 2005. Similarly, notable estimates were made for 2005 sales of online sports merchandise (US $5.8 billion) and ticketing sales (US $2.9 billion). In Australia, the AFL signed a five-year Internet rights contract with Telstra in 2002 for a reported $30 million. These massive figures indicate why online revenue strategies are critical to the future of sports organisations. Having generated 'attention', interest' and 'desire', providing suitable online products that consumers are able to access via the organisational website is paramount. Online revenue-generating schemes are limited only by administrators' imagination; however, six typical revenue streams are reviewed below:

- Virtual stores (including merchandising and ticketing);
- Online advertising;
- Netcasting;
- Online memberships;
- Online gaming; and
- Online gambling.

VIRTUAL STORES

With customers growing propensity to make purchases online, revenue from virtual stores is a growing concern for sports organisations. Generally, a sports organisation's online store is simply an electronic version of a traditional outlet, and will contain all of the items typically available from such channels, such as merchandise, memorabilia and match tickets. Importantly, the Internet's ability to overcome geography also presents sports organisations with an effective opening into the global marketplace. Organisations like the Los Angeles Lakers and Manchester United, for example, which have large followings outside their national borders, can now efficiently tap that market via their virtual stores.

As explored earlier, there are also potential disintermediation advantages generated through the use of virtual stores. Sporting organisations have traditionally distributed merchandise through a combination of privately run stores and licensed retailers. Virtual stores, however, have few of the typical overheads and costs associated with 'actual' stores, and can bypass the commissions payable to licensed retailers.

Online Advertising

There are a number of reasons for sporting websites being among the most attractive available to advertisers. According to Church (2000), the typical online sports visitor has a higher net worth and propensity to buy online than visitors to other sites. In addition, the 'stickiness' of sports sites (or their ability to hold a visitor for longer) makes them more attractive to advertisers and sponsors.

The growing popularity of online gambling and the power of major sports to attract global audiences are also contributing to the propensity for advertisers to be interested in sports sites. Sports-related websites are already making a significant impact online. We have already noted the US$612 million spent on advertising on sports-related sites in 1999, and the projections of US $6.27 billion for advertising through the same channels in 2005. Online advertising, therefore, will presumably form an important part of Internet strategy for sporting organisations.

Netcasting

Using the Internet to compete with television's dominance of broadcasting is perhaps the most exciting development presented by the medium. Netcasting is much cheaper than launching a television channel, and users can log in from any computer and, increasingly, from mobile telephone devices. With the steady penetration of broadband cabling, netcasting is increasingly being considered the platform for media ownership by sports organisations. Manchester United supporters, for example, can currently watch delayed highlights of any of their club's games from the past 10 years for £25 a year, or £3.99 a month.

As sports audiences on the Internet grow, organisations are assessing their ability to use disintermediation and bypass television broadcasting. The number of sporting events being broadcast on the Internet is certainly growing, the medium's global access and interactivity being highly attractive to sponsors and marketers. Although the rewards associated with Internet broadcasting are compelling, the path forward is not completely clear.

GazeTV can offer sponsors a global audience and is well placed to incorporate interactive technology. In addition, the service has the potential (subject to contractual agreements) to offer packages similar to those provided by Manchester United, or even to provide live coverage, and already enables supporters not present to feel a part of home games. Given GazeTV is a relatively low-cost production, with similarly low levels of e-commerce, the major query here would involve video quality.

At present the broadcasting status quo is precarious. The benefits associated with Internet broadcasts are significant, and the disadvantages, while present, are far from insurmountable. Improving technology and society's growing use of the Internet for both communication and financial transactions is going a long way to overcoming its disadvantages. For sports marketers, the implications of a significant increase in Internet broadcasting are momentous.

Online Memberships

Sports organisations are also moving towards generating revenue through the sale of online memberships that provide subscribers with access to exclusive information releases and value-added services. AFL clubs expe-rimenting with the concept in 2001 had positive experiences, with at least one club boasting an online membership in excess of 1000. Multiplied by the $ 25 fee, the preliminary results augur well for this Internet-based revenue stream in the future.

Online Gaming

As distinct from online gambling, various small payment games available to sports enthusiasts such as fantasy leagues, tipping, or variations of the traditional 'spot the ball' competitions, are having considerable success online. These interactive types of gaming both generate revenue and assist in the formation of online communities. As such they are an important element of Internet strategy for sports organisations.

Online Gambling

The final element of online revenue to be considered is online gambling. Investment bank Merrill Lynch expects e-sports betting to rise, from its current US$142 million, to US$2.8 billion by 2015 (Gerlis 2001). Some industry experts feel this to be a very conservative estimate. In fact, it can be argued that, with the development of wireless Internet access (through mobile devices), online gambling will become so 'instant' that it can be done anywhere, anytime, anyway.

Savvy sports organisations will incorporate strategies to gain a share of this significant market. Australia is a key market within an online sports betting industry that investment bank Merrill Lynch recently predicted would be worth US$173 billion by 2015. Although Australian online gambling legislation is currently quite restrictive, it seems inevitable that AFL clubs will one day follow the 'leed' of sporting clubs like Premier League soccer club Leeds United.

Leeds supporters can currently use a Leeds United-branded mobile phone to access unique mobile content from the official Leeds website—and to place a bet on their team! Having signed a revenue-sharing deal with Wap Integrators, a technology company with a UK betting licence, Leeds is well placed to benefit from online gambling as part of a wider Internet strategy. Leeds followers in Australia and globally can get the Leeds URL and pay a local phone rate for bets, or order tickets, merchandise or even travel (Gellatly 2001).

The concept of online communities has emerged as critical to the success of sports organisations' online sorties. For the sports marketer, the successful manufacture of these audiences represents an exiting new market ripe for exploitation. Creative sports marketers have the opportunity to influence consumers as they move through the buying process of attention, interest, desire and, crucially, action.

Six distinct types of online revenue streams were considered that in combination have the capacity to radically alter the sports business landscape. Although rhetoric surrounding the global potential of the Internet abounds, there is growing evidence that, for the sports industry in particular, the World Wide Web offers marketers unique opportunities. Indeed, for sports, the Internet has rapidly moved from the ranks of a potential marketing channel to a critical nexus—the Internet-sports nexus.

CHAPTER

Attracting Sponsorship

The *Penguin English Dictionary* defines sponsorship as 'somebody who pays for a project or activity'. In today's (sports) business environment, however, nothing is less true. As an important marketing tool for many organisations, sponsorship involves a reciprocal relationship. One party puts something in and the other party returns the favour. Sleight (1989: 4), in his pointed definition of sponsorship, acknowledges the importance of the reciprocal relationship. His definition is used in the remainder of this book: Sponsorship is a business relationship between a provider of funds, resources or services and an individual, event or organisation which offers in return some rights and association that may be used for commercial advantage.

In marketing it is common to look at the different marketing tools, like sponsorship, from an applied point of view. In other words, how can we use this tool (i.e. spend money, resources or services) to reach sales-related goals? This is the sponsoring organisation. From the sporting organisation's point of view, the main goal of sponsorship is not sales-related. Sporting organisations or athletes mainly use sponsorship to accumulate funds, resources or services. These funds, resources or services are then used to run the operations of the organisation. This is the *sponsored* organisation.

The Market for Sponsors

A market, as a collection of buyers, consists of all those organisations and individuals in need of something. The collection of organisations and individuals in competition for sponsors (funds, resources or services) therefore makes up the market for sponsors. Expenditure in this market worldwide needs to be considered in light of the global growth of sports sponsorship, growing in value from US$1.5 billion in 1989, US$5.5 billion in 1996 and US$10 billion in 1999, to an extrapolated value of approximately US$20 billion in 2005. The United States alone would account for almost half of that amount, of which 85% would be sports-related sponsorship (SportBusiness 2000: 58; Boyle & Haynes 2000: 49).

According to Sports and Recreation Victoria (2000), A$429 million was spent in Australia in 1996, growing to A$519 million in 1998, A$1.16 billion in 1999, A$1.252 billion in 2000, and plateauing at A$1.248 billion (approximately US$700 billion) in 2001 (O'Riordan 2002: 48). This 'plateau' can largely be attributed to the fact that Australia hosted the 2000 Olympic Games. Obviously, sponsorship investments of Australian companies increased dramatically in relation to the Games, returning to more 'natural' levels in 2001. Figures for the United Kingdom indicate a sports sponsorship expenditure of US$500 million in 1998, with expectations that the UK will hit the US$1 billion mark somewhere around 2003. Although these figures are only estimates, it can be argued that this is a huge pool of potential funds for sporting organisations. There are two major trends that have to be taken into consideration before we arrive at a final conclusion about available funds:

1. The move to big event sponsorship; and
2. The growing competition for sponsorship dollars.

As stated earlier, the Sydney Olympic Games exemplified the move to big-event sponsorship in 2000. The Sydney 2000 Games needed to attract close to A$500 million in sponsorship. Local sponsors accounted for A$300 million; the worldwide International Olympic Committee (IOC) TOP sponsors contributed the rest. During the Olympic Games period, local (Australian) companies redirected their sponsorship dollars from local, regional or national sporting organisations to the Olympic Games.

This drained sponsorship budgets of Australian sporting organisations. This happens also with other media-attractive events (e.g. Grand Prix, World Swimming Championships) that are able to attract mass television audiences. In other words, a relatively large portion of sponsorship funds goes to relatively few organisations. Although it will be shown later that even global corporations increasingly attempt to apply their sponsorship locally, it remains a fact that much of the attraction of the sponsorship opportunity lies in its media attractiveness, with the bigger events being the more likely beneficiaries. As a matter of fact, Westerbeek and Smith (2002) observed that 'Sponsors will simply not spend such amounts of money without the committed support of major broadcasters to the event. It is unsurprising therefore that sponsorship of youth sporting events accounts for as little as 0.5% of all sports sponsorship'. The Commercial Economic Advisory Service of Australia (CEASA) found that the top five sponsored sports in Australia are motor racing, Formula One, Australian Rules football, rugby league and horseracing, in that order (O'Riordan 2002).

In the market for sponsors, competition is also increasing. Global figures indicate a rise in sponsorship expenditure with most funds being channelled into sports (85%), but the picture in Australia is much more sobering. Sports and Recreation Victoria (2000) figures indicate that as much as 67% of all Australian-based sponsorship funds in 1996 were spent in industries other than sports. Although expenditure on sponsorship is still growing, the increasing dominance of big sporting events and powerful sporting organisations, and increasing competition from organisations other than sports, are making it more difficult for many (smaller) sporting organisations to attract funds, resources or services through sponsorship.

SPONSORSHIP GOALS: THE RIGHT TO ASSOCIATE

Historically, the sponsorship tool can be seen as a derivative of either advertising or public relations, as elements of the promotion mix, or a combination of the two. Throughout the past decade, however, sponsorship has developed as an independent and important element of the promotion mix. In other words, sponsorship clearly stands apart from other promotion mix elements, potentially to be considered as the dominant promotional tool in a marketing communications programme.

From the sponsor's point of view, the difference between sponsorship and advertising is the actual message communicated, and how the message is communicated. In advertising, the content of the message and the moments of communication are determined by the paying organisation. When using sponsorship, however, the sponsor provides financial or material support for what are often independent organisations, individuals or activities. Less control can be exercised over the communication through these entities, and the timing of communication cannot be controlled. Although indirect (through the sponsored organisation), the actual message is often communicated at a more personal level (e.g. to people visiting an event). These points are returned to when discussing the advantages and disadvantages of sports sponsorship.

Public relations goals such as 'earning understanding and acceptance' and 'creating goodwill' can be sponsorship goals as well. The fact that the organisation has to pay for the association with the sponsored organisation, and that communication takes place through an independent organisation, distinguishes sponsorship from pure public relations. The sponsored organisation is used as the means of communication, which in effect can make sponsorship a public relations tool.

A general goal of sponsorship is described by Wilmshurst (1993: 377). Elements of both advertising and public relations can be found in this goal, which reads: sponsorship is usually undertaken to encourage more favourable attitudes towards the sponsoring company or its products within a relevant target audience, such as consumers, trade customers, employees or the community in which it operates. Earlier in this chapter we described the difference in goal orientation between the sponsoring organisation (sponsor) and sponsored organisation (sponsee). Because the sporting organisation most of the time is the sponsee, neither advertising nor public relations goals seem to fit! In order to obtain sponsors, it is important to know about the sponsor's goals, but sponsee goals are often different.

The reality of the sponsorship opportunity, however, is that what is really bought by the sponsor, as outlined in our definition at the beginning of the chapter, is the right to 'associate'. In other words, the sponsor attempts to forge a connection between the sponsorship property (i.e. event or athlete) and the company or brand. The assumption is that a value transfer from the event or athlete to the company or brand occurs, in the process achieving sponsorship objectives. (We will further introduce this 'image transfer' concept later in this chapter when discussing celebrity marketing.)

For example, a high-profile event can best be used to attract attention to a new brand, a high-profile athlete to generate further interest, a special niche event (e.g. Xtreme Games) to create 'desire' to own the product and, finally, a community-based event to make people buy the product in a convenient and comfortable environment. In other words, sponsorship, when applied to different properties, can be used to achieve a wide range of objectives. (We use the AIDA model again in chapter 14 when we discuss measuring the effect of sponsorship programmes.)

Advantages and Disadvantages of Sports Sponsorship

It was shown above that sponsorship has distinctly different characteristics from other elements of the promotion mix such as advertising and public relations. Sponsorship in a sports context allows the sponsor to communicate more directly and intimately with its target market (in this case the people interested in the sporting organisation and its products). First, sports consumers tend to identify themselves personally with the sports, which creates opportunities for enhancing brand loyalty in products linked to the sports.

Sports evokes personal attachment, and with this the sponsor can be linked to the excitement, energy and emotion of the sporting contest. In other words, sports has the potential to deliver a clear message. Sports has universal appeal and pervades all elements of life (geographically, demogra-phically and socioculturally). This characteristic presents the opportunity to cross difficult cultural and language borders in communication, enabling the sponsor to talk to a (global) mass audience. At the same time the variety in sports available makes it possible to create distinct market segments with which to communicate separately. The universal appeal and strong interest in sports give sports a high media exposure, resulting in free publicity.

Free publicity can make a sponsorship deal very cost-effective. Thousands of dollars in advertising expenditure can be saved when a sporting organisation or athlete attracts a lot of media attention. This makes many organisations want to be associated with sports. Also, because of the clear linkage of the sponsor to a sporting organisation or athlete, sponsorship stands out from the clutter, contrary to mainstream advertising, in which people are bombarded with hundreds of messages each day.

With so many advantages, why do organisations not simply spend their complete promotional budget on sponsorship? Well, there are some disadvantages to be considered before entering into a sponsorship agreement. In ambush marketing, non-sponsors take advantage of the efforts of real sponsors in that they try to be associated with the sponsored organisation, event, product or athlete. Lack of control over media coverage is another disadvantage of sports sponsorship. Also, the media are sometimes reluctant to recognise the sponsor's name when reporting on events or the achievements of athletes. Achievements of teams or athletes are another area that cannot be controlled. A non-performing team or athlete will have direct influence on the perception the public holds of the sponsor. The implications of this for the sponsorship of individual athletes are considered later in this chapter.

Creating Win-win Situations

If both sponsor and sponsee have to benefit from a cooperation, certain goals of both need to be satisfied. The main question that sponsor and sponsee have to ask themselves is: How can we successfully reach our own goals by assisting the sponsor/sponsee to reach their goals? The assumption in the framework is that certain benefits will satisfy certain goals. Those benefits can be delivered only by an entity other than the organisation. If two entities, both in search of benefits to satisfy their own goals, are able to deliver the benefits needed by the other entity, they can become engaged in an exchange of benefits. By exchanging benefits, both organisations 'benefit' from the cooperation; therefore, a win-win situation is created.

It must be noticed though that in today's sporting environment it is often not enough to 'create' a win-win situation and leave it at that. It is rapidly becoming common practice for sponsor and sponsee executives to organise regular strategic-planning meetings, in order to maximise the effectiveness of the sponsorship. During these meetings it is evaluated whether the goals of both the sponsor and sponsee are being reached and whether any new insight and ideas can increase the effectiveness of the sponsorship.

More and more, executives discuss new business opportunities beyond the scope of the (current) sponsorship through which the actual sponsorship can lead into a strategic alliance. A strategic alliance is a commitment and relationship between two organisations from which both organisations hope to benefit. It is now time to examine the conceptual sponsorship framework in practice. There are a variety of issues to consider before a deal can be closed and a win-win situation is created. Now we take a closer look at a typical sports industry sponsee: the individual athlete.

Sponsoring Individual Athletes and Celebrity Marketing

Belch and Belch (1998) suggest that when communicating a message the credibility and attractiveness of the source are of particular importance. Credibility and attractiveness are therefore the concepts to consider when organisations choose to use athletes as their source of communication. Consider this example (Beydemuller & Fiedler 2001: 29): After his third world championship title, Michael Schumacher is established as a cult figure among his fellow countrymen. He has become a license to print money. His incomparable driving skills alone are worth a fee of 46 million Euro per year to the Ferrari team. In addition he earns an estimated 22.5 million Euro from advertising contracts and merchandising. Renowned companies (DVAG, L'Oreal, Omega, Nike, Hilfiger and RTL among others) are investing about 15,300 Euro in the smart smile of the man from the Rhein—per second of each commercial.

Credibility and Attractiveness

Why is Michael Schumacher so successful in conveying the message of so many companies? Why is he such a powerful source? Are there limitations to the credibility and attractiveness of sporting celebrities like Schumacher? To answer these questions, it is first necessary to elaborate on the concepts of credibility and attractiveness. The model shows that when a source is credible and attractive, the message will become more powerful and will have a higher impact on the receiver of the message. This in turn will lead to a positive association with the source and message, eventually leading to a planned change in the perception, awareness or buying behaviour of the receiver. If the source is not credible and attractive, the opposite is more likely to happen.

According to Belch and Belch (1998), a source is credible when it has expertise about the message. When Michael Jordan endorses the sports drink Gatorade, he is a more credible source than golfer John Daly endorsing basketball shoes. It is more likely that Jordan has expertise about the sports drink than that Daly has any about the shoes. A source also becomes more credible when it is trustworthy. Brazilian soccer star Rivaldo will probably be more honest and believable in supporting the wellbeing of the Amazon rainforest than in endorsing the benefits of being a member of the Turkish Automobile Club. Information from credible sources will influence the receiver in that the message communicated will become the opinion of the receiver. This opinion will have an influence on the (buying) behaviour of the receiver.

A source becomes more attractive when there is a similarity between the source and the receiver. The more similarities a person can (or wants to!) identify between the athlete and him/herself, the more likely that person is to be influenced by the message of the athlete. Many juniors aspire 'to be like Mike'. Linking this message to drinking Gatorade, Michael Jordan successfully influences the buying behaviour of many juniors around the world. Likeability is another determinant of attractiveness. Sporting celebrities are admired for their performances and become well known to the public, given the high visibility and hence media coverage of sports. Rather than a plain advertisement, Ferrari uses Michael Schumacher to draw attention to its message, in order to stand out in the very cluttered advertising media.

How important the attractiveness of an athlete is to organisations associated with the athlete is exemplified by golfer Tiger Woods. When the American PGA renegotiated its television contract, it agreed on a new four-year deal worth US$870 million, some US$90 million per annum up from the last deal. It has been argued that Tiger Woods single-handedly is accountable for this rise, and the proof is in the pudding. Sports television ratings in 2000 in the USA showed the PGA tour to be up 22% over the 1999 season. This increase is even more spectacular when compared to the 2000 ratings of the NFL (down 7.2%), Nascar (down 7.3%), the NBA (down 11.9%; Jordan was still in retirement) and the MLB (down 22.2%) (Wilner 2001a). Credibility and attractiveness, however, are influenced by other factors when using an athlete celebrity.

Considerations when Using Athlete Celebrities

Using a single athlete, as opposed to a sporting organisation, team or event, brings with it advantages and disadvantages. The single athlete can stand out in myriad advertising messages, especially when performance is high. Nike athletes like Andre Agassi and Richard Krajicek, both considered huge tennis talents, did not perform up to the expectations of the general public over the longer period. Agassi's world ranking fell to as low as 30, and Krajicek never seemed to perform when it really mattered (in Grand Slam tournaments). Nike even considered discontinuing the agreement until Agassi, with a new coach, became number 1 in the world and Krajicek won Wimbledon in 1996.

Another uncontrollable factor is the personality of the star athlete. Athletes who find it hard to control themselves when they lose, say things to the press they regret later or always seem to run into trouble are risky investments for organisations trying to build a consistent image or sell more products. More recently, Nike seemed to have hit the mark again when Australian tennis star Lleyton Hewitt reached the number 1 position in the world and then won Wimbledon in 2002, after much publicised difficulties controlling his on-court temper and initial struggle to building rapport with audiences. 'Winners are grinners' and, although the performance and personality of athletes cannot be controlled, it can heavily influence their credibility. Organisations also have to realise that young people are more likely to be influenced by athlete celebrities than older people.

Therefore the target publics that organisations want to communicate with by using athlete celebrities have to be carefully selected. When using high-profile celebrities, organisations run the risk that the message or product they want endorsed will be overshadowed by the celebrity. Because high-profile celebrities are attractive to a mass audience, many organisations want them to endorse their messages. This can easily lead to overexposure of the athletes, which will make the messages they communicate less credible. Overexposure is noted when it becomes too obvious that the celebrities are being paid to endorse the message, and the public can become very sceptical.

Marketing Michael

According to Forbes magazine, in 1995 Michael Jordan received more than US$40 million for endorsing such products as Nike basketball shoes, Big Macs, Gatorade, cars for Chicago-area Chevy dealers, basketballs for Wilson, lottery tickets for the state of Illinois, calendars, school suppliesand greeting cards, underwearfor Hanesand Oakley sunglasses (part of this deal with Oakley was a seat on the board). His alignment with Wheaties is so strong that the cereal's manufacturer, General Foods, has printed a special edition Wheaties box with Jordan and the Chicago Bulls on the cover. When the Bulls won the NBA title in June 1996, Michael Jordan Wheaties boxes were in supermarkets within hours. It seems Wheaties needs Jordan more than he needs the cereal. Its share of the $US7.9 billion ready-to-eat cereal market is only 1.6%. The idea of having to do without Jordan is a nightmare for General Foods. Jordan's endorsement power, which barely waned during his two seasons of retirement, continues to grow. *Forbes* estimates that since 1990, when he started getting major product endorsements, he has earned $170 million as a 'pitch man' (Hay 1996:18).

David Falk, Jordan's marketing agent from ProServ says, 'we haven't packaged Michael Jordan, we have done a good job exposing who he is and what he is to corporate decision makers. Once they saw what he was firsthand, the rest flowed from there'. It was clear from the beginning that Jordan was a made-for-the-media athlete. He had natural ability to communicate, to provide intelligent answers to questions, to delicately handle the tough questions.

The 1984 Olympic gold medal enhanced Jordan's image as an all-American kid, and unlike other Olympic heroes, his star only has risen from there. His visibility was a key factor in reversing the declining fortunes of the NBA in the 1980s and when Nike and Jordan developed the first Air Jordan basketball shoes, Jordan told his former roommate at the University of North Carolina to 'better get some Nike stock; they are going to make a shoe for me, these Air Jordans, and someday it's going to be worth a lot of money'. At Nike the director of design, after releasing the Air Jordan No. 6 says, 'one of the things about Michael Jordan is we can take incredible risks in the product because his wearing them validates it. The fact that Michael Jordan is wearing this plain-toed shoe will make it all right for a lot of people'.

Jordan's fame presents him with a range of moral dilemmas. In 1989, kids began murdering one another for the $115 sneakers that bore his name. Jordan was first informed about sneaker violence by Sports *Illustrated* reporter Rick Telander, whose May 14, 1990, cover story 'senseless' helped focus attention and sharpen debate on the issue. 'I thought I'd be helping out others and everything would be positive', a visibly shaken Jordan told Telander. 'I thought people would try to emulate the good things I do, they'd try to achieve, to do better. Nothing bad. It is kind of ironic, though, that the press builds people like me up to be a role model and then blames us for the unfortunate crimes kids are committing'.

Although Jordan's image has suffered some minor damage in 1993, when rumours regarding selfishness, aloofness and serious gambling problems surfaced, David Falk remains confident his client will remain among the few celebrity legends, who will not lose their public appeal.

Although Michael will lose the principal platform from which he addresses the public, he will not fade into obscurity. It is assumed that when you stop playing the impact dramatically goes a way. Quickly because you are not in the public eye. In his case I don't think that is going to be the situation at all. I think he is going to be very much before the public eye, and he is still going to be doing Nike commercials and other commercials. (Naughton 1992:11-29)

In the NBA of 2002 though, Michael is still pulling in the crowds and his consistent high performance keeps him at the top of the list of the most ubiquitous endorsers of our time. Michaels' new team, the Washington Wizards, suddenly sell out all their matches, both at home and on the road, and before Jordan's return became official, NBC [television] didn't have the Wizards on their schedule, and Turner had Washington just once. Now, the Wizards plan to make the maximum number of appearances on both networks—11 on NBC, 15 on Turner—with NBC actually planning to shuffle its entire schedule and occasionally televise Jordan and the Wizards in prime time (Wilner2001:15).

The Integrated Marketing Approach

Sponsorship support activities complement the sponsor's goals. Given the sponsorship framework, the sponsee can either supply support activities or participate in support activities in order to chance the value of the sponsorship for the sponsor. Examples of different sponsorship support activities are given below. Fuji Xerox Australia, as an Olympic sponsor, serves as a case example, presented from the sponsor's point of view.

Sponsorship Support Activities

A personal letter (direct mail) notified business relations that, on 5 September 1995, Fuji Xerox Australia would host a special Olympic event in the central business district of Melbourne. The media were informed through a press release (publicity), and around 400 general managers and marketing managers of a variety of organisations were invited to the Victorian Arts Centre to witness and participate in Fuji Xerox's Olympic sponsorship launch. A well-organised introductory show, in which the Olympic flame was lit, led into a video presentation of Australia's Olympic achievements throughout the years. The motivator of the Australian Olympic team, Mr Laurie Lawrence, followed the video presentation and entertained the crowd with sports stories in which the importance of teamwork was stressed. Fuji Xerox's marketing manager then highlighted his organisation's commitment to the Olympic team, enabling Australian athletes to represent their country.

Four Olympic athletes were honoured and awarded before a variety of new Fuji Xerox products were introduced. Guests were invited to take drinks and food after the formal presentation and to see the new products in action in the different demonstration areas (personal selling). Different Olympic prizes were given away by the present Olympic athletes, and every guest deciding to buy Fuji Xerox products in the following weeks automatically entered the draw for a trip to the Atlanta Games in 1996 (sales promotion). Opportunities for interviews and photo sessions were given after the event (public relations). In the months following the Olympic launch several television commercials and newspaper advertisements backed up the Olympic sponsor involvement of Fuji Xerox.

Sponsoring Internationally but Making it Works Locally

Cousens and Slack (1996) state that sports sponsorship can be a very effective tool to enhance corporate image at the international level. However, consumer awareness of the fact that McDonald's was the sponsor of the 1994 World Cup of the World Soccer Federation (FIFA) might not have been enough to strengthen consumer demand at the local level. McDonald's franchisees needed to have the opportunity to leverage the sponsorship to make it work in their local store. For example, McDonald's, as the sole retail sponsor of the World Cup, was able to feature the games in its restaurants. It organised local franchise-backed soccer tournaments and hosted local McKicks mobile soccer clinics. Although optional for franchisees, these local tie-in promotions proved to be very successful in boosting sales, developing relationships with the local community and targeting new market segments.

An Olympic sponsor since 1986, VISA has gained a reputation as one of the most successful sponsors of sports in the world. The credit card business is extremely fragmented when considering the face-to-face communication with customers. VISA has 1.2 billion cardholders worldwide, who obtain their cards through one of the 21,000 member financial institutions. VISA is responsible for some US$2 trillion in business. As an Olympic sponsor it has to create alliances with local partners in order to talk to (potential) customers, both on the Olympic site and through the various media outlets. In Salt Lake City, VISA created partnerships with the Salt Lake Visitors and Convention Bureau as early as 1996.

It further aligned with the local Chamber of Commerce, Ski Utah, Park City, Deer Valley and the USA ski team. Many banks have historically not been involved with the Olympic Games, yet VISA managed to convince twelve of the USA's largest banks to become active Olympic VISA marketers, representing 80% of the financial market in the USA: Throughout the world, thousands of member banks are running marketing programmes which utilise Olympic branding and messages. Millions of VISA cards now bear the famous five rings and the presence of Olympic branding at point of sale further cements the relationship (Roberts 2002: 22-3). Smaller sponsorships (e.g. the local bakery sponsoring the local hockey club) can be leveraged according to the same principle: tie-in promotions making customers aware of the association between sponsor and sponsee.

The above examples show the importance of leveraging the sponsorship through support activities and tie-in promotions. If sponsorship is seen as a single, separate tool, benefits resulting from it will be much less. Leveraging the sponsorship is as much in the interest of the sporting organisation as it is in the interest of the sponsor. An unsuccessful sponsorship deal is less likely to be renewed, leaving the sporting organisation without a sponsor. When the sporting organisation is able to supply or participate in support activities, sponsorship will more successfully operate as part of the total promotion and marketing plan. This ultimately will lead to a win-win situation. To distinguish a win situation from a not-win situation, it is important for the sports marketer to measure the effectiveness of sponsorship. Now we take a brief look at some of the current trends in relation to sports sponsorship.

Current Trends in Sports Sponsorship

The first sports sponsorship trend is the move from sponsoring the big, established sports to the new, exciting, up-and-coming sports. For example, extreme sports such as skateboarding, inline skating, surfing and snowboarding offer affordable sponsorship opportunities, especially when compared with the established global sports. The 'new' sports also boast a highly identified and segmented following. In other words, 'niche' sports offer excellent opportunities for sponsors to talk one-on-one with a target market, because the segmentation information that is available about the target market is much more specific than the bigger sports mass market segments. The extension of exploiting 'niche' market opportunities through sponsorship relates to another interesting trend, so-called sponsor-funded programming.

The increasing demand for quality content by broadcasters has been identified as a new opportunity for sponsors. Rather than broadcasters funding and producing sports programming, sponsors become partners in this process. For example, the Trans World Sports programme, often screened as part of in-flight entertainment, is now called Samsung World Sports. One of the major disadvantages of sponsorship—the perceived lack of control over the sponsored property—can now largely be overcome because the sponsor becomes a co-producer. It has even been suggested that a consortium of sponsors may become involved in the bidding process for broadcast rights in order to obtain complete control over the production of their sponsored property (*SportBusiness International* 2002).

Another important generic marketing trend that is emerging is the move from 'commercial' marketing approaches to 'cause-related' marketing approaches. This trend may be considered in the 'ethics' or 'corporate social responsibility' framework. In the context of sponsorship, the move to cause-related marketing is critical for sports organisations in particular. Big corporate sponsors increasingly are looking for opportunities to show to their customers that 'they care', especially after corporate scandals such as Enron and Worldcom in the United States, or the corporate collapses of insurer HIH and Ansett Airlines in Australia.

The general public demands evidence of corporations (sponsors and sponsees!) that they are 'good corporate citizens', that they behave ethically, and that they give back to the communities they receive from. Sports organisations should therefore carefully balance their on-the-field ambitions with those in the world outside the arena. On-field success requires significant resources to pay the superstars responsible for victory, in turn raising the price for fans at the gate and through pay-television subscriptions. The latter may damage the public's (fans') opinion about the sports organisation, ultimately leading to a decline in attractiveness as a vehicle for sponsorship because the sports organisation is not viewed as an exemplar of community friendliness. Hence, sponsors may direct their marketing resources to organisations such as the Salvation Army or UNICEF. In other words, sports is no longer the natural 'number 1' choice of sponsors.

Finally, some soccer clubs in Europe are exploring new opportunities through the application of virtual advertising technology to shirt sponsorship. Some of the clubs that have signed players from different continents are keen to offer virtual shirt sponsorships to different markets. Viewers in Asia will see Feyenoord's Japanese star player Shinji Ono promoting a Japanese brand (in Japanese writing), whereas hometown fans were exposed to the current sponsor, a local insurance company. According to the experts, though, the technology needs at least a few more years of maturing before it is ready to be exploited through virtual shirt sponsorship (Hancock, 2001).

For both sponsor and sponsee, sponsorship can be used to satisfy multiple goals, particularly advertising-and public relations-related for the sponsor and fundraising-related for the sponsee. The relationship between the goals of sponsor and sponsee were shown in the sponsorship framework for how to create win-win situations. Relationships between sponsor and sponsee can even lead to a strategic alliance between the two organisations. Sponsorship as a tool of the promotion mix is still growing in popularity because it is generally seen as a cost-effective manner of achieving the sponsor's communication goals. Because of the high visibility and attractiveness of sports as a communication medium, many sporting organisations tend to overemphasise the importance of sponsorship as a potential source of income.

Sporting organisations should be aware that this 'sponsorship myopia' can lead to an underusage of the other elements of the marketing mix in developing a broad-based marketing programme. From the sponsor's point of view, sponsorship alone will not satisfy the communication goals set. A comprehensive set of sponsorship support activities and tie-in promotions is required to optimise the sponsorship effort and make the sponsorship as successful as possible in the overall marketing effort. Sponsoring individual athletes has distinct advantages and disadvantages. The sponsorathlete relationship is similar to the sponsor-sporting organisation relationship in that both involve mutual commitment and obligations. Sponsorship support activities need to be considered in both relationships.

CHAPTER 14

Measuring Sponsorship Effectiveness

As we have already indicated, how effective a sponsorship is, or has been, depends on the goals the sponsor and sponsee have set before they enter the sponsorship agreement. For example, Heineken has different goals when sponsoring the Australian Open Tennis Championships from those when sponsoring the Heineken Classic golf tournament. The goal at the tennis is global attention-related, whereas the goal at the golf is more related to direct sales—through, for example, business relationship marketing activities.

How the public perceives the association between sponsor and sponsee determines what can be measured as the effect of the sponsorship. If, for example, the public links the name of the sponsor only to the event, and does not change its buying behaviour, it makes little sense to measure after-sponsorship sales. In this section, it is assumed that the overall effectiveness of the sponsorship is based on the achievement of the sponsor's goals. Achievement of sponsee goals are partly met at the agreement of the sponsorship (i.e. receiving funds, goods or services). Other goals, like brand positioning, can be measured in a similar fashion to the sponsor's goals. Hansen and Scotwin (1995) identify four levels of measuring sponsorship effectiveness:

- Exposure;
- Attention;
- Cognition; and
- Bbehaviour.

As is shown in the case study, exposure is the broadest measure of sponsorship effectiveness. It measures how many times (in seconds on television, or number of columns and photographs in print media) an organisation or brand is observable. Television exposure, for example, is measured by multiplying seconds by the number of viewers; hence exposure is expressed in 'exposure per 1000 viewers in 30 seconds'. Exposure value can be compared with advertising value by multiplying seconds (30) by advertising rates for 30-second commercials. The resulting value presents the sponsor with the money figure that would have been paid had the sponsor invested the money in 30-second commercials.

However, there are significant problems with these measures of effectiveness. For example, how do we know that viewing a 30-second commercial equals the value of viewing 30 seconds of scattered brand exposure throughout an event broadcast? This problem is compounded when one realises how hard it is to accurately measure the number of viewers. These problems relate to the fact that exposure is one thing, but what really matters is the impact of exposure.

In other words, volume of exposure is only the start of measuring the effect of sponsorship. A better measure of impact is how much attention people pay to a brand or an organisation. Attention can be measured in terms of changes in recall or recognition by individual target-market members. Recall is the more powerful measure of effectiveness in that research subjects are not aided in recalling sponsors' names. In recognition, subjects are asked to choose from a list of possible sponsors. The benchmark for attention measures has to be the recall or recognition measure before entering the sponsorship agreement. This may be achieved through pre-testing. Otherwise, changes in recall or recognition cannot be measured.

Cognitive effects also can be measured in individuals who are part of the target markets of the sponsor. The association between a car manufacturer and a car-racing event evokes a stronger cognitive effect than the association between a car manufacturer and a tennis event. The car manufacturer-car race link is logical and requires little explanation. The car manufacturer-tennis event link is expected to evoke a more general association, and tries to link the image of the event to the image of the car. Both effects are often measured in associative tests.

For example, given the Australian Open tennis championships, the question 'Which sponsors do you associate with this event?' can be asked. One can even consider using research techniques that compare attitudes people have about different brands, including the brands that compete with the sponsor. Tracking studies, where factors such as the brand image are researched over an extended period of time, also fit the category of measuring cognitive effects. Cognitive tests are better described as qualitative research techniques because they deliver information that allows the researcher to explain consumer behaviour, rather than the quantified measures that result from media monitoring. Cognitive research becomes more important towards the 'desire' and 'action' stages of buyer readiness.

The most direct measure of sponsorship effectiveness is buying behaviour. What are the effects of the sponsorship on attitudes towards buying, or even the direct sales figures or turnover of the organisation, or the sales figures of certain product lines? In this case, the benchmark for measurement has to be set before the sponsorship. Behavioural measurement of sponsorship has often been criticised because of the difficulties in isolating the effects of sponsorship on sales and turnover from those of other promotion mix tools. Experimental research designs or historical analysis of prior promotion impact may help the researcher to isolate the impact of sponsorship investment. Measurement of sponsorship effectiveness is a difficult issue. How effectiveness is measured strongly depends on the goals of the sponsor, and even then many variables can influence effectiveness. One of the most important variables to influence sponsorship effectiveness is the choice of the sponsored object or sponsorship property.

The Sponsorship Properties: Events and Athletes

It can be argued that there are literally hundreds of sponsorship opportunities, including sponsoring the name or title of an event or stadium, broadcast sponsorship, location sponsorship (e.g. the fifteenth green), leader board sponsorship, corporate hospitality suites, athletic outfit sponsorship (e.g. shoes, apparel)—the list goes on. It is largely up to the creativity of sports marketers to come up with new ways of packaging 'rights to associate with' for sponsors to buy and use. Irrespective of how this is done, the majority of sponsored properties in sports can be categorised either as events or athletes. As we noted earlier, what principally determines the success of the sponsorship is the amount of exposure received, and the impact exposure has on the sponsorship objectives. Geographic diffusion of the sports property really relates to the diffusion of appeal of the sports: in other words, do a broad selection of people know about and like the sports, or is the potential audience narrowly defined? Geographic distribution and sports diffusion are used as the key drivers of (potential) sponsorship.

The SPONSEFFECT Model

It has been noted that the formulation of specific sponsorship objectives is critical when selecting the right sponsorship entity, in turn affecting the different measures to be used when assessing the effectiveness of the sponsorship partnership. We have also argued that both objectives and effectiveness measures are strongly linked to the buyer readiness sequence. The practical value of the AIDA model lies in its strong focus on moving consumers from being unaware of a product to buying it.

Ultimately sponsorship is about only one thing bringing as many customers to the sponsor's company and enabling them to buy as many products as possible, preferably many, many times! In reality, the stages of attention, interest and desire are therefore quite awkward. We don't want consumers to be in those stages for too long. As can be observed from the model, it is much harder to define clearcut objectives and sponsorship properties for the interest and desire stages than it is for the attention and action stages. It is therefore very important to remember that the mid-stages of buyer readiness are transitory. In the SPONSEFFECT all these issues are summarised. The model can be used by sponsors and sponsees to assist them in planning and executing sponsorship agreements. We briefly introduce the concept of ambush marketing here, because it may strongly influence the effectiveness of the sponsorship deal, from the perspective of both sponsor and sponsee.

Ambush Marketing

The Australian *Trade Practices Act 1974* defines ambush marketing in an indirect manner under Section 53 as follows: A corporation shall not, in trade or commerce, in connection with the supply or possible supply of goods or services or in connection with the promotion by any means of the supply or use of goods or services: (c) represent that goods or services have sponsorship, approval, performance characteristics, accessories, uses or benefits they do not have; (d) represent that the corporation has a sponsorship, approval or affiliation it does not have.

Ambush marketing is a problem for the sponsor in that funds or services are invested in an association with a sporting organisation of which non-investing organisations reap the benefits. Ambush marketing is a problem for the sponsee in that the effectiveness of the sponsorship will diminish and a prolonged business relationship with the sponsor will be put in jeopardy. More and more, sponsors are demanding that sponsees take precautions to prevent ambush marketing. In servicing the sponsor, sponsees should therefore take a proactive stance in preparing for potential 'ambushers'. A proactive strategy can consist of the following actions:

- Identification of potential ambushers (these are often potential sponsors the sporting organisation did not sign up);
- Identification of the commercial value of the sponsorship (which benefits the sponsee can deliver, and how potential ambushers can obtain these benefits without being involved as an official sponsor);
- Detailed contracts (including exclusivity rights, detailed descriptions of what is being considered as conflicting signage/advertising, sponsor/sponsee obligations to prevent ambush marketing); and
- Joint sponsor/sponsee counteract strategies (which determine how sponsor and sponsee will react in terms of public relations, advertising—for example buying 'strategic' media time during potential 'ambush time slots'—or public appearances when commenting on an ambusher's actions).

This is a limited and certainly not complete list of actions to prevent ambushers from taking advantage of a sponsorship relationship. Although ambush marketing can never be eliminated, solid preparation can assist sports marketers in servicing the sponsor to the best of their ability. It needs to be noted that ambush marketing, in the context of 'ethics' in sports marketing, increasingly is an activity that is viewed as unethical behaviour. Consumers are increasingly aware of and sensitive to 'corporate abusive practices', ambushing being an obvious example. In the very near future 'to ambush' may not be worth the effort. Behaving in a societally responsible manner may prove to be the best marketing medicine of them all.

Ambush Marketing at the Olympics

The Olympic Games attract global interest and can deliver tremendous exposure. Billions of spectators watched the combined 1988 Summer and Winter Olympics and many corporations would therefore like to benefit from the exposure of being associated directly or indirectly with the Olympic Games. Research evaluating the effectiveness of sponsorship and ambush marketing at the 1988 Olympic Winter Games investigated the recall and recognition of official sponsors, ambushers and other organisations. The large drawing power of the Olympics was evidenced by the fact that 82 per cent of the people surveyed watched some part of the Olympic telecast. Of the respondents, 41.4 per cent were light viewers (watched one to four days), 27.2 per cent were moderate viewers (five to nine days) and 31.3 per cent were heavy viewers (ten to sixteen days).

Overall, 20 per cent of the respondents correctly recalled the official sponsors, with recall varying by product category: from 50 per cent correct for credit cards to 7 per cent for airlines. Recognition (choosing from a list with names) of sponsors was higher, with 39 per cent of respondents correctly recognising offical sponsors. Recognition also varied by product category, from a high 59 per cent for fast foods to 25 per cent for hotels. To determine the effect of viewing the Olympic telecast on consumer perceptions, the three viewer groups were used to analyse sponsor awareness. The ability to both recognise and recall sponsors varied directly with viewership: light viewers averaged 18.9 per cent correct recall, moderate viewers 33.5 per cent and heavy viewers 37.5 per cent. For recognition, the numbers ranged from 37 per cent to 46 per cent to 52.2 percent.

Ambush marketers attempt to avoid the up-front high investment of sponsorship while gaining the glamour and benefits of an Olympic tie-in; their hope is that consumers associate their products with the Olympic Games and thus weaken any major advantage of their competitors who paid for official sponsorship. To determine the effect that ambushers had on sponsorship awareness, the number of correct sponsor identifications were compared with the number of ambushers as sponsors. Seven product categories, each with one official sponsor and one major ambusher, were chosen. The results for recall and recognition were aggregated. Across the overall sample an average of 2.57 official sponsors were correctly identified (out of a possible seven). In comparison, on average 1.43 ambushers were identified as official sponsors. Ambushers were significantly less recognised as official sponsors.

A closer look at these data by product category, however, leads to some interesting cautions for advertisers. In only four out of seven product categories studied were the correct official sponsors identified more than the non-sponsors (ambushers and others). In the other three cases the sponsor was not number one when it came to sponsor identification; in two of these three cases the official sponsors, while engaging in other promotional activities, were not major advertisers on the Olympic telecast, and in the third case (cars), the ambushers were engaged in very heavy advertising (Ford and Chrysler bought all available advertising time for domestic cars). This might indicate that to achieve any benefits from being a sponsor it is necessary not only for a company to sponsor an event such as the Olympics but to heavily advertise the fact that they are *official sponsors*. Buying the right to be an "official sponsor" may, in reality, only be buying a licence to spend more money!

Atlanta 1996 Olympic sponsors did everything within their power to combat the ambush strategies of competitors. But it seems that ambushers are always one step ahead of their 'official partner' competition. Nike, as the pre-eminent ambusher in Atlanta, achieved great exposure through building-high billboards and 'precinct theming', to the extent that parts of the inner city were transformed into Nike town suburbs. Although Nike was gladly accepted into the Olympic sponsorship family of Sydney 2000 when Reebok decided to discontinue its relationship with the five rings, the IOC had learned its lesson the hard way. The Salt Lake City Organising Committee (SLOC) installed a 'Brand Protection Programme', obtaining a permit from city authorities to close all streets directly connected with the Salt Lake Ice Centre and the Olympic Medals Plaza.

The streets of Salt Lake became an Olympic venue in their own right, 100% controlled by SLOC. To prevent ambushers from using tall buildings as advertising banners, the SLOC launched a 'Cityscape Programme'. Through negotiations with building owners, nominal fee contracts were drawn up allowing the SLOC to completely wrap the buildings in Games-related imagery. If space could not be leased, the contract stated that building owners would not lease the space to anybody for the duration of the Olympic Games. Life for an ambusher is becoming increasingly difficult!

Location Dependency of Sponsorship

In this final section it is appropriate to reflect on the increasing specialisation in regard to sponsorship as a promotional tool. Here we would like to introduce the concept of 'location dependency' as a special characteristic of sports sponsorship. Westerbeek (2000) tested the hypothesis: 'revenue maximisation of tenants of sports facilities is dependent on geographical location of the facility (location of distribution)'. Revenue maximisation was operationalised pertaining to sponsorship. A survey instrument was sent to all sponsors of a Melbourne-based football club.

Sponsors were grouped as location-dependent and location independent based on the location of their head office and financial turnover achieved in the area around the sports facility. The survey collected information on three different steps in the sports consumption process, including 'coming to the sports facility', 'being in and around the sports facility' and 'being serviced in the sports facility'. Indicative evidence was found in support of the general hypothesis. Smaller, low-spending sponsors with an important percentage of turnover in the area around the sports facility were less likely to move with the football club to a (remote) new facility. In relation to sponsors' objectives, it was found that objectives of location-dependent sponsors are directed more towards direct sales, whereas location-independent sponsors' objectives seem to be indirectly related to sales and more towards obtaining exposure.

In a follow-up study, Westerbeek and Smith (2002) found that location-dependent organisations had fewer employees, and spent less on sponsorship, and on sponsoring sports in particular, than their location-independent counterparts. Where location-dependent organisations predominantly operated in metropolitan or state territories, location-independent organisations operated largely on a domestic or international level. Location-dependent sponsors perceive issues in relation to 'location' of the sports facility (such as an attractive environment, close proximity to head office, distribution outlets and major residential areas) to be significantly more important than do location-independent sponsors.

Location independent sponsors perceive 'corporate exposure' issues (such as quality television coverage of the game, frequent telecasts from the stadium and excellent corporate hospitality facilities at the stadium) to be significantly more important than do location-dependent sponsors. The location dependency of sponsorship shows that the complexity of effectiveness measurement will only grow, when sponsors become aware of how they would like to maximise their sponsorship investment.

A range of measures that can be used to measure the effectiveness of sponsorship were introduced, discussed in direct relation to the sponsor's objectives, and placed in the buyer readiness continuum. Following the measures of effectiveness it was argued that the amount of exposure and the potential impact of this exposure will make sponsors decide which sponsorship properties they can consider purchasing. Ultimately, sponsorship effectiveness is a combination of choosing a suitable sponsorship properly, setting specific objectives that can be fitted to the buyer readiness continuum and linking this to the appropriate qualitative or quantitative effectiveness measures. In order to further protect the sponsorship rights, ambush-marketing opportunities need to be detected in order to prepare for potential ambushers taking advantage of the sponsor's rights.

CHAPTER

The Importance of Public Relations

DEFINING PUBLIC RELATIONS

Griswold (1995: 7) defines public relations as: the management function which evaluates public attitudes, identifies the policies and procedures of an individual or an organisation with the public interest, and plans and executes a programme of action to earn public understanding and acceptance. Three critical activities can be derived from this definition:

- Evaluating public attitudes;
- Identifying the policies and procedures of an individual or an organisation with the public interest; and
- Planning and executing a programme of action.

EVALUATING PUBLIC ATTITUDES

Marketing research techniques are also used in identifying and evaluating the attitudes that publics have towards the sporting organisation, its products and its employees (often the athletes). In order to communicate effectively, however, it is important not only to identify public attitudes but also to convey these attitudes to the management of the organisation.

Management can then adjust organisational strategies to more effectively influence public attitudes. If, for example, the local soccer club is suddenly losing members, attitudinal research might find that members did not understand why the club sold the league's top scorer to a rival club and sebsequently cancelled their memberships. With this information, management of the soccer club could put public relations strategies in place to improve members' understanding of this decision. Public relations objectives and their relationship to promotion and marketing objectives. Because public relations is part of the promotion mix, and the promotion mix is part of the marketing mix, it is obvious that marketing objectives are the basis for both promotion and public relations objectives. Returning to the soccer example, one of the club's marketing objectives might be to boost memberships by 10% in the next year. A promotion objective to support the marketing objective might be to sign up at least fifteen new youth members during a weekend shopping-mall promotion.

This objective could more easily be achieved if the club had a favourable image over three other soccer clubs in the area. A public relations objective therefore might be to become the preferred soccer club in the area with 75% of the population. If this percentage were not reached (e.g. as a result of selling the top scorer), a public relations programme of action might help the promotion and marketing activities to become more successful. In general, the following broad public relations objectives can be formulated to support promotion and marketing objectives:

- Earning understanding and acceptance for organisational activities;
- Explaining certain behaviour;

- Educating and informing publics;
- Raising awareness for the organisation or new products;
- Creating trust (in the organisation or its products); and
- Creating goodwill.

These objectives show that most public relations objectives, and hence activities, will not be aimed directly at increasing sales or, in the soccer example, increasing memberships. Linked to the other marketing functions in the organisation, public relations becomes part of an integrated marketing approach. This integrated approach should lead to a more efficient and effective achievement of overall marketing objectives. To know where to start, the organisation needs to be aware of public opinion about the organisation and its product range.

Public Opinion

Evaluating public attitudes has been defined above as one of the critical activities of the public relations function. Seitel (1995: 52) defines an attitude as an evaluation people make about specific problems or issues. A public then is a group of people who share an evaluation about specific problems or issues. When certain group attitudes become important and strong enough, they turn into opinions. Opinions about certain issues can lead to behaviour.

It is the opinion of the larger public that influences the buying behaviour of target markets. Consider the following example by Rhoden (1993: Bll); By the summer of 1993, Michael Jordan, the most widely recognised athlete in the world, had begun to develop serious public opinion problems. After leading the U.S. Dream Team to an Olympic victory and then his Chicago Bulls to an unprecedented third straight National Basketball Association title, Jordan was the focus of nasty rumours regarding selfishness, aloofness, and serious gambling problems. Then, late in the summer of 1993, tragedy struck. Jordan's father, James, was found murdered in his car. The nation mourned with Michael. Scarcely two months later, in the midst of major league baseball's playoffs, Michael Jordan stunned the world by announcing his retirement from basketball. The news was so jarring that President Clinton even took time out to address a statement of support to Michael. In the space of one traumatic quarter of the year, Michael Jordan's public opinion ratings had rebounded from questionable to sky high.

It was in the commercial interest of the multiple organisations that Michael Jordan was associated with to turn the negative public opinion around. Since his second return to the game of basketball, not many people in cities other than Washington will become season ticket holders of the Wizards (they are a public, not a target market), but their opinion about Jordan and hence the Washington Wizards will influence Washington citizens to affiliate with the Wizards. Not many senior citizens will consider drinking Gatorade (a sports drink endorsed by Jordan) because Jordan does (they are a public, not a target market), but their opinion of Jordan will influence young people in their decision to drink Gatorade.

In other words, public opinion highly influences the buying behaviour of target markets and therefore becomes one of the primary areas of public relations activity. Reinforcing existing positive public opinions and changing negative public opinions are the underlying aims of all public relations strategies. Depending on marketing objectives and public opinion, certain publics will become the target audience for public relations activities. ANZAC Day 1995, as introduced in the headline story, was the catalyst for the AFL to recognise issues associated with racial vilification. It also understood that this was a significant social issue that had the potential to polarise the community. The AFL had to take action, and it had to work at shaping public opinion about the sensitivity of the issue and how it was to be managed.

PUBLICS OF SPORTING ORGANISATIONS

Target market implies a focus on exchange between the sporting organisation and its customers. It was shown above that publics have a much wider scope. The Michael Jordan example showed that the public at large can be the target audience of public relations activities without being a target market. In other cases, such as a product recall after a manufacturing mistake, the target market may be the target audience Reactive public relations: Why have we done the things we've done? Reactive public relations actions are put in place when unplanned events occur that negatively influence the attitudes of the organisation's publics. Preventing the problem is always better than fixing the problem, but sometimes even careful planning does not prevent things from happening. Sporting organisations and their athletes receive high-level attention from the media and hence are more likely than other organisations or persons to become involved in crisis situations. Just consider the ongoing saga of the racial vilification case. It can be argued that a crisis, like a positive drug test or racial abuse, might be expected and prepared for.

During major events like the Olympic Games, national sporting bodies know that the chances of athletes being caught using banned drugs are much higher. How can a sporting organisation employ a proactive public relations strategy in preparing for a crisis situation? Sporting organisations cannot always prevent a crisis from happening, but anticipation and preparation will reduce the damage.

Ethics

Seitel (1995: 121) defines an individual's or organisation's ethics as the 'standards that are followed in relationships with others—the real integrity of the individual or organisation'. If one of the most important goals of the public relations function is to enhance public trust in an organisation, clearly the public relations professional must act in an honest and trustworthy manner. Linking the policies and procedures of the organisation to the public interest means that no other organisation or individual should be harmed by the actions of the organisation. Spreading rumours about rival athletes or clubs not based on facts, to enhance one's own image, is therefore unethical behaviour. Bribing the media to report favourably on important issues is also unethical behaviour. Much can be written about this topic. The bottom line is that, in the interest of the publics and the organisation, honest information and genuine procedures will benefit most in both the short and long run.

Media Relations

It is the task of the sports marketer to influence public opinion in order to create a favourable image of the sporting organisation. In this decade of globalisation and booming communications technology, the media, communicating to a global mass audience, are unequivocally the most powerful means of influencing the public opinion. This is both good and bad for sporting organisations: good because, as we discuss later in this chapter, sporting organisations receive a lot of free publicity; bad because the content and timing of this free publicity cannot be controlled. This makes sporting organisations dependent on the media. This dependency, however, can be managed to a certain extent. This is done through fostering media relations. To create and maintain favourable media relations, three actions are important to consider:

- Form;
- Inform;
- Be informal.

Depending on the type of sporting organisation and its strategies, certain media channels are more important than others. The local tennis club, for example, will benefit more from local newspaper coverage and local radio, whereas a Grand Slam tennis tournament will need global television and newspaper coverage to satisfy sponsor needs. That is why a comprehensive form of potential media outlets has to be put together. This form, or media database, will enable the sports marketer to inform the media. This is done through formal channels, but communication may also be successful if informal communication can be developed with media representatives. Different ways of how to form, inform and be informal are now discussed.

Planning and Executing a Programme of Action

Once the sports marketer has identified the attitudes of the sporting organisation's publics, and thought of ways of linking their interests to the activities of the organisation, it is time to develop a programme of action. With the media as one of the sports marketer's most powerful means of communication, a large part of this section will be devoted to public relations communication through the media. To start this process, it is first necessary to know which media are available and how to get in contact with them. Form—the media database Helitzer (1996) lists three main sources that have to be included in the sporting organisation media database:

- The media that routinely cover sports;
- Personal contacts; and
- Media directories.

These sources have to be categorised in a logical order. This is, the media outlets and contacts must be ordered according to the most relevant publics for individual sporting organisations. Contact persons and addresses are vital and should be updated regularly.

Form—the Communications Plan

Planning communications is nothing more (and nothing less!) than putting together a plan of what to tell which media when. As previously discussed, proactive public relations communications should support the promotion and marketing goals of the sporting organisation. In relation to setting goals for the organisation, public relations action plans can be put together and, with the help of the database, distribution of information can be planned.

Returning to the soccer example cited earlier in this chapter, when aiming to become the preferred soccer club in the area with 75% of the population, the local television station, regional newspaper 1 and community newsletters can be selected as the preferred media outlets. The local television station is targeted (once) for the finals at the end of the season, regional newspaper 1 is approached every week in relation to the weekend's results, and the community newsletters are targeted at least twice during the season in every suburb, with information about youth activities at the club. Simple planning boards can be used to create a comprehensive annual overview of planned communications.

Inform: The Press Release

Press releases, as a means of informing the media, can be used for long-term proactive, short-term proactive and reactive public relations. Many organisations issue press releases on any topic of interest for one or more of their publics. The main goal of the press release is to inform the publics through the media in the way the organisation wants. Ideally, it will generate positive publicity for the sporting organisation or sports persons. A few standard rules apply to the format of press releases:

- Use a catching and informative short title.
- Present the backbone information in the first paragraphs. Answer the questions who, what, when, where, why and how.
- Put facts first. Give accurate information. Use correct grammar.
- Include the name and address of a contact person.

- Use current media contacts and addresses when sending the press release.
- State the source of the press release, and date it.

The major causes of rejection of some press releases are: limited reader interest;

- Poorly written;
- Conflicts with media outlet policies;
- Hard to distinguish from advertising;
- Material obviously faked or exaggerated;
- Apparent inaccuracies in story; and
- Duplicates story previously used.

If an issue is important enough to create widespread media attention, a press release can be used to announce a press conference. Inform—the press conference. A press conference presents the sporting organisation with the opportunity to inform all present media at once. Also, when media representatives consider the issue of the conference important enough to attend, it is very likely that some kind of publicity will be the result. When the media attend, they often use the provided information. Conference organisers should realise that, besides printed publicity, photographs and audiovisual information also will be collected by the media. This has implications for who the spokesperson will be, how he/she will dress, and how and where the names and logos of sponsors and the organisation will be presented. Helitzer (1996: 179-81) states eleven reasons for sporting organisations to call a press conference:

- A major change in personnel;
- A major change in the status of a star player;
- An important event scheduled;
- A major investigation (e.g. into illegal drug use);
- A change in a major facility;
- Award presentations;
- Crisis developments;
- Post-game interviews;

- the sports banquet speaker;
- the introduction of a new product; and
- a new rule that is complex or controversial.

A press conference should be called only when the general public or specific publics of the sporting organisation are interested enough to be informed. One of the above reasons might be applicable to a sporting organisation. If, however, the people or issues involved are still insignificant to the public, the media will not show up and the unsuccessful press conference will only damage the reputation of the organisation.

Inform and Informal—Interviews

Both a press release and a press conference can serve as an invitation for interviews. Interviews are one-on-one contact opportunities in which disseminated information can best be controlled. The interviewee has the opportunity to tell only what he/she wants to tell. However, conducting an interview and taking part in an interview are both skills in their own right. Poor preparation or failing to recognise an interviewer's leading questions can turn the opportunity into disaster for the organisation. Helitzer (1996: 273) provides a list of the do's and don'ts of interviews:

- Don't permit off-the-record statements. Don't try to become a major part of the interview.
- Don't assume that every fact will be used.
- Don't complain if the result is not totally satisfactory.
- Do pick the best spokesperson.
- Do try to limit the subject to areas where your spokesperson is an authority.
- Do provide suggested quotes, anecdotes and statistics that can be used.
- Do rehearse fully
- Do select the site where the spokesperson will be most comfortable.
- Do provide the press with full background.

- Do keep every promise to supply supplementary information.
- Do show your appreciation in a letter. It's even better than a call.

The interview presents the experienced sports marketer with an opportunity to use personal media contacts and disseminate information in an informal way. Informal contacts do not imply less care when supplying the information! The opportunity to talk informally to media representatives should not be turned into a disadvantage by accidentally releasing confidential information.

Form, Inform and Informal—Publicity

Publicity, according to Belch and Belch (1998: 528), refers to 'the generation of news about a person, product, service [or organisation] that appears in broadcast or print media [at no cost to the organisation]'. Although not every public relations effort necessarily has to result in news appearing in broadcast or print media, it can be an effective and efficient means of public relations communication. As a subset of the overall public relations exercise, planning and executing a programme of action (press release, press conference, interview) often lead to the generation of publicity. Mullin et al. (1993: 260) state that: sports is the most interesting specimen examined by the media... and it prospered because it received at no cost reams of publicity in daily and Sunday papers... This coverage, for which any other business would have had to pay, was given freely because of its entertainment value and because a newspaper that contained information about sports would sell more copies, creating both higher circulation and higher advertising rates.

Publicity is generated when the information has news value. Because the sporting organisation does not pay for the publicity, content is very hard to control. Also, the release time and accuracy of information are hard to control. But because the sporting organisation is not the direct source of information (other than in advertising or sales promotions), positive publicity can become very powerful and credible. Negative publicity, however, has the opposite extreme effect. In an integrated public relations strategy, the content, timing and generation of publicity are as much as possible controlled in the proactive strategy, and as much as possible prepared for in the reactive strategy.

Advantages and Disadvantages of Public Relations

At the beginning of this chapter, public relations was introduced as one element of the promotion mix. Public relations has some distinct advantages over other elements when applied under certain conditions. Belch and Belch (1998: 524-7) list the following advantages:

- ***Credibility:*** Contrary to advertising, the source of the public relations message is often not the organisation itself, which makes the message more credible to the receiver.
- ***Cost:*** Apart from the public relations personnel cost, few other expenditures have to be incurred.
- ***Avoidance of Clutter:*** Because many public relations efforts lead to news generation, information will stand apart from, for example, advertising or sales promotions.
- ***Lead Generation:*** For example, when Tiger Woods—one of the longest drivers on the Professional Golf Association Tour—was seen using a Cobra golf club, the club manufacturer received inquiries from all over the United States, Europe and Japan.
- ***Ability to reach specific groups.***
- ***Image Building:*** Effective public relations programmes lead to the development of a strong image, one that can resist negative publicity for a while.

The main disadvantage of public relations is the uncontrollability of publicity. When proactive or reactive public relations results in negative publicity, all potential public relations advantages turn into disadvantages. Negative information will hit more powerfully, and it will cost more to repair the damage. The avoidance of clutter, lead generation and ability to reach specific groups will now work against the organisation, damaging the favourable image. This is an important tool for the sports marketer because of the high visibility and attractiveness of the sports product. Three critical activities were derived from a public relations definition in order to describe the main public relations activities:

- Evaluating public attitudes;
- Identifying the policies and procedures of an individual or organisation with the public interest; and
- Planning and executing a programme of action.

It is important for the sports marketer to know how the sporting organisation's publics perceive the organisation and its product range. Knowledge of public opinion and how to influence opinion is vital in order to create proactive public relations strategies. Therefore, public attitudes need to be evaluated. Proactive strategies enable the sports marketer to 'control and adjust' public opinion, whereas reactive strategies always require changing negative public opinions. Prevention is better than repairing damage.

As a very influential public of many sporting organisations, relations with the media were considered, and the public relations tools of press release, press conference and interviews were introduced. There are basically three things that need to be considered when communicating with the media. The sports marketer has to know with whom to communicate, what information to supply and how to maintain excellent relationships with media representatives. In sports marketing special attention needs to be given to the concept of publicity, as it is probably the most important means (and opportunity) of conveying information in the sports industry.

Brand and Promotional Licensing

TRADEMARK LICENSING

A trademark is 'a sign used, or intended to be used, to "distinguish" goods or services of the plaintiff from those of any other person'. A sign, then, includes the following, or any combination of the following: any letter; word; name; signature; numeral; device (i.e. symbol or logo); brand; heading; label; ticket; aspect of packaging; shape; colour; sound; or scent. Trademark licensing is a multi-billion-dollar industry, and is defined by Wilkof (1995: 1) as 'an arrangement by which one party consents to the use of its trade mark in accordance with specified terms and conditions'. It is used in many industries for different purposes, which can be appreciated by considering the following examples:

- Using the Calvin Klein clothing trademark to sell perfume (using the established brand/trademark to sell new products);
- Coca-Cola using an overseas franchisee to sell in new markets (using the established brand/trademark to sell in new markets);

- McDonald's using the Olympic rings to sell more hamburgers (using the established brand / trademark to boost sales); and
- licensing the sporting organisation's logo to an apparel manufacturer (building brand/ trademark awareness and raising funds).

For a trademark to become the property of an organisation, it needs to be registered. When a trademark is registered, the owner will have the exclusive rights to:

- Use the trademark; and
- Authorise other persons to use the trademark (Section 20(1)).

Registration of the trademark is of extreme importance to the sporting organisation. Without this registration the original owner of the trademark has little legal protection when other organisations use the trademark in one way or the other. This point is reinforced by the Australian Olympic Committee's (AOC) decision to seek additional protection for its insignia. The *Olympic Insignia Protection Act 1987* came into force in 1987 to enable the AOC to regulate the use of the Olympic symbol and other nominated Olympic designs.

The Sydney Olympic Organising Committee for the Olympic Games (SOCOG) also sought added protection via the proclamation of the *Sydney 2000 Games (Indicia and Images) Protection Act 1996* (repealed). Use of a trademark is important for an organisation in many ways. Some of the reasons are discussed in the next section. Functions of a trademark Wilkof (1995) identifies six different functions of trademarks. These functions developed over time, and hence the merchandising function incorporates elements of all other, earlier developed functions.

The functions are:

- Identification;
- Physical source;

- Anonymous source;
- Quality;
- Advertising; and
- Merchandising.

Identification

The most obvious function of the trademark is to identify ownership or who is responsible for producing the product. When Juventus played Ajax in the European Champions League final, for example, soccer consumers knew that the 'black and white' Italians played the 'red and white' Dutchmen.

Physical Source

Without being able to witness the production of certain products, the trademark can be seen as acknowledgement of the physical source of the purchased goods. The trademark serves as a stamp of approval. When licensing trademarks, however, the licensee is not the actual source of the goods. T-shirts with National Basketball League (NBL) logos printed on them are not produced by the NBL. Manufacturers are granted a licence to produce merchandise, and hence licensing seems incompatible with this function of the trademark. To reduce this incompatibility, it is important that the sporting organisation put in place stringent quality control procedures to ensure that products will be of a quality that the 'physical source' organisation would deliver itself.

Anonymous Source

When the scope of production and marketing of an organisation expands, it becomes less likely that consumers of goods will know the actual name of the producer. The anonymous source function ensures that purchasers of goods or services with a given established trademark know that these goods or services emanate from a source that established those trademarks. In other words, the trademark products have proven their quality, validating their anonymous source. Large consumer good producers like Procter & Gamble and Unilever have hundreds of trademarks validating the 'anonymous source'. Sporting organisations are less likely to use this function of the trademark, although large entertainment companies involved in the sports industry actually do.

For instance, sports properties such as the Mighty Ducks of Anaheim (National Hockey League) and the Anaheim Angels (Major League Baseball) not only are cartoon characters, they also are professional sporting franchises owned by the Disney Corporation. These sports properties are distributed through channels like ESPN, ESPN2 and ABC Sports, also owned by Disney. Disney also owns the names, logos and trademarks of all these organisational entities. In the case of the two professional teams—the Mighty Ducks of Anaheim and the Anaheim Angels—there are also licensing restrictions on the use of the logos and names placed by the National Hockey League (NHL) and Major League Baseball (MLB) as part of the franchise agreements.

Quality

Licensing of sports trademarks has become so popular because of the quality function of trademarks. If a trademark has the power to convey a quality perception, surely this perception can be transferred to products or entities linked to the trademark. From a legal perspective this concept changed the position of licensing. Provided that the licensor establishes sufficient quality control measures and procedures, it does not really matter whether the products emanate from the licensor (i.e. owner of the trademark) or another source. The quality level provided to the end consumer by the licensee should be similar to the quality level if the product had been provided by the licensor.

Advertising

Fuji Xerox using the Olympic rings, Heineken using Tennis Australia's logo and Vodafone using Manchester United's logo are all examples of trademark usage going beyond the creation of goodwill (as exemplified in the previous functions). Trademarks have become symbols with the power to sell goods and services. Although advertising can be criticised as an effort to manipulate the consumer's mind through slick, high-impact campaigns, it does serve as a way to mass-communicate the source and quality of a product through the trademark. It complements the source and quality functions. The positive perception that consumers have of Manchester United, Tennis Australia or the Olympic organisation is transferred to the associated organisations and products, stimulating these consumers to use Vodaphone communication products, drink Heineken or use Fuji Xerox products.

Merchandising

The trademark becomes a product in itself when it is not serving to sell other goods or services but serving to sell itself. Examples are the teenage fans of a rock band buying all possible merchandise with the name of the band on it, or football fans buying shirts, mugs, jackets and pens with the name of their team on them. The consumer wants to be identified with the trademark organisation. Which merchandise they buy is secondary. Often, the only criterion is that it is visible to others, showing the consumer's allegiance to the trademark organisation.

Quality Control

Quality control is a vital and integral component of trademark licensing. We have shown that the legal position of licensing changed when the concept of quality control was included. As long as the licensor establishes sufficient quality control measures and procedures, it does not really matter whether the products emanate from the licensor (i.e. owner of the trademark) or another source. The trademark identifies the source and distinguishes the products from those of others. The law loosely formulates standards for quality control in that the owner of the trademark should be capable of exercising control over the users of the trademark.

Wilkof (1995) distinguishes between two types of quality control: contractual and financial. *Contractual control* exists between two unrelated parties whose only mutual interest is the exploitation of the trademark. *Financial control* exists when two parties are related, in that one of them has an ownership relation to the other (e.g. a holding or subsidiary relation). Financial control is more stringent, as the aims of benefiting from the trademark are more likely to be in line with each other because of the ownership relation between the organisations. In the sports industry, contractual control is the most frequently used type of quality control. A contractual specification of quality control terms and con-ditions should identify at least the following aspects of quality control:

- Specification of standards;
- Inspection of products and methods of production; and
- Supply of samples.

The Trademark Licensing Agreement

The trademark licensing agreement sets out the broader relationship between the licensor and licensee. Ownership of the trademark, who can use the trademark as the licensee and how the trademark can be used (contractual, i.e. quality control) are described first. Then the commercial and financial terms and conditions are described. Issues like how merchandise is going to be marketed and which royalties have to be paid by the licensee are described in this part of the agreement. Sherman (1991: 330-1) describes several key areas that need to be addressed when preparing the trademark licensing agreement. In summary, the key areas are:

- Scope of the territorial and product exclusivity;
- Assignability and sublicensing rights;
- Definition of the property and the licensed products;
- Quality control and approval;
- Ownership of artwork and designs;
- Term renewal rights and termination of the relationship;
- Initial licence and ongoing royalty fees;
- Performance criteria for the licensee;
- Liability insurance;
- Indemnification;
- Duty to pursue trademark and copyright infringement;
- Minimum advertising and promotional requirements;
- Accounting and record keeping of the licensee;
- Inspection and audit rights of the licensor;
- Right of first refusal for expanded or revised characters and images;
- Limitations on the licensee's distribution to related or affiliated entities;
- Representations and warranties of the licensor with respect to its rights to the property;
- Availability of the licensor for technical and promotional assistance; and miscellaneous provisions, such as law to govern, inurement of goodwill, nature of the relationship notice, and force- majeure.

It goes beyond the scope of this text to specify further the contents of the trademark licensing agreement. Before taking a closer look at building the sporting organisation's licensing programme, we outline the trademark licensing agreement briefly from both licensor's and licensee's perspectives.

Licensor's and Licensee's Perspectives

The trademark licensing agreement from the licensor's perspective should serve one most important goal. If the trademark is used by the licensee in any other manner than was intended by the licensor when entering the agreement, contractual arrangements must be in place to entitle the licensor to take action. Although this point is of obvious importance to the licensee as well, the focus of the licensee should be on the terms and conditions related to commercial and financial matters.

Sports Excitement Video Games (fictitious name) wants to create a game called The All Blacks/ Wallabies/ Springboks conquer the world. The game will be marketed in New Zealand, Australia and South Africa. When sold in New Zealand, the game will be marketed as 'The All Blacks conquer the world', in Australia as The Wallabies conquer the world and in South Africa as The Springboks conquer the world'.

Sports Excitement has several licensing considerations. The company needs to develop the actual game, which includes writing the software code for graphical display, play options, opponents and voice enhancement features (cost can go up to $400000). Sports Excitement also needs to pay the New Zealand, Australian and South African national governing bodies of rugby union their licensing fees. In this case all organisations have negotiated a minimum advance fee ($100000) plus a percentage of sales royalty fee (4%). On top of the licensing fees, Sports Excitement has to undertake the packaging, warehousing and shipping costs. Then it has to obtain the other necessary licences, from either the International Rugby Football Board (IRFB) or the Players Association, to feature indentifiable teams and/or players other than the three already identified. Next, Sports Excitement has to decide which game platforms it will develop for (e.g. Sega, CD-Rom, Nintendo). Depending on which platform the manufacturer develops, the cartridges will add extra costs.

An analyst calculates the revenue streams and forecasts the potential return on investment. The net revenue per platform for an average game is $32 per game *sold through,* meaning purchased at a retail outlet such as Target. The All Blacks royalty would likely be 4% of that, less the advance. Therefore, if 100000 unit sold through, the All Blacks' royalties would amount to: 100000 (units) x (0.04)($32)-$100000 = $28000. In this case, the sporting teams are not the catalyst for the game. The developer seeks a category and the teams are merely the well-known vehicles to differentiate the product. In the competitive video-game development industry, the sophisticated marketplace will weed out poorly conceived games, and they will fail in spite of a fabulous licensor. Licensors, in this case, will help to sell the products, if those products are good!

Sports Team Logos are Big Business

Have you ever considered using the logo of your favourite professional sports team in a promotional campaign? Did you know it would cost you? Apparently not all marketing professionals realise that sports teams, like other companies that produce products or services, own protectable trademarks that others may not use unless they first obtain the trademark owner's permission and usually pay a licensing fee. In a recent case, the Angels baseball team defended its trademark rights when it sued the Broadway department store after it ran an ad for women's dresses featuring three children wearing Angels uniforms. Broad way had failed to first obtain the requisite permission from the Angels and later refused to pay the Angels' requested licensing fee. Broadway claimed that it did not know it was supposed to pay a licensing fee, even though the Angels uniforms used in the ad contained registered trademark notations.

Professional sports teams aggressively protect their trademark rights, which include its name and its logos. This is done by demanding licensing fees on other contexts which may, at first glance, appear worlds apart from the department store advertisement case. Recently, Major League Baseball has even cracked down on Little League and amateur adult teams that use major-league nicknames. Because Major League Baseball owns trademark rights in the names of all its teams when they are used in connection with baseball, it can legally require amateur teams using these names to wear only licensed apparel. This can add about $6 to the cost of each uniform.

Trademark licensing increased the marketing opportunities for many companies. Instead of diversifying directly into a new product line, a trademark proprietor could license an existing producer in another industry to manufacture a line of goods under the licensor's trademark. This became very common, for exam pie, between perfume companies and apparel manufacturers. It is now also common between professional sports organisations and apparel and novelty manufacturers. The sports organisation must specify the products on which any licensee is permitted to use the trademark, as well as supervise and control the quality of those products. The public will benefit because it will receive a guarantee that the sports organisation stands behind the goods bearing its trademarks. What would happen if Major League Baseball ignored the Little Leaguers' use of its nicknames? Major League Baseball could lose its trademark rights and that would mean the loss of millions of dollars a year in royalties from its extremely lucrative licensing business. 'Professional sports organisations have much to lose if they do not adequately control the use of their trademarks. In addition, it is safe to say that many consumers want to know that the products they buy are both high quality and "approved".'

Building the Sporting Organisation's Licensing Programme

An Operational Protocol

Irwin and Stotlar (1993) investigated the operational protocol employed by six major US sporting organisations in their sports licensing programmes. The six organisations were Major League Baseball (MLB), National Football League (NFL), National Basketball Association (NBA), National Hockey League (NHL), National Collegiate Athletic Association (NCAA) and the US Olympic Committee.

Key Factors

Baghdikian (1996) has devel SPONSEFFECT model a model to assist the sports marketer in identifying the key factors when building a licensing programme.

Organisational Objectives

Like the other marketing tools discussed in this text, licensing should serve the broader purpose of achieving the marketing goals of the organisation, which in turn should support the achievement of overall strategic goals. In sports, licensing the organisation's trademark for merchandising purposes often aims to raise funds or to increase brand awareness.

Programme Protection and Enforcement: Legal specialist consultation; Majority of logos registered as trademarks; Licensee application and screening process; Licence issuance and renewal procedures; Non-exclusive basic agreement; Execution of joint-use agreements; Execution of international licences; Product sample required for quality control 'Licensed product' identification required; Counterfeit logo detection procedures; Counterfeit logo reduction procedures.

Programme Promotions and Public Relations: Proactive recruitment of licensees; Proactive recruitment of retailers; Licensee/retailer public relations programme; Advertising used to promote products/programme; Licensing programme information published.

Revenue Management: Advance payment required; Uniform loyalty charged on all products; Written royalty exemption policy; Royalty verifications routinely conducted; Royalty verifications conducted by specialist; Written royalty distribution policy.

Choice of Licensee

In light of the functions of the trademark and the organisational objectives, it is important to find the right licensee. Pertaining to the functions of the trademark, the potential licensee should be capable of satisfying the quality control standards and should maintain the function of identifying the source of the products. From an organisational perspective it is important for the sporting organisation to find reputable partners with an ability to deliver quality on time with regular payments.

Commitment

Rather than leaving the work to the licensee and simply 'licensing' it to use the sporting organisation's trademark, the sporting organisation should commit itself to doing the preliminary market research and financial analysis. Baghdikian (1996: 38) states that: the San Jose Sharks, during their first season, compiled the worst on-field record in the National Hockey League (NHL). However, due to the organisations spending 13 months on consumer research, and planning a name and design that would create an exciting image in the market, the Sharks outsold all other NHL team-licensed products.

Resource

In investigating sports and collegiate licensing programmes, Irwin and Stotlar (1993: 15) concluded that 'with nearly half of all colleges assigning programme administrators less than 10% of their time to licensing, the complex administrative tasks associated with a licensing programme cannot effectively be addressed'. Although the resources invested in managing a sports licensing programme might be high, the resulting benefits are likely to be proportionately higher than the investment.

Communication

Although the licensing agreement (including contractual agreements) should serve as the basis for business communication, regular and open channels of communication should be established. A clear understanding of both parties' goals, the early detection of problems and effective quality control are the results of open and frequent communication between licensor and licensee.

Relationship

The more formal business communication described above can be complemented with more informal communication (e.g. between the two chief executive officers). An afternoon on the golf course with the aim of fostering personal relationships has often proven vital to the maintenance of business relationships.

Contractual Agreement

The contract represents the written agreement that both licensor and licensee are legally obliged to fulfil. Examples of areas, suggested by Sherman (1991), to be included in a contract were listed earlier in this chapter. The contract is the agreement that licensor and licensee can turn to when they feel that one or the other party is not fulfilling the requirements of the agreement.

Legal Protection

The practice of ambush marketing is of particular interest when considering the power of trademarks. Without the law and legal advisers, the sporting organisation has little to protect it from organisations ambushing its trademarks and other properties. The specialised nature of licensing in general, contracts, interpretations of law and the management of licensing programmes requires the support and advice of legally qualified experts. For example, the Nick Faldo Golf Company has entered into a partnership with sports brand and business development consultancy WSM, which will police the licensing of his name (Gillis 2002).

Issues that can Arise

The second part of this chapter has first provided a range of activities to be executed by sports licensing programme managers and then the different steps that need to be taken when building the organisation's licensing programme.

Using the Established Brand to Enter New Markets

Although the market for licensed merchandise towards the end of the 1990s has experienced some difficult times, especially in the USA, the prospects for the future are bright Partly due to the baseball strike and the NBA lockout in 1997/98, sales dropped dramatically towards the end of the 1990s. However, the NFL and NBA are revitalising and innovating the industry by entering previously untapped markets. For example, the NBA launched the Global Retail Environment Programme through which they aimed to create unified NBA-branded visual impact zones at retail all overthe world...looking at direct TV selling models, selling products in adspots during matches, and alternative retailing and merchandising, with the aim of getting the brand message at the point of sale (Glendinning 1999:10).

The Copyright Promotions Group (CPG), in their association with the 1999 World Cup Cricket in England, are a good example of licensing in the context of a one-off event Of the five product categories that included apparel, toys and gifts, publishing, fast-moving consumer goods and promotions, 60% of revenue came from the apparel product category. The success of their licensing programmes was based on their integral involvement in discussions that ranged from television rights to on-site sales of produce. This allowed them to come up with the best licensing strategies that not only protected and leveraged the rights of (often exclusive) licensees but provided the best possible value and return for the licensor as well. Even when fans are not able to attend the event or purchase memorabilia from event-specific merchandise stores, online shopping allows them to be part of the event by ordering merchandise unique to the event (Westerbeek & Smith 2003).

With the opportunity that is the Internet, online sales of licensed merchandise may receive a welcome boost in the first part of the new decade. In particular, the market for soccer merchandise remains potentially very lucrative. Sales in relation to the Japan/South Korea World Cup were expected to generate US$1.5 billion, some 20% up from France 1998. The global opportunity presented to clubs such as Italian power brokers Juventus and Premier League giants Manchester United are there for the taking.

Twenty percent of the hits on the Juventus website are from Asia. The Asian opportunity consists of a potential 2-billion-person marketplace. The red devils' signed a new merchandising and licensing deal with Japan Sports Vision (JSV), the official World Cup distributor for Japan. JSV is a major client of Nike, and Nike in turn, has signed a 13-year deal with Manchester United, reported to be worth US$427 million, to become an official sponsor and the official merchandise partner of the club. By the way, Nike and its swoosh, as a strong yet vulnerable brand (and symbol) in its own right, have taken the 'unprecendented step of releasing a detailed report on its child labour policy. Its "Corporate Responsibility Report" offers an open assessment of the lobbyist's claims and details other ethical issues such as the effect of its activities on the environment and the company's involvement in local communities. Conscious of the impact even an isolated case can have on the image of the Nike brand—a commodity that has taken tens of millions of pounds to position.' (Clarke 2002: 26)

Only five years ago European soccer clubs handled most of their licensing programmes in house. Because the scope of merchandising operations was mostly domestic, many clubs felt that spending sparse resources on an outside licensing agency could not be justified. However, this attitude is changing rapidly. In order to maximise profiting from the club's brand equity, more and more clubs are selecting licensing agents. Chris Protheroe, director of the Copyright Promotions Licensing Group, argues that 'if they keep their merchandising rights in-house they avoid paying agency commission but they will naturally in curover heads of man-power, design, legal advice and accounting expenses' (Wallace 2002:31). However, Edward Friedman of Zone Marketing thinks differently. He argues that 'licensing firms will never do as good a job as you can do yourself. Afirm like Levi's, for exam pie, wouldn't just hand everything over so why should football clubs?...You become only as good as the people who look after you' (Wallace 2002:32).

BRANDING

The Branding Process

Chernatony and McDonald (1992: 18) define a successful brand as: an identifiable product, service, person or place augmented in such a way that the buyer or user perceives relevant unique added values which match their needs most closely. Furthermore its success results from being able to sustain these added values in the face of competition.

We can all associate with the practical application of the brand concept. Powerful brands are immediately associated with the product or service they represent. Coca-Cola is a softdrink, McDonald's sells hamburgers, Manchester United deals with soccer and the Indy 500 is about car racing. A brand represents the combination of the core product and the perceptions that consumers have about the product and its unique added values.

A SPORTS BRAND

Developing successful brands is important for organisations because the brand can be used as a means to communicate with consumers. Branding, as the process of developing and sustaining successful brands, has strategic relevance for the marketing function. In other words, the full marketing mix is used in the strategic branding process. The marketer tries to position the brand 'in the mind' of the consumer. Consumers start perceiving the brand as the symbolic total of the packaging, design, recall advertising, quality of product, price paid, and store or outlet where the product can be bought. This total brand perception enables the marketer to link mental visions to the organisation's branded products—expressing, for example, a lifestyle, a personality or a feeling. Powerful brands differentiate themselves from similar products of competitors and provide the opportunity to build long-term relationships with consumers, developing brand-loyal buyers.

Brand equity, according to Gladden, Milne and Sutton (1998), is the combined tangible and intangible value of the brand, and can be broken down into four constituents: perceived quality (of the brand), brand awareness (recall, recognition), brand associations (in sports often emotionally loaded), and brand loyalty (the ability of the brand to retain customers). In the sports industry, the antecedents to brand equity are team-related (e.g. success, star players), organisation-related (e.g. reputation and tradition, overall entertainment package, service reputation) and market-related (e.g. media coverage and reach, competitive forces).

The marketer can use the brand as a symbol of, for example, prestige, status, lifestyle or personality, and can position the symbol in such a way that it expresses physical and psychological comfort to the target market. If the sports marketer chooses to build the registered trademark into a brand, licensing in many ways can assist in achieving branding objectives.

Branding and Licensing

Trademark licensing, as an arrangement by which one party consents to the use of its trademark in accordance with specified terms and conditions, makes sense only if the trademark is in any way valuable to the potential licensee. The trademark can have value as an established brand, making it a powerful means of communication. If the trademark has the potential value of becoming an established brand, it has future earning power, making it an interesting investment. Sporting organisations can capitalise on this potential value by using other organisations to raise their own brand awareness.

The Potential Power of Sports Brands

Earlier we discussed the advantages of sports sponsorship. These advantages also explain why sports brands, or sports trademarks, are potentially powerful tools to add value. The advantages, explaining the potential power of sports brands, may be summarised as follows:

- Sports consumers tend to identify themselves personally with the sports, which creates opportunities for increasing brand loyalty in products linked to the sports.
- Sports evokes personal attachment, and with this the licensee can be linked to the excitement, energy and emotion of the sporting contest. In other words, sports has the potential to deliver a clear message.
- Sports has universal appeal and pervades all elements of life (geographically, demographically and socioculturally). This characteristic presents the

opportunity to cross difficult cultural and language borders in communication, enabling the licensee to talk to a global mass audience.
- The variety of sports available makes it possible to create distinct market segments with which to communicate separately.
- The universal appeal and high interest that sports has in society give sports a high media exposure, resulting in free publicity. Free publicity can make a licensing deal very costeffective.
- Because of the clear linkage of the licensee to the sporting organisation's trademark, the relationship stands out from the clutter, contrary to advertising, in which people are bombarded with hundreds of 'sender unknown' messages each day.

Earlier, this chapter presented some examples of how organisations use licensing and for which purposes. These purposes are repeated here in the context of the sports industry.

USING THE SPORTS BRAND TO ADD VALUE

Adding value, as the most important activity of creating powerful brands, can be done in many ways. It has been explained that branding is a strategic effort in that the marketer should use the whole marketing mix to build the brand. Using an established trademark or brand to add value to another brand is one means of applying the marketing mix. The Olympic sponsors are licensed to link the Olympic rings to their products. A variety of consumer good licensees (e.g. Four'n'Twenty pies, Carlton Draught, Volkswagen) are licensed to use the AFL logo on their products. The potential licensees of Nick Faldo's name in the headline story use the brand equity he has built over the years to add value to already existing brands or general products. More specifically, this added value is needed to fulfil one of the following purposes:

- To sell in new products using the established brand/ trademark;
- To sell in new markets using the established brand/ trademark; or
- To boost sales using the established brand/ trademark.

The major aim of the sporting organisation in this process is to use its established brand/ trademark to raise funds for the organisation. An extra bonus is the widespread attention that is given to its brand name through the promotional efforts of licensees. This is why careful selection of licensees is important, because the established sports brand should not be associated with a wrong or inferior product or organisation. The branding process in a sporting organisation can be enhanced by using licensing as a means of raising brand awareness.

Using Licensing to Add Value to the Sports Brand

If the sports brand is not established yet, but careful preparation and commitment have been put into preparing an appropriate and attractive brand name and symbols, licensing can be used as one way of informing consumers about the brand. The San Jose Sharks, used as an example earlier, raised their brand awareness and raised funds by offering a potentially profitable trademark to a selection of merchandise licensees. Using the marketing mix elements to integrate pricing, distribution and promotion of the merchandise, they successfully established the San Jose Sharks brand. More specifically, licensing is used to fulfil the following purpose:

- Licensing the unknown trademark to build brand/ trademark awareness and raise funds.

The previous examples have shown that licensing plays a vital role in adding value to the licensor's, licensee's or both organisations' brands. The realisation that brands/ trademarks are successful only if they add value to the product or the organisation, as perceived by the consumer, highlights the strategic importance of branding. Powerful brands can be developed only if the organisation views the branding process as integral to the marketing function, using all marketing mix elements to build powerful brands.

This section discussed the licensing of the sporting organisation's intellectual property (name and/or logo registered in a trademark) to a third party. It was shown that promotional licensing in the sports industry basically serves two purposes: promotion of the sporting organisation, and promotion of a third party or its products through use of the sporting organisation's name or logo. In the latter case, the major benefit the sporting organisation derives is a royalty fee, often calculated as a percentage of sales of licensed products.

The importance of registering a trademark was shown by discussing the different functions of the trademark. Registration of the trademark is always important because trademarks can become valuable organisational assets, namely brands. Through careful management, trademarks linked to products can be built into powerful brands. This was discussed in the last part of this chapter. A powerful sports brand is a valuable organisational asset because it has the power to represent multiple consumer perceptions. Consumers perceive a brand as a symbolic total of the organisation's product—in sport's case the excitement, speed and action orientation of the core product and its star players. Sports brands therefore are capable of linking powerful messages to other products through licensing.

CHAPTER

Coordination and Control of Marketing Strategy

TYPES OF CONTROL

There are three types of organisational control:

- Feed forward;
- Concurrent; and
- Feedback.

Feed forward control takes place before production and operations begin and commences during the strategic sports-marketing planning process (SSMPP). Determining the operating procedures and setting standards for the operation of a facility prior to a season commencing are examples of feed forward control. As part of this review of operational procedures, appropriate staff training will be provided consistent with service quality policies. This form of control ensures all inputs are of the highest quality for optimum spectator enjoyment.

Concurrent control occurs during the sporting fixture or, in other words, while the plans are being carried out. Often in sports this will be a major event or the weekly fixtures in a season. In the sports facility, monitoring the quality of service delivery exemplifies concurrent control. Supervisors will be responsible for checking that staff carry out their jobs in a manner consistent with the organisation's policy. In some cases it is possible to fine-tune the activity as it occurs or to rectify problems immediately, which is an example of concurrent control. Concurrent control can also occur during a major event or a season when monitoring attendances. If these are lower than expected, advertising may need to be intensified or altered, or sales promotions implemented to return the organisation to a satisfactory level of performance. Determining acceptable levels of performance requires the identification of appropriate measures during the strategic sports-marketing planning process.

Feedback control focuses on the final performance measured against the standards or targets foreordained. As a consequence of this feedback, the marketing plan can be reviewed and modified where necessary to ensure that the defined performance standards can be achieved during the next season or event.

Measures of Success

On-field Success

On-field success is typically the most obvious and visible measure of success by which to assess the performance of sporting organisations. Unlike most products, where the marketer has some input into design and packaging, the sports marketer has no control over the quality of the team selected. The selection and development of players are not the purview of the sports marketer. The sports marketer, however, is responsible for promoting the team based on its quality and its star athletes. Elements of this marketing effort will be seen in ticketing and games promotions, advertising, public relations and sponsorship strategies, all discussed in earlier chapters. It has been stressed in this book that the sports marketer needs to ensure that overpromising is not a feature of the promotion mix. It could be argued, for example, that the head coach of the Australian swimming team at the 1996 Olympic Games overpromised in relation to the success of his athletes.

Ultimately, the Australian swimming team performed well, but expectations were so high that the actual performance (in terms of medals) was seen to be relatively poor. What could have been a perfect situation on which to build future marketing strategies turned into an exercise in managing negative public relations. On-field success, then, is an organisation-wide measure not specific to the efforts of marketing personnel. The derivates, however, of on-field or off-field success are the purview of the sports marketer. These are now discussed.

Attendance and Participation

Attendance and participation are two key measures of marketing performance. They are linked, as elite athletes serve as role models for those participating at lower levels of sporting competition. Known as the 'Norman factor' in Australia, or globally as the 'Tiger Woods' factor, the effect that Greg Norman and Tiger Woods have on golf participation and attendance when they visit Australia to play in major golf tournaments is undisputed. Typically, attendances at the event and interest in golf both rise. Increased participation in a sports has the added benefit of contributing to increased attendances, as people's affinity to a sports grows with participation and they are therefore more likely to watch it, either live or on television.

Sporting organisations are therefore concerned with boosting the numbers of registered participants. Strategies designed to ensure participation have been discussed in this book. The introduction of modified rules for juniors has been the main strategy designed to attract juniors to play sports. These modified rules programmes become integral parts of marketing strategy as all sports strive to capture a finite group of participants. Registration numbers are important measures of success, in particular of the success of marketing programmes. Attendance also is a frequently cited measure of success for an association, club or league. Elements of the promotion mix, pricing policies, service quality and facility management have been important factors discussed contributing to the likely success of maximising attendances.

Club Membership

Club membership is another important measure. As discussed, club members represent heavy attendance on the frequency attendance escalator and are thus an important source of revenue. More importantly, this revenue often comes well before the season, providing much-needed income during a period when no games are conducted to generate weekly revenues. Marketing programmes should be designed to reward longevity and minimise defection, or season ticket holders falling off the frequency attendance escalator.

Sponsorship

Sponsorship is another key measure of success in the marketing programme. In fact, sponsorship has been considered so important that many sports have developed unidimensional marketing programmes aimed at attracting sponsorship revenue. In the long term, this myopic view is detrimental to the sporting organisation for two reasons:

1. It negates the extent to which the sporting organisation can devise a full range of marketing-related benefits that can be provided to the sponsor; and

2. It concentrates the success of the marketing programme on one objective.

Concentration on any one objective is potentially poor strategy. Sporting organisations need to diversify their range of marketing strategies to ensure that there is not an overreliance on any one area.

For example, if sponsorship income falls well below anticipated projections, the overall success of the organisation will be threatened because no effort has been made to raise revenues by ensuring attendance, attracting members and selling merchandise. As noted, sponsorship myopia is caused by the capacity of sports to attract sponsors seeking a relatively inexpensive way to promote their products. As some sporting organisations have the capacity to fulfil sponsor objectives easily, this adds to the potential to concentrate solely on sponsorship income at the expense of developing a broad-based marketing programme, including all elements of the marketing mix.

Television

The importance of television to the marketing effort has been stressed throughout this book. Television has the capacity to provide significant streams of revenue as well as to act as an important promotion vehicle for sports, even if no television revenue is forthcoming. Therefore, television as a measure of success is very important. Sports marketers must carefully determine the role of television in their marketing plans. Questions to be answered in relation to setting marketing objectives include: Is the sports capable of attracting television rights revenue? If so, how much? If not, can some coverage be obtained to help promote the sports? Answers to these questions determine the marketing objectives set in relation to television and thus the measures used to assess performance.

Successful sports marketers need to have an intimate knowledge of the way in which the television business operates to ensure that television revenues or promotions are successfully implemented in the overall marketing strategy. Television's impact on sports is an important strategic issue for sports marketers. To what extent are sports required to modify their game to make it more attractive to television? Although the need to appease television can be a potential problem, in some instances it has also forced sports to modernise and therefore present a more attractive product. Cricket, as discussed in this book, has been better off for the World Series Cricket revolution in 1977. The introduction of the one-day game, with a variety of new rules better suited to television, has brought an added dimension to playing standards through improved fielding, more creative batting and an array of tactics not seen previously.

It is not the purpose of this book to take one view as to whether television's impact on sports in relation to changing the game is either good or bad. Clearly, there are examples of such changes benefiting sports and others working to the detriment of the sports. This is an important issue, and rather than adopt an extreme position either way sports marketers should carefully think through the implications of change. The sports marketer should conduct research, consult past and current players and trial changes, in just the way marketers do when preparing to introduce new products.

Merchandising and Licensing

Merchandising and licensing are important marketing objectives. Sporting organisations license their logos and trademarks for two reasons:

1. To create awareness of the sports, club or league; and
2. To endorse product lines outside of sports as a means of generating additional revenue.

Revenue from licensing income becomes the main measure in determining the success of such a programme. Clearly, this revenue can easily be measured.

Service Quality

Another important but less tangible measure is service quality. It also indirectly affects everything that is concerned with attracting spectators, members and sponsors, contributing to the likelihood of repeat purchase. Strategically, it is significant because it has the capacity to even out the fluctuations in enjoyment governed by winning or losing. An enjoyable night at the basketball, for example, may to some extent offset the disappointment of losing. This raises the critical question in relation to this intangible area of assessing how much participants and spectators enjoy the sports experience.

Equally, this question relates to winning. Clubs, associations and leagues are increasingly realising that their marketing programmes should be designed to build loyalty—loyalty that has the capacity to withstand periods of poor on-field performance. The reality of most sporting competitions is that it is in their own interests to ensure that winning is shared by all, and therefore mechanisms will be put in place to even out the competition. Clubs will experience periods during which they are successful and periods when they perform poorly. Success on the field does not guarantee success off the field, but poor on-field performance almost certainly guarantees poor off-field success based on the measures discussed above. Reducing the impact of these periods of poor on-field performance enhances the likelihood of achieving financial stability.

Financial Stability

Despite an earlier statement in this chapter that profit is not the sole goal of sporting organisations, it has grown in importance during the past 15 years. Many sporting organisations typified the extreme position, where debt could be freely incurred without considering the consequences. Fortunately, this culture is changing, reinforcing the importance of control in the implementation of marketing activities. Modern sporting organisations more readily understand the balance between on-field success and sound off-field success. Most of the measures of success discussed in this section contribute to the incomegenerating potential of the organisation. The ability to reign in costs is the subject of broader texts in the management domain, covering the issue of control in more detail.

Coordinating and Implementing Marketing Strategy

Coordination and implementation of this strategy are primarily the responsibility of the marketing department. Kotler et al. (1989: 635) define marketing implementation as 'the process that turns marketing strategies and plans into marketing actions in order to accomplish strategic marketing objectives'. Coordination cannot occur, however, without the support of the entire organisation. Marketing staff are often reliant, for example, on sports operations staff to allow star players to become involved in promotion activities. Typically, these star players are in high demand for such promotion activities, often conflicting with training and playing schedules.

Implementation is primarily about staff management, and in essence deals with the who, what, where and when of the marketing plan. The who, what, where and when activities are the result of the strategies determined, otherwise referred to as the what and why. Implementation is often difficult—more difficult than determining the strategies. It is easy to dream up a range of interesting and creative strategies; however, when it comes to actual implementation it may be found that they are totally unrealistic or impractical.

Added to the difficulties of coordinating marketing strategies is the relatively recent introduction of marketing personnel, even marketing departments, to sporting organisations. In fact, in some sporting organisations in Australia, a national development officer or state development officer is responsible for the marketing programme, based on his/her responsibility for promoting and encouraging participation. In some sports, specialist sportmarketing staff are now employed. The Australian Cricket Board (ACB), for example, has for some time employed a general manager of marketing, sales manager, events and sponsorship manager, events assistant and sponsorship officer, licensing manager and marketing officer. Careers in sports marketing are beginning to flourish.

Careers in Sports Marketing

The ACB is indicative of the range of career options emerging in this field. Professional sports in particular offer the greatest range of career options. Marketing staff employed in Australian Football League (AFL) clubs have multiplied markedly during the 1990s and early 2000s. The Port Adelaide Football Club, for example, employed twelve staff in its marketing division in 2001 plus three staff in media and public relations. Jobs covered include a membership and database manager, sponsorship executive, merchandise manager, sales executives and assistants and marketing assistants, media and public relations manager, assistant and communications coordinator. All staff were responsible for the implementation and coordination of all the club's marketing activities. Also, their employment is indicative of the breadth and range of activities undertaken by the club.

Most large sporting organisations now incorporate media relations in their marketing department, or as a related department such as at Port Adelaide. Tennis Australia is one such organisation, with a marketing and media department. The importance of public relations has been stressed throughout this book as a vital function within the marketing mix and should be integrated in, or closely associated with, the activities of the marketing department.

Slowly there is evidence that marketing personnel are being employed in a greater variety of sporting organisations. The biggest hurdle to overcome in expanding an organisation's staff expertise has been the view that sports promotes itself and therefore does not require marketing staff. This complacency has been responsible for the slow pace at which sports has embraced the need for marketing expertise. There is evidence of this changing.

Interestingly, the pace of change has become more urgent as sporting organisations realise the capacity of a skilled marketing team's potential to contribute to the full range of revenueearning possibilities via marketing programmes. It is true that in some instances it is necessary to spend money up front to ensure that revenue-earning potential is maximised. Advertising, public relations launches and staff training in terms of service delivery are examples of this. However, they are also the means of communicating with a public increasingly subject to an attractive range of recreation and leisure pursuits capable of detracting from interest in sports. The past decade in particular has seen a rapidly intensifying range of competitive forces within the recreation and leisure industry. In many ways this has been good for sports, as sports have been forced to professionalise their operations and modernise the way they deliver the overall sports package. The overall sports package remains the domain of all staff and board members associated with various sports, but the sports marketer's input to the package is rapidly growing.

SPORTS-MARKETING PLANNING REVISITED

Stage 1, 'Identification of marketing opportunities', should remain fairly constant. As each organisation prepares to enter a new three-to five-year plan, a renewed analysis of the environment and review of the organisation's capabilities should be undertaken. Importantly, this review should recognise the changing forces driving competition in the sports and recreation industry. This book has already noted changes in the competitive forces confronted by sporting organisations during the past 10-15 years. Decisions taken in regard to the overall analysis of the organisation filter down to the marketing mission and objectives set, to allow marketing activities to contribute to broader organisational goals. Most of these decisions are based on the market research and data available to accurately assess buying patterns and consumer behaviour in general. Understanding consumer behaviour in sports and market research and segmentation were covered in Part I of this book. In general, these stages remain constant components of the SSMPP.

Stage 2, 'Strategy determination, represents the greatest detail provided in this book. This is because it is at this stage of determining the core marketing strategy that the range of marketing mix variables can be varied to suit the circumstances confronting an organisation. The reason for selecting the mix of variables also changes depending on whether a repositioning exercise is required, such as that described for the NBL during this book, or the development of product offerings aimed at specific market segments. Stage 2 also represents the greatest unknown in terms of' Have we chosen the right core marketing strategy?' There is no correct answer to the question. It can be answered only over time, and even this is subject to the ability of staff to implement marketing plans.

Stage 3, Strategy implementation, consists of measuring performance based on standards determined earlier in the process and, where necessary, modifying or altering the way in which the core marketing strategy is implemented. Control, implementation and coordination, as discussed in this last chapter, are crucial to the overall success of the marketing strategy. Implementation, like strategy determination, is an ongoing process. As one season or event rolls into the next, it becomes important for marketing personnel to step back every so often to assess progress and to ensure that strategies are not subject to rapid change based on short-term success. In particular, for seasonal sports it is important that week-by-week winning or losing does not unduly interfere with strategic marketing plans, usually prepared for three to five years. This is one of sport's greatest pitfalls: reacting to short-term poor on-field performance. It also represents the main difficulty confronted by the sports marketer: to market a product over which there is little control.

Implementation is also guided by the assumptions made during the planning process. Because all strategies and action plans are based on these assumptions about the future, they are subject to considerable risk. It is necessary for marketing managers to assess continually the assumption on which strategies were based. It is here that the beginning and end of the planning process meet. In fact, there is never an end, as the cycle continues in a feedback loop that sometimes blurs beginning and end. To some extent this is a good sign. It indicates that once the plan and associated strategies are formulated they are not simply put on the shelf. Plans put into action are subject to contingency planning to correct assumptions that do not prove to be true. Therefore the SSMPP is dynamic, rarely stagnant, and laden with challenges to ensure that the full potential of marketing's contribution to the overall functioning of a sporting organi-sation is optimised.

BIBLIOGRAPHY

Anderson, L. K. and Sollenberger, HJVL, *Managerial Accounting*, South-Western Publishing, Cincinnati, OH., 1992

Ansoff, H. I. *'Strategies for diversification'*, Harvard Business Review, 1957

ANZ McCaughan *'Broadcasting Bounces Back: A Financial Evaluation of Australian Commercial Metropolitan Television'*, Industry Overview, ANZ McCaughan, Melbourne, 1993

Armstrong, C. P. and Sambamurthy, V. *Information Technology Assimilation in Firms: The Influence of Senior Leadership and IT Infrastructures*, Information Systems Research, 1999

Armstrong, K. *Black Women's Participation in Sports and Fitness: Implications for Sports Marketing*, Sports Marketing, Quarterly, 2001

Australian Bureau of Statistics, *Sports Attendance*, AGPS, Canberra, 2000

Australian Bureau of Statistics, *Participation in Sports and Physical Activities*, Australia, AGPS, Canberra, 2000

Australian Bureau of Statistics, *Australians Less Active*, AGPS, Canberra, 2000

Australian Football League (AFL). *AFL Strategic Plan 1994*, Melbourne, 1994

Australian Football League (AFL). *AFL 99th Annual Report-1995*, Melbourne, 1995

Australian Sports Commission *2002-2005 Strategic Plan*, ABC, ACT, 2002

Baghdikian, E. *Building the Sports Organisation's Merchandise Licensing Program: The Appropriateness, Significance, and Considerations*, Sports Marketing Quarterly, 1996

Baker, M. *Marketing Strategy and Management,* Macmillan Business, London, 2000

Beikoff, K. *Packaged to Sell,* The Advertiser, 2002

Belch, G. E. and Belch, M. A. *Introduction to Advertising, and Promotion: An Integrated Marketing Communications Perspective,* Irwin, Homewood, IL, 1998

Belch, G. E. and Belch, M.A. *Advertising and Promotion: An Integrated Marketing Communications Perspective,* McGraw-Hill/Irwin, New York, 2001

Beydemuller, K. and Fiedler, M. *The Schumacher Effect, Germany 2001,* SportBusiness Group, 2001

Bishop, B. *Strategic Marketing for the Digital Age,* NTC Contemporary Publishing Group, Chicago, 1998

Bitner, MJ. *Servicescapes: The Impact of Physical Surrounding on Customers and Employees,* Journal of Marketing, 1992

Bitner, M.J., Booms, B.H. and Tetreault, M.S. *The Service Encounter: Diagnosing Favorable and Unfavorable Incidents,* Journal of Marketing, 1990

Boon, G. *Deloitte & Touche Annual Review of Football Finance (1997-1998 Season),* Deloitte Touche, Manchester, 1999

Boon, G. *Deloitte & Touche Annual Review of Football Finance (1999-2000 Season),* Deloitte & Touche, Manchester, 2001

Boyd, H.W. and Walker, O.C. *Marketing Management: A Strategic Approach,* Irwin, Homewood, IL, 1990

Boyd, H.W., Walker, O.C and Larreche, J.C. *Marketing Management,* Irwin, Sydney, 1995

Boyle, R. and Haynes, R *Power Play: Sports, the Media and Popular Culture,* Pearson Education, Harlow, 2000

Branch, D. *Rethinking Sport's Product Position and Program Concept,* Sports Marketing, Quarterly, 1992

Britcher, C. *Kirch's World Cup Web Cops,* SportBusiness International, 2001

Brooks, C.M. *Sports/Exercise Identity Theory and Participation Marketing: Theory Formation and Theoretical Justification,* Sports Marketing, 1998

Brown, M. *The Big Gamble,* The Age, Green Guide, 1992

Brown, M. *NBL Rethinks its Strategy as Crowds Fall,* Sunday Age, Sports Extra, 1993

Bryden-Brown, S. *OzTAM Figures to Get no Respect,* The Australian, 2001

Burchett, J. *News Limited v Australian Rugby League Limited and Others, NG 197 of 1995,* Federal Court of Australia, Sydney, 1996

Buzzard, K. *Electronic Media Ratings: Turning Dollars into Sense,* Focal Press, Boston, MA., 1992

Campbell, D. *Is the People's Game Going Back to its Roots?,* SportBusiness International, 2001

Carroll, J. *In Awe of a Tiger out in the Open,* The Age, 2002

Chase, RB. and Stewart, D.M. *Make Your Service Fail-safe,* Sloan Management Review, 1994

Chernatory, de L. and McDonald, M.H.B. *Creating Powerful Brands,* Butterworth/Heinemann, Oxford, 1992

Cheverton, P. *Key Marketing Skills,* Koran Page, London, 2000

Church, R *Sports on the Internet,* Screen Digest, 2000

Churches, D. *Sydney 2000,* Panstadia International, 1994

Churchill, G.A., Jr. and Surprenant, C. *An Investigation into the Determinants of Customer Satisfaction,* Journal of Marketing Research, 1982

Cialdini, R.B., Borden, R.J., Thorne, A., Walker, M.R, Freeman, S. and Sloan, L.R. *Basking in Reflected Glory: Three (football) Field Studies,* Journal of Personality and Social Psychology, 1976

Clarke, R *Wearing out the Opposition,* SportBusiness International, 2002

Cockington, J. *Speed Freaks,* The Sydney Morning Herald, 2002

Collins, J. *Athens Opts for Old Fashioned Values,* The SportsVine, 2002

Connolly, R *Oakley Denies AFL Code Acts as Censor*, The Age, Melbourne, 1995

Cousens, L. and Slack, T. *Using Sports Sponsorship to Penetrate Local Markets: The Case of the Fast Food Industry*, Journal of Sports Management, 1996

Cravens, D.W *Strategic Marketing*, Irwin, IL, 1994

Dampney, J. *NBL's Rocky Road—Teams Tighten Belts*, The Daily Telegraph, 2002

Darby, J. *Rocky Mountain High*, The Herald Sun, Melbourne, 2002

Dauncey, H. and Hare, G. *World Cup France' 98 Metaphors, Meanings and Values*, International Review for the Sociology of Sports, 2000

Delpy L. and Bosetti, H.A. *Sports Management and Marketing via the World Wide Web*, Sports Marketing Quarterly, 1998

Denham, G. *Dons to Act on Long Racism Complaints*, The Age, 1995

Denham, G. *Lewis Supports Fines for Racial Abuse*, The Age, 1995

Dennis, A. *Gay Games Showing the Critics a Racy Pair of Heels*, The Sydney Morning Herald, 2002

Department of Industry, Science and Resources / Australian Services Network (DISK), *The Australian Service Sector Review 2000*, Commonwealth of Australia: Author, 2000

DeSensi, J.T. and Rosenberg, D. *Ethics in Sports Management*, Fitness Information Technology, Morgantown, WV., 1996

DeVito, J.A. *Essentials of Human Communication*, Addison Wesley Longman, New York, 1999

Dietz-Uhler, B. and Harrick, E.A. *Sex Differences in Sports Fan Behaviour and Reasons for Being a Sports Fun*, Journal of Sports Behavior, 2000

Eccles, J. *It's Big, Beautiful and a Touch Shambolic*, The Canberra Times, 2002

El Sawy, O.A., Malhotra, A., Gosain, S. and Young, K.M. *IT-intensive Value Innovation in the Electronic Economy: Insights from Marshall Industries*, MIS Quarterly, 1999

Evans, J.R and Berman, B. *Marketing*, Macmillan, New York, 1987

Farber, B. and Wycoff, J. *Customer service: Evolution and Revolution*, Sales and Marketing Management, 1991

Fink, J., Trail, G. and Anderson, D. *Environmental Factors Associated with Spectator Attendance and Sports Consumption Behavior: Gender and Team Differences*, Sports Marketing Quarterly, 2002

Friedman, W. *Hockey Comeback Tied to Engaging its Core Audience*, Advertising Age, 2000

Friedman, W. *Super Bowl Ads Sell Super Early*, Advertising Age, 2002

Funk, D. and James, J. *The Psychological Continuum Model: A Conceptual Framework for Understanding and Individual's Psychological Connection to Sports*, Sports Management Review, 2001

Funk, D., Haugtvedt, C. and Howard, D. *Contemporary Attitude Theory in Sports: Theoretical Considerations and Implications*, Sports Management Review, 2000

Funk, D., Mahony, D. and Ridinger, L. *Characterizing Consumer Motivation as Individual Difference Factors: Augmenting the Sports Interest Inventory (SII) to Explain Level of Spectator Support*, Sports Marketing Quarterly, 2002

Gaudron, M. *Sydney Builds on Olympic Success*, SportBusiness International, 2002

Gellatly, A. *Online Gambling: The Buzz becomes a Roar*, SportBusiness International, 2001

George, W. and Berry, L. *Guidelines for Advertising Services*, Business Horizons, 1981

Gerlis, S. *Gambling on Online Future*, SportBusiness International, 2001

Gillis, R *Being Nick Faldo*, SportBusiness International, 2002

Gillis, R *Delivering on the Deal*, SportBusiness International, 2002

Gladden, J., Milne, G.R and Sutton, W. *A Conceptual Framework for Assessing Brand Equity in Division I College Athletics*, Journal of port Management, 1998

Glendinning, M. *Mapping Out the Future of Sports Licensing*, Sports Business, 1999

Griswold, D. *The Practice of Public Relations*, Prentice-Hall, Englewood Cliffs, NJ., 1995

Gritsi, S. *Volunteer Attrition at the Olympic Games: The Case of Sydney 2000 Olympic Games*, Sports Management Project, UTS, Sydney, 2000

Gronroos, C. *Service Management and Marketing*, Lexington Books, MA., 1990

GTV Nine Network *Australian Grand Prix 2002*, Wide World of Sports, Nine Network, 2002

Haigh, G. *The Cricket War: The Inside Story of Kerry Packer's World Series Cricket*, The Text Publishing Company, Melbourne, 1993

Halbish, G. *Developing Professional Sporting Leagues*, Sports Management and Marketing Conference, Sydney, 1995

Hancock, S. *Feyenoord Gearing up for Change*, SportBusiness International, 2001

Hansen, F. and Scotwin, L. *Advertising, Sponsorship and Promotions: Understanding and Measuring the Effectiveness of Commercial Communication*, ESOMAR, Amsterdam, 1995

Hawkins, D.I., Best, RJ. and Coney, K.A. *Consumer Behavior—Implications for Marketing Strategy*, Irwin, Boston, MA., 1992

Hay, D. *Jordan Plays the Money Game*, Sunday Age, 1996

Helitzer, M. *The Dream Job: Sports Publicity, Promotion and Marketing*, University Sports Press, Athens, OH., 1996

Henderson, I. *AFL Kicks a Goal on Marketing Strategy*, The Australian, 1996

Hickman, B. *To Get Interactive, Viewers Must Box Clever*, The Australian, 2002

Hirons, M. *Nice Lookin' Result Among Sponsorship Swirl*, Sweeney Sports Media Release, 2002

Hirsley, M. ABC, *ESPN Gobble Rest of NFL Rights: Networks Pay $17.6 billion for 8 Years*, Chicago Tribune, 1998

Hoffman, K.D. and Bateson, J.E.G. *Essentials of Services Marketing*, The Dryden Press, Orlando, FL., 1997

Howard, D.R. *The Changing Fanscape for Big-league Sports: Implications for Sports Managers*, Journal of Sports Management, 1999

Huggjns, M.H. *Marketing Research: A Must for Every Sports Organisation*, Sports Marketing Quarterly, 1992

Hunt, K., Bristol, T. and Bashaw R.E. *A Conceptual Approach to Classifying Sports Fans*, Journal of Services Marketing, 1999

Hyman, M. *Masters of Anti-sports Marketing*, Business Week, 2000

International Olympic Committee *Marketing Matters*, The Olympic Marketing Newsletter, Lausanne, 1996

Irwin, R.L. and Stotlar, D.K. *Operational Protocol Analysis of Sports and Collegiate Licensing Programs*, Sports Marketing Quarterly, 1993

Irwin, R.L., Sutton, W.A. and McCarthy, L.M. *Sports Promotion and Sales Management*, Human Kinetics, Champaign, IL, 2002

Jefkins, F. *Public Relations Techniques*, Butterworth/ Heinemann, Oxford, 1994

Jones, TO. and Sasser, W.E. Jr. *Why Satisfied Customers Defect*, Harvard Business Review, 1995

Judson, B. and Kelly, K. *Hyperwars-Eleven Strategies for Survival and Profit in the Era of Online Business*, Scribner, New York, 1999

Kahn, R. *The Boys of Summer*, Harper & Row, New York, 1972

Kates, S. *Consumer Research and Sports Marketing: Starting the Conversation between Two Different Academic Discourses*, Sports Marketing Quarterly, 1998

Kim, D. and Kim, S.Y. QUESC: *An Instrument for Assessing the Service Quality of Sports Centers in Korea*, Journal of Sports Management, 1995

Klattell, D.A. and Marcus, N. *Sports for Sale*, Oxford University Press, New York, 1988

Kotler, P. and Andreasen, A.R. *Strategic Marketing for Nonprofit Organisations*, Prentice-Hall, Englewood Cliffs, NJ., 1991

Kotler, P., Chandler, P., Gibbs, R, and McColl, R. *Marketing in Australia*, PrenticeHall, Englewood Cliffs, NJ., 1989

Kotler, P., Chandler, P.C., Brown, L. and Adam, S. *Marketing: Australia and New Zealand*, Prentice-Hall, Englewood Cliffs, NJ., 1994

Langeard, E., Bateson, J., Lovelock, C. and Eiglier, P. *Services Marketing: New Insights from Consumers and Managers*, Marketing Science Institute, Cambridge, MA., 1981

Lans, M.S. *Sports Team Logos are Big Business*, Marketing News, 1995

Lapidus, R.S. and Pinkerton, L. *Customer Complaint Situations: An Equity Theory Perspective*, Psychology & Marketing, 1995

Lawrence, M. *High Stakes keep Growing and there can Only be One Winner*, The Age, 1995

Legg, D. and Baker, J. *Add Value to Your Service*, American Marketing Association, Chicago, 1987

Linnell, S. *How Channel Seven Scored the Rights to TV Football*, The Age, 1991

Lovelock, C.H. *Services Marketing*, Prentice-Hall, Englewood Cliffs, NJ., 1991

Lovelock, C.H., Patterson, P.G. and Walker, R.H. *Services Marketing: An Asia-Pacific Perspective*, Pearson Education, Sydney, 2001

Lyons Jr., R. and Jackson Jr., E.N. *Factors that Influence African American Gen-Xers to Purchase Nikes*, Sports Marketing Quarterly, 2001

M2 PressWIRE *Di3: Sky Gamestar Invests in Interactive TV Software for World Cup 2002*, M2 Communications, 2002

McCarthy, J.E. and Perreault, WD. *Basic Marketing*, Irwin, Homewood, IL., 1990

McCarthy, L. *Marketing Sports to Hispanic Consumers*, Sports Marketing Quarterly, 1998

McDonald, M.A., Sutton, W.A. and Milne, G.R. *TEAMQUAL: Measuring Service Quality in Professional Team Sports*, Sports Marketing Quarterly, 1995

McGeoch, R. and Korporaal, G. *The Bid: How Australia Won the 2000 Games*, William Heinemann, Melbourne, 1994

McGuire, M. *On the Ball—Why Advertisers Keep Sponsoring Sports: Sport's Fevered Pitch*, The Australian, 2002

Macnow, G. *A Winning Game Plan*, Nation's Business, 1990

Martin, C. *The Digital Estate—Strategies for Competing, Surviving, and Thriving in an Internetworked World*, U.S.A., Mcgraw-Hill, 1997

Matthews, B. *More Courses for New Mecca*, The Herald Sun, Melbourne, 2002

Menary, S. *Clubs Profit from Good Groundwork*, Football Business International, 2001

Miller, J.A. *Conceptualization and Measurement of Consumer Satisfaction and Dissatisfaction*, Marketing Science Institute, Cambridge, 1977

Mullin, BJ. *Sports Management: The Nature and Utility of the Concept*, Arena Review, 1980

Mullin, BJ. *Successful Sports Management*, Michie Co., Charlottesville, 1985

Mullin, B.J., Hardy, S. and Sutton, W.A. *Sports Marketing*, Human Kinetics, Champaign, IL., 2000

National Basketball League *Chief Executive Annual Report*, NBL, Melbourne, 1994

National Basketball League *Chief Executive Annual Report*, NBL, Melbourne, 1995

National Basketball League *Chief Executive Annual Report*, NBL, Melbourne, 2000

Naughton, J. *Marketing Michael: The Making of a Commercial Superstar*, Washington Post Magazine, 1992

Nowell, M. *The Women's Golf Market: An Overview of Spectators and Participants*, Sports Marketing Quarterly, 1995

O'Riordan, B. *Sports Sponsorship on the Road to Recovery*, Financial Review, 2002

Oldfield, S. *Long's Abuse Claim to Test Code of Conduct*, The Age, 1995

Oliver, R.L. *Advances in Services Marketing, and Management*, JAI Press, Greenwich, CT., 1993

Oliver, R.L. *Satisfaction: A Behavioral Perspective on the Consumer*. McGraw-Hill, Singapore, 1997

OzTAM, *Enter the Discovery Guide*, Sydney, 2002

Peek, A. *Personal Interview Held at the Offices of the Australian Football League*, Brunton Ave, Melbourne, 1998

Peterson, RA. and Wilson, WR. *Measuring Customer Satisfaction: Fact and Artifact*, Journal of the Academy of Marketing Science, 1992

Porter, M., *Competitive Strategy*, Free Press, New York, 1980

Porter, M. *Competitive Advantage: Creating and Sustaining Superior Performance*, The Free Press, New York, 1985

Rhoden, WC. *High Stakes: Low Sense of Values,* New York Times, 1993

Richards, C. *Schools to Join Fight against Racism in Sports,* The Age, 1995

Ries, A. and Trout, J. *Positioning: The Battle for Your Mind,* Warner Books, New York, 1986

Roberts, K. *Visa Playing its Cards Right*, SportBusiness International, 2002

Sandier, D.M. and Shani, D. *Olympic Sponsorship vs. "ambush" Marketing: Who Gets the Gold?*, Journal of Advertising Research, 1989

Schaaf, P. *Sports Marketing: It's Not Just a Game Anymore,* Prometheus Books, Amherst, NY., 1995

Seitel, F.P. *The Practice of Public Relations*, Prentice-Hall, Englewood Cliffs, NJ., 1995

Sherman, AJ. *Franchising and Licensing: Two Ways to Build Your Business,* American Management Association, New York, 1991

Shilbury, D. *Characteristics of Sports Marketing: Developing Trends,* ACHPER National Journal, 1989

Shilbury, D. *Delivering Quality Service in Professional Sports,* Sports Marketing Quarterly, 1994

Shilbury, D. *Ticketing Strategy in the Australian National Basketball League,* Sports Marketing Quarterly, 1994

Shoebridge, N. *The Sprint to Atlanta becomes a Marathon to Sydney,* Business Review Weekly, 1996

Shoham, A. and Kahle, L.R, *Spectators, Viewers, Readers: Communication and Consumption in Sports Marketing,* Sports Marketing Quarterly, 1996

Sleight, S. *Sponsorship: What is it and How to Use it,* McGraw-Hill, Sydney, 1989

Smith, A. and Stewart, B. *Sports Management: A Guide to Professional Practice,* Allen & Unwin, Sydney, 1999

Smith, G. *A Strategy to Sell the Swans,* The Age, 1996

Smith, G. *Swans Kick Goals with Marketing Research*, Niche, Melbourne, 1996

Smith, P. *AFL is Out of Step in Attempt to Solve Race Row*, The Age, 1995

Sofios, S. *They Displayed the Spirit of Sydney and we Thank them*, The Daily Telegraph, 2002

Spolestra, J. *How to Sell the Last Seat in the House*, SRO Partners, Portland, OR., 1991

Standing, C. *Internet Commerce Development*, Artech House, Boston, 2000

Stanton, W.J., Miller, K.E. and Layton, R. *Fundamentals of Marketing*, McGraw-Hill, Sydney, 1995

Stensholt, J. *Rugby's Dream Run*, Business Review Weekly, 2002

Stotlar, D. *Successful Sports Marketing*, Brown & Benchmark, Dubuque, IA., 1993

Stotlar, D. *Sports Grill Demographics and Marketing Implications*, Sports Marketing Quarterly, 1995

Strategy Planning Group, *Towards the Millennium: Building a Strategic Vision for the* MCC, Melbourne Cricket Club, Melbourne, 1992

Sutherland, M. *Advertising and the Mind of the Consumer*, Allen & Unwin, Sydney, 1993

Sutton, W.A. and Parrett, I. *Marketing the Core Product in Professional Team Sports in the United States*, Sports Marketing Quarterly, 1992

Swan, J.E. and Trawick, I.F. *Refining Concepts and Measures of Consumer Satisfaction and Complaining Behavior*, Indiana University, Bloomington, IN., 1980

Swan, J.E., Trawick, I.F. and Carroll, M.G., *New Findings on Consumer Satisfaction and Complaining*, Indiana University, Bloomington, IN, pp. 11-14, 1982

Taylor, L. *The Marketing and Sponsorship of Sports in Australia*, *Sports Coach*, 1984

Team Marketing Report, *Team Marketing Report's NBA Fan Cost Index 2000-2001*, Team Marketing Report Inc., Chicago, IL., 2001

Tennis Australia, *The Perfect Match for Australia: Tennis Australia Strategic Plan, 2002-2004*, Melbourne, 2001

Teutsch, D., *All You Need is Gloves*, The Sun-Herald, 2002

Thamnopoulos, I., *Ticketing the Sydney 200 Olympic Games: Marketing and Operational Aspects in Olympic Marketing*, Management in Sports Management Project, UTS, Sydney, 2000

Timms, D., *Plenty to Crow About*, Herald Sun, 2002

Todreas, T.M. *Value Creation and Branding, in Televisions Digital Age*, Quorum Books, Westport, CT., 1999

Turner, P. and Shilbury, D., *Sports on Television: A Study of the Australian Football League Television Rights*, Sports Marketing Quarterly, 1997

Van Leeuwen, L., *Determinants of Customer Satisfaction with the Season Ticket Service of Professional Sports Clubs*, University of Technology, Sydney, 2001

Veeck, B. and Linn, E., *Veeck—as in Wreck*, New American Library, New York, 1962

Veeck, B. and Linn, E., *Hitting an all-time Low*, The Sydney Morning Herald, 2002

Wakefield, K.L. and Blodgett, J.G., *The Importance of Servicescapes in Leisure Service Settings*, Journal of Services Marketing, 1994

Wakefield, K.L., and Blodgett, J.G., *The Effect of the Servicescape on Customers*, Journal of Services Marketing, 1996

Wakefield, K.L., Blodgett, J.G., and Sloan, HJ., *Measurement and Management of the Sportscape*, Journal of Sports Management, 1996

Wakefield, K.L., and Sloan, HJ., *The Effects of Team Loyalty and Selected Stadium Factors on Spectator Attendance*, Journal of Sports Management, 1995

Wallace, T., *Expanding the Branding,* Football Business International, 2002

Walmsley, D., *Is the Rights Party Over?*, Sports Business International, 2001

Warren, I. and Tsaousis, S., *Racism and the Law in Australian Rules Football: A Critical Analysis*, Sporting Traditions, 1997

Westerbeek, H.M., *Is Sponsorship Retention Dependent on the Geographic Location of the Sports Facility?*, Journal of Marketing Communications, 2000

Westerbeek, H.M. and Smith, A., *Understanding the Criteria for a Winning Bid Strategy*, SportBusiness Group, 2001

Westerbeek, H.M. and Smith, A., *Location Dependency and Sports Sponsors: A Factor Analytic Study,* Sports Marketing Quarterly, 2002

Westerbeek, H.M. and Smith, A., *Sports Business in the Global Marketplace,* Palgrave Macmillan, London, 2003

Westerbeek, H.M. and Turner, P., *Market Power of Sports Organisations: An Australian Case Study,* Montpellier, France, 1996

Westland, J.C. and Clark, T.H.K., *Global Electronic Commerce: Theory and Case Studies,* The MIT Press, London, 2000

Whyte, J., *Adelaide's Wheel of Fortune,* Australian Financial Review, 2001

Wilkof, NJ., *Trade Mark Licensing,* Sweet & Maxwell, London, 1995

Wilmoth, P., *TV Ratings Systems Favors the Young,* The Age, 2001

Wilmshurst, J., *Below-the Line Promotion,* Butterworth/ Heinemann, Oxford, 1993

Wilner, B., *Internet Leading NFL Development,* Sports Business, 2000

Wilner, B., *Tiger Helps PGA Paw $870m TV Deal,* SportBusiness International, 2001

Zbar, J.D., *Ball's Bounce Goes ESPN, TNT's Way*, Advertising Age, 2002

Zeithaml, V.A., Parasuraman, A. and Berry, L., *Problems and Strategies in Services Marketing*, Journal of Marketing, 1985

Zeithaml, V.A., Parasuraman, A. and Berry, L., *Delivering Service Quality: Balancing Customer Perceptions and Expectations*, Free Press, New York, 1990

Zhang, J.J., Pease, D.G., Lam, T.C., Bellerive, L.M., Pham, U.L., Williamson, D.P., Lee, J.T. andWall, K.A., *Sociomotivational Factors Affecting Attendance at Minor League Hockey Games*, Sports Marketing Quarterly, 2001